Walter Hilton

The Scale of Perfection

Middle English Texts

General Editor

Russell A. Peck
University of Rochester

Associate Editor

Alan Lupack
University of Rochester

Advisory Board

Rita Copeland
University of Pennsylvania

Thomas G. Hahn
University of Rochester

Lisa Kiser
Ohio State University

Thomas Seiler
Western Michigan University

R. A. Shoaf
University of Florida

Bonnie Wheeler
Southern Methodist University

The Middle English Texts Series is designed for classroom use. Its goal is to make available to teachers and students texts that occupy an important place in the literary and cultural canon but that have not been readily available in student editions. The series does not include those authors, such as Chaucer, Langland, or Malory, whose English works are normally in print in good student editions. The focus is, instead, upon Middle English literature adjacent to those authors that teachers need in compiling the syllabuses they wish to teach. The editions maintain the linguistic integrity of the original work but within the parameters of modern reading conventions. The texts are printed in the modern alphabet and follow the practices of modern capitalization and punctuation. Manuscript abbreviations are silently expanded, and *u/v* and *j/i* spellings are regularized according to modern orthography. Hard words, difficult phrases, and unusual idioms are glossed on the page, either in the right margin or at the foot of the page. Explanatory and Textual notes appear at the end of the text, along with a brief glossary. The editions include short introductions on the history of the work, its merits and points of topical interest, and also briefly annotated bibliographies.

Walter Hilton

The Scale of Perfection

Edited by
Thomas H. Bestul

Published for TEAMS
(The Consortium for the Teaching of the Middle Ages)
in Association with the University of Rochester

by

Medieval Institute Publications

WESTERN MICHIGAN UNIVERSITY

Kalamazoo, Michigan — 2000

Library of Congress Cataloging-in-Publication Data

Hilton, Walter, d. 1396.
   The scale of perfection / Walter Hilton ; edited by Thomas H. Bestul.
     p. cm.
   Includes bibliographical references.
   ISBN 1-58044-069-X (pbk. : alk. paper)
    1. Mysticism--Early works to 1800. I. Bestul, Thomas H. II. Title.

BV5082.2 .H55 2000
248.4'82--dc21

                                                        00-064749

ISBN 1-58044-068-01

Printed in the United States of America

Cover design by Linda K. Judy

Contents

Acknowledgments   vii

Introduction   1
    Select Bibliography   14

Table of Contents   21

The Scale of Perfection
    Book I   31
    Book II   134

Textual Notes   263

Glossary   287

Acknowledgments

In the making of this edition I have received help from several persons and institutions. Michael Sargent generously shared important information on manuscripts of *The Scale of Perfection* resulting from his work in preparing an edition of Book I of *The Scale* for the Early English Text Society. I am deeply grateful for the consistently good advice given to me by Russell Peck from the beginning to the end of the project. I wish to thank John Sutton for reading my manuscript against a photocopy of its source, and I am especially grateful to Mara Amster for her excellent work in the demanding task of formatting the volume. Tom Seiler reviewed the manuscript for Medieval Institute Publications, for which I am also grateful, and shepherded the volume through the press.

For permission to publish the text from Lambeth Palace, MS 472, I am grateful to the Archbishop of Canterbury and the Trustees of Lambeth Palace Library. I must also thank the members of the staff of that library for their assistance and hospitality. I am grateful to the Institute for the Humanities of the University of Illinois at Chicago for assistance in the form of a grant-in-aid. Finally, it is a pleasure to acknowledge the generous support given to the Middle English Texts Series by the National Endowment for the Humanities.

The Scale of Perfection

Introduction

Among the major religious treatises written in fourteenth-century England, *The Scale of Perfection* of Walter Hilton maintains a secure place. *The Scale* is a guide to the contemplative life in two books of more than 40,000 words each and is notable not only for the careful exploration of its religious themes, but as a principal monument of Middle English prose.

Although we know relatively little about the author of the treatise, we have more information about Walter Hilton than is known about many authors of medieval texts. He was a member of the religious order known as the Augustinian Canons, and died at the Augustinian Priory of Thurgarton in Nottinghamshire in 1396.[1] There is reason to believe that he was trained in canon law and studied at the University of Cambridge. The exact date of his birth is unknown, but it is thought to be around 1343.

Besides *The Scale of Perfection,* Hilton is the author of a number of other surviving works in both English and Latin. Among the English works, all of which are much shorter than either of the books of *The Scale*, are a treatise *On the Mixed Life*, which deals in briefer form with some of the same topics taken up in *The Scale*; *Eight Chapters on Perfection*; *Of Angels' Song*; quite probably an English commentary on Psalm 90 (Vulgate), *Qui habitat*; and less certainly a commentary on Psalm 91, *Bonum est.*[2] On the basis of the content of certain of his works it can be safely inferred that Hilton was actively involved in some of the religious controversies current in England in the 1380s and 1390s. His principal concern, which is present in *The Scale*, is to defend orthodox belief, especially in the conduct of the contemplative life. One treatise, the *Conclusiones de imaginibus* ("Conclusions Concerning Images"), which cannot unequivocally be assigned to him, suggests that he defended the veneration of images against the kind of critique characteristic of the heterodox movement known as Lollardy.[3] The dates of Hilton's works cannot be known with certainty. In the case of *The Scale of Perfection* it is generally agreed, on the basis of the greater depth and maturity of approach in Book II, and

---

[1] See John P. H. Clark and Rosemary Dorward, trans., *Walter Hilton: The Scale of Perfection*, p. 13 [hereafter cited as Clark].

[2] For discussion of the English and Latin works, with full bibliographical information, see Lagorio and Sargent, pp. 3075–80.

[3] See Clark, p. 16; Lagorio and Sargent, p. 3075.

the fact that manuscript evidence suggests that Book I circulated independently, that some time separated the writing of the two books. A date range for the composition of the whole from about 1380 to Hilton's death in 1396 seems reasonable.[4]

The title *The Scale of Perfection*, or in Latin *Scala perfectionis*, is found in several manuscripts; *The Scale* of the title has the proximate Latin meaning of ladder or stairway. The treatise itself is addressed to a female who has taken religious vows. It is thereby connected to an extensive Western European tradition of works of devotion or spiritual guidance directed at women, written either in Latin or the vernaculars. Representative of such works are the *De institutione inclusarum* ("Rule of Life for Recluses") of Aelred of Rievaulx (d. 1167), a work translated from Latin into Middle English in the fourteenth century, the *Ancrene Wisse* ("Guide for Anchoresses") written in English in the thirteenth century, and the extremely popular *Meditationes vitae Christi* ("Meditations on the Life of Christ") extant in several fifteenth-century English versions or adaptations from the original Latin of the late thirteenth century.[5]

Hilton's *Scale of Perfection* is always counted among the masterpieces that constitute the great efflorescence of English mystical writing of the fourteenth century and the early years of the fifteenth. Along with Hilton the other members of the canon of great mystical writers of the age are Richard Rolle (d. 1349); the unknown author of *The Cloud of Unknowing*; Julian of Norwich (d. 1413); and Margery Kempe (d. ?1440) who has a less secure but steadily solidifying position in the roster.[6] Although there are certainly similarities among them, Hilton is quite distinct from each of the others. In very general terms, his understanding of contemplation is less material, less dependent on imagery and sensation, than that of Richard Rolle, whose approach he seems to counter directly in *The Scale*. Despite some superficial similarities between the *myrknesse* ("darkness") and the cloud of forgetting or the cloud of unknowing of *The Cloud* author, Hilton's use of this imagery is quite different. Hilton's *myrknesse* is the darkness of sin and separation from God; there is no signifying of the pseudo-Dionysian annihilation of the self so prominent in *The Cloud*.[7] Although both Hilton and Julian of Norwich are concerned with the recovery of the image of God and the meaning of sin, Hilton manages to be more orthodox and less innovative, and at the same time less personal and ultimately less theologically profound than Julian. Margery Kempe is justly said to be

---

[4] See Underhill, pp. xliii–xlv; Gardner (1936), pp. 12–14.

[5] For the versions of Aelred, see Ayto and Barratt; *Ancrene Wisse*, ed. Robert Hasenfratz for the Middle English Texts Series; for the English versions of the *Meditationes*, see Sargent (1992) and Lagorio and Sargent, pp. 3103–07.

[6] See the METS editions of *The Cloud of Unknowing*, ed. Patrick Gallagher; *The Shewings of Julian of Norwich*, ed. Georgia Crampton; and *The Book of Margery Kempe*, ed. Lynn Staley.

[7] The use of the phrase "I am nought" in *Scale*, Book II, chapter 21, has to do with the acquisition of humility.

incomparable; nevertheless, one readily notices in Hilton's *Scale* that very little is said of the author's spiritual or mystical experiences (Hilton at one point declares that he is writing about prayer at a level that has been beyond him),[8] experiences of a kind which are the heart and soul of *The Book of Margery Kempe*.

The two books of Hilton's treatise are quite different from each other. Book I is divided into 92 chapters, and although Book II is more than a quarter again as long, it has only 46. This difference is more than superficial. Hilton rarely develops a line of thinking for more than a few chapters in Book I, whereas in Book II several of the chapters, particularly those in the middle sections of the book on the reforming of the soul to the image of God, contain profound and detailed analyses of certain aspects of advanced stages of the contemplative life, some of which he had already examined in Book I. The obviously greater intellectual depth is the strongest internal evidence for the theory that the books were written at different times in Hilton's life.

Book I begins with definitions of the active and contemplative lives, and distinguishes three degrees of contemplation. The first is in knowledge of God through reason and learning only; the second is knowing God in the affections (or emotions) only; the third, and highest stage attainable on earth, lies in knowing God in both cognition and affection. This constitutes perfect knowledge and love of God and happens only when the soul is purged of sins and reformed to the image of Jesus. This is the "perfection" of the title.

Hilton also explains what contemplation is not, in a passage that is usually taken to be a direct criticism of the kind of spirituality advocated by Richard Rolle (whose name, of course, is not mentioned). Hilton notes that some persons would associate spiritual visions with bodily sensations, such as music in the ear, a sweet tasting in the mouth, or a heat that can be felt by the body. This enumeration corresponds closely with Rolle's celebrated trio, *calor, dulcor, canor* (heat, sweetness, song). Such physical sensations, Hilton says, are at best only secondary phenomena, and are not contemplation, which is exclusively spiritual (chapter 10).[9]

Hilton then considers how contemplation is initiated by reading of Scripture, meditation, and prayer. Since reading the Bible would not be a means ordinarily available to his female readership, Hilton concentrates on prayer and meditation, including the impediments and distractions that often stand in the way. The last half of the book takes up Hilton's major theme, one Hilton returns to in greater depth in Book II, the use of contemplation to assist in the recovery in the individual of the image of God that has been distorted by sin. The topic, and Hilton's treatment of it, is generally Augustinian, beginning with the analysis of the soul

---

[8] See *Scale*, Book I, chapter 33.

[9] See Clark, p. 163n36, for a discussion and reference to Rolle's *Incendium amoris*. There is also criticism of excessive materialism in Book II, chapter 32. Lagorio and Sargent (p. 3074), however, doubt that Hilton is directly criticizing Rolle.

as a reflection of the Trinity (chapter 43). Hilton's thinking is appropriately consistent with his membership in an Augustinian order, but the ideas expressed are the general possession of late medieval intellectual life.

The last half of the book also gives advice about overcoming the seven deadly sins, advice which is specifically tailored to the circumstances of a person leading a contemplative life. This section of the book contains Hilton's brief excursions into practical advice of the kind that enlivens a work such as the *Ancrene Wisse* (*Scale*, Book I, chapter 83, tells an anchorite how she should handle an intrusive visitor). The importance of humility, charity, and self-knowledge is stressed and advice is given about how to control the senses. All this is necessary preparation for destroying what Hilton calls "the myrke image of synne" (chapter 84; "the dark image of sin"), which must be broken down before man can be reformed to the image of Jesus.

Hilton's second book is less wide ranging, focused on a smaller number of topics, and more logically arranged. He begins by explaining how the divine image in man was deformed by original sin and how only the sacrifice of Christ makes it possible for that image to be restored and reformed. Such reformation, and with it, salvation and eternal life, is open only to believers in Christ, and is not available to Jews and pagans. Hilton's stance on the question of the salvation of the heathen, a topic of active concern in the later Middle Ages, is distinctly hard line.[10] It can be contrasted, for example, with Dante's more generous treatment of virtuous pagans in *The Divine Comedy*.[11]

Hilton then discusses how the restoration of the divine image can take place, distinguishing between reformation in faith and reformation in feeling. The process begins with the sacrament of baptism, which allows the image to be reformed from the distorting effect of original sin; the sacrament of penance allows reformation from the effects of sin actually committed by an individual. Hilton explains that some persons are reformed only in faith but not in feeling; the highest state, which corresponds to the limits of human perfection, is to be reformed in both faith and feeling. This state is reached only after a lengthy and often arduous process of spiritual growth, is limited to those leading a contemplative life, and is attained by very few. At the same time, Hilton makes clear that the attainment of such a state is not a requirement of salvation, which is open to all, learned and unlearned, whether leading a life in the world or a life of contemplation. This point is consistent with Hilton's defense of orthodoxy; he is very careful to avoid the appearance of advocating a special way to salvation that stands outside of or competes with the universal message of salvation proclaimed by a universal church.

Using the metaphor of a pilgrim going to Jerusalem, Hilton explains how the soul should attain restoration of the divine image, and the difficulties and obstacles that must be overcome.

---

[10] See notes on chapter 3 and references given there.

[11] See, for example, Statius who, in *Purgatorio* 22.73–93, is identified as a secret Christian — "per paura chiuso cristian fu'mi."

Introduction

In this section (especially chapters 24–27) Hilton adopts paradoxical imagery of light and darkness that superficially resembles that used in *The Cloud of Unknowing*. In Hilton's usage, the brightness of day is a false light representing love of the world and is therefore evil. The night represents withdrawal from the world, a desire to love Jesus, and longing for spiritual fulfillment. It is therefore a good night and an illuminated darkness ("this is a gode nyght and a lighti merkenesse," chapter 24), because it blocks out love of the world, and enables love of Jesus, which in turn destroys in the soul all sinful impulses ("stirynges of synne," chapter 25). The soul must be careful to recognize the difference between the true light of knowledge sent from God and false illuminations that are the work of the devil. Chapter 30 articulates a familiar medieval theme, that knowledge of spiritual themes begins with knowledge of self, a theme treated also in Book I (chapter 42).[12] Chapter 31 of Book II is especially important because it contains Hilton's explicit connection of his conception of reforming the soul in feeling with Pauline ideas of reformation and renewal, putting off the old man of sin and taking on the new man reformed in the image of God, ideas notably expressed in Colossians 3:9–10, verses which are quoted and commented upon by Hilton.

Once the soul is reformed in faith and feeling, the inner eye of the soul can be opened, which allows knowledge of God in perfect love for him. It is at this point that Hilton comes closest to describing what might be called a mystical vision of the deity. Hilton stresses that the vision is not to be equated with a picture formed in the imagination of Christ seated in majesty in the firmament. The vision is not physical or material, or capable of definition by images constructed by the human imagination, but it is spiritual only (chapter 32).

Hilton then affirms the importance of the love of Jesus for such reformed souls. Love is the greatest gift of Jesus to his followers; it helps to overcome sin and to achieve a quiet humility. Once Jesus is beheld through the opening of the inner eye, the soul increases in virtues, which are gifts of grace, but require spiritual striving as well.

The last section of the book (chapters 41–44) deals with the problems caused when the vision of Jesus is sometimes withdrawn from the soul. Even though the soul may feel his absence, Hilton affirms that Jesus is always present in the soul, but his presence or absence is a matter of his grace. Finally, Hilton explains that the opening of the spiritual eye to the vision of Jesus brings true wisdom, allowing the soul to recognize the difference between good angels and the reprobate, the distinction and unity of the persons of the Trinity, and to see that Jesus as man is above all creatures.

Knowledge of Hilton's spiritual vocabulary and terminology is important in understanding *The Scale*. Among Hilton's most frequently used words, *goostly* (or spiritual) is constantly

---

[12] See Pierre Courcelle, *Connais-toi toi-même: De Socrate à saint Bernard* (Paris: Études Augustinennes, 1975); and R. Bultot, "Les 'Meditationes' pseudo-Bernardines sur la connaissance de la condition humaine: Problèmes d'histoire littéraire," *Sacris Erudiri* 15 (1964), 256–92.

contrasted with its opposite, worldly. Hilton makes frequent reference to his *even Cristene* ("fellow Christians"), a collocation also prominent in Julian's *Revelations of Divine Love*. *Liknesse* is the term usually used for the image of God in the soul that has been distorted by sin; *merknesse* ("darkness") is the consequence of sin and is used for any attachment to the things of this world. The word *gracious* in Hilton almost always carries the specific meaning of having to do with the operation of divine grace (for example: "He moste bicome man thorugh a gracious generacioun, bi wirkynge of the Holi Goost," II.57–58). *Ransake* ("ransack") is used to describe the act of making a thorough examination of the conscience in preparation for penance; *ravysche* ("carried off, ravish") is the Englishing of Latin *raptus*, used in St. Paul's account of his experience of being swept away into the third heaven (2 Corinthians 12:2), and often in later writing on mysticism and contemplation. The *goostly iye* ("spiritual eye") is the means by which the soul receives knowledge of God, once the barrier of sin has been removed.

Among the most important terms in *The Scale* are those that describe the non-intellectual, non-rational aspects of the soul, or broadly speaking, the emotions. *Affeccioun* ("affection") is used often, and is the technical term derived from the *affectio* of Latin writing on the psychology of the soul; in Hilton, however, the word also sometimes assumes its modern meaning of affection or love. Hilton speaks of contemplation "in cognicion and in affeccion," which he defines as "in knowyng and in perfight lovynge of God" (I.147–48). Hilton's usual term is *styringe* ("stirring"), which means some kind of arousal of the emotions. The term most often describes a sinful impulse. Hilton speaks of fleshly stirrings, such as stirrings of pride and envy; but there are also stirrings to devotion and prayer, stirrings of meekness and charity, and stirrings of grace.[13] *Feelynge* ("feeling") is the other major term, which is especially important in the second book. *Feelynge* again refers to the non-intellectual part of the soul, the source of love and desire for God. Reforming in feeling is contrasted to reforming in intellect through study and reason. The state of earthly perfection for Hilton is reformation of the soul in both intellect and in feeling, a state attained when God is both perfectly known and perfectly loved. Reformation in feeling is harder to describe and understand, but love of Jesus is at the base of it. It is for Hilton the chief reward of contemplation.

Hilton's *Scale* was one of the most popular religious texts of late medieval England. Its popularity is attested by the large number of manuscripts that survive — some forty-two containing one or both of the books, with a relatively large number of manuscripts with Book

---

[13] On the term "stirring" in Margery Kempe, Rolle, and Julian, see Lynn Staley, *The Book of Margery Kempe*, p. 236; and Aers and Staley, *The Powers of the Holy*, pp. 107–78.

I alone, suggesting it may have been the more popular of the two.[14] The manuscript evidence suggests a fairly broad readership for the work, which certainly extended beyond the female anchorites who were its putative first audience. Michael Sargent has gathered evidence to show that *The Scale* was a well-known text in monastic foundations in or near London, such as the Carthusian houses of London and Sheen and the important Brigittine abbey of Syon.[15] Another sign of its popularity is that it was translated into Latin by the Carmelite monk Thomas Fishlake, perhaps around the turn of the fifteenth century.[16] *The Scale* was printed by Wynkyn de Worde in 1494 and several times thereafter, and, as Helen Gardner notes, it was the first English mystical work to appear in print.[17] Hilton's book clearly reached a lay as well as clerical audience. Margery Kempe was familiar with "Hyltons boke," and lists it with other spiritual classics.[18] As we shall see, the manuscript that is the basis of the present edition is likely to have been prepared for a London merchant early in the fifteenth century.

About this edition

This edition is made from London, Lambeth Palace, MS 472, written early in the fifteenth century, possibly in London.[19] The manuscript has been chosen because it contains a well-written text of a type that would have been read in early fifteenth-century London, but it is also significant for other reasons. The manuscript seems to be a purposely assembled collection or anthology of Hilton's work, although it is noteworthy that his name is not mentioned in a contemporary inscription, and none of the works is ascribed to any author. Besides both books of *The Scale of Perfection*, the manuscript includes Hilton's *Mixed Life*, *Eight Chapters on Perfection*, and work that is likely to be his, the commentaries on the psalms *Qui habitat* and

---

[14] See Lagorio and Sargent, p. 3075, and the listing of manuscripts, pp. 3430–31; including collections of extracts and fragmentary texts, the total given is forty-nine manuscripts. Lagorio and Sargent has the most recent account of the manuscripts; slightly different counts are given in Clark, p. 33, following information from S. S. Hussey and A. J. Bliss. Ignoring the extracts, Hussey (1992, p. 101), counts forty-one manuscripts with Book I and 24 with Book II. Clark (p. 33) suggested that the simpler treatment of the subject in Book I contributed to its greater popularity.

[15] Sargent (1983), pp. 189–90; see also Gardner (1936), pp. 27–28.

[16] On the Latin translation, see Sargent (1983), pp. 189–90; Clark, pp. 56–57; Lagorio and Sargent, p. 3076, where it is noted that Fishlake's Latin version circulated also on the continent.

[17] Gardner (1936), p. 11.

[18] *Book of Margery Kempe*, 1.17 (ed. Staley, p. 51).

[19] See Gardner (1936), pp. 25–26; *Walter Hilton's Mixed Life*, ed. Ogilvie-Thomson, pp. xii–xiv; *Linguistic Atlas of Late Medieval English*, 1.118.

Bonum est, and a commentary on the *Benedictus*. The manuscript can also be regarded as an interesting document reflecting the growth of lay piety in fifteenth-century England. The anthology appears to have been made for John Killum, a grocer of London, who died in 1416. An inscription in the manuscript describes it as a "common profit" volume, intended to benefit the spiritual welfare of its owner, then to be passed down to benefit another reader at his death, and so on from person to person "as longe as the booke endurith."[20] Inscriptions in the manuscript indicate that such a procedure was followed by a series of London owners until the end of the fifteenth century.[21]

This is a scribal, not an authorial edition; that is, it does not seek to recover the words that Hilton actually wrote (if such a thing were possible). Neither should it be thought of as a "best-text" edition, as that term is usually defined.[22] The edition represents a coherent text from a well-written manuscript as produced by a scribe (or scribes), with emendations made only to correct obvious mistakes or when necessary to preserve the sense. In my opinion, there are good theoretical reasons for preferring this editorial method, but the justification for such a procedure is also practical.[23] As noted above, *The Scale* exists in many manuscripts, and the textual tradition is unusually complicated, so much so that an edition based on more comprehensive principles would be difficult to accommodate within the scope of this series. But the chief practical reason for the present procedure is that an edition is in progress for the Early English Text Society that will be based on an entirely different editorial method. That edition, for example, will be based on examination of the known manuscripts, and attempt, through the traditional methods of recension and collation, to recover a sound authorial text.[24] The fact that this edition has been so long in progress and is still some time from completion indicates the complexity of the editorial task, and also, I believe, provides a warrant for the more modest undertaking presented here.

---

[20] Inscription quoted and discussed by Ogilvie-Thomson, p. xii (fol. 260r).

[21] More information on the common profit books and the succession of owners may be found in Sargent (1983), pp. 205–06.

[22] See Moffat, "A Bibliographical Essay," pp. 31–36.

[23] The editing of Middle English texts is a topic that has inspired much recent scholarly debate; much of this is admirably summarized in Moffat, "A Bibliographical Essay," pp. 25–57. All the essays in this volume, *A Guide to Editing Middle English*, may be consulted with profit; see also the important essays in Minnis and Brewer (1992), especially S. S. Hussey, "Editing *The Scale of Perfection*," pp. 97–107; and R. Allen Shoaf's Introduction to his edition of Thomas Usk's *Testament of Love* (1998), pp. 1–5.

[24] For the EETS, the edition of Book I begun by A. J. Bliss is being completed by Michael Sargent; Book II is being edited by S. S. Hussey; see Clark, pp. 53–54; I am grateful to Michael Sargent for informing me of the present state of the EETS edition.

Introduction

Most of the textual complexities of *The Scale* are found in Book I. Although a full discussion is not appropriate here, it should be noted that at least two versions of Book I were in circulation, the second being an expansion of the first, with alterations and additions that Evelyn Underhill described as "Christo-centric," for example the substitution of "Jesus Christ" for "God."[25] By no means all of the changes, however, can be characterized in this way.[26] Whether Hilton was responsible for the revisions or whether they were the work of a scribe or another reviser is a matter of doubt, but scholarly consensus leans to the view that they are not authorial.[27] An exception to this conclusion is the long passage on the Holy Name of Jesus which has been added to the end of chapter 44 of Book I in many manuscripts, including the Lambeth manuscript edited here.[28] This is widely accepted as Hilton's work, the result of conscious authorial revision.

The Lambeth manuscript is an example of the expanded version of Book I, including both the "Christo-centric" and other additions as well as the Holy Name passage.[29] Not only that, Gardner notes that a feature of this manuscript is that there are slight expansions of the expansions, so that it appears there is little doubt that the text contains words and phrases that are unlikely to be authentically Hilton's.[30] Gardner concludes that the Lambeth text is a representative of an enlarged revision of *The Scale* that appears to have originated in the major Carthusian or Brigittine religious houses in or near London and was widely circulated there;[31] as such it has a claim on our attention.

In this edition, the text of the Lambeth manuscript is compared with Cambridge, University Library MS Additional 6686, which is a good representative of the unexpanded version. This manuscript also has been chosen for comparison because it will form the base text of the EETS edition of Book I now in progress.[32] The Textual Notes identify the considerable number of major variations between the two versions, and are thus more extensive than is usual for this

---

[25] Underhill, p. xxvi.

[26] See Gardner's (1936) critique, pp. 23–25; and Sargent (1983), p. 197.

[27] Clark, p. 55; Gardner (1936, p. 26) notes among other evidence that the expansions are not in the Latin translation; see also Sargent (1983), p. 197.

[28] See the Textual Notes, where the passage is identified.

[29] On the classification and affiliations of the Lambeth manuscript, see Gardner (1936), pp. 15–18 (the Lambeth manuscript belongs to Gardner's type A); Sargent (1983), pp. 190–93.

[30] Gardner (1936), pp. 25–26.

[31] On the London origin of this version, see Gardner (1936), pp. 26–28; Hussey (1992, p. 106) agrees on the London (probably Carthusian) origin, but rejects Gardner's notion that the great houses near London, Sheen and Syon, could have been involved.

[32] See Clark, pp. 53–56.

series. The reader should be aware that not every variation has been recorded; the decision of what to include under the category of major is inevitably subjective and depends on editorial judgment. The aim is to give the reader an idea of the nature and extent of the revisions. A complete list of variants must await the publication of the EETS edition.

The assumption is usually made that the text as represented by the Cambridge manuscript is the earlier form of Book I. This is a reasonable assumption, but it should be noted that the Cambridge manuscript includes several passages, some of them quite lengthy, that are not found in the Lambeth version (these too are recorded in the Textual Notes). It is possible to consider these as scribal deletions made to the earlier version, or it may be that the Cambridge version itself is based on a somewhat different interpolated tradition. In any case, the important point is that the text in the Lambeth manuscript is not simply an enlarged version of the Cambridge text.

For the student, the practical consequences of the editorial decisions I have made will be that the text of this edition will differ from what eventually appears in the EETS edition. In some sections of the book, the variation will be considerable, where in others the variations will be relatively minor.[33] It should also be noted that the text of this edition will differ to the same extent from the modern English translation of Clark and Dorward, which is based on the Cambridge manuscript.

The textual situation of Book II is less complicated. There are many fewer manuscripts, and the textual variations, though considerable, are less substantial.[34] Despite the relatively uniform textual tradition, there appear to have been two versions of the book, and manuscript categories can be constructed on the basis of the variants.[35] Hussey's EETS edition of Book II will be based on the uncorrected text in London, British Library, MS Harley 6579, a member of a group of manuscripts designated by Hussey as x, and regarded by him as prior to another group of manuscripts designated as y.[36] Since the Lambeth manuscript belongs to Hussey's type y, in the Textual Notes I record variations with a representative of Hussey's type x, namely Oxford, Bodleian Library, MS Bodley 100. This manuscript was chosen in preference to

---

[33] This is because it appears that the Lambeth manuscript followed two exemplars for different parts of the book, one with the expansions, and the other close to the Cambridge manuscript; this can be seen, for example, in the small number of variants in chapters 1–10; I owe this information to a personal communication from Michael Sargent.

[34] Hussey (1992), p. 103.

[35] Hussey (1992, p. 103) inclines to think that the revised version is at least in part authorial.

[36] Sargent (1983), pp. 193–95; x and y include most of the existing manuscripts of *The Scale* II; the situation is further complicated because both x and y have several subgroups: Harley is subgroup a of the x group; Bodley is subgroup c of the x group; Lambeth is subgroup d of the y group; Hussey (1964), pp. 85–86. The textual complexities will presumably be addressed in the EETS edition.

Harley 6579 because the Harley manuscript includes many erasures and corrections, which must be evaluated in order to recover the type *x* text. This is a task Hussey will undertake in his edition.[37]

The Lambeth manuscript, too, has been subject to much correction. There are insertions of words and phrases from the margin; insertions of words and letters above the line; words and phrases written over erasures by a second hand; occasional glosses; and cancellations and expunctions. Some of this activity is no more than a typical scribe's routine correction of his own work, but in other cases, the insertions from the margin are the passages and phrases that are not found in the Cambridge manuscript. Not all this activity has been recorded in the Textual Notes, especially in cases where the alterations are simply corrections of obvious errors. An attempt has been made, however, to give an idea of the extent of the scribal correction, and I have tried not only to record the significant variations from the Cambridge text, but to signal when they are inserted from the margin or above the line. I have not indicated where another hand has written over erasures in the main text when the original readings are not recoverable, which is usually the case. Ogilvie-Thomson claims that the corrections in the Lambeth manuscript have been made by three different hands, with one contemporary hand being responsible for most of them.[38] It is not always easy to distinguish the activity of this corrector from the corrections of the main scribe, and I have accepted the corrections into my text without trying to distinguish between them. The corrections and additions I take as integral to the scribal text that this edition aims to reproduce. As Ogilvie-Thomson notes, because of the authoritative correcting activity, the Lambeth text is in some senses already an edited text.[39]

Although the Lambeth manuscript is likely to have been written in London, its language is distinctly more northern. Whether this language represents the dialect of the scribe or the dialect of his exemplar, or a combination of both, is not easy to determine. The language of the Lambeth manuscript has been analyzed by the editors of the *Linguistic Atlas of Late Medieval English* and localized to northern Cambridgeshire, near the borders with Huntingdon and the Isle of Ely.[40] Although there is no necessary connection between the language of a manuscript and the language of the author, the location in northern Cambridgeshire accords well with the known facts of Hilton's life. Thurgarton Priory is further north, in Nottinghamshire, but in the

---

[37] See Hussey (1964), pp. 91–92.

[38] Ogilvie-Thomson, pp. xii–xiii.

[39] Ogilvie-Thomson, p. xlii.

[40] *Linguistic Atlas of Late Medieval English*, 1:118; 3:25–26 (the linguistic profile); 4:336 (the map location). See also Hideo Yamaguchi, "A Short Descriptive Study," pp. 110–71.

same general north-east midland dialect area; and there is strong reason to believe, as noted above, that Hilton spent considerable time in Cambridge and its environs.[41]

The reader will notice in the Lambeth text a mixture of northern and southern forms, such as the variation between northern *-ande* and southern *-ynge* for the ending of the present participle, and the northern *mykil* beside the southern *moche* or hybrid *mychil*. The third person plural pronoun system is usually the *thei/hire/hem* of Chaucer's London, but occasionally the northern oblique forms *ther(e)* and *them* are encountered. The first person singular pronoun is *I* or *y*. The third-person singular ending of present tense verbs is invariably *-eth*. Readers can expect to find standard orthographic variations, such as *thou /thu*; modern English *too* spelled as *to*; modern English *one* rendered as *o* or *oo*.

For modern readers, Middle English pronouns are often confusing: their forms differ from modern forms and sometimes they appear to overlap because of multiple spellings, particularly in the possessive and third person forms. Moreover, because the forms undergo change within a single dialect at the time a manuscript is being copied, the referents are often ambiguous. Forms most likely to be confusing are *here*, usually meaning "their" but occasionally meaning "her," and *hem*, usually meaning "them." Normally, the third person feminine pronoun is *hire*, though occasionally it is *her*, and thus easily confused with the word for "their." So too the third person masculine pronoun is usually *hym*, not to be confused with *hem*, meaning "them." But it is the strings of *he*, *his(e)*, and *hym*, referring to a male person, or a hypothetical male, or God, or the devil, without clearly defined antecedents that are likely to give the modern reader the greatest trouble. To assist the reader in such situations, I have followed the practice of the Middle English Texts Series and capitalized personal pronouns referring to God. This should help to clarify the sense where strings of pronouns with different referents occur. The ambiguity of readings created by such repetitions of the same pronoun may be attractive to modern readers, but ambiguity in these matters was certainly not the intention of the author.

Hilton's syntax is generally clear, the prose vigorous and easy to read, although there are sometimes very long paratactic sentences that are loosely constructed by modern standards. On a very few occasions, Hilton uses a construction based on the Latin ablative absolute, especially when he is closely following a Latin source, such as in the second chapter of Book II, which is based on Anselm's *Cur deus homo*. Such constructions are awkward stylistically and can create confusion for the modern reader, as, for example, "stondinge the rightwisenesse of God" (II.38), which means "the righteousness of God being maintained" or "were the justice of God to stand."

In reproducing the text, the editorial principles followed are those of the Middle English Texts Series. Manuscript spelling is followed, but *u/v* and *i/j* are normalized in accord with modern spelling conventions. Initial *ff* is given as *F* or *f*, depending on context; thorn is

---

[41] Clark, pp. 13–14.

rendered as *th*. Manuscript yogh is given as *g*, *gh*, *y*, or *z*, depending on modern equivalents. When palatal yogh is rendered as *y* before or after a front vowel also symbolized by the graph *y*, spellings result that may at first confuse. Examples are *yyf* (for *yif*, modern English "if"), and *yye* (*iye*, modern English "eye"). The use of yogh in this manuscript is particularly interesting. It is found unhistorically in such spellings as *oughte* ("out") and *though* ("thou"), and is sometimes not present where it would be historically expected, in spellings such as *mait* ("might") and *not* ("nought"). These spellings suggest that yogh no longer has specific phonemic value for this scribe.

When the second person singular pronoun is spelled *the* in the manuscript, this is rendered as *thee*; conversely, the very few instances when the definite article is spelled *thee* are rendered *the*. The final *e* of French loan words that eventually came to be spelled as *y* is given as *é* to indicate that the final *e* is syllabic. Examples are such words as *charité* ("charity"), *cité* ("city"), *plenté* ("plenty"), and *freelté* ("frailty").

Abbreviations in the manuscript are silently expanded in accordance with the way the word is usually spelled out in full;[42] roman numerals are written out; word division and capitalization are modern; paragraphing, sentence division, and punctuation are modern, although guided by manuscript practice.

In this manuscript, each book is preceded by a Table listing chapters and their titles. The Table of Contents for this edition does not reproduce the Tables in the Lambeth manuscript, but is made from the chapter titles as found in the main text. Readers should be aware that chapter divisions as well as titles of individual chapters are not uniform in all manuscripts.[43] In comparing this edition with Underhill's translation, for example, there are several differences in chapter breaks; in the case of the Clark-Dorward translation, on the other hand, the chapter divisions correspond exactly.

Hilton uses many biblical quotations, which are given here in the Latin form as they are found in the manuscript, since Hilton always translates the Latin in the immediately following lines. Sources of the biblical quotations are placed in parentheses in my text. The practice is of course editorial, although in the Lambeth manuscript each biblical quotation is identified in the margin. Readers will notice occasional differences from the standard Vulgate. Like many medieval writers, Hilton seems to quote from memory, a practice which sometimes results in small inaccuracies; or, he may quote the biblical text as cited in one of his patristic sources, such as Augustine or Gregory, where a version of the Bible may have been used

---

[42] Among the most frequently abbreviated words is the sacred name Jesus, almost always rendered as *ihu* (*Ihesu*), as is customary scribal practice; on two occasions, however, the name is written in full as *Jhesus*, supporting the expansion in the edition as *Jhesus* rather than the more linguistically accurate *Jesus*.

[43] The textual tradition of the tables and titles has its separate complexities; see Hussey (1992), p. 106.

different from what became the standard late-medieval Vulgate. Students should remember that the numbering of the Psalms (and occasionally a few of the verses) will differ from that in Protestant Bible translations.

Translations of *The Scale* are listed in the Bibliography. Until the EETS edition appears, the present edition is the only published modern edition of the entire Middle English text. Special mention should be made of the translation of Evelyn Underhill published in 1923; her semi-modernized version of the Middle English, prepared from an examination of ten manuscripts, has been the foundation for most modern scholarship on *The Scale* as well as the basis of subsequent modern translations, such as that by Leo Sherley-Price in the Penguin series. The 1991 translation by John P. H. Clark and Rosemary Dorward, on the other hand, was made directly from the manuscripts which will form the base texts of the EETS edition, with doubtful readings checked against Fishlake's contemporary Latin translation. The Clark-Dorward translation has an extensive introduction discussing Hilton's sources and the relation of *The Scale* to his other writings, as well as a particularly detailed analysis of the spirituality of the text. The annotations, the work of Clark, are also exceptionally thorough, especially in the matter of sources, and I have made much use of them in my own annotations, indicating my obligation by appropriate citations. The Clark-Dorward translation, which also has a valuable bibliography, should be consulted by any student of *The Scale*.

A hypertext version of the present edition will be made available on the world wide web, so that corrections may be entered, and space made available for clarification of the relationship of the version edited here with the text in the EETS edition when it appears. Folio breaks for the Lambeth MS will be indicated in the Web edition.

Select Bibliography

Manuscripts

London, Lambeth Palace, MS 472. [The base text of this edition.]

Cambridge, University Library, MS Additional 6686. [Used as a comparison text for Book I; the base text for the forthcoming EETS edition of Book I.]

Oxford, Bodleian Library, MS Bodley 100. [Used as a comparison text for Book II.]

Introduction

Translations

Clark, John P. H., and Rosemary Dorward. *Walter Hilton: The Scale of Perfection.* New York: Paulist Press, 1991. [Valuable notes, introduction, and bibliography.]

del Mastro, M. L. *The Stairway of Perfection.* Garden City, NY: Image Books, 1979.

Sherley-Price, Leo. *Walter Hilton: The Ladder of Perfection.* Harmondsworth: Penguin, 1957.

Underhill, Evelyn. *The Scale of Perfection.* London: J. M. Watkins, 1923. [A modernization as much as a translation, based on manuscripts; in the absence of a critical edition of the Middle English, this has become the standard edition.]

Other Works by Hilton

Hilton, Walter. *The Goad of Love: An Unpublished Translation [by] Walter Hilton, of the Stimulus Amoris formerly Attributed to St. Bonaventura.* Ed. and trans. Clare Kirchberger. London: Faber and Faber, 1952. [It is not certain that this is the work of Hilton.]

———. *An Exposition of "Qui habitat" and "Bonum est" in English.* Ed. Björn Wallner. Lund: C. W. K. Gleerup, 1954.

———. *Two Minor Works of Walter Hilton.* Ed. Fumio Kuriyagawa and Toshiyuki Takamiya. Tokyo: T. Takamiya, 1980. [Editions of *Of Angels' Song* and *Eight Chapters on Perfection.*]

———. *The Prickynge of Love.* Ed. Harold Kane. 2 vols. Salzburg: Institut für Anglistik und Amerikanistik, 1983. [Middle English edition of *The Goad of Love.*]

———. *Walter Hilton's Mixed Life: edited from Lambeth Palace MS 472.* Ed. S. J. Ogilvie-Thomson. Salzburg: Institut für Anglistik und Amerikanistik, 1986.

———. *Walter Hilton's Latin Writings.* Ed. J. P. H. Clark and C. Taylor. Salzburg: Institut für Anglistik und Amerikanistik, 1987.

Horstman, C., ed. *Yorkshire Writers: Richard Rolle of Hampole, an English Father of the Church and His Followers.* 2 vols. London: S. Sonnenschein & Co., 1895–96. [Includes editions of Hilton's *Of Angels' Song* (1:175–82) and *On the Mixed Life* (1:264–92).]

The Scale of Perfection

Studies and Texts

Aelred of Rievaulx. See Ayto and Barratt.

Aers, David, and Lynn Staley. *The Powers of the Holy: Religion, Politics, and Gender in Late Medieval English Culture*. University Park: Pennsylvania State University Press, 1996.

Ancren Riwle: The English Text of the Ancrene Riwle. Ancrene Wisse, edited from Ms. Corpus Christi College, Cambridge 402. Ed. J. R. R. Tolkien. EETS o.s. 249. London: Oxford University Press, 1962.

Ancrene Wisse. See Hasenfratz.

Ayto, John, and Alexandra Barratt, eds. *Aelred of Rievaulx's De institutione inclusarum: Two English Versions*. EETS o.s. 287. London: Oxford University Press, 1984.

Clark, John P. H. See **Translations**, above.

Cleve, Gunnel. *Mystic Themes in Walter Hilton's Scale of Perfection, Book I*. Salzburg: Institut für Anglistik und Amerikanistik, 1989.

———. *Basic Mystic Themes in Walter Hilton's Scale of Perfection, Book II*. Salzburg: Institut für Anglistik und Amerikanistik, 1994.

The Cloud of Unknowing. See Gallacher.

Crampton, Georgia Ronan, ed. *The Shewings of Julian of Norwich*. Kalamazoo, MI: Medieval Institute Publications, 1994.

Fletcher, Alan J. "A Suggested Place of Origin of the Huntington 112 Copy of Walter Hilton's *Scale of Perfection*." *Notes and Queries* n.s. 32 (1985), 10–11.

Gallacher, Patrick J., ed. *The Cloud of Unknowing*. Kalamazoo, MI: Medieval Institute Publications, 1997.

Gardner, Helen. "Walter Hilton and the Authorship of *The Cloud of Unknowing*." *Review of English Studies* 9 (1933), 129–47.

———."The Text of *The Scale of Perfection*." *Medium Aevum* 5 (1936), 11–30.

————. "Walter Hilton and the Mystical Tradition in England." *Essays and Studies* 22 (1937), 103–27.

Hasenfratz, Robert, ed. *Ancrene Wisse*. Kalamazoo, MI: Medieval Institute Publications, 2000.

Hodgson, Phyllis. *Three Fourteenth-Century English Mystics*. London: Longmans, 1967. [Hilton, Rolle, the *Cloud* author.]

Hughes, Alfred C. *Walter Hilton's Directions to Contemplatives*. Rome: Pontifica Universitas Gregoriana, 1962.

Hughes, Jonathan. *Pastors and Visionaries: Religion and Secular Life in Late Medieval Yorkshire*. Woodbridge, Suffolk: Boydell and Brewer, 1988.

Hussey, S. S. "The Text of *The Scale of Perfection*, Book II." *Neuphilologische Mitteilungen* 65 (1964), 75–92.

————. "Latin and English in *The Scale of Perfection*." *Medieval Studies* 35 (1973), 456–76.

————. "Editing *The Scale of Perfection*: Return to Recension." In *Crux and Controversy in Middle English Textual Criticism*. Ed. A. J. Minnis and Charlotte Brewer. Cambridge: D. S. Brewer, 1992. Pp. 97–107.

Julian of Norwich. See Crampton.

Kempe, Margery. See Staley.

Knowles, David. *The English Mystical Tradition*. New York: Harper, 1961. [Chapter 6 is on Hilton.]

Lagorio, Valerie, and Michael G. Sargent. "English Mystical Writings." In *A Manual of the Writings in Middle English, 1050–1500*. Ed. J. Burke Severs. Rev. Albert Hartung. 9 vols. New Haven: Connecticut Academy of Arts and Sciences, 1967–. 9:3049–3137.

LeClercq, Jean. *The Love of Learning and the Desire for God: A Study of Monastic Culture*. New York: Fordham University Press, 1982.

Linguistic Atlas of Late Medieval English. See McIntosh.

Love, Nicholas. See Sargent (1992).

McCarren, Vincent P., and Douglas Moffat, eds. *A Guide to Editing Middle English*. Ann Arbor: University of Michigan Press, 1998.

McIntosh, Angus, M. L. Samuels, Michael Benskin, with the assistance of Margaret Laing and Keith Williamson. *A Linguistic Atlas of Late Medieval English*. 4 vols. Aberdeen: Aberdeen University Press, 1986.

Milosh, Joseph E. *The Scale of Perfection and the English Mystical Tradition*. Madison: University of Wisconsin Press, 1966.

Minnis, A. J. "Affection and Imagination in *The Cloud of Unknowing* and Hilton's *Scale of Perfection*." *Traditio* 39 (1983), 323–66.

————. "*The Cloud of Unknowing* and Walter Hilton's *Scale of Perfection*." In *Middle English Prose: A Critical Guide to Major Authors and Genres*. Ed. A. S. G. Edwards. New Brunswick: Rutgers University Press, 1984. Pp. 61–81.

————, and Charlotte Brewer, eds. *Crux and Controversy in Middle English Textual Criticism*. Cambridge: D. S. Brewer, 1992.

Moffat, Douglas. "A Bibliographical Essay on Editing Methods and Authorial and Scribal Intention." In *A Guide to Editing Middle English*. Ed. Vincent P. McCarren and Douglas Moffat. Ann Arbor: University of Michigan Press, 1998. Pp. 25–57.

Ogilvie-Thomson, S. J. See **Other Works by Hilton**, above.

Riehle, Wolfgang. *The Middle English Mystics*. Trans. Bernard Standring. London: Routledge, 1981.

Ross, Ellen M. "Submission or Fidelity? The Unity of Church and Mysticism in Walter Hilton's *Scale of Perfection*." *Downside Review* 106 (1988), 134–44.

Sargent, Michael G. "Walter Hilton's *Scale of Perfection*: The London Manuscript Group Reconsidered." *Medium Aevum* 52 (1983), 189–216.

————. *Nicholas Love's Mirror of the Blessed Life of Jesus Christ: A Critical Edition Based on Cambridge University Library Additional MSS 6578 and 6686*. New York: Garland, 1992.

Shoaf, R. Allen, ed. *Thomas Usk: The Testament of Love*. Kalamazoo, MI: Medieval Institute Publications, 1998.

Staley, Lynn, ed. *The Book of Margery Kempe*. Kalamazoo, MI: Medieval Institute Publications, 1996.

Usk, Thomas. See Shoaf.

Vitto, Cindy L. *The Virtuous Pagan in Middle English Literature*. Philadelphia: American Philosophical Society, 1989.

Whiting, Bartlctt Jere. *Proverbs, Sentences, and Proverbial Phrases from English Writings Mainly Before 1500*. Cambridge, MA: Harvard University Press, 1968.

Yamaguchi, Hideo. "A Short Descriptive Study of Dialectical Variations in the Language of Walter Hilton's *Scala Perfectionis* or the *Scale of Perfection*." *Poetica* (Japan) 25–26 (1987), 110–71.

Table of Contents

Book I

Chapter One: That the innere havynge schulde be like to the uttere.

Chapter Two: Of actif lif and of the werkes of it.

Chapter Three: Of contemplatif lif and the werkes of hit.

Chapter Four: Of the first partye of contemplacioun.

Chapter Five: Of the secunde partye of contemplacion.

Chapter Six: Of the lower degré of the secunde partie of contemplacioun.

Chapter Seven: Of the highere degree of the secunde partie of contemplacion.

Chapter Eight: Of the thridde partie of contemplacion.

Chapter Nine: Of the twynynge of the thridde partie of contemplacion fro the secunde, and of praysynge of it.

Chapter Ten: How the schewynges to the bodili wittis and the feelynge of hem may be bothe good and yvel.

Chapter Eleven: Hou thu schal knowe whanne the schewinges to thi bodili wittes and the feelynge of hem aren good or yvele.

Chapter Twelve: What knetteth Jhesu to mannys soule and what looseth Hym therfro.

Chapter Thirteen: How and in what thynges a contemplatif man schuld ben occupied.

Chapter Fourteen: Hou in resoun and in wille vertues bigynnen, and in love and in likynge it is eendid and maad perfight.

Chapter Fifteen: Of the meenes that bryngen a man to contemplacioun.

Chapter Sixteen: What a man schal use and refuse bi vertu of mekenes.

Chapter Seventeen: Who schulde blame mennys defautis and deme hem, and who not.

Chapter Eighteen: Whi meke men schal worschip othere, and lowe hemself in her owen herte undir alle othere.

Chapter Nineteen: Hou men schullen don that wanten the feelynge of mekenes in affeccioun, not dredynge over mykil therof.

Chapter Twenty: Hou heretikes and ypocrites, for wantynge of mekenesse, highen hemself in herte bifore alle othere.

Chapter Twenty-one: What thinges men owen to trowe bi siker trouthe.

Chapter Twenty-two: How a stable entent is nedefulle to thise that schal plese God and discrecioun in bodili werkes.

Chapter Twenty-three: Of a litil rehersynge of thynges biforseid, and of makynge offrynge of that schulde be offrid to God.

Chapter Twenty-four: Of praier that is spedful to gete clennes in herte and vertues.

Chapter Twenty-five: Hou men schulde praie, and whereon the poynt of the thought schal be sette in prayere.

Chapter Twenty-six: Of the fier of love.

Chapter Twenty-seven: That certayn praier in speche ordeyned of God and of Holi Chirche is best to hem that aren bounden and ordeyned therto, and to hem that gyven hem newli to devocion.

Chapter Twenty-eight: What peril it is to men that in the bigynnynge of here turnynge to God leeven to sone the comone praier of the ordenaunce of Holi Chirche and gyven hem to meditacion hooli.

Chapter Twenty-nine: Of the secunde maner of praier, that is in speche not certayn, but folweth the stirenges that aren in devocioun.

Chapter Thirty: That this maner of praier pleseth moche God, and maketh a man to have him as he were dronken, and maketh his soule to be woundid with the suerd of love.

Table of Contents

Chapter Thirty-one: Hou fier of love wasteth alle fleischli lustes, as othir fier wasteth alle bodili thynges here.

Chapter Thirty-two: Of the thridde maner of praier, oonli in herte withouten speche.

Chapter Thirty-three: How men schal do that aren traveylid with veyn thoughtes in her preier.

Chapter Thirty-four: Of meditacion of synful men, aftir that thei ben turned hooli to God.

Chapter Thirty-five: That the meditacion of the manhede of Crist or of His passion is gyven of God, and how it schal be knowen whanne it is geven.

Chapter Thirty-six: That the meditacioun of the passioun of Crist is withdrawen from hem that it is gyven to ofte sithes for divers skyles.

Chapter Thirty-seven: Of divers temptaciouns of the feend of helle.

Chapter Thirty-eight: Of sere remedies agennes temptaciounes of feend.

Chapter Thirty-nine: Hou God suffreth hem that He cheseth for to be tarid and temptid; and aftirwarde He comfortith hem and stableth hem yn grace.

Chapter Forty: That a man schulde not geve him to idelnesse ne lightli leve the grace that were gyven to him of God.

Chapter Forty-one: That a man schulde knowe the mesure of his gifte, and evere desire more, and take a betere, whanne God wole gyve it.

Chapter Forty-two: That a man schulde travaile for to knowe his owen soule and the myghtes of it, and breke doun the ground of synne therinne.

Chapter Forty-three: Hou a man schal knowe the worthinesse and the worschipe of his soule that it oweth to have bi kynde, and the wrecchidnesse and myschief that it is fallen in thorw synne.

Chapter Forty-four: Hou everi man mai be saved bi the passioun of Crist, be he never so wrecchid, yif he aske it.

Chapter Forty-five: That a man schulde be besi for to recovere agen his worthynesse, and reforme in him the ymage of the Trinité.

Chapter Forty-six: Hou Jhesu schal be sought, desired, and founden.

23

Chapter Forty-seven: What profite is to have the desire of Jhesu.

Chapter Forty-eight: Where and wherewith Jhesu schal be sought and founden.

Chapter Forty-nine: Where Jhesu is loste and founden thorugh His mercy.

Chapter Fifty: What letteth a man to heere and see Jhesu withinne hymsilf.

Chapter Fifty-one: That mekenesse and charité are the special lyveré of Jhesu, thorugh the whiche mannys soule is reformed to the liknes of Him.

Chapter Fifty-two: Hou a man schal see the gr<!-- -->oround of synne in hymsilf.

Chapter Fifty-three: Unto what thinge is the ymage of synne like, and what it is in itsilf.

Chapter Fifty-four: Whoso wole fynde Jhesu, hym bihoveth abide and traveile in this goostli merkenesse of this ymage of synne.

Chapter Fifty-five: What propirli is the ymage of synne and what cometh thereof.

Chapter Fifty-six: What pride is and whanne it is synne.

Chapter Fifty-seven: Whanne pride is deedli synne, and hou it is in fleischli lyvande men deedli synne.

Chapter Fifty-eight: Hou pride is in heretikes deedli synne.

Chapter Fifty-nine: Hou pride is in ypocrites deedli synne.

Chapter Sixty: Hou stirynges of pride and veynglorie in good men are but venial synne.

Chapter Sixty-one: Hou sere states in Holi Chirche schulle have sere medes in the blisse of hevene, and of two medes, sovereyn and secundarie.

Chapter Sixty-two: A schort stirynge to mekenesse and to charité.

Chapter Sixty-three: Hou a man schal knowe hou mykil pride is in hym.

Chapter Sixty-four: Of envie and ire and of here braunchis, and hou sumtyme instide of synne mannys persoone is hated.

Table of Contents

Chapter Sixty-five: That it is mykil maistrie sothfastli to love men in charité and hate here synne.

Chapter Sixty-six: That for the same deedis outewarde sere men schal have seere medis.

Chapter Sixty-seven: That alle menys good deedis schal be appreved that hath likenes of good, save of the opyn heretik and the opyn cursid man.

Chapter Sixty-eight: That no good deede mai make a man sikir withoute charité; and that charité is oonli had of the gifte of God to hem that are meke, and who is parfightli meke.

Chapter Sixty-nine: Hou a man schal wite hou moche ire and envie is hid in the ground of hys herte.

Chapter Seventy: Bi what tokenes thou schalt wite yif thou love thyn enemye and what ensample thou schalte take of Crist for to love Hym also.

Chapter Seventy-one: Hou a man schal knowe hou mochel coveytise is hid in hys herte.

Chapter Seventy-two: Hou a man schal knowe whanne he synneth not in etynge and drynkynge and whanne he synneth deedli and whan veniali.

Chapter Seventy-three: The ground of leccherie schulde be distroied with goostli travaile and not with bodili.

Chapter Seventy-four: That a man schulde be bisi for to putte awai alle stirynges of synne but more bisili goostli synnes than bodili.

Chapter Seventy-five: That hunger and othere peynes of the bodi letteth moche goostly wirkynge.

Chapter Seventy-six: What remedie a man schal use agenes defaute maad in etynge and drinkynge.

Chapter Seventy-seven: That thorwgh besi desire and travaile in mekenesse and charité, a man cometh sunnere to othere vertues to travaile in hemself.

Chapter Seventy-eight: What cometh of the merkenese of the image of synne and what cometh bi the wyndowes thereof.

Chapter Seventy-nine: That a soule for defaute of knowynge of hitsilf wendith out bi the fyve wittes for to sek liking outward.

Chapter Eighty: That a soule schulde not seke withoute, but aske withinne of Jhesu, al that it nedeth.

Chapter Eighty-one: That the hoole of ymaginacion nedeth to be stopped, als wel as the wyndowes of the wittes.

Chapter Eighty-two: Whanne the use of the wittes and of the imaginacioun is deedli synne, and whanne venyal.

Chapter Eighty-three: Hou an ankir schal have hir to hem that comen to hir.

Chapter Eighty-four: Of the myrke image of synne and of the clothinge therof.

Chapter Eight-five: Whiche aren the lymes of the ymage of synne.

Chapter Eighty-six: Whereof the image of Jhesu is maad, and the ymage of synne and hou we aren passynge forth by the image of synne.

Chapter Eighty-seven: What profite cometh of the kepynge of the herte, and hou moche the soule is.

Chapter Eighty-eight: Hou the ymage of synne schal be broken doun.

Chapter Eighty-nine: How a man schal have hym agens stirynges of pride and of alle othere vices.

Chapter Ninety: What thynge helpith most a mannys knowynge, and geteth him that hym wanteth, and distroieth synne in hym.

Chapter Ninety-one: Hou a man schal be schapen to the image of Jhesu, and Jhesu schapen in hym.

Chapter Ninety-two: Hereinne is told the cause whi this writynge is maad, and hou sche schal have hire in the redynge that it was maad unto.

Book II

Chapter One: This chapitle scheweth that a man is seid the image of God aftir the soule and not aftir the bodi.

Table of Contents

Chapter Two: Hou it nedide to mankynde that oonli thorugh the passioun of oure Lord it schulde be restorid and reformed that was forsaken bi the first synne.

Chapter Three: That Jewes and paynymes and also fals Cristene men are not reformed effectuali thorugh vertu of this passioun for here owen defaute.

Chapter Four: Of two maner reformynge of this image, oon in fulnesse and othir in partie.

Chapter Five: That the reformyng in partie is on two maneres. Oon in feyth, anothir in feith and in felynge.

Chapter Six: That thorugh the sacrament of baptym that is groundid in the passioun of Crist this image is reformed fro the original synne.

Chapter Seven: That thorugh the sacrament of penaunce that stondeth in contricion and in confessioun and in satisfaccioun this image is reformed fro actuel synne.

Chapter Eight: Hou in the sacrament of baptym and of penaunce thorugh a privei unperceivable wirkynge of the Hooli Goost this image is reformed though it be not seen ne feelid.

Chapter Nine: That we schul trowe stidefasteli reformynge of this image, yif oure conscience wittenesse us a ful forsakynge of synne and a trewe turnynge of oure wil to good lyvynge.

Chapter Ten: That alle the soules that lyven mekeli in the trouthe of Holi Chirche and han here trouthe quykened with love and charité aren reformid bi this sacrament, though it so be that thei mown not fele the special gift of devocion or of goostli feelynge.

Chapter Eleven: That soules reformed neden ai for to fighten and stryven agen stirynges of synne whiles thei lyven heer, and hou a soule mai witen whanne he assenteth to ille stirynges and whanne not.

Chapter Twelve: That this image is bothe fair and foule whilis it is in this lif, though it be reformed; and of dyversité of felyng priveli had atwixe thise soulis that aren reformede and othere that aren nought reformed.

Chapter Thirteen: Of thre maner of men, of the whiche summe aren not reformed, and summe ben reformed oonli in feythe, and summe in feithe and in feelynge.

Chapter Fourteen: Hou men thorugh synne forschapen hemsilf into seere bestis liknesse and thise aren callid the loveres of this world.

Chapter Fifteen: Hou loveris of this world unable hemsilf on seere wise to the reformynge of here owen soulis.

Chapter Sixteen: A litil conceile hou loveres of this world schullen doon yif thei wolen be reformed in heer soules bifore that thei passen hennys.

Chapter Seventeen: That reformynge in feith and in feelynge mai not sodeynli be geten, but thorugh grace and mochil traveile bodili and goostli.

Chapter Eighteen: On encheson whi so fewe soulis as in regarde of the multitude of othere comen to this reformynge in feith and in feelynge.

Chapter Nineteen: Anothir encheson of the same, and hou wilful bodili custum undiscreteli rewarded and usid, sumtyme hyndren soulis fro felinge of more grace.

Chapter Twenty: Hou that withouten moche bodili and goostli bisynesse and withoute moche grace of mekenes of soulis mowen not be reformed in feelinge ne be kept in it whan thei mai come therto.

Chapter Twenty-one: That a man that wil come to Jerusalem, that is undirstonde to the cité of pees, the which is contemplacion, muste hoolde him lowe in mekenesse and in feith, and suffir disese bothe bodili and gosteli.

Chapter Twenty-two: Of a general remedie agens wikkid stirynges and peynful taryynges that fallen in here hertis of the fleisch, the world, and the feend, and hou a stidefast desire to Jhesu mayntened and strenthed with devout praiere and bisi thenkynge on Him is a sovereyn remedye.

Chapter Twenty-three: Hou thou that art thus in this weie and wolt not be put out bi no diseses; thyne enemyes wolen than forgen thee and sette thee bifore alle thi good deedes and commende thee of hem and hou than thou schalt putte hem awey.

Chapter Twenty-four: Hou a soule whan it is hid thorugh grace fro the vyle noise and besynesse of the world is a gode nyght and a lighti merkenesse, for thane may it freli praien and thenken on Jhesu.

Chapter Twenty-five: Hou that desire of Jhesu sothfastli feelid in this lightli myrkenesse sleeth alle stirynges of synne, and ableth the soule for to perceyve goostli lightnynges for the goostli Jerusalem, that is Jhesu.

Chapter Twenty-six: Hou a soule mai knowe fals illuminacions feyned bi the feend fro the trewe light of knowing that cometh oute of Jhesu; and bi what tokenes.

Table of Contents

Chapter Twenty-seven: Hou grete profite it is to a soule for to be brought thorugh grace into this lighti merkenes, and hou a man nedeth to dispose him yif he wole come therto and hou it is oonli the gate and the entré to contemplacioun.

Chapter Twenty-eight: That in reformynge of a soule the wirkynge of oure Lord is departed in foure tymes, that aren callynge, rightynge, magnifyyng, and glorifyynge.

Chapter Twenty-nine: Hou it falleth sumtyme that soulis bigynnynge and profitynge in grace han more fervour of love as bi outeward tokenes than sum men han that are perfite and netherelees yit is it not so.

Chapter Thirty: On what manere a man schal have the knowing of his owen soule and hou a man schal setten his love in Jhesu God and man, oo persone and netherelees yit is the love that is caused of biholdynge of Him as God and man worthiere and betere than that that is causid of Him oonli as man.

Chapter Thirty-one: Hou this maner of spekyng reformynge of a soule in feelynge and in what wise it is reformed is founden in Seynt Poulis wordis.

Chapter Thirty-two: Hou grace openeth the innere iye of a soule into goostli biholdynge of Jhesu, and hou there is thre maner of knowynge of Jhesu bi example of thre men stondynge in the sunne, on blynd, anothir hath his iyen sperid, and the thridde forth lokynge.

Chapter Thirty-three: Hou Jhesu is hevene to the soule; and hou a soule schal seke Jhesu above itself and withinne itsilf; and whi Jhesu is callid fier and light.

Chapter Thirty-four: Of two maner of love formed, what it meeneth, and unformed; and hou we aren biholden for to love Jhesu moche for oure makynge, but moche more for oure biynge, but most for oure ful savynge whanne He geveth the Holi Goost to us and maketh us saaf thorugh love.

Chapter Thirty-five: Hou sum soulis loven Jhesu bi bodili fervours, and bi ther owen affeccions that aren stired bi grace and bi resoun; and sum loven Jhesu more restfulli, bi gostli affeccions onli, stired inward thorugh grace of the Hooli Gost.

Chapter Thirty-six: That the gifte of love amonge alle the giftes of Jhesu is worthiest and most profitable; and hou Jhesu doth al that is wel don in His chosen onli for love. And hou love maketh the usynge of alle vertues and alle good dedis, light and esy.

Chapter Thirty-seven: Hou love, thoru a gracious biholding of Jhesu, sleth alle stirynges of pride and maketh the soule perfiteli meke; for it maketh the soule for to lese savour and delite in al ertheli worschip.

Chapter Thirty-eight: Hou love sleeth alle stirynges of ire and envie softeli, and reformeth in the soule the vertues of pees and pacience and of perfite charité to his even Cristene, as he deede speciali in the apostelis and martyres.

Chapter Thirty-nine: Hou love sleeth coveitise, leccherie, glotonye, and accidie, and the fleschli savour and delite in alle the fyve bodili wittes in the perfite love of Jhesu softli and esili thorugh a gracious biholdynge of Hym.

Chapter Forty: What vertues and graces a soule receyveth thorugh openynge of the innere iye into the gracious biholdynge of Jhesu, and hou it mai not be geten oonli thorugh mannes traveile, but thorugh special grace and traveile also.

Chapter Forty-one: Hou special grace in biholdynge of Jhesu withdraweth sumtyme from a soule, and hou a man schal han him in absence and presence of special grace, and hou a soule schal desiren that in it is ai the gracious presence of Jhesu.

Chapter Forty-two: A commendacioun of praiere offrid to Jhesu in a soule contemplatif, and hou stablenesse in praiere is a siker werk to stonden in, and hou every feelynge of grace in a chosen soule mai be seid Jhesu, but the more clene that the soule is, the worthiere is the grace.

Chapter Forty-three: Hou a soule thorugh openynge of the gosteli iye receyveth a gracious ablenesse for to undirstonden Holi Writ, and hou Jhesu, that is hid in Hooli Writte, scheweth Hym to Hise loveris.

Chapter Forty-four: Of the privei vois of Jhesu sounned in a soule, wherebi it mai be knowen; and hou alle the gracious illuminaciouns maad in a soule aren called the spekynges of Jhesu.

Chapter Forty-five: Hou thorugh openynge of the goostli iye a soule is maad wise, mekeli and sothfastli for to seen Hooli Chirche as travalynge and as blissid, and for to seen angelis kynde repreved for ther malice.

Chapter Forty-six: Hou bi the selve light of grace the blissed aungeles kynde mai be seen; and hou Jhesu as man aboven alle creatures, and as God aftir that the soule mai seen Hym heere.

The Scale of Perfection

Book I

Chapter One

That the innere havynge schulde be like to the uttere.

Goostli suster in Jhesu Crist, y praye thee that in the callynge whiche oure Lord hath callyd thee to IIis servyse, thu holde thee paied and stond stedefastli thereinne, travailynge bisili with alle thyne myghtes of thy soule bi grace of Jhesu Crist to fullefille in
5   sothfastnesse of gode lyvynge the staat whiche that thou hast take thee too in likenesse and in semynge. And as thu hast forsaken the world, as it were a deed man turnyd to oure Lord bodili in sight of men, right so that thyn hert myght be as it were deed to alle ertheli loves and dredes, turnyd hooli to oure Lord Jhesu Crist. For wite thu weel, a bodili turnynge to God without the herte folwynge is but a figure or a likenes of vertues
10   and no soothfastnesse. Wherfore a wrecchid man or a woman is he or sche that leveth al the inward kepinge of hymself and schapith hym withoute oonli a fourme and likenes of hoolynesse, as in habite and in speche and in bodili werkes, biholdynge othere mennys deedys and demyng here defaughtes, wenynge hymsilf to be aught whanne he is right nought, and so bigileth hymsilf. Do thou not so, but turne thyne herte with thy body
15   principali to God, and schape thee withinne to His likenesse bi mekenesse and charité and othere goostli vertues, and thanne art thou truli turned to Hym.

    I sey not that thou so lightli on the first day may be turnyd to Hym in thi soule bi fulheed of vertues as thu may with thi bodi be speryd in an hous, but that thu schuldest

---

1 havynge, conduct; **uttere**, outer. **2 Goostli suster**, Spiritual sister; **callynge**, her vocation as an enclosed anchorite. **3 paied**, satisfied. **4 bisili**, diligently; **myghtes**, powers. **5 sothfastnesse**, truthfulness; **staat**, estate. **6 semynge**, appearance; **deed**, dead. **8 dredes**, fears; **hooli**, wholly; **wite**, know. **11 kepinge**, maintaining; **schapith**, forms; **withoute**, on the outside. **13 demyng here defaughtes**, judging their faults; **wenynge**, supposing; **aught**, something. **14 nought**, nothing. **15 schape thee**, conform yourself. **16 goostli**, spiritual. **17 lightli**, easily. **18 fulheed**, fullness; **speryd**, locked.

31

20 knowe that the cause of thy bodili enclosynge is that thu myght the betere come to goosteli enclosynge; and as thi bodi is enclosid fro bodili conversacioun of men, right so that thyn hert myght be enclosid from fleisschli loves and dredis of alle ertheli thynges. And that thu myght the betere come therto, I schalle telle thee in this litel wrytinge, as me thynketh. Thou schalt undirstonde that ther ben in Holi Chirche two maner of lyves, as Seynt Gregor seith, in the whiche Cristene men schul be saaf. That on is callid actif

25 lif, that other contemplatif lif. Withoutin the ton of thise two may no man be saaf.

Chapter Two

Of actif lif and of the werkes of it.

Actif lif lieth in love and charité schewyd outward in good bodili werkes, in fulfillynge of Goddis comaundementes and of the sevene deedys of mercy, bodeli and goostli, to a mannys even Cristene. This lif longeth to alle worldeli men whiche han richesse and

30 plenté of worldli goodes, and also to alle othere whiche eithir han staat, office, or cure over other men and han goodis for to spende, leryd or lewyd, temporal or spiritual; and generali alle worldli men. They aren bounden to fulfille up here myght and here connynge, as reson and discrecion asketh. Yif he mykil have, mykil doo; yif he litil have, litil doo; yif he nought have, that thanne he have a good wille. These aren werkes of actif lif,

35 eyther bodili or goostli.

Also a partie of actif lif lieth in grete bodili deedes whiche a man dooth to hymsilf, as greet fastynge, mykil wakynge, and other scharp penaunce-doynge for to chastise the fleissch with discrecioun for trespaces that been bifore doon, and bi sich penaunce for to refreyne lustes and likynges of it, and make it buxum and redi to the wil of the Spirit.

19 **bodili enclosynge**, enclosure in a cell as an anchorite. 20 **conversacioun**, interaction. 21 **fleisschli**, carnal; **dredis**, fears. 23 **me thynketh**, it seems to me; **ben**, are. 24 **saaf**, saved. 25 **ton**, one. 27 **schewyd**, shown. 29 **even Cristene**, fellow Christians; this is Hilton's frequent usage; **longeth**, belongs; **han**, have. 30 **plenté**, plenty; **staat**, status; **cure**, reponsibility. 31 **leryd**, learned; **lewyd**, ignorant. 32 **up here myght**, according to their ability; **connynge**, knowledge. 33 **asketh**, requires; **mykil,**, much. 34 **nought**, nothing. 36 **partie**, part. 38 **fleissch**, flesh; **trespaces**, trespasses. 39 **lustes**, desires; **likynges**, pleasures; **buxum**, obedient; **redi**, prompt.

40   Thise werkes, though thei ben actif, not for thi they helpen mykel and ordaynen a man in the bigynnynge to come to contemplatif lif, yif thei ben usid bi discrecion.

Chapter Three

Of contemplatif lif and the werkes of hit.

Contemplatif lif is in perfight love and charité feelid inwardli bi goostli vertues and bi soothfaste knowynge and sight of God in goosteli thynges. This lif longeth speciali to

45   hem whiche forsaken for the love of God al worldli richesse and worschipes and outeward besynesse and oonly gyven hem body and soule, up her myght and here kunnynge, to the service of God bi goosteli occupacioun. Now sithen it is so that thy staat asketh to be contemplatif, for that is the ende and the entent of thyn enclosynge, that thu myght more freli and entierli gyve thee to gosteli occupacioun — thanne bihoveth thee for to be

50   right bisy nyght and day with travaile of bodi and of spirit, for to come to that lif as neer as thu may bi swich meenys as thu hopist were best unto thee.

    Neverthelees bifore that I telle thee of the meenys, I schal telle firste a litil more of this lif contemplatif that thu myght sumwhat see what it is and sette it as a mark in the sight of thi soule wherto thu schalt drawe in al thyn occupacion.

Chapter Four

55   Of the first partye of contemplacioun.

Contemplatif liyf hath three parties. The first is in knowynge of God and goosteli thynges geten by resoun, bi techynge of man and bi studie of Hooly Writ, withouten goostli

---

40 not for thi, nevertheless; **ordaynen**, dispose. **43 perfight**, perfect; **feelid**, felt. **44 soothfaste**, true; **goosteli**, spiritual; **longeth**, belongs. **45 hem**, them. **46 besynesse**, activity; **gyven hem**, give themselves. **47 occupacioun**, activity; **sithen**, since. **48 thu**, you. **49 freli**, freely; **entierli**, entirely; **thee**, yourself; **bihoveth thee**, it is necessary for you. **50 right**, very. **51 meenys**, means. **54 occupacion**, activities. **55 partye**, part. **56 liyf**, life; **parties**, parts. **57 geten**, obtained.

affeccion and inward savour feelid bi the special gift of the Hooli Goost. This party han speciali summe lettred men and grete clerkes whiche bi longe studé and travaile in

60   Hooli Writ comen to this knowynge, more or lesse, after the sutelté of kyndeli wit and contynuance of studie after the general gift that God gyveth to everi man that hath use of reson. This knowyng is good, and it may be called a partie of contemplacioun in as mykil as it is a sight of soothfastnesse and knowynge of goostli thynges.

     Neverthelees, it is but a figure and a schadewe of verry contemplacioun, for it hath

65   no gosteli savoure in God ne the inwarde swetnesse of love, whiche may no man feele but he be in mykil charité. For that is the propir welle of oure Lord, to the whiche cometh noon alien. But this maner of knowinge is comone to gode and to badde, for it may be had withoute charité. And therfore it is not veri contemplacion, as ofte sithes heretikes, ypocrites, and fleisschly lyvynge men han more sich knowynge than many

70   trewe Cristene men, and yit han thise men noo charité. Of this maner of knowynge speketh Seynt Poul thus: *Si habuero omnem scienciam et noverim misteria omnia, caritatem autem non habuero, nichil sum* (1 Corinthians 13:2). Yif I hadde ful knowynge of alle thyngis, yhe, and y knewe al privytees and I hadde no charité, I am right nought. Neverthelees, yif they that han this knowynge kepe hem in mekenesse and charité, sich

75   as thei han, and fleen worldli and fleischly synnes up her myght, it is to hem a good wey and a gret disposynge to veri contemplacion yif thei desiren and prayen devouteli after the grace of the Hooli Goost.

     Othere men whiche have this knowyng and turnen it into pride and veynglorie of hemsilf, or into coveityse or desirynge of worldli staatis, worschipes or richesses, not

80   mekeli taken it in praisynge of God, ne charitabli spenden it in profight of here evene Cristene, summe of hem fallen oither into errours and heresies, or into othere opyn synnes bi the whiche thei sclaundren hemsilf and al Holi Chirche.

---

58 affeccion, affection; **savour,** taste; **feelid,** felt; **han,** have. **59 studé,** study. **60 after,** according to; **sutelté,** subtlety; **kyndeli wit,** natural intelligence. **63 mykil,** much. **64 schadewe,** shadow; **verry,** true. **65 savoure,** taste; **swetnesse,** sweetness. **66 propir,** belonging to; **welle,** source. **67 noon,** no. **68 veri,** true; **ofte sithes,** often times. **69 ypocrites,** hypocrites; **han,** have; **sich,** such. **72 Yif,** If. **73 yhe,** yea; **privytees,** mysteries. **74 hem,** themselves. **75 han,** have; **fleen,** flee; **up her myght,** according to their ability. **76 disposynge,** disposition; **yif,** if. **77 after,** for. **79 hemsilf,** themselves; **coveityse,** covetousness; **staatis,** positions; **worschipes,** honors. **80 ne,** nor; **profight,** profit; **here,** their. **82 sclaundren,** slander.

Of this knowynge seyde Seynt Poul thus: *Sciencia inflat, caritas autem edificat* (1
Corinthians 8:1). Knowynge aloone bolneth up the hert into pride, but medle it with
85   charité and thanne turneth it to edificacion. This knowynge aloone is but water, unsavery
and cold; and therfore yif thei wold mekeli offre it up to oure Lord and praye Hym of
His grace, He schulde with His blissinge turne the water into wyn as He dide for the
praier of His moder at the feest of Architriclyn. That is for to seie, He schulde turne the
unsavery knowynge into wisdoom and the colde naked resoun into goosteli light and
90   brennynge bi the gift of the Holi Goost.

Chapter Five

Of the secunde partye of contemplacion.

The secunde partie of contemplacion lieth principali in affeccioun, withoute
undirstondynge of gosteli thynges, and this is comonli of simple and unlettrid men
which gyven hem hooli to devocion. And this is feelid on this maner. Whan a man or a
95   woman in meditacioun of God feelith fervour of love and gostli swettenesse, bi mynde
of His passioun or of ony of His werkes in His manhede; or he felith greet trust in the
goodnesse and in the merci of God, of forgyvenesse of his synnes and for Ilis grete
giftes of grace; or ellis he feeleth drede in his affeccioun with gret reverence of the
pryvey doomes of God which he seeth not, and of His rightwisenesse; or in praier he
100   feelith the thought of his herte drawe up from alle ertheli thynges, streyned togedre with
alle the myghtes of it, upstiande into oure Lord bi fervent desire and goostili dylite; and
neverthelees in that tyme he hath noon opyn sight in undirstondyng in goostli thynges,
ne of pryvitees of Holi Writ in special, but oonly that hym thenketh for the tyme nothyng
liketh hym so mykil as for to praie or for to thynke as he dooth for savour, delite, and

84 bolneth, swells; **medle**, mingle. **85 unsavery**, unsavory. **86 yif**, if. **88 Architriclyn**, ruler of
the feast, mistakenly taken as a proper name; see John 2:9 and Clark, p. 162n14. **90 brennynge**,
burning. **91 partye**, part. **92 affeccioun**, the emotions. **93 gosteli**, spiritual. **94 hem**, themselves; **hooli**, wholly. **95–96 bi mynde of**, by remembering. **96 manhede**, humanity. **98 drede**,
fear. **99 pryvey**, secret; **doomes**, judgments; **rightwisenesse**, righteousness. **100 streyned**,
contained. **101 upstiande**, ascending; **dylite**, pleasure. **103 hym thenketh**, it seems to him.
104 liketh, pleases.

105   comfort that he fyndeth thereinne; and yit he can not telle weel what it is, but he feelith it wel, for oute of it springeth many good sweet teres, brennande desires, and many stille mornynges, whiche schoure and clensyn the herte fro al the filthe of synne, and maken hit melten into a wondirful swettenesse of Jhesu Crist, buxum, souple and redi to fulfulle al Goddis wille, in so mykil that hym thynketh he maketh no charge what

110   come of hymsilf then, so that Goddis wille were folfillid, with siche many styrynges moo thanne y can or may seye. Thes felynges mai not be had without greet grace, and whoso hath hem, for the tyme I hope that he is in charité. Which charité may not be lorn ne lassed, though the fervour of it passe away, but bi a deedli synne; and that is counfortable. This may be called the secunde partie of contemplacioun.

Chapter Six

115   Of the lower degré of the secunde partie of contemplacioun.

Neverthelees this partie hath two degrees. The lowere degré of this feelynge, men whiche aren actif may have bi grace whanne thei be visited of oure Lord, as myghtili and as ferventli as thei that gyven hem hooli to contemplatiff liyf and han this gift. But it lasteth not so longe. Also this feelynge in his fervour cometh not alwey whanne a man

120   wolde, ne it lasteth not wel longe. It cometh and gooth as he wole that gyveth it. And therfore whoso hath it, meke hymsilf and thanke God, and kepe it prevey, but yif it be to his confessour, and holde it as longe as he may with discrecion. And whanne hit withdraweth, drede not to mykil, but stond in feith and in meke hope, with pacient abidynge til it come agen. This is a litil tastynge of the swetenesse in the love of God, of

125   the whiche David seith thus in the sautier: *Gustate et videte quam suavis est dominus* (Psalms 33:9). Tasteth and seeth the swettenesse of oure Lord.

106 brennande, burning. **107 mornynges**, mournings; **schoure**, scour; **clensyn**, cleanse. **108 buxum**, obedient; **souple**, compliant. **109 fulfulle**, fulfill (the second *u*, if it is not the result of a minim error for *i*, indicates a southern spelling). **110 folfillid**, fulfilled; **styrynges**, stirrings. **111 moo**, more. **112 hope**, suppose. **113 lorn**, lost; **lassed**, diminished. **114 counfortable**, comforting. **116 degrees**, stages. **121 meke**, humble; **prevey**, secret; **but yif**, unless. **123 to mykil**, too much. **125 sautier**, psalter.

Chapter Seven

Of the highere degree of the secunde partie of contemplacion.

But the highere degré of this partie may not be had ne halden, but of thoo that aren in grete reest of bodi and soule, the which bi grace of Jhesu Crist and longe travaile bodili
130 and goostli felen rest of herte and clennesse in conscience, so that hem liketh nothynge so mykil for to do as for to sitte stille in reste of bodi and for to alwey pray to God and to thynke on oure Lord, and for to thynke sum tyme on the blissid name Jhesu, which is maad confortable and delitable to hem, that they bi the mynde of it, felen hem feed in here affeccion. And not oonli bi that name, but alle othere praieres, as the Pater Noster
135 or the Ave Maria or ympnys or psalmes or other devoute seyynges of Holi Chirche aren turnyd as it were into gostli mirthe and swete songe, bi the which thei aren comfortid and strengthed agens alle synnes, and mykil relevyd of bodili dishese. Of this degree spekcth Seynt Poul thus: *Nolite inebriari vino sed impleamini spiritu sancto, loquentes vobismetipsis in ympnis et psalmis, et canticis spiritualibus, cantantes et psallentes in*
140 *cordibus vestris domino* (Ephesians 5:18–19). Be not drunken with wyn, but be ye fulfilled of the Holi Goost, seiande to youresilf in ympnes and psalmes and goostli songes, syngynge and phalmynge in youre hertes to oure Lorde. Whoso hath this grace, kepe hymself in lowenesse, and that he be evermore desirynge for to come to more knowyng and feelynge of God in the thridde partie of contemplacioun.

Chapter Eight

145 Of the thridde partie of contemplacion.

The thridde partie of contemplacioun, whiche is perfite as it may be here, lieth bothe in cognicion and in affeccion: that is for to seie, in knowyng and in perfight lovynge of

128 halden, held; **of thoo**, by those. **129 reest**, rest. **130 clennesse**, purity; **hem liketh**, it pleases them. **132 blissid name Jhesu**, devotion to the name of Jesus was popular in the later Middle Ages; see Clark, p. 162n20. **133 confortable**, comforting; **delitable**, pleasant. **134 Pater Noster**, the Lord's Prayer. **135 Ave Maria**, the prayer, "Hail Mary"; **ympnys**, hymns. **137 dishese**, distress. **141 seiande**, saying; **ympnes**, hymns. **142 phalmynge**, psalming (see Textual Notes). **144 thridde**, third. **146 perfite**, perfect.

God. And that is whanne a mannys soule first is cleensid from alle synnes and reformyd
bi fulheed of vertues to the ymage of Jhesu; and after whanne he is visitid and is taken
150   up from alle ertheli and fleisschli affecciones, from veyn thoughtis and veyn ymaginacions
of alle bodili thynges, and as it were mykil ravysschid out of the bodili wittes and thanne
bi the grace of the Holi Gost is illumyned for to see bi undirstoondynge soothfastnesse,
whiche is God, and also goostli thynges, with a soft swete brennande love in hym, so
perfightli that bi ravyschynge of this love the soule is ooned for the tyme and conformyd
155   to the ymage of the Trinité. The bigynnyng of this contemplacioun may be felid in this
lif, but the fulheed of it is kepid in the blisse of hevene. Of this onynge and conformynge
speketh Seynt Poul thus: *Qui adheret deo unus spiritus est cum illo* (1 Corinthians 6:17).
That is for to seie, whoso bi raveschynge of love is fastned to God, thanne God and a
soule aren not two but bothe oon. Not in fleisch, but in oo spirit. And sotheli in this
160   onynge is the mariage maad bitwixe God and the soule, which schal nevere be brokyn.

Chapter Nine

Of the twynynge of the thridde partie of contemplacion fro the secunde, and of praysynge
of it.

That othir partie mai be called brennande love in devocioun, but this is brennande love
in contemplacion. That is the lowere, this is the highere. That is the swettere to the
165   bodili felinge, this is swettere to the goostli felynge, for it is more inward, more goostli,
and more worthi and more wonderful. For this is verili a taastynge, and as it were a
sight of heveneli joye, not cleerli, but half in derkenesse, which schal be fulfillid and
opynli clerid in the blisse of hevene, as Seynt Poul seith: *Videmus nunc per speculum in
enigmate; tunc autem videbimus facie ad faciem* (1 Corinthians 13:12). We seen now
170   God bi a myrour, as it were in deerkenesse, but in hevene we schulen see openli face to

---

148 mannys, man's; **cleensid**, cleansed. **149 fulheed**, fulness. **150 ymaginacions**, imaginings.
151 ravysschid, ravished; the term is from St. Paul's description of his mystical experience on
the road to Damascus (2 Corinthians 12:2) and is typically associated with contemplation.
153 brennande, burning. **154 ooned**, united. **156 fulheed**, fulness; **kepid**, kept; **onynge**, union.
159 oo, one. **161 twynynge**, separation. **166 verili**, truly. **168 clerid**, made clear.

face. This is the illuminacion of undirstondynge in delites of lovynge, as David seith in the sautier: *Et nox mea illuminacio mea in deliciis meis* (Psalms 138:11). Mi nyght is my light in my delitees. That othere partie is mylk for children, this is hool mete for perfite men, which han assaied wittes to knowe the gode from the yvel, as Seynt Poul

175 seith: *Perfectorum est solidus cibus qui habent sensus exercitatos ad discrecionem boni et mali* (Hebrews 5:14).

The wirkynge and the ful use of this gift may no man have, but yif he bee first reformed to the likenesse of Jhesu bi fulheed of vertues. Ther may no man lyvande in fleisch dedli have contynueli it in his fulheed, but bi tymes whanne he is visited. And as

180 I conceyve of the writynge of holi men, it is ful schort tyme, for soone after he falleth into sobirté of bodili felynge. And alle this werke maketh charité. Thus, as I undirstonde, seid Seynt Poul of hymsilf: *Sive excidimus, deo, sive sobrii sumus, vobis; caritas Christi urget nos* (2 Corinthians 5:13–14). Whether we overpasse oure bodili wittes to God in contemplacion, or we aren more sobre to yow in bodily felynge, the charité of Crist

185 stireth us. Of this partie of contemplacioun and conformynge to God speketh Seint Poul: *Nos autem revelata facie gloriam domini speculamur, transformati in eandem ymaginem, a claritate in claritatem tanquam a domini spiritu* (2 Corinthians 3:18). This is thus moche for to seie, Seynt Poul in the persone of hymsilf and of perfight men seith thus: We, first reformed bi vertues to the likenes of God se the face of oure soule

190 unhiled bi openynge of the goostli iye, bihalden as in a myrour heveneli joye, ful schapen and oned to the ymage of oure Lord, fro brightnesse of feith into brightnesse of undirstondynge, or elles from clerté of desire into cleerté of blissid love. And al this is wrought of the sprite of oure Lord in a mannes soule, as Seynt Poule seith. This part of contemplacioun God gyveth where that he wole, to lerid or to lewed, men or women

195 occupied in prelacie, and to solitarie also, but it is special and not comone. And also though a man which is actif have the gifte of it bi a special grace, neverthelees the ful use of it as I hoope may no man have, but he be solitarie and in liyf contemplatif.

172 **sautier**, psalter. 173 **delitees**, delights. 173–74 **mylk for children . . . for perfite men**, a commonplace contrast based on 1 Corinthians 3:1–2; used also in *Scale*, Book II, chapters 10 and 31. 173 **mete**, food. 174 **assaied**, tested; **wittes**, sense. 178 **lyvande**, living. 181 **sobirté**, soberness. 183 **overpasse**, surpass; **wittes**, senses. 184 **felynge**, feeling. 190 **unhiled**, revealed; **iye**, eye; **schapen**, formed. 191 **oned**, united. 192 **clerté**, brightness. 193 **sprite**, spirit. 194 **lerid**, learned; **lewed**, ignorant. 195 **prelacie**, prelacy; Clark notes (p. 163n33) that the women prelates referred to must be heads of religious houses. 197 **hoope**, suppose; **liyf**, life.

Chapter Ten

How the schewynges to the bodili wittis and the feelynge of hem may be bothe good and yvel.

200   By this that I have seid myght thu sumwhat undirstonde that visiones or revelaciouns of ony maner spirite, bodili apperynge or in ymagynynge, slepand or wakand, or ellis ony othere feelinge in the bodili wittes maad as it were goosteli; either in sownynge of the eere, or saverynge in the mouth, or smellynge in the nose, or ellis ony felable heete as it were fier glowand and warmand the breest, or ony othere partie of the bodi, or onythinge 205   that mai be feelyd bi bodili wit, though it be never so comfortable and lykande, aren not verili contemplacion; ne thei aren but symple and secundarie though thei be good, in regard of goostli vertues and in goosteli knowynge and loovyng of God.

     For in vertues and in knowynge of God with love is noo disceit. But al swich maner of feelyng thei mowe by gode, wrought bi a good angil, and they may be deceyvable, 210   feyned bi a wikkid angel whan he transfigurith him into an angel of light. Wherfore sithen thei moun be bothe good and yvel, it semeth that thei aren not of the beste; for wyte thou weel that the devyl may, whanne he hath leve, feyne in bodili felinge the liknes of the same thinges whiche a good angil may worche. For as the good angil cometh with light, so can the devel, and so of othere wittes. Whoso hadde felid bothe, 215   he schulde kunne telle whiche were gode and whiche were yvele, but he that nevere feelid neither, or elles but that oon, may lightli be disseyved.

     Thei aren like in maner of feelynge oughtward, but thei aren ful diverse withinne; and therfore thei aren not to desire greetli, ne for to resseyve lightli, but yif a soule myght bi spirite of discrecioun knowe the gode from the yvele, that he were not bigiled. Seynt 220   Joon seith thus: *Nolite credere omni spiritui, sed probate si ex deo sit* (1 John 4:1). Seynt

---

198 schewynges, revelations; **wittis**, senses. **201 slepand**, sleeping; **wakand**, waking. **202 sownynge**, sounding. **203 saverynge**, tasting. **204 glowand**, glowing; **warmand**, warming. **205 wit**, sense; **comfortable**, comforting; **lykande**, pleasant. **205–06 aren not verili contemplacion**, are not truly contemplation; the first of several critiques of the association of sensible phenomena with contemplation, an association found in the works of Richard Rolle; see also *Scale*, I.669–79; Clark, p. 163n36. **209 mowe by**, may be; **deceyvable**, deceitful. **211 moun**, may; **yvel**, evil. **212 wyte**, know. **213 worche**, work. **215 kunne**, know how to. **216 lightli**, easily; **disseyved**, deceived. **217 oughtward**, outward.

Joon biddeth us, we schulde not leve everi spirit, but we schullen assaien frist whether he be of God or no. Therfore bi oon assaie, I schal telle thee as me thenketh.

Chapter Eleven

Hou thu schal knowe whanne the schewinges to thi bodili wittes and the feelynge of hem aren good or yvele.

225 If it be soo that thou see ony maner of light or brightnes with thi bodili iye or in ymagynynge, othir than every man mai see; or yif thou here ony meri or wondirful sowninge with thi bodili eere; or in thi mouth ony swete sodayne savour, othir than of kynde; or ony heete in thi breest as it were fier; or ony maner of deelighte in ony partie of thi bodi; or yif a spirit bodili appere to thee as hit were an angel for to conforte thee

230 and teche thee; or ony swich feelynge which thu woost weel it cometh not of thiself ne of noo bodili creature — be thanne waar in that tyme or soone aftir and wisili bihoold the stirynge of thyne herte. Yif thou be stired bicause of that likinge that thu feelist, for to drawe oute thyn herte from biholdinge of oure Lord Jhesu Crist and fro goostli occupacions, as from preiers, and thenkinge of thisilf and of thi defautis, fro the inward

235 desire of vertues and of goostli knowynge and the feelinge of God, for to sette the sight of thin herte and thyn affeccioun, thi delite and thi reest principali therinne, wenynge that bodili feelinge schulde be a partie of heveneli joie and of angilis blisse, and for thi thee thynketh that thu schuldest never pray ne thinke not elles, but al hooli tende therto, for to kepe it and delite thee therinne: this feelinge is suspect and of the enemye. And

240 therfore, yif it be never so likinge and wondirful, refuse it and assente not therto, for this is the sleighte of the enemy. Whanne he seeth that a soule gyveth him entierli to goostli occupacioun, he is wondirful wrooth, for he hateth nothinge more thanne for to see a soule in bodi of synne feele verili the savour of gostli knowinge and the love of God, the whiche he withouten bodi of synne loste wilfulli. And therefore yif he may not

221 leve, believe; **frist**, first. **222 bi**, by; **assaie**, test. **225 iye**, eye. **227 sowninge**, sound. **228 kynde**, nature; **fier**, fire. **230 woost weel**, know well. **231 waar**, aware. **232 stirynge**, stirring; **likinge**, pleasure. **234 occupacions**, activities; **defautis**, faults. **236 wenynge**, supposing. **237–38 for thi thee thynketh**, because it seems to you. **239 the enemye**, one of Hilton's regular terms for the devil. **240 likinge**, pleasant. **241 sleighte**, deception. **242 wrooth**, angry.

245 lette him bi opyn bodili synnes, he wole dere hym and bigile him bi swich a vanité of bodili savoures or swettenesse in the wittis, for to bringe a soule into goostli pride and into a fals sikernesse of himsilf, wenande therbi that he hadde a feelinge of heveneli joye, and that he were half in paradise for delite that he feeleth al aboute hym, whanne he is neer atte helle gates, and so bi pride and presumpcion he myght falle into errouris

250 or into fantasies or into othere bodili or goostli myschevys.

Neverthelees, yif it so be that this maner of feelynge lette not thyn herte fro goostli occupacion, but it maketh thee the more devoute and the more fervent for to pray, it maketh thee the more wise for to thenke goostli thoughtes; and though it be so that it stonyeth thee in the first biginnynge, neverthelees aftirward it turneth and quykeneth

255 thyn herte to more desire of vertues and encreseeth thi love more bothe to God and to thyn evene Cristen; also it maketh thee more meke in thyn owyn sight. Bi thise tokenes may thu knowe thanne that it is of God, maad bi the presence and the touchinge of the good angil, and that is of the goodnesse of God in confort of symple devoute soulis for to encrese ther trust and there desire to God, for to seke therbi the knowynge and the

260 love of God more perfightli for swich a confort, or ellis, yif thei be perfight, that thei fele suyche a delite: it semeth than that it is an ernest, and as it were a schadewe of glorifyynge of the bodi which it schal have in the blisse. But I not whether ther be ony siche man lyvande in erthe. This pryvylegie hadde Marie Mawdeleyn, as hit seemeth to my sight, in tyme whanne sche was visited, whanne sche was aloone in the cave thritti

265 wyntir and iche day was born up with angelis into the eyr, and was feed bothe bodi and soule bi the presence of hem. Thus we reden in the legend of hire.

Of this maner of assayinge of wirkynge of spirites speketh Seynt Joon in his epistil thus, and techeth us: *Omnis spiritus qui solvit Jhesum, hic non est ex deo* (1 John 4:3). Eche a spirit that looseth Jhesu or ellis unknitteth Hym, he is not of God. Thise woordes

---

245 lette, prevent; **dere**, harm. **247 sikernesse**, security; **wenande**, supposing. **250 myschevys**, misfortunes. **251 lette**, hinder. **254 stonyeth**, astonishes; **quykeneth**, enlivens. **255 encreseeth**, increases. **260 perfightli**, perfectly; **swich**, such. **261 suyche**, such. **262 not**, know not. **263 pryvylegie**, privilege; **Mawdeleyn**, Magdalene. Mary Magdalene was identified with Mary, the sister of Martha, thus becoming a type of the contemplative; the story of her dwelling in a cave was a widely known medieval legend. See Jacobus de Voragine, *The Golden Legend*, trans. William Granger Ryan (Princeton: Princeton University Press, 1993), 1:379–80. **265 eyr**, air. **267 assayinge**, testing.

270   may be undirstonde on many manerys; neverthelees upon oon maner I mai undirstonde
       to that purpos whiche y have seid.

Chapter Twelve

What knetteth Jhesu to mannys soule and what looseth Hym therfro.

The knyttyng and the festenynge of Jhesu to a mannys soule is bi good wille and a greet
desire to Hym oonli, for to love and for to have Hym and see Him in His blisse. The
275   more goostli that he desireth, the fastere is Jhesu knyt to the soule; and the lesse that he
       desireth, the lousere He is knyt. Than what spirit or what felyng that it be that leeseth
       this desire and wolde drawe hit doun fro stable mynde of Jhesu Crist, and from the
       kyndeli stiynge up to Hym, for to sette it upon himsilf, thys spirit wole unknytten and
       undo Jhesu from the soule, and therfore it is not of God, but it is of the wirkynge of the
280   enemye. Neverthelees, yif a spirit, or a felynge, or revelacion maketh his desire more,
       knytteth the knotte of love and of devocion to Jhesu fastere, openeth the sight of the
       soule into goostli knowynge more cleerli, and maketh it more meke in itsilf, this spirit is
       of God. Here mai thu see sumwhat that thu schalt not suffre thyn herte wilfulli for to
       reste, ne for to delite hooli, in no bodili thynge of sich maner felinge, confortes or
285   swettenessis, though thei were gode; but thou schalt holde hem in thyn owen sight as
       thei were right nought or litil in regard of gostli desire, ne sette not to mykil thyn herte
       upon hem. But thou schalt ay seke that thou myght come to goostli feelynge of God;
       and that is that thou myght knowe the wisdom of God, the eendelees myght of Hym,
       the grete goodnesse of Hym in Hymsilf and in His creatures. For this is contemplacion
290   and that othir is noon. Thus seith Seynt Poul: *In caritate radicati, et fundati, ut possitis*
       comprehendere cum omnibus sanctis, que sit longitudo, et latitudo, sublimitas, et
       profundum (Ephesians 3:17–18). Be ye rootid and groundid in charité, that ye may
       knowe, he seith, neither the sound of the eere, ne the swete savour in the mouth, ne
       siche bodili thyng, but that ye myght knowe and fele with alle halewes, whiche is the
295   lengthe of the eendelees beynge of God, the brede of the wondirful charité and goodnes

276 lousere, looser; **leeseth**, loses. **278 kyndeli stiynge**, natural rising. **287 ay**, always. **294
halewes**, saints. **295 brede**, breadth.

of God, the heighte of the almyghti magesté of Hym, and the groundlees depnesse of the wisdom of God.

Chapter Thirteen

How and in what thynges a contemplatif man schuld ben occupied.

In knowynge and in felinge gostly, in thise schulde be the occupacion of a contemplatif man, for in thise mai be undirstonden the ful knowynge of gosteli thynges. This occupacion is that thynge that Seynt Poul coveitede, seiynge thus: *Unum vero, que retro sunt obliviscens, in anteriora me extendam sequor si quomodo comprehendam supernum bravium* (Philippians 3:13–14). O thynge, as who seith, is left to me for to coveite, and that is that I may forgeten al thynges whiche aren hyndward, and y schal strecche unto myn herte ay forward for to feele and for to gripe the sovereyne meede of the endelees blisse. Hyndward aren alle bodili thingis, foreward aren alle goostli thinges; and therfore Seynt Poul wolde forgeten al bodili thyng, and his owen bodi also, forthi that he myght see goostli thynges.

Chapter Fourteen

Hou in resoun and in wille vertues bigynnen, and in love and in likynge it is eendid and maad perfight.

Now have y toolde thee a litil of countemplacion, what it schulde be, for this entent, that thu myght knowe it and sette it as it were a mark bifore the sight of thi soule, and for to desire al thy lyvetyme for to come to ony partie of it bi the grace of oure Lord Jhesu Crist. This is the confoormynge of a soule to God, which may not be had but he be first reformyd bi fulheed of vertues turnyd into affeccion. And that is whanne a man loveth vertu, for it is good in the silf.

300
305
310
315

303 O, One; **as who seith**, as is said; **coveite**, desire. **304 hyndward**, behind. **305 gripe**, grasp; **meede**, reward.

There is many man that hath vertues, as lowenesse, pacience, charité to his even Cristene, and siche othere, onli in his resoun and wille and hath no goostli delite ne love in hem. For ofte tyme he felith grucchinge, hevynesse, and bittirnesse for to doo hem,

320 and neverthelees yit he doth hem bi strengthe and stirynge of resoun for drede of God. This man hath vertues in resoun and in wille, but not the love of hem in affeccion. But whanne bi the grace of gode Jhesu, and bi goostli and bodili exercise, reson is turnyd into light and wil into love, thanne hath he vertues in affeccion, for he hath so wel gnawen upon the bittir bark of the note that he hath broken it and fedeth him with the

325 swete kirnel. That is for to seie, the vertues whiche weren first hevy for to do aren now turnyd into delite and savour, as whanne a man liketh in mekenesse, in pacience, in clennesse, in sobirté and in charité, as in ony delices. Sothli whanne vertues be turned thus into affeccioun, he may have the secunde partie of contemplacioun, but to the thridde soothfastli he schal not come. Now sithen vertues aren so disposynge to

330 contemplacion, than bihoveth thee for to use certayn meenes for to come to vertues.

Chapter Fifteen

Of the meenes that bryngen a man to contemplacioun.

Thre meenys there ben whiche men most comonli use that gyven hem to contemplacioun: redynge of Holi Writ and of hooli techynge, goosteli meditacion, and besi praeris with devocioun. Redynge of Holi Writ mai thu not wel use, and therfore thee bihoveth more

335 occupye thee in prayer and in meditacioun. By meditacion schalt thou see hou mykil thee wanteth of vertues; and bi prayer schalt thou gete hem. Bi meditacion schalt thou see thi wrecchidnesse, thi synnes, and thi wikkidnessis, as pryde, coveytise, glotonye,

317 lowenesse, humility. **319 grucchinge**, complaining; **hevynesse**, gloom. **320 drede**, fear. **324 note**, nut. **327 clennesse**, purity; **sobirté**, soberness; **delices**, delights. **329 sithen**, since. **330 bihoveth thee**, it is necessary for you. **332 gyven hem**, give themselves. **333 besi praeris**, diligent prayers; with *redynge* and *meditacion* just mentioned, the conventional triad, *lectio, meditatio, oratio*, associated with the contemplative life. See Leclerq, *Love of Learning*, pp. 15–17, 72–74. **334 mai thu not wel use**, Clark notes (p. 165n52) that the (female) reader addressed by Hilton presumably could not read Latin. **336 wanteth**, lack. **337 pryde**, an expanded list of the seven capital (or deadly) sins begins here; the others of the seven included leccherie, wikide stiryngis of envye, ire, haterede, malincolie, angrynesse, bittirnesse, sleughthe, and unskilful hevynesse. Thou schalt also see thyn herte ful of veyn schames

340 and dredes of thi fleisch and of the world. Alle thise stirynges wole alwey boylen ought of the herte as watir wole renne from the sprynge of a stynkande welle, and letten the sight of thi soule, that thu mai neither see ne fele clenli the love of Jhesu Crist; for wite thou wel, til thyn herte be mykil yclensid from sich synnes thorugh stedefaste trouthe and bisi biholdynge on Jhesu Crist in praieres and in othir good werkes, thou mai not

345 perfightli have goostli felynge of Hym. Witnessinge Hymsilf in the Gospel thus: *Beati mundo corde quoniam ipsi deum videbunt* (Matthew 5:8). Blissid be the clene of herte, for thei schullen see God. Also in meditacioun thou schal see vertues whiche aren needful to thee for to have, as mekenesse, myldenesse, pacience, rightwisenesse, goosteli strengthe, temperaunce, pees, clennesse, and sobirnesse, feith, hope, and charité. Thise

350 vertues schalt thou see in meditacion, hou goode, hou faire, hou profitable thei aren, and bi prayer thou schalt desire hem and gete hem, withoute whiche thu may not be contemplatif. For Job seith thus: *In habundancia ingredieris sepulcrum* (Job 5:26); that is for to seie, thou schalt in plenté of gode bodili werkes and goostli vertues entre thi grave, that is the reste in contemplacioun.

Chapter Sixteen

355 What a man schal use and refuse bi vertu of mekenes.

Now yif thou schuldest use wiseli thise goostli werkis and sikirli travaile in hem, thee bihoveth bigynne right lowe. Thre thinges thee nedith to have first, upon whiche as

here are avarice (*coveytise*), gluttony, lechery, envy, ire, and sloth (*sleughthe*). **338 haterede**, hatred; **malincolie**, melancholy. **339 unskilful hevynesse**, unreasonable sadness; **schames**, shames. **340 stirynges**, stirrings. A frequent term in Hilton, as in other devotional writers; Staley (*Kempe*, p. 236) notes that it could refer to either physical or spiritual arousal; **boylen ought**, boil out. **341 letten**, obstruct. **342 clenli**, purely. **343 yclensid**, cleansed. **344 bisi**, active. **346 clene**, pure. **347 schullen**, shall. **348 rightwisenesse**, righteousness, justice; in the list of virtues of which this is part are found the four cardinal virtues (justice, fortitude, mercy, temperance) and the three theological virtues (faith, hope, charity). **349 clennesse**, purity. **353 entre**, enter. **356–57 thee bihoveth**, it behooves you [to].

upon a siker ground thu schalt sitte al thi werk. These three aren mekenesse, siker feith, and hool entencion to God. First thee bihoveth to have mekenesse in this maner. Thou

360 schalte holde thi silf in thi wille and in thi felynge, yif thou may, unable for to duelle amonge men or women, and unworthi to serve God in conversacion with his servauntis, unprofitable to thi even Cristene, wantynge bothe connynge and myght to fulfille gode werkes of actif lif in helpe of thyn even Cristene, as othere men and women doon; and therfore as a wrecche, outcaste and refuse of alle men and women, art spered in an

365 hous aloone, that thou schuldest dere no man ne woman bi yvel ensaumple, sithen thou canst not profiten hem bi good wirkynge. Over this, thee bihoveth loke forthere that sithen thou art so unable to serve oure Lord bi bodili werkis outeward, hou mykil more thee bihoveth holde thee unable and unworthi to serve hym goosteli bi inward occupacion. For oure Lord is a spirit, as the prophete seith: *Spiritus ante faciem nostram Christus*

370 *dominus est* (Lamentations 4:20). Bifore oure face a goost is oure Lord Jhesu Crist. And the kyndeli service to Him is goostli, as He seith Himsilf: *Veri adoratores adorabunt patrem in spiritu et veritate* (John 4:23). Sothfast servauntes schullen worschipen the fadir in spirit and sothfastnesse. Thanne thou that art so boystous and so lewed, so fleischli, so blynd in goostli thinges, and nameli of thyn owyn soule, which thee bihoveth

375 first to knowe yif thu schuldest come to the knowynge of God, hou schuldest thu thanne fele thisilf able or worthi to have that staat and the likenes of lif contemplatif, the which liyf, as y have seid, lith principali in goostli knowynge and lovynge of God? This y seie to thee, not for thou schuldest forthynke thi purpos and be myspaide with thyn enclosynge, but that thu schuldest fele this lowenesse soothfastli, yif thu myght, in thyn

380 herte, for it is sooth and noo lees. And though thou fele thus, yit schalt thou yerne nyght and day up thi myght for to come as neer as thou myght to the staat that thou hast taken, trowand stedefastli that it is best to thee bi the merci of God for to travaile inne. And though it be so, that thu myght not come to the fulheed of it heere in this lif, that thu myghttest be here in the bigynnynge of hit; and truste sikirli for to have the fulheed of it

385 bi the merci of God in the blisse of hevene. For soothli that is my liff. I feele me so

---

358 siker, secure. **360 duelle**, dwell. **361 conversacion**, community. **362 wantynge**, lacking; **connynge**, knowledge. **364 refuse of**, rejected by; **spered**, locked. **365 dere**, harm; **ensaumple**, example. **371 kyndeli**, natural. **372 Sothfast**, True. **373 boystous**, unruly; **lewed**, ignorant. **377 lith**, lies. **378 forthynke**, reject; **myspaide**, dissatisfied. **380 lees**, lies. **381 up thi myght**, according to your ability. **382 trowand**, believing. **384 sikirli**, certainly; **fulheed**, fulness.

wrecchid, and so freel, and so fleischli, and so fer fro the trewe feelynge fro that that I speke and have spoke, that y ne can not ellis but crie merci, and desire after as y may with hope that oure Lord wol brynge me therto of His grace in the blisse of hevene. Do thou soo, and betir, after that God geveth thee grace. The felynge of this lowenesse

390 schal putte oute of thyn herte unskilful bihooldynge of othere myslyvynge and demynge of othere mennys dedes, and it schal dryve thee oonli to biholde thisilf, as ther were no man lyvynge but God and thou; and thow schalte deeme and holde thisilf more vile and more wrecchid thanne is ony creature that berith liyf, that unnethes thou schal mowe suffre thisilf for mykilnesse of synne and filthe that thu schalt fynde and fele in thisilf.

395 Thus bihoveth thee for to feele sum tyme, yif thou wolt be verili meke; for I telle thee soothli, yif thou wolt be truli meke, thee schal thenke a venial synne more grevous and more peyneful to thee, and gretter schal be in thi sight sumtyme, thanne grete deedli synnes of othere men. And that for this skile, that thynge whiche putteth thi soule or letteth it moost from the felynge of love and knowynge of God, bihoveth to be moost

400 grevous and peynful to thee. But a venyal synne of thisilf letteth thee more fro the felynge and fro the perfight love of Jhesu Crist thanne othere mennys synnes mai do, be it never so mykil. Thanne semeth it that thou schuldest arise up in thyn owen herte agens thisilf, for to hate and deme in thisilf al maner of synne which letteth thee from the sight of God, more bisili thanne agens defautes of ony othir man. For yif thyn herte

405 be clene of thyn owen synnes, sothli the synnes of alle othere men schullen not dere thee; and therfore yif thou wolt fynde reest here and in the blisse of hevene, up the counseil of oon of the hooli fadres seie every dai, "What am I?" and deme no man.

Chapter Seventeen

Who schulde blame mennys defautis and deme hem, and who not.

But now seist thou, hou mai this bee, sithen it is a dede of a charité for to undirneme

410 men of here defautis, and for to deme hem for here amendynge, it is a dede of merci. As

386 freel, frail. **393 unnethes**, scarcely. **393–44 mowe suffre**, be able to bear. **394 mykilnesse**, greatness. **398 skile**, reason. **399 letteth**, hinders. **405 sothli**, truly; **dere**, harm. **406 up**, upon. **407 oon of the hooli fadres**, Clark (p. 165n60) cites the *Vitae patrum,* 5.9.5 (PL 73:910); **deme**, judge. **409 sithen**, since; **undirneme**, reproach.

to this I answere as me thenketh, that to thee or to ony othir which hath the staat and the purpos of lif contemplatif it fallith not for to leve the kepynge of youresilf and underneme othir men of here defautis, but it were in wel greet nede, that a man schulde perische but yif he undernemyd hym. But to men which aren actif and han sovereynté and cure of
415 othere, as prelatis and curates and swich othere, thei aren bounden bi there office and by wai of charité for to see and seke and deme rightfulli othere mennys defautis, not of desire and delite for to chastise hem, but oonli for nede, with drede of God and in His name, for love and savacioun of here soulis. Othere men that aren actif and han no cure over othere men, thei aren boundyn for to undirnyme othere men of her defautis bi wei
420 of charité, oonly thanne whanne the synne is deedli and may not wel be correctid bi noon othir man, and whanne he troweth that the synnere schulde be amendid bi undirnymyng. Ellis it is betere that he cese. That this is sooth, it semeth bi Seynt Joon, which hadde the staat of contemplatif lif, and Seynt Petir, whiche hadde the staat of actif lif. Whanne oure Lord in His laste sopeer with His disciples, atte the pryvey stirynge
425 of Seynt Petir to Seynt Joon, toolde Seynt Joon how Judas schulde bitraie Hym, Seynt Joon tolde it not to Seynt Petir, as he askide, but he turnede him and leide his heed upon Cristis brest and was raveschid bi love into contemplacion of Goddis privetees, and so medfulli to hym he forgaat bothe Judas and Petir — in tokenynge and in techynge of othere men which wolden ben contemplatif that thei schulden dispose hem for to doo
430 the same.

Thanne seest thou heere sumwhat that thu schalt neither deme othere men, ne conceyve agens hem wilfulli noon evel suspicion. But thu schalt love hem in thyn herte, sich as leden in the world actif lif and suffren many tribulacions and greet temptaciones which thu sittynge in thyn hous felist not of. And thei han wel mykil travaile for here owen and
435 othir mennys sustenaunce, and manye of hem hadde wel lyvere serve God, yif thei myghten, as thou doost in bodili reste; neverthelees thei in here worldli bisynesse fleen many synnes, which yif thou were in here astaat schuldest falle in, and thei doon many good deedes whiche thou kowdest not doo. It is no doute that many doon thus; whiche thei are, thou wost not.

414 cure, responsibility. **419 undirnyme**, reproach. **421 troweth**, believes. **422 Seynt Joon**, for St. John as type of contemplative life and St. Peter as active life, see Augustine, *Tractatus in Iohannis Evangelium,* 124.5 (Clark, p. 166n63). **424 sopeer**, supper. **427 privetees**, secrets. **428 medfulli**, worthy of reward. **434 travaile**, trouble. **435 sustenaunce**, support; **lyvere**, rather. **436 bisynesse**, activity; **fleen**, flee. **437 astaat**, estate, position. **439 wost**, know.

Chapter Eighteen

440 Whi meke men schal worschip othere, and lowe hemself in her owen herte undir alle
othere.

And therfore thou schalt worschipe alle, and sette hem in thyn herte al above thee as thi
sovereynes, and caste thee doun undir her feet, that thou be vileste and lowest in thyn
owen sight. For it is no drede ne peril to thee, how mykil thou may lowe thiself binethe
445 alle othere, though it were so that in Goddis sight thou hadde more grace than anothir.
But it is peril to thee for to highe thee and lifte thisilf in thi thought wilfulli above ony
othir man, though he were the mooste wrecche or the most synful caytif that is in
erthe. For oure Lord seith: *Qui se humiliat exaltabitur, et qui se exaltat humiliabitur*
(Luke 14:11). Whoso higheth hymsilf, he schal be lowed, and whoso loweth himsilf, he
450 schal be highed. This partie of mekenesse thee bihoveth for to have in thi bigynnynge,
and bi this and bi grace schalt thou come to the fulhede of it and of alle othere vertues.
For whoso hath oon vertu, hath alle. As mykil as thu hast of mekenesse, so mykil haste
thou of charité, of pacience, and of othere vertues, though thei be not alle schewid
outward. Be thanne besi for to gete mekenesse and for to holde it; for it is the first and
455 the laste of alle vertues. It is the firste, for it is the ground, as Seynt Austyn seith: Yif thu
thynke to bigge an high hous of vertues, ordeyne thee firste a deep grounde of meknes.
And also it is laste, for it is savynge and kepynge of alle vertues, as Seynt Gregor seith:
He that gadreth vertues withouten mekenesse, he is like to hym that maketh and berith
poudre of spicerie in the wynde. Doo thou nevere so many good dedis, fast thou or
460 wake thou, or ony good dede that thu doo, yif thu have no mekenesse it is nought that
thou doost.

Chapter Nineteen

Hou men schullen don that wanten the feelynge of mekenes in affeccioun, not dredynge
over mykil therof.

440 **lowe**, humble. 446 **highe**, exalt. 447 **mooste**, greatest. 454 **besi**, diligent. 455 **Seynt
Austyn seith**, *Sermo* 69.1.2 (Clark, p. 166n67). 456 **bigge**, build. 457 **Seynt Gregor seith**,
Homilia in Evangelia, 7.4 (PL 76:1103) (Clark, p. 166n68). 459 **spicerie**, spices.

465 Neverthelees, yif thou mai not fele this mekenesse in thyn herte with affeccion as thu
woldest, do as thou may: meke thisilf in wille bi thi resoun, trowynge that it schulde be
so as I seie, though thou fele it not. And in that holde thee a more wrecche, that thou
may not feele sothfastli as thou art. And yif thu doo so, though thi fleisch rise thereagen
and wole not assente to thi wille, be not to mykil adraad, but thu schalt bere thanne and
suffre the fals feelynge of thi fleisch as a peyne. And thou schalt thanne dispise and
470 repreve that feelynge, and breke doun that risynge of thyn herte, as though thou woldest
be wel paide for to be troden and spurnyd undir every mannys feet as a thynge whiche
is outcast. And so bi grace of Jhesu Crist thorugh devoute biholdynge on His manhede
and His mekenesse schalt thu mykil abate the stirynge of pride, and the vertu of mekenesse
that was first in the nakid wille schal be turnyd into feelynge of affeccion. Withoutin
475 which vertu, either in a trewe wil or in felynge, whoso disposeth hym for to serve God
in lif contemplatif, as the blynde he schal stumble and nevere schal he come therto. The
highere he clymbeth bi bodili penaunce and othere vertues and hath not this, the lowere
he falleth. For as Gregor seith, he that cannot perfightli dispice hymsilf, he fond yit
nevere the meke wisdom of oure Lord Jhesu.

Chapter Twenty

480 Hou heretikes and ypocrites, for wantynge of mekenesse, highen hemself in herte bifore
alle othere.

Ypocrites ne heretikes feele not this mekenesse, neither in good wille, ne in affeccioun;
but wel drie and wel cold aren here hertis and here reynes fro the softe feelynge of this
vertu; and so mykil thei aren the ferther fro it, that they wenen for to have it. Thei
485 gnawen upoun the drie bark withoutyn, but the swete kirnel of it and the inli savoure
may he not come to. Thei schewen outward mekenesse, in habite, in hooli speche, in
loweli berynge, and, as it semeth, in many grete bodili and goostli vertues. But neverthelees
in the wille and the affeccioun of here herte, where mekenesse schulde principali be, it
is but feyned. For thei dispisen and setten at nought alle othere men that wolen not doo

465 **trowynge**, believing. 466 **more**, greater. 467 **thereagen**, against it. 468 **adraad**, afraid. 469
peyne, punishment. 470 **repreve**, reject. 471 **paide**, content. 478 **Gregor seith**, *Moralia*,
34.32.43 (Clark, p. 166n69); **dispice**, despise. 483 **reynes**, kidneys, loins. 484 **wenen**, suppose.

51

490 as thei doon and techen. Thei holden hem fooles bi unkunnynge, or blyndid bi fleischli likynge; and therfore thei liften hemsilf upoun high in there owen sight, above alle othere, wenynge that thei lyven betere than othere and that they haave oonli the soothfastnesse of good lyvynge and singuler grace of God, bothe in knowynge and

goostli feelynge, passynge othere men. And of this sight in hemsilf riseth a grete delite
495 in here hertes in the which thei worschipen and preisen hemself, as ther were noon but thei. Thei preisen and thanken God with here lippes, but in her hertis thei stelen as theves the worschip and the thankyng from God and setten it in hemself. And so thei have neither mekenesse in wille ne in felynge. A fleischli caytif or a synnere which falleth al day, and is sori for that he doth so, though he have not mekenesse in affeccioun,
500 he hath in a gode wille. But an heretik or an ipocrite hath neither, for thei han the condicion of the pharisee, the which com as oure Lord seith in the Gospel with the publican to the temple for to prey. And whanne he com he prayde not ne he askide not of God, for hym thoughte he hadde no nede, but he bigan for to thanke God, and seide thus: "Lord, y thanke Thee that Thu gyvest me more grace thanne another, that y am
505 not as othere men aren, robbours, lecchours, and sich synneres." And he lokide bisides hym, and sigh the publican, whiche he knew for a wrecch, knokkand upon his brest onli, criande after merci. Thanne he thanked God that he was not sich oon as he was. "For Lord," he seide, "I faste twies in the woke, and I paye truli my tithes." And whanne he hadde doon, oure Lord seide he yede hoom agen withouten grace as he
510 com, and gaat right nought. But now seist thou, "Whereinne thanne trespacide this pharisee, sithen he thankid God, and was soth as he seide?" As to this I answere and seie, that this pharisee trespacide in as mykil as he demede and reprovede in his herte the publican, which was justifyed bi oure Lord. And also he trespacide, for he thanked God oonly with his mouth, but he delitede willfulli by a pryvé pride in hymsilf of the
515 giftes of God, stelande the worschipe and the loovynge from God and sette it in hymsilf. This same condicioun of this pharisee soothli han heretikes and ypocrites. Thei wolen not gladli praie, and yif thei praien they meke not hemself knowelechynge truli here wrecchidnesse, but thei maken hem by a feynynge for to thanke and loove God, and speken of Hym with here mouth. But her delite is veyn and fals and not in God, and yit

490 **unkunnynge**, ignorance. 491 **likynge**, pleasure. 494 **passynge**, surpassing. 495 **here**, their. 501 **in the Gospel**, Luke 18:10–14. 502 **not₂**, nothing. 503 **hym thoughte**, it seemed to him. 506 **sigh**, saw. 507 **criande**, crying. 508 **twies**, twice; **woke**, week. 509 **yede**, went. 510 **gaat**, got. 515 **loovynge**, praising. 517 **knowelechynge**, acknowledging. 518 **loove**, praise.

520   thei wenen not so. They conne not love God, for the wise man seith: *Non est speciosa laus in ore peccatoris* (Ecclesiasticus 15:9). It is neither fair ne semeli praisynge of God in the mouth of a synnere. Wherfor it is profitable to thee and to me, and sich othere wrecchis, for to leve the condicion of this pharisee and feyned lovyng of God, and folwe the publican first in lowenesse, askynge merci and forgifnesse of synnes and

525   grace of goosteli vertues, that we myght afterward with a clene herte sothfastli thanke Hym and love Hym and gyve Him hooli the worschipe withouten feynynge. For oure Lord asketh bi His prophete thus: *Super quem requiescet spiritus meus nisi super humilem contritum spiritu et trementem sermones meos?* (Isaiah 66:2). Upon whom schal My spirit reste? And He answereth Himsilf and seith: upon noon but upon the meke, poverli

530   and contrite in herte and dredynge My wordes. Thanne yif thou wolt have the spirit of God rulynge thyn herte, have mekenesse and dreede of Hym.

Chapter Twenty-one

What thinges men owen to trowe bi siker trouthe.

Secunde thynge which thee bihoveth for to have is a siker trouth in articlis of the feith and the sacramentes of Holi Chirche, trowand hem stidefastli with al the wille of thyn

535   herte. And though thu feele ony stirynge in thyn herte agens ony of hem bi suggestion of the enemye, for to putte thee in doute and in dweer of hem, be thu stidefast and not to mykil have drede of sich stirynges ne of the feelynge of hem, but forsake thyn owen witte withoute disputynge or ransakynge of hem, and sette thi feith generali in the feith of Hooli Chirche, and charge not the styrynge of thyn herte whiche, as thee thenkith, is

540   contrarie therto. For that stirynge that thu felist is not thi feith, but the feith of Holi Chirche is thi feith, though thou neither see it ne fele it. And bere thanne sich stirynges pacienteli as a scourge of oure Lord, bi the which He wole clense thyn herte and make thi feith stidefast. Also thee bihoveth love and worschipe in thyn herte the lawes and the ordenaunces maad bi prelates and rulers of Hooli Chirche, either in declarynge of the

545   feith, or in the sacramentis, or in general governance of alle Cristen men.

520 love, praise. **523 lovyng**, praise. **526 love**, praise. **529 poverli**, poor. **533 siker**, certain; **trouth**, faith. **536 dweer**, uncertainty. **538 witte**, intelligence; **ransakynge**, examining. **543–44 lawes and the ordenaunces**, Hilton regularly defends orthodoxy and ecclesiastical authority.

Mekeli and truli assente to hem, though it be so that thou knowe not the cause of here ordenaunce; and though thee thenketh that summe were unskileful, thu schalt not deme hem, ne reprove hem, but receyve and worschipe hem alle, though thei longen but litil to thee; ne thou schalt not resseyve noon opynioun, ne fantasie, ne singuler conceyt undir
550 colour of more holynesse, as summe doon that aren not wise, neither bi thyn owen ymaginacion ne bi kunnynge of noon othir man, whiche is contrarie to the leeste ordenaunce of general techynge of al Hooli Chirche.

And over this, thou schalt hopen stidefastli that thou art ordaynyd of oure Lord to be saaf as oon of His chosene, bi His merci, and stire not fro this hope, whatso thou herist
555 or seest, what temptacion thou be inne. And though thou thenke thee so greet a wrecche that thou were worthi to synke to helle for that thu doost no good, ne servest God as thu schuldist doo, yit holde thee in this hope, and aske merci, and al schal be right weel. Yhe, and though alle the develis of helle appereden in bodili likenesse, slepynge or wakynge, seiden to thee that thou schulde not be saaf, or alle men lyvyng in erthe or alle the angelis
560 in hevene, yif it myght be seid to thee the same, thou schulde not leve hem, ne bee myche stirid fro this truthe and hope of salvacioun. This y seie to thee, for summe aren so weyke and so symple, that whanne thei have gyven hem al hooli to serve God up here kunnynge, yif thei feelen ony styrynge withinne bi incastynge of the enemye, or fro withouten of ony word of the develis prophetis, whiche men callen soothseieris, that thei
565 schulde not bee saaf, or here astaat or maner of lyvynge were not plesant to God, thei ben astonyed and stired with sich wordis, and so for unkunnynge thei fallen sum tyme into grete hevynesse, and as it were into dyspeir of savacioun. Wherfore as me thenketh it is spedeful to everi creature whiche bi grace of oure Lord Jhesu Crist is in ful wille to forsake synne, and as clerli as his conscience telleth hym he suffreth no deedli synne
570 reste in hym that he ne schryveth hym sone therof, and meketh hym to the sacramentis of Holi Chirche, for to have a trust and hope of savacion. And mykil more thanne they

547 thee thenketh, it seems to you; **unskileful**, unreasonable; **deme**, judge. **548 reprove**, reject; **longen**, belong. **549 conceyt**, conception. **551 kunnynge**, knowledge; **leeste**, least. **553 hopen**, think. **554 saaf**, saved; **hope**, expectation; **herist**, hear. **557 hope**, expectation; **Yhe**, Yea. **558 appereden**, appeared. **560 leve**, believe. **562 weyke**, weak. **562–63 up here kunnynge**, according to their knowledge. **563 incastynge**, insertion. **565 astaat**, condition; **plesant**, pleasing. **566 astonyed**, astonished; **unkunnynge**, ignorance. **567 hevynesse**, gloom. **568 spedeful**, advantageous. **570 schryveth hym sone**, confesses himself immediately; **meketh**, humbles. **571 thanne**, then.

that gyven hem hooli to God, and flen venyal synnes up here myght. And on the contrarie wise, as perilous it is to hym whiche lieth wityngeli in a deedli synne for to hafe truste of savacion, and in hope of that trust wole not forsake his synne, ne lowe him trewli to

575 God and to Hooli Chirche.

Chapter Twenty-two

How a stable entent is nedefulle to thise that schal plese God and discrecioun in bodili werkes.

The thridde thynge whiche is nedeful thee to have in the bigynynge is an hool and a stable entencioun, that is for to seie, an hool wille and a desyre oonli to plese God. For

580 that is charité, withoute whiche al were not that thou doost. Thu schalt sette thyn entente alwey for to seke and traveile how thou myghttest plese oure Lord Jhesu Crist, no tyme for to cese wilfulli of good occupacion either bodili or gostli. For thu schalt not sette in thyn herte a tyme, as thus longe thou woldest serve God, and sithen to suffre thyn herte wilfulli to falle doun into veyn thoughtes and ydel occupacions, wenande that

585 it were nedeful to thee for savynge of thi bodili kynde, levynge the kepynge of thy herte and gode occupacion, sekynge reste and confort oughtward bi the bodili wittes or in worldeli vanytees, as it were for recreacion of the spirit, that it schulde be more scharp afterward to goostli traveile. For y trowe it is not sooth. I seie not that thou schal mowen in deede ay performe thyn entent; for ofte sithes thi bodili nede in etynge,

590 slepynge, and spekynge, and the freelté of thi fleisch schal lette thee and hyndre thee, be thu nevere so bisy. But I wolde that thyn entente and thi wille were alwey hool for to traveil bodili or goostli, and no tyme to be ydel, but alwey liftynge up thyn herte bi desire to thy Lord Jhesu Crist and to the blisse of hevene, whethir thu ete or drynke, or ony othir bodili traveile that thu usist, as mykil as thou mai wilfulli leve it not. For yif thou

595 have this entent, it schal make thee ay quyk and scharp in thi traveile; and yif thou falle

---

572 flen, flee; **up here myght**, according to their ability. **573 hafe**, have. **580 not**, nothing. **582 no tyme**, at no time. **583 sithen**, since. **584 wenande**, supposing. **588 trowe**, believe; **sooth**, true; **seie**, say. **589 mowen**, be able to; **ofte sithes**, often times. **590 freelté**, frailty. **594 usist**, practice; **leve**, leave.

bi freelté or necgligence to ony idel occupacion, or in veyn speche, it schal smyte upon thyn herte scharpeli as a prikke and make thee for to yrke with alle vanitees, and for to turne agen hastili into inwarde biholdynge of Jhesu Crist bi praieres or bi summe gode dede or occupacion. For as anemptis thi bodili kynde, it is good to use discrecion in

600 etynge, and drynkynge, and in slepynge, and in alle maner bodily penaunce, or in longe praier bi speche, or in bodili feelynge bi greet fervour of devocioun, eyther in weepynge or in swiche othere, and also in ymagynynge of the spirit. Whan a man feeleth no grace in alle thise werkes, it is good to kepe discrecion and for to breke of summe tyme, for the mene is the beste. But in destroyynge of synne bi kepynge of thyn herte fro alle

605 maner of unclennesse, and in ay lastynge desire of vertues, and of the blisse of hevene, and for to have the goostli felynge and lovynge of God, halde thou noo meene, for the more it is of this, the betere is it. For thu schalt hate synne, and alle fleischli loves and dredis, in thyn herte withouten cesynge, and thou schalt love vertues and clennesse, and desire hem withouten stintynge, yif thou myghtest. I sey not that this is nedeful to

610 savacion, but y hope that it ys spedeful; and yif thou kepe it thou schalt profite more in a yeer in vertues thanne thu schalt withoutin this entent profite in sevene.

Chapter Twenty-three

Of a litil rehersynge of thynges biforseid, and of makynge offrynge of that schulde be offrid to God.

Now have y tolde thee first of the ende which thou schalt biholde in thi desire and

615 drawe toward as myche as thou may. Also y have seide of the bigynnynge, what thee nedeth for to have, as mekenesse, siker trowth, and an hool entente to God, upon whiche ground thou schalt sette thy goostli hous, bi praier and meditacioun and othere goostli vertues. Thanne sei I to thee thus: praie thou, or thenke thou, or ony othir deede that thou doost, good bi grace or badde bi synne or bi thin owne freelté, or what that

620 thou feelist, seest, or smellest or savours, withouten in thi bodili wittes, or withinne in ymagynynge or feelynge in thi resoun or knowynge: brynge hit al withynne the trowthe

---

597 yrke, be annoyed with. **599 as anemptis**, in regard to; **kynde**, nature. **602 swiche**, such. **603 of**, off. **604 mene**, mean. **606 halde**, keep. **610 spedeful**, helpful. **612 that**, what. **616 siker trowth**, certain faith; **hool**, whole. **618 sei**, say.

and rulis of Hooli Chirche and caste it al in the morter of mekenesse and breke it smal
with the pestel of drede of God, and throw the pouder of alle thise in the fier of desire,
and offre it soo to thi Lord Jhesu Crist. And y telle thee forsothe, wel schal that offrynge
625   like in the sight of oure Lord Jhesu, and swete schal the smoke of that ilke fier smelle in
the face of thi Lord Jhesu. This is for to seie, drawe al this that thou felist withinne the
trowthe of Holi Chirche and breke thisilf in mekenesse, and offre the desire of thin herte
oonli to thi Lord Jhesu Crist, for to have Hym and not ellis but Hym. And yif thou doo
thus, I hope bi the grace of Jhesu Crist thou schalt nevere be overcomen with thyn
630   enemye. Thus techeth us Seynt Poul, whanne he seide thus: *Sive manducatis, sive
bibitis, sive quicquid aliud facitis, omnia in nomine domini facite* (1 Corinthians 10:31).
Whether ye eten or ye drynken or what maner of dede that ye doon, dooth al in the
name of oure Lord Jhesu Crist, forsakynge youresilf, and offreth up to Hym. Menes
whiche thu schalt most use, as I have biforseid, aren praier and meditacion. First I schal
635   schewe thee a litil of praier, and sithen of meditacion.

Chapter Twenty-four

Of praier that is spedful to gete clennes in herte and vertues.

Preyer is profitable and spedful to use for to gete clennesse of herte bi distroynge of
synne and receyvynge of vertues. Not for thou schuldest bi thi praier kenne oure Lord
what thou desirest, for He knoweth wel ynowgh al that thee nedeth; but for to make
640   thee able and redi bi thi praier that thou myght receyve as a clene vessel the grace that
oure Lord wole freeli gyve to thee, whiche grace mai not be felid til thou be purified bi
fier of desire in devoute praier. For though it be so that praier is not the cause for
whiche our Lord geveth grace, neverthelees it is a weie bi the whiche grace freli gyven
cometh to a soule.
645   But now desirest thou peraventure for to knowe hou thu schuldest praie and upon
what thynge thu schal sette the poynt of thi thought in thi praier, and also what preier
were best to thee for to use. As unto the first, I answere and seie thus: That whan thou
art waken of thi sleep and art redi for to preie, thou schalt fele thisilf fleischli and hevy

625 like, please; **ilke**, same. **629 hope**, expect; **with**, by. **633 Menes**, Means. **636 spedful**,
useful. **639 ynowgh**, enough. **642 fier**, fire. **645 peraventure**, perhaps.

650 and ai dounward into veyn thoughtes, either of dreemes or of fantasies, or unskilful bisynesse of the world, or of thi fleisch. Thanne bihoveth thee for to quykene thyn herte bi praier and stire it als mykil as thou mai to sum devocioun.

Chapter Twenty-five

Hou men schulde praie, and whereon the poynt of the thought schal be sette in prayere.

And in thi praier thou schalt not sette thyn herte in ony erthly thynge, but al thi travail schal be for to drawe in thi thoughtis fro alle bihooldynges of alle erthli thinges, that thi

655 desire myght be, as it were, bare and nakid from alle ertheli thinges, evermore upward stiynge into Jhesu Crist as yif thu were in His presence whom thou may neither see bodili as He is in His Godhede, ne bi bodili liknes in ymaginacion; but thou may thorugh devout biholdynge of His precious manhede fele His godenesse and the grace of His Godhede, whanne thi desire is esid and holpen and as it were maad free and myghti

660 from alle fleschli thoughtes and affeccions, and is mykil lifted up bi a goostli myght into gosteli savour and delite of His goostli presence, and holde stille thereinne mykil of the tyme of thi praiere, so that thou hast no grete mynde of noon ertheli thynge, or elles the mynde dereth thee but litil. Yif thou praye thus, than can thou preyen wel; for praier is not ellis but a stiynge desire of the herte to God bi a withdrawinge of thi mynde from

665 alle ertheli thoughtes. And so is praier likenyd to a fier whiche of the owen kynde leeveth the lowenesse of the erthe and alwei stieth up into the eir. Right so desire in praier, whanne it is touchid and lightned of the goostli fier whiche is God, it is ay upstyande to Hym kyndeli whom it com fro.

Chapter Twenty-six

Of the fier of love.

649 unskilful, unreasonable. **650 bisynesse**, activity; **quykene**, enliven. **656 stiynge**, ascending. **659 esid**, eased; **holpen**, helped. **663 dereth**, harms. **666 stieth**, ascends. **667 lightned of**, illuminated by. **668 upstyande**, ascending; **kyndeli**, by nature; **fro**, from.

670   Alle men and women that speken of the fier of love knowe not wel what it is, for what
it is I can not telle thee, save this may I telle thee, it is neither bodili, ne it is bodili feelid.
A soule mai fele it in praiere or in devocioun, whiche soule is in the bodi, but he felith it
not bi no bodili witt. For though it be so, that yif it wirke in a soule the bodi mai turne
into an heete as it were chafid for likynge travaile of the spirit, neverthelees the fier of

675   love is not bodili, for it is oonly in the goostli desire of the soule. This is no doute to no
man ne woman that felith and knoweth devocion, but summe aren so symple and
wenen bicause that it is callid fier that it schulde be hoot as bodili fier is. And forthi I seie
that I have seid. Now as to that othir, for to knowe what prayer were best for to use, y
schal seie as me thenkith. Thou schalt undirstonde that there are thre maner of praieres.

Chapter Twenty-seven

680   That certayn praier in speche ordeyned of God and of Holi Chirche is best to hem that
aren bounden and ordeyned therto, and to hem that gyven hem newli to devocion.

The first is praier of speche maad speciali of God, as is the Pater Noster, and maad also
more generali bi the ordenaunce of Holi Chirche, as mateyns and evesonge and houres;
and also maad bi devout men of othere special seiynges, as to oure Lord and oure Ladi,

685   and to His seyntis. As unto this matier of praier, whiche is callid vocal, me thenketh unto
thee that art religious, and bi custum of rule art bounden for to seie mateyns and houres,
I holde it moost spedful for to seie hem as devouteli as thou mai. For whanne thou seist
thi mateyns, thou seist also thi Pater Noster principali; and over more to stire thee to
more devocioun was it ordeyned for to seie psalmys and ympnys and siche othere

690   whiche are maad bi the Holi Goost, as the Pater Noster is. And therfore thou schalt not
seie hem gredili ne rekleesli, as thou were yvel paid that thou art bounden with hem, but
thou schalt gadre thyn affeccioun and thi thought for to seie hem more sadli and more
devouteli than ony othir special praier of devocioun, trowande for sothe, that sithen it is

671 **bodili feelid**, felt in the body; see also *Scale*, Book I, chapter 11, for similar analysis. 673
witt, sense. 674 **chafid**, warmed; **likynge**, pleasant. 677 **wenen**, suppose. 683 **mateyns . . . and
houres**, matins, evensong, and hours, regular times of public prayer appointed by the Church.
686 **religious**, in religious orders. 687 **spedful**, helpful. 688 **Pater Noster**, the Lord's Prayer.
689 **ympnys**, hymns. 691 **gredili**, greedily; **yvel paid**, ill-satisfied. 692 **sadli**, seriously.

695 the praiere of Holi Chirche there is no praier so profitable to thee whiche is vocale for to use comounli as that is. And so schalt thou put awey al the hevynesse, and bi grace thou schalt turne thi nede into good wille and thi boond into gret freedom, that it schal no lettynge be to thee of goostli occupacion. And after thise, yif thou wolte, thou mai use othere, as the Pater Noster or ony swiche othir. And in thise, in whiche thou felist most savour and most gostli confort, inne that holde y best for thee. This maner of praier is
700 spedful to everi man comonli in the bigynnynge of his conversioun, for to use most of ony othir goostli occupacioun. For a man in the biginnynge is rude and boistous and fleiscli, but yif he have the more grace, and cannot thenke gostli thoughtis in meditacioun, for his soule is not yit clensid from olde synne. And therfore y hope it is most spedful to use this maner of praiere, as for to seie his Pater Noster and his Ave Marie and rede
705 upon his sautier and sich othere. For he that cannot renne lightli bi goostli praier, for his feet of knowynge and lovynge aren syke for synne, hym nedeth for to have a siker staaf for to holde him bi. This staaf is special praier of speche ordayned of God and of Holi Chirche in helpe of mennys soulis, bi the whiche praier a soule of a fleischli man that is alwei fallynge dounward into worldli thoughtis and fleschli affeccions schal be liftid up
710 from hem, and holden bi hem as bi a staaf, feed with suete wordis of the praier as a childe with mylk, and rulid bi it that he falle not in errours ne fantasies bi his veyn meditacioun. For in this maner of praiere is no disceite, whoso wole stidefastli and mekeli travaile thereinne.

Chapter Twenty-eight

715 What peril it is to men that in the bigynnynge of here turnynge to God leeven to sone the comone praier of the ordenaunce of Holi Chirche and gyven hem to meditacion hooli.

Thanne mai though bi this see, that thise men, yif ony ben siche, that in the bigynnynge of here conversioun or soone aftir, whanne thei han felid a litil of goostli comfort either in devocion or in knowynge, and not aren stablid yit therinne, thei leven siche praier

697 **lettynge,** hindrance. 698 **swiche,** such. 701 **boistous,** rough. 702 **fleiscli,** fleshly. 705 **sautier,** psalter. 706 **staaf,** staff. 710 **suete,** sweet. 712 **disceite,** deceit. 714 **to₃,** too. 716 **though,** you; **yif,** if; **siche,** such. 718 **stablid,** established.

vocal to sone, and othere bodili exercise, and gyven hem hooli to meditacion. Thei aren
720   not wise, for ofte in reste of here meditacion thei ymagen and thenken of gostli thinges
after here owen wittes, and folwen here bodili felyng, and han not yit receyved grace
therto. And therfore thei bi undiscrecion, ofte sithes overtravailen hire wittes and breken
here bodili myght, and so thei fallen into fantasies and singulere conceites, or into open
errours, and letten the grace that God gyveth hem bi sich vanytees. The cause of al this
725   is a prevei pride and presumpcion of hemself, as whanne thei han felid a litil grace thei
wenen that it is so mykil, passand othere, that thei fallen in veynglorie and so thei leesen
it. Yif thei wisten how litil it were that thei feelen in regard of that God geveth or mai
geven thei schulde be aschamed for to speke ought therof, but if it were in grete nede.
Of this maner of praiere bi speche speketh David in sautier thus: *Voce mea ad dominum*
730   *clamavi; voce mea ad dominum deprecatus sum* (Psalms 141:2). David the prophete,
for to stire othere men bothe with herte and with mouth seide: With my vois I criede to
God, and with my speche y bisoughte oure Lord.

Chapter Twenty-nine

Of the secunde maner of praier, that is in speche not certayn, but folweth the stirenges
that aren in devocioun.

735   The secunde maner of praiere is bi speche, but it is not of noon certayn special seiynge;
and this is whanne a man or a woman felith grace of devocioun bi the gifte of God, and
in his devocioun speketh to Hym as yif he were bodili in presence, with sich wordis and
acordande most to his stirynge for the tyme as comen to his mynde after sondri rewardes
which he felith in his herte, either rehersynge hise synnes and his wrecchidnesse or the
740   malice and the sleightes of the enemye, or ellis the godenesse and the merci of God. And
with that he crieth with desire of herte and with speche of his mouth to oure Lord for
socour and help, as a man that were in peril amonge his enemyes or as a man in
sikenesse, schewynge his sooris to God as to a leche, seiynge thus: *Eripe me de inimicis*

720 reste, quiet. **722 ofte sithes**, often times; **overtravailen**, overburden. **724 letten**, hinder.
725 prevei, secret. **726 passand**, exceeding; **leesen**, lose. **727 wisten**, knew. **728 ought**, any-
thing. **729 sautier**, psalter. **738 rewardes**, concerns. **740 sleightes**, tricks. **743 leche**, physician.

745 *meis, deus meus* (Psalms 58:2) Lord, delyvere me fro myn enemyes, or ellis thus: *Sana, domine, animam meam, quia peccavi tibi* (Psalms 40:5). A, Lord, heele my soule, for I have synned agenys Thee, or sich othere that come to mynde. And also hym thenketh so mykil godenesse, grace, and mercy in God, that hym liketh with grete affeccioun of the herte for to love Hym and thanke Hym by siche wordes and psalmys as acorden to the lovynge and preisynge of God, as Davyd seith: *Confitemini domino, quoniam bo-*

750 *nus, quoniam in seculum misericordia eius* (Psalms 135:1). Loveth and preiseth oure Lord for He is good and merciful, and bi siche othere as he is sterid for to seie.

Chapter Thirty

That this maner of praier pleseth moche God, and maketh a man to have him as he were dronken, and maketh his soule to be woundid with the suerd of love.

This maner of praier mykil pleseth God, for it is oonli in the affeccion of the herte, and

755 therfore it goth nevere awey unsped withoutin sum grace. This praier longeth to the secunde partie of contemplacioun, as I have bifore seide. Whoso hath this gift of God ferventli, hym bihoveth for the tyme flee presence and cumpanye of alle men and to be alone that he be not lettid. Whoso hath it, holde it while he may, for it mai not longe laste in the fervour. For yif grace come plenteuously, it is traveilous wondirfulli to the spirit,

760 though it be likande; and it is mykil wastande the bodili kynde, whoso mykil useth it, for it maketh the bodi, yif grace come myghtili, for to stire and turne heer and theer as a man that were mad or dronken and can have noo reste. And this is a poynt of the passion of love, the whiche bi grete violence and maistrie breketh doun alle lustis and likynges of alle ertheli thinges, and it woundeth the soule with the blisful swerd of love,

765 that the bodi faileth and falleth doun and mai not bere it. This touchynge is of so grete myght that the moste vicious or fleschli man lyvand in erthe, yif he were wel touchid ones myghtili with this scharp suerd, he schulde be right saad and sobre a grete while after, and lothe alle likynges and the lustis of the fleisch, and of alle ertheli thinges whiche he hadde bifore most likynge inne.

752 have him, conduct himself. **753 suerd**, sword. **755 unsped**, unsuccessful. **759 plenteuousli**, copiously. **760 likande**, pleasant; **wastande**, wasting. **767 saad**, serious.

Chapter Thirty-one

770   Hou fier of love wasteth alle fleischli lustes, as othir fier wasteth alle bodili thynges here.

Of this maner of felynge speketh the prophete Jeremye thus: *Et factus est in corde meo quasi ignis estuans, claususque in ossibus meis, et defeci, ferre non sustinens* (Jeremiah 20:9). This is thus mykil to undirstonde: The love and the felynge of God was maad in myn herte not as fier, but as fier glowand; for as bodili fire brenneth and wasteth al

775   bodili thyng where it cometh, right so gosteli fier, as is love of God, brenneth and wasteth fleischli loves and likynges in a mannys soule, and this fier is stokyn so in my boonys, as the prophete seith of himsilf. That is for to seie, this love filleth ful the myghtes of the soule, as mynde, wille, and resoun, of grace and goostli swettenesse, as marwe filleth fulle the boon; and that is withinne, not withouten in the wittis. Neverthelees,

780   it is so myghti withinne that it smyteth oute into the bodi, and dooth al the bodi quake and tremble, for it is so feer from the bodili kynde and so uncouthe that he can no skile of it and mai not bere it, but faileth and falleth doun, as the prophete seide. Therfore oure Lord temprith it and withdraweth the fervour and suffreth the herte for to falle into sobirté of mor swettenesse. Whoso can preie thus ofte, he spedeth swithe in his travaile.

785   He schal gete more of vertues in a litil tyme thanne sum man withoutyn this, or anothir as gode schal doo in a longe tyme, for al the bodili penaunce that he myght doo; and whoso hath this, it nedeth not to charge the bodili kynde with more penance than he bereth yif he have it ofte.

Chapter Thirty-two

Of the thridde maner of praier, oonli in herte withouten speche.

790   The thridde maner of praier is oonli in herte withoute speche, bi grete reste of the bodi and of soule. A clene herte him bihoveth for to have that schulde prai wel thus, for it is of sich men and women that bi longe travaile bodili and goostli, or cllis bi swich smert

---

776 stokyn, stuck. **781 feer**, far; **uncouthe**, unknown; **can**, knows; **skile**, reason. **784 sobirté**, soberness; **spedeth swithe**, succeeds greatly. **786 as gode schal doo**, as good shall do. **787 charge**, burden. **792 smert**, smart.

smytynges of love, as I bifore seide, comen into reste of spirit, so that here affeccioun is turnyd into goostli savoure, that thei moun neer contynueli praie in here herte, and
795 love and praise God withoutyn grete lettynge of temptacions or of vanitees, as I bifore seide in the secunde partie of contemplacioun. Of this maner of preier seith Seynt Poul thus: *Nam si orem lingua, spiritus meus orat, mens autem mea sine fructu est. Quid ergo? Orabo spiritu, orabo et mente, psallam spiritu, psallam et mente* (1 Corinthians 14:15). This is thus mykil for to seie: Yif y praie with my tunge oonli, bi wille of spirit
800 and bi traveil, the preier is meedful, but my soule is not fed, for it felith not the frughte of goostli swettenesse bi undirstondynge. What schal y thanne doo? seith Seynt Poul. And he answereth and seith: I schal praie bi travaile and bi desire of the spirit, and I schal pray also more inward in my spirit withouten travaile, bi felinge of goosteli savour and the swettenesse of the love and the sight of God, bi the whiche sight and felynge of
805 love my soule schal be fed. Thus, as y undirstonde, Seynt Poul cowde preie. Of this maner of preier speketh oure Lord in Holi Writ bi figure thus: *Ignis in altari meo semper ardebit, et cotidie sacerdos surgens mane subiciet ligna, ut ignis non extinguatur* (Leviticus 6:12). This is for to seie thus mykil: The fier of love schal be ay light in the soule of a devoute man or woman, the whiche is the autier of oure Lord, and the prest schal every
810 dai at morwe lei to stikkes and norissch the fier. That is to seie, this man schal bi hooli psalmes, clene thoughtes, fervent desires, norische the fier of love in his herte, that it goo not out noo tyme. This reste oure Lord geveth to summe of Hise servauntis, as it were for a reward of here traveyle and a shadwe of the love whiche thei shullen have in the blisse of hevene.

Chapter Thirty-three

815 How men schal do that aren traveylid with veyn thoughtes in her preier.

But now seist thou that y speke over highe to thee in this manere of praier, for it is no maistrie to me for to seie it, but for to doo it is the maistrie. Thou seist that thu cannot

---

794 moun, are able. **800 meedful**, worthy of reward; **frughte**, fruit. **801 swettenesse**, sweet-ness. **805 cowde**, could. **808 light**, lit. **809 autier**, altar. **810 morwe lei to**, morning lay on. **813 here traveyle**, their labor. **817 maistrie**, feat of skill.

so hoolili ne thus devoutli prai in thyn herte as y speke of. For whanne thou woldest have the mynde of thyn herte upward to God in praier, thou felist so many veyn thoughtis
820 of thyn owen deedis bifore doon, or what thu schalt doon, or of othir mennys dedis, and siche many othire lettynge and taryynge thee, so that thou mai nevere fele savor ne reste in thi praiere ne devocioun in thi seiynge. And ofte sithes the more thu traveilest to kepe thyn herte, the ferthere it is fro thee and the hardere, sumtyme fro the bigynnynge to the laste ende, that thee thenketh it is but loste, al that thou doost. As unto this that I
825 speke to highe to thee of praier, I graunt wel that y speke othirwise than y can do or mai do. Neverthelees y sei it for this entent, that thu schuldest knowe hou we oute to praie yif we dede wel. And sithen we mowen not do so, that we knowe thanne mekeli oure feblenesse and crie God merci. Oure Lord seide so himsilf whan he seide: *Diliges dominum tuum ex tote corde tuo, et ex tota anima tua, et ex omnibus viribus tuis* (Luke
830 10:27). Thou schalt love God of al thyn herte and al thi soule and al thi myghtis. It is inpossible to ony man for to fulfille this biddynge soo fulli as it is seid, lyvynge in erthe, and yit neverthelees oure Lord bad us for to love soo; for this entent, as Seynt Bernard scith, that we schulde knowe therbi oure feblenesse and thanne mekeli crie merci and we schul have it. Neverthelees, I schal telle thee as me thenketh in this askyng.
835 Whenne thu schalt praie, make thyn entente and thi wil in the biginnynge as hool and as clene to God as thou mai schorteli in thi mynde, and than bigynne and do as thou mai; and though thou be never so mykil lettid agens thi first wil, be not to mikil adreed, ne to angri with thisilf, ne unpacient agens God, that he gyveth not thee that savour and goostli swettenesse with devocioun as thee thenketh that he gyveth to othere creatures.
840 But se therbi thyn owen feblenesse and bere it esili, holdynge in thyn owyn sight thi praier, simple as it is, with mekenesse of herte, trustynge also sikirli in the merci of oure Lord, that He schal make it good more thanne thou knowyste or feeliste. And yif thou doo thus, al schal be wel. For wite thou weel that thou art excusid of thi dette, and thou schalt have mecde for it as for anothir good dede that thou doost in charité, though thyn
845 herte were not thereupon in the doynge. Therfore doo thou that longeth to thee, and suffre oure Lord to gyve what He wole, and kenne Hym not; and though thee thenketh

---

821 taryynge, troubling. **822 seiynge**, saying. **826 oute**, ought. **827 mowen**, are able. **832–33 Seynt Bernard seith**, *In Cant.* 50.1.2 (see Clark, p. 169n115). **834 askyng**, request. **835 hool**, whole. **838 unpacient**, impatient. **843 wite**, know; **dette**, debt. **844 meede**, reward. **845 longeth**, belongs. **846 kenne**, teach.

850

855

thee reklees and necgligent, and as thou were in greet defautis for sich thinges, yit nevertheleos schalt thu for this defaute and for alle othere veniales, whiche moun not alle been eschewed in this wrecchid lif, lift up thyn herte to God, knowelechynge thi wrecchid-nesse, and crie merci with a good truste of forgyvenesse, and God schal forgyve thee. Stryve no more therewith, ne hange noo lenger therupon, as thou woldest bi maistrie not fele siche wrecchidnesse. Leve of and goo to sum good deede, bodili or goostli, and thenke to doo betere another tyme. But though thou falle another tyme in the same, yhe an hundrid tymes, a thousand tymes, yit doo as I have seid, and al schal be wel. For ther is many a soule that never mai fynde reste of herte in praiere, but al here liftyme aren stryvande with here thoughtis and taried and troblid with hem. Yif thei kepe hem in mekenesse and charité in othir sides, thei schul have wel mykil mede in hevene for here gode travaile.

860

865

870

Now of meditacioun schal y telle thee as me thenketh. Thou schalt undirstonde that in meditacion mai no certayn rule be sette ai a man for to kepe, for thei aren the free gift of oure Lord, aftir the sondrie disposynges of chosen soules and aftir the staat that thei ben inne. And also aftir that thei profiten in vertues and in here astaat, so He encreseth here meditacion, in goostli knowynge and lovynge of Him; for whoso is ai likewise in knowinge of God and of goosteli thinges, it semeth he wexith but litil in the lovynge of God. And that mai be schewid opynli in the apostelis, whanne thei in the dai of Pentecost weren fulfilled with brennynge love of the Holi Gost; thei weren noo foolis ne fooltes, but thei were maad wondir wise in knowynge and spekynge of God and goostli thinges, als mykil as a man might have in fleschly lyvyng. Thus seith Holi Writ of hem: *Repleti sunt omnes spiritu sancto et ceperunt loqui magnalia dei* (Acts 2:4, 11). Thei weren fulfillid of the Holi Goost, and thei bigan to speke the grete merveiles of God. And al that knowynge thei hadden bi ravyschynge of love of the Hooli Goost.

Chapter Thirty-four

Of meditacion of synful men, aftir that thei ben turned hooli to God.

847 thee reklees, yourself reckless. **849 knowelechynge,** acknowledging. **852 maistrie,** force; **of,** off. **854 yhe,** yea. **856 taried,** disturbed. **857 sides,** aspects. **862 profiten,** advance; **astaat,** estate. **864 wexith,** grows. **867 fooltes,** fools.

Sundrie meditacions ther aren whiche oure Lord putteth in a mannys herte. Sum schal y telle thee, as me thenketh, for this entent, yif thou fele ony of hem, that thou schulde the betere travaile in hem. In the bigynnynge of conversioun of siche a man as hath ben mykil foulid with worldli or fleschli synnes, comounli his thought is most upon his synnes, with gret conpuccion and sorwe of herte, grete wepynges and many teeris of the iye, mekeli and bisili askynge merci and forgyvnesse of God for hem. And yif he be touchid scharpeli, for oure Lord wole make him soone clene, hym schal thenke that in his sight his synnes aren ai so foule and so horrible that unnethes schal he mowe bere himsilf for hevynesse of synne. And though he schryve him never so cleerli, yit schal he fynde bitynge and fretynge of conscience, that him schal thynke that he is not schriven aright. And unnethe schal he mowe have ony reste, in so mykil that he schulde not endure in siche traveile, ne were it that oure Lord of his merci comforteth him sum tyme as He wole, bi grete devocioun of His passioun or bi sum othir wai. Upon this maner werketh oure Lord in sum mennys hertis, more or lasse as He wole. And this is the grete merci of oure Lord, that not oonli wole forgyve the synne and the trespace, but He wole forgyve bothe trespas and peyne for it in purgatorie, for siche a litil peyne here of bitynge of conscience. And also yif He wole dispose a man for to receyve ony special gift of His lofe, him bihoveth first to be scourid and clensid bi siche a fier of conpunccioun for alle the grete synnes bifore doon. Of this maner of travaile speketh David in many psalmes of the sautier, and speciali in the psalme *Miserere mei deus, secundum magnam misericordiam tuam* (Psalms 50:3).

Thanne after this traveile, and sum tyme with alle, sich a man or ellis anothir, whiche bi grace of God hath ben kepid in innocence, oure Lord gyveth a meditacion with gret conpunccioun and with plenté of teeris of His manhede, as of His birthe or of His passioun, or of the compassioun of oure Ladi Seynt Marie.

Chapter Thirty-five

That the meditacion of the manhede of Crist or of His passion is gyven of God, and how it schal be knowen whanne it is geven.

877 **conpuccion**, compunction. 878 **iye**, eye; **bisili**, diligently. 879 **soone clene**, immediately pure. 880 **unnethes**, scarcely; **mowe**, be able to. 881 **schryve**, confess. 882 **fretynge**, eating. 883 **unnethe**, scarcely. 885 **wole**, will. 890 **lofe**, love. 896 **teeris**, tears.

900   Whanne this meditacion is maad bi the Holi Goost, thanne it is right profightable and
gracious, and that schalt thou wite bi this tokene: whanne it is so that thou art stired to
devocion, and sodeynli thi thought is drawen up from alle worldli and fleischli thinges,
and thee thenketh as thu seighe in thi soule thi Lord Jhesu Crist in bodili liknesse as He
was in erthe, how He was taken of the Jewes and bounden as a theef, beten and
905   dispisid, scourgid and demed to the deeth; hou mekeli He baar the Cros upon his bak,
and hou crueli He was nailed therupon; also of the crowne of thornes upon His heed,
and upon the scharp spere that stonge Him to the herte. And thou in this goostli sight
thou felist thyn herte stired into so greet compassioun and pité of thi Lord Jhesu that
thou mornest, and wepist, and criest with alle thy myghtes of thi bodi and of thi soule,
910   wondrynge the goodnesse and the love, the pacience and the mekenesse of oure Lord
Jhesu, that He wolde for so synful a caitif as thou art suffre so mykil peyne. And also
over this thou felist so mykil goodnesse and merci in oure Lord that thi herte riseth up
into love and glaadnesse of Him with manye swete teeris, havynge greet trust of
forgyvenesse of thi synnes and of savacioun of thi soule bi the vertu of this precious
915   passioun. Thanne whanne the mynde of Cristis passioun or ony poynt of His manhede
is thus maad in thi herte bi siche goostli sight, with devout affeccioun answerynge
therto, wite thou wel thanne that it is not thyn owen werkynge, ne feynynge of noo
wikkid spirit, but bi grace of the Holi Goost, for it is an openynge of the goostli iye into
Cristis manhede. And it mai be called the fleischli love of God, as Seynt Bernard callith
920   it, in as mekil as it is set in the fleischli kynde of Crist. And it is right good, and a greet
help in distroyynge of grete synnes, and a wei for to come to vertues. And so aftir to
come to comtemplacioun of Jhesu Crist in His Godhed. For a man schal not come to
goostli delite in comtemplacioun of His Godhede, but yif he come first in ymaginacion
bi bitirnesse and compassioun and bi stable trouthe and stidefaste mynde of His manhede.
925   Thus Seynt Poul dide. For first he seide thus: *Nichil iudicavi me scire inter vos, nisi
Jesum Christum, et hunc crucifixum* (1 Corinthians 2:2). I schewed yow right nought
that y couthe, but oonli Jhesu Crist and Him crucified. As yif he had seid: My knowynge
and my trust is oonli in the passioun of Crist. And therfore seide he thus also: *Michi
autem absit gloriari, nisi in cruce domini nostri Jhesu Cristi* (Galatians 6:14). Forbed be

---

900 profightable, profitable. **903 seighe**, see. **907 stonge**, pierced. **911 caitif**, wretch. **918 iye**,
eye. **919–20 Seynt Bernard callith it**, *In Cant.* 20.2.3–5.9 (Clark, p. 169n120, with other
references). **920 kynde**, nature. **924 trouthe**, faith; **mynde**, thought. **927 couthe**, knew.

930 it fro me al maner of joie and of likynge, but in the Cros and in the passioun of oure Jhesu Crist. And aftirward he seid thus: *Predicamus vobis Christum dei virtutem, et dei sapientiam* (1 Corinthians 1:24). As who seie: First he prechid to yow of the manhed and of the passion of Crist; now y preche to yow of the Godhede and Cristis myght and the eendeles wisdom of God.

Chapter Thirty-six

935 That the meditacioun of the passioun of Crist is withdrawen from hem that it is gyven to ofte sithes for divers skyles.

This maner of meditacioun with gracious conpunccion a man hath not alwei whan he wolde, but whanne oure Lord wole gyve it. Unto sum men and women He geveth it al here lyvetyme, bi sithes whan He visiteth hem; as summe devout men and women aren

940 so tendre in here affeccion that whanne thei here men speke or ellis that thei thenken of this precious passioun, her hertis melten in devocion and thei are fed and confortid bi vertu of it agens al maner temptacions of the enemye, and that is a grete gift of God. To summe men He gyveth it first plenteuousli, and aftirward He withdrawith it for dyverse causis, either yif a man wex proud of it in his owen sight, or for sum othir synne bi the

945 whiche he maketh himsilf unable for to resseyve the grace; or ellis oure Lord withdrawith it and al othir devocion sumtyme from a man or a woman, for He wole suffre hem for to be assaied bi temptacions of His enemye, and so wole He dispose a man for to knowe and fele Him more goostli. For he seide so Himsilf to His disciples: *Expedit vobis ut ego vadam; si enim non abiero, paraclitus non veniet ad vos* (John 16:7). It is spedful to

950 you that y goo fro yow bodili; for yif y goo not, the Holi Goost mai not come to yow. For as longe as He was with hem, thei lovyd Him mykil, but it was flesschli oonli in the manhed; for thei trowed not fulli that Jhesu man was God, and therfore it was spedful to hem that He schulde drawe the bodili forme from here sight that the Hooli Goost myght come to hem, and kenne hem for to love Him and knowe Hym as God more

932 **As who seie,** As if to say. 934 **eendeles,** endless. 936 **ofte sithes,** often times; **skyles,** reasons. 939 **bi sithes,** at times. 943 **plenteuousli,** plentifully. 945 **resseyve,** receive. 947 **assaied,** tested. 949 **spedful,** advantageous. 953 **drawe,** withdraw. 954 **kenne,** teach.

955   goostli, as He dide on the dai of Pentecost. Right so it is spedeful to summe that oure Lord withdrawe a litil the bodili and the fleschli likenesse from the iye of her soule, that the herte myght be set and ficchid more bisili in gosteli desire and felynge of His Godhed.

Chapter Thirty-seven

Of divers temptaciouns of the feend of helle.

Neverthelees it bihoveth a man for to suffre many temptacions first, and thise temptacions
960   fallen ofte sithes to sum men and women after whanne comfort is withdrawen upon divers maneres bi the malice of the enemye, as thus. Whanne the devyl perceyveth devocioun mykil withdrawen, that the soule is left as it were nakid for a tyme, thanne he sendeth to summe men temptacions of leccherie or glotonye, so hoot and so brennynge that hem schal thenke thei felid nevere noon so grevous in al here lif bifore whanne thei
965   gave hem to synne most. In so mykil that thei schul thenke it impossible for to stonde longe and suffre, that thei ne schul nedynges falle but yif thei have helpe. And therfore han thei than mykil sorwe, bothe for lakkynge of comfort and devocioun that thei weren wonte to have, and mykil drede of fallyng from God bi siche open synnes. And al this worcheth the devel for to doo hem forthenke here good purpos and turne agen to
970   synne as they were wont to doo; but whoso wole abide awhile and suffre a litil peyne, the hande of oure Lorde is ful neer and helpeth swithe soone. For He kepeth hem wel sikirli, and thei wot not how; as the prophete David seide in the persoone of oure Lord: *Cum ipso sum in tribulacione, eripiam eum et glorificabo eum* (Psalms 90:15). I am with him in tribulacion and in temptacion; I schal delivere him and y schal make him
975   glorious in my blisse. Sum men he tempteth bi gosteli synnes maliciousli, as of mystrowynge of the articles of the feith or of the sacrament of Goddis bodi, also dispeir or blasphemye in oure Lord or in ony of His seyntis, or lothynge of here lif, or bittirnesse and unskilful hevynesse, or to mykil drede of hemsilf or of here bodi, yif thei putten

956 iye, eye. **957 ficchid**, fixed. **963 hoot**, hot. **966 nedynges**, necessarily. **969 worcheth**, works; **doo hem forthenke**, cause them to reject. **971 swithe**, very. **972 sikirli**, securely. **975–76 mystrowynge**, disbelieving; the items of doubt enumerated here — about the eucharist and devotion to the saints — were among those characteristic of the Lollard movement, the heretical outgrowth of the teachings of John Wycliffe; see Clark, p. 170n131, 132.

980 hem hooli to Goddis service. Sum men he tempteth also, and nameli solitarie men and women, bi dredes and ugglynesse and quakynges and schakynges, either apperynge to hem in bodili liknesse or ellis in ymagynyng, slepynge and wakynge, and tarieth hem so that thei mai unnethes have ony reste. And also on many othere wises he tempteth mo than I can or mai seie.

Chapter Thirty-eight

Of sere remedies agennes temptaciounes of feend.

985 Remedie unto siche maner of men and women that aren thus travaled, or ony othir wise, mai be this: first that thei wolen putten al hire trust in oure Lord Jhesu Crist and bringe thanne to mynde His passioun and His peynes that He suffride, and that thei trowe thanne stidefastli that al this sorwe and traveile that thei suffren in siche temptacions, whiche to an unkunynge man semeth forsakynge of God, is no reprovynge 990 of God, ne non forsakynge, but assayynge for here betere, either for clensynge of here synnes bifore doon, or for grete encresynge of here mede, or for greet disposynge to mykil grace, yif thei wole abide and suffre a litil while and stonde faste with a nakid trouthe and stidefaste mynde of Jhesu Crist, so that thei turne not wilfulli agene to synne. Another remedye is that thei drede not ne sette not at herte siche malicious 995 stirynges of despeir or blasfemye, or of the sacrament or ony siche othere that were uggly to here, for the felynge of thise temptacions foulen the soule no more than yif thei herde an hound berke or felid a flee bite. Thei tarie the soule, but thei apeire not the soule, yif a man wolde despice hem and sette hem at nought. It is not good to stryve with hem, for to putte hem ought bi maistrie; for the more that men stryven with siche 1000 thoughtes the more thei cleve to hem. And therfore thei schullen as mykil as thei moun drawe oute the thought from hem, as yif thei chargiden hem not, and sette it to summe

---

980 ugglynesse, frightfulness. **981 tarieth**, troubles. **982 unnethes**, scarcely; **wises**, manners. **984 sere**, various. **989 unkunynge**, ignorant; **reprovynge**, blaming. **990 assayynge**, testing. **991 mede**, reward; **disposynge**, disposition. **993 trouthe**, faith. **996 uggly**, horrible. **997 tarie**, trouble; **apeire**, injure. **998 despice**, despise. **1000 moun**, are able. **1001 chargiden**, concerned.

othir good occupacion. And yit yif thei wolen ai hange upoun hem, thanne it is good to hem that thei ben not angri ne hevy for to fele hem, but that thei with a good trust in God wole bere hem as it were a bodili peyne and a scourge of oure Lord for clensynge
1005 of here synnes, as longe as He wole. And over this it is good to hem, to schewe hire hertes to sum wise man in the bigynnynge bifore thei ben rooted in the herte, and that thei leve here owen witte and folwe the counsel of him; and that thei schewe hem not lightli to noon uncouth man, that is to seie, to noon unkunnynge man and worldli, which never hadde felid siche temptacions, for thei myghte lightli bringe a symple soule into
1010 despeir bi unkunynge of hemsilf. Of this maner of temptacions, bi the whiche a man semeth forsaken of God and is not, in comfort of hem that aren temptid oure Lord seith thus bi His prophete: *In modico dereliqui te et in memento indignacionis mee percussi te, et in miseracionibus meis multis congregabo te* (Isaiah 54:7). In a litil y forsook thee, that is for to seie, I suffrid thee for to be taried a litil, and in a poynt of my wraththe y
1015 smoot thee, that is to seie, al the penaunce and the peyne that thou suffrest heere is but a poynt of my wraththe in reward of peyne of helle or of purgatorie. And yit in my manyfold mercies y schal gadre thee togedre, that is for to sai, whanne that thee theenketh that thou art forsaken, thanne schal y of my greet merci gadre thee agen to me, for thanne whanne that thu wenest that thou art but lost, thanne schal oure Lord helpe thee,
1020 as seith Job: *Cum te consumptum putaveris, orieris ut lucifer et habebis fiduciam* (Job 11:17). That is for to seie, whanne thou art brought so lowe bi traveil in temptacion that thee thenketh noon help ne comfort, but as it were a fordoon man, yit stond stifli in hope, and prai God, and sotheli thou schalt sodaynli springe up as the dai sterre in gladnesse of herte, and have a veri trust in God, as Job seide.

Chapter Thirty-nine

1025 Hou God suffreth hem that He cheseth for to be tarid and temptid; and aftirwarde He comfortith hem and stableth hem yn grace.

1008 uncouth, ignorant; **unkunnynge**, unknowing. **1009 felid**, felt; **lightli**, easily. **1016 poynt**, small amount; **reward of**, comparison to. **1022 fordoon**, ruined; **stifli**, resolutely. **1023 sterre**, star. **1025 tarid**, troubled. **1026 stableth**, establishes.

And also in confort of sich men that thei schulde not despeire, the wise man seith thus of oure Lord: *In temptacione ambulat cum eo. In primis eligit eum. Timorem et metum et approbacionem inducit super illum; et cruciabit illum in tribulacione doctrine sue,* 1030 *donec temptet illum in cogitacionibus suis, et credat anime illius, ad iter directum adducet illum et firmabit illum et letificabit illum; et denudabit abscondita sua illi, et thesaurizabit super illum scienciam et intellectum iusticie* (Ecclesiasticus 4:18–21). This is thus mykil for to sai: The wise man, for he wolde not that men schulde dispeire in temptacion, in comfort of hem he seith thus: In tribulacion, ne in temptacioun oure Lord forsaketh not 1035 a man, but He goth with him fro the bigynnynge to the laste ende, for He seith, first He cheseth him, and that is whanne He draweth a man to him bi confort of devocion; and aftirward sorwe and drede and assaiynge He bringeth upon him, and that is whanne He withdraweth devocion and suffreth him to be temptid. Also He seith He tormenteth him in tribulacion, until He hath assaied hym wel in his thoughtis, and til a man wole putte al 1040 his trust fulli in Him. And thanne aftir this oure Lord bringeth hym oute to the right wai and festeneth him to Hym, and gladith hym, and sithen scheweth him His pryvetees, and geveth him His tresour of knowynge and undirstondinge and rightwisenesse.

Bi thise wordes of Holi Writ mai thou see that thise temptacions, or ony othere, be thei nevere so uggli to a man that bi grace is in ful wille to forsake synne, aren spedful and 1045 profitable, yif he wole suffre as he mai and abide Goddis wille, and not turne agen to synnes which he hath forsake for no sorwe ne peyne ne drede of siche temptacioun, but ai stondeth stille in travaile, and in praiere. Oure Lord of His endelees godenesse, havynge pité and merci of alle His creatures, whanne He seeth tyme He leith to His hond, and smyteth doun the devel and al his power; and eseth hem of here travaile, and 1050 putteth awei dredis and sorwes and merkenesse oute of here hertes and bringeth into hire soules light of grace, and openeth the sight of here soule, gyvynge hem a newe goostli myght to agenstonde al the fondynges of the fende and alle deedli synnes withoutin gret travaile, and ledeth hem into saddenesse of good vertues lyvynge. In the which, yif thei be meke, He kepeth hem to here laste ende, and thanne taketh He hem al hooli to 1055 Hym. This thyng y seie to thee, yif thou be taried or traveiled with ony siche manere of temptacions, be not to mykil adred, but doo as I have seide, and betere yif thou may; and y hope bi the grace of Jhesu Crist thou schal nevere be overcome with thyn enemy.

1041 festeneth, fastens; **gladith**, cheers. **1044 uggli**, horrible; **spedful**, useful. **1047 stille**, constantly. **1050 merkenesse**, darkness. **1052 agenstonde**, resist; **fondynges**, temptations. **1053 saddenesse**, firmness; **vertues**, virtuous. **1057 hope**, expect.

Chapter Forty

That a man schulde not geve him to idelnesse ne lightli leve the grace that were gyven to him of God.

1060   Aftir this, whanne thou hast ascapid siche temptacions, or ellis oure Lord hath so kepid thee, as He hath doon many of His merci, that thou hast not ben mykil taried with non siche, thanne it is good to thee that thou turne not thi reste into idelnesse; for there is many man that taketh reste upon Him to sone. But thou schalt, yif thou wolt, bigynne a newe travaile, and that is for to entre into thyn owen soule bi meditacion, for to knowe what it is, 1065   and bi the knowynge therof for to come to the goostli knowynge of God. For as Seynt Austyn seith: "Bi the knowynge of mysilf, I schalle gete the knowing of God." I seie not that it is nedeful to thee and dette for to travaile so, ne to noon othir man, but yif he fele him stired bi grace and as it were callid therto. For oure Lord gyveth sundri giftes whereso He wole, not oon man al, ne alle men oon, outaken charité whiche is comyn to alle. And 1070   therfore, yif a man or a woman have receyved a gifte of oure Lord, as devocion in praier or in the passion of Crist, or ony othir be it nevere so litil, leve it not to soone for noon othir, but yif he felid sothfastli a betere, whanne God wole give it. Neverthelees aftirward yif hit be withdrawen sumwhat, and he see a betere and felith his hert stired therto, thanne semeth it a callynge of oure Lord to the betere, and thanne is tyme for to folwe aftir for to gete it.

Chapter Forty-one

1075   That a man schulde knowe the mesure of his gifte, and evere desire more, and take a betere, whanne God wole gyve it.

Oure holi fadres heere bifore kenned us that we schulde knowe the mesure of oure gifte, and up that werk, not takynge upon us bi feynynge more thanne we han in felynge. We moun ai desire the beste, but we moun not ay werke the beste, for we han 1080   not yit receyved the grace. An hound that renneth aftir the hare oonli for he seeth othir

1060 **ascapid**, escaped. **1065–66 Seynt Austyn seith**, *Soliloquia*, 2.1.1; see Clark, p. 171n144. **1067 dette**, debt. **1069 outaken**, except for. **1077 kenned**, taught. **1078 up that werk**, work according to that. **1079 moun₂**, are able to; **werke**, perform. **1080 An hound**, the story of the hound and the hare is common, based on *Vitae patrum*, 5.7.35 (PL 73:901) (Clark, p. 171n146).

houndes renne, whanne he is weri he resteth him and turneth hym agen. But yif he
renne for he seeth the hare, he wole not spare for werynesse til he have geten it. Right
so it is gosteli. Whoso hath a grace, be it never so litil, yif he leve wilfulli the werkynge
of it, and make himsilf for to traveile in anothir whiche he hath not yit, oonli for he seeth
1085 or heereth that othere men doo soo, sothli he may renne a while til he be weri, and
thanne schal he turne him agen, and but yif he be waar, he mai hurte his feet bi sum
fantasies, or thanne he come hoom. But he that worcheth in siche grace as he hath, and
desireth mekeli and lastandli aftir more, and aftir felith his herte stired for to folwe the
grace whiche he hath desired, he mai sikirli renne, yif he kepe mekenesse. And therfore
1090 desire of God as mykil as thou mai, withoutyn mesure or discrecioun, of alle that
longith to His love, and to the blisse of hevene; for woso can best desire of God, most
schal fele of Hym. But worche as thu mai, and crie God merci for that that thou mai not.
Thus it semeth Seynt Poule seide: *Unusquisque habet donum suum a deo, alius autem
sic, alius vero sic* (1 Corinthians 7:7). *Item: unicuique nostrum data est gracia secun-*
1095 *dum mensuram donacionis Christi* (Ephesians 4:7). *Item: divisiones graciarum sunt,*
alii datur sermo sapiencie; alii sermo sciencie (1 Corinthians 12:4, 8). *Item: ut sciamus*
que a deo donata sunt nobis (1 Corinthians 2:12). Seynt Poul seith that everi man hath
his gift of God, oon thus, and anothir thus. For to everi man that schal be saaf is geven
grace aftir the mesure of Cristis gifte, and therfore it is spedful that we knowe the giftis
1100 whiche are gyven us of God, that we myght worche in hem, for bi hem we schullen ben
saaf; as summe bi bodili werkes and bi dedes of merci, summe bi grete penaunce, summe
bi sorwes and wepyngis for here synnes al here liyftyme, sum bi prechynge and techynge,
sum bi divers graces and giftes of devocioun schullen ben saaf and comen to blisse.

Chapter Forty-two

That a man schulde travaile for to knowe his owen soule and the myghtes of it, and
1105 breke doun the ground of synne therinne.

1081 **weri**, weary. **1086 but yif**, unless; **waar**, wary. **1087 or thanne**, before; **worcheth**, works.
1088 lastandli, constantly. **1091 woso**, whoever. **1098 saaf**, saved.

Neverthelees, there is oon werke whiche is nedful and spedful for to traveile inne. And that is a man for to entre into himsilf, for to knowe his owen soule and the myghtes therof, the fairenesse and the foulenesse therof. In this inward biholdinge thou schalt mow see the worschipe and the dignité whiche it hadde bi kynde of the firste makynge, 1110 and thou schalt see also the wrecchidnesse and the myschief of synne whiche thou art fallen in. And of this sight schal come grete desire with longynge in thyn herte for to receyve agen that clennesse and that worschipe whiche thou hast lost. Also thou schalt fele a lothynge and a grisynge of thisilf, with a grete wil for to distroie and bere doun thisilf and al that synne that letteth thee fro that dignité and fro that clennesse. This is a 1115 goostli travaile hard and scharp in bigynnynge, whoso wole quykli travayle thereinne, for it is a traveile in the soule agens the ground of al synnes litil or mykil, which ground is not ellis but a fals mysrulid love of a man to himsilf. Oute of this love, as Seynt Austen seith, spryngeth alle manere of synne deedli and venial; and sothli until this ground be wel ransakid and depe dolven, and as it were up dried bi outecastynge of alle 1120 worldli and fleischli loves, a soule mai nevere fele goostli the brennande love of oure Lord Jhesu Crist, ne have hoomlinesse of His gracious presence, ne cleer sightis of goostli thinges bi light of undirstondynge. This is the travaile that a man bihooveth drawe out his herte from the fleischli love of alle ertheli creatures and from veyn love of himsilf, that his soule schulde no reste fynde in noo fleischli thought, ne in eertheli 1125 affeccion. And yif he doo thus, thanne in as mykil as the soule mai not fynde redili his goostli reste in the love and in the hoomli presence and in the sight of Jhesu, it schal nedynge fele peyne. This travaile is sumdel streit and narwgh, and neverthelees it is a wai whiche Crist techid to hem that wolden ben His perfight folweres in the Gospel, seiande thus: *Contendite intrare per angustam portam; quoniam arta est via que ducit* 1130 *ad vitam, et pauci inveniunt eam* (Luke 13:24; Matthew 7:13–14). Stryve ye for to entre bi this streite gate, for the wai that ledeth to hevene is narw, and fewe men fynden it. And hou streite this wei is, oure Lord tellith in another place thus: *Si quis vult post me venire, abneget semetipsum, et tollat crucem suam, et sequatur me* (Matthew 16:24).

1106 nedful, necessary; **spedful**, helpful. **1107 entre**, enter. **1109 mow**, be able to. **1112 clennesse**, purity; **worschipe**, respect. **1113 grisynge**, horror. **1117–18 Seynt Austen seith**, possible reference to *De civitate dei*, 14.28; see Clark, p. 172n158. **1119 ransakid**, examined; **dolven**, dug; **outecastynge**, casting out. **1120 brennande**, burning. **1127 nedynge**, necessarily; **narwgh**, narrow. **1129 seiande**, saying. **1131 narw**, narrow.

Item: qui odit animam suam in hoc mundo, in vitam eternam custodit eam (John 12:25).

1135 That is for to seie: Whoso wole come aftir Me, forsake hymsilf and hate his owen soule. That is for to seie: Forsake alle fleischli love and hate his owen fleschli lif and the likynge of alle his fleischli wittis for the love of Me; and take the Cros, that is to seie suffre the peyne of this for awhile, and thanne folwe, that is to seie in contemplacioun of My manhede and of My Godhede. This is a streit weie and narwe, for it is a sleynge of alle

1140 synnes, as Seynt Poul seith: *Mortificate membra vestra, que sunt super terram, immundiciam, libidinem, concupiscenciam malam* (Colossians 3:5). Slee youre membris upoun erthe — not youre membris of bodi, but the membris of thi soule, as unclenne lust and unskilful love to youresilf and to erthili thinges. Therfore as thi travaile hath ben here bifore for to agenstonde grete bodili synnes and open temptaciouns of the enemye

1145 as hit were fro withoutin, right soo thee bihoveth now in this gostli werk withinne thisilf, bigynnynge for to distroie and breke doun the ground of synne in thisilf, as mykil as thou mai. And that thou myghtest redili bringe it aboute, I schal telle thee as me thenketh.

Chapter Forty-three

Hou a man schal knowe the worthinesse and the worschipe of his soule that it oweth to have bi kynde, and the wrecchidnesse and myschief that it is fallen in thorw synne.

1150 The soule of a man is a liyf, made of thre myghtes — mynde, resoun, and wille — to the ymage and the likenes of the blissid holi Trinité, hooli perfight and rightwise. In as myche as the mynde was maad myghti and stidefaste bi the Fadir almyghti, for to holde Hym withoughte forgetynge, distractynge, or lettynge of ony creature, and so it hath the likenes of the Fader. The resoun was maad cleer and bright withouten errour or

1155 derkenesse, as perfightli as a soule in a bodi unglorifiede myght have; and so it hath the likenes of the Sone, whiche is endelees wisdom. And the love and the wille was maad clene, brenynge into God withouten beestly lust of the fleisch or of ony creature, bi

1139 sleynge, slaying. **1143 unskilful**, unreasonable. **1144 agenstonde**, resist. **1148 worschipe**, respect. **1149 kynde**, nature. **1150 liyf**, life; **myghtes**, powers; **mynde, resoun, and wille**, the influential association of these powers of the soul with the persons of the Trinity is found in Augustine, *De Trinitate*, 10.11.17–12.19; see Clark, p. 168n108 and p. 172n167. **1151 perfight**, perfect; **rightwise**, righteous. **1153 withoughte**, without.

sovereyne goodnesse of God; and so it hath the likenes of the Hooli Goost, the whiche is blissid love. So that a mannys soule, whiche mai be callid a maad trinyté, was fulfillid
1160 in mynde, sight, and love, of the unmaad blissed Trinité, whiche is oure Lord. This is the dignité, the state and the worschipe of a mannys soule, bi kynde of the firste makynge. This staat haddest thou in Adam bifore the first synne of man; but whanne Adam synnede, chosynge love and delite in himsilf and in creaturis, he loste al this worschipe and his dygnyté and thou also lostest it in hym and felle from that blissid Trinité into a
1165 foule merk wrecchid trinité, that is into forgetynge of God and unknowynge of him, and into beestli likynge of thisilf, and that skilefulli, for as David seith in the sautier: *Homo, cum in honore esset, non intellexit; comparatus est iumentis, et similis factus est illis* (Psalms 48:21). A man whanne he was in worschipe, he knewe it not, and therfore he loste it and was maad like to a beest. See now thanne the wrecchidnesse of thi soule,
1170 for as thi mynde was sum tyme stable in God, right so now it hath forgeten Hym, and seketh his reste in creatures now froo oon to another, and never may fynde ful reste, for he hath lost Him in whoom is ful reste. And right so it is of the resoun and of the love also, whiche was clene in goostli savoure and suettenesse; now it is turned into foule beestli lust and likynge into thisilf and into creatures and in fleischli savoures,
1175 bothe in the wittes, as in glotonye and leccherie, and in the ymagynynge, as in pride, veynglorie and covetise — in so mykil that thou mai unnethes doo ony good dede but yif thou be defouled by veynglorie, ne thou may not wel use noon of thi five wittes cleenli in noon creature delitable but yif thyn herte be take and gleymed with veyn lust and likynge of it, whiche putteth oute the love of God from the herte, as in felynge and
1180 the goosteli savour, that it may not come therinne. Everiche man that lyveth in spirite knoweth wel al this. This is the wrecchidnesse of thi soule and the myschief for the firste synne of man, withouten al othir wrecchidnesse and synnes whiche thou hast put therto wilfulli. And wite thou wel, though thou hadde nevere doo synne with thi bodi deedli ne venyal, but onli this that is callid origynal — for it is the first synne, and that is
1185 not ellis but the loesynge of thi rightwisenesse whiche thou were maad inne — yit schuldest thou nevere have ben saaf yif oure Lord Jhesu Criste bi His precious passioun hadde not delyvered thee and restored thee agen.

1159 **maad**, made. 1160 **of**, by. 1165 **merk**, dark. 1166 **skilefulli**, reasonably. 1168 **worschipe**, honor. 1176 **unnethes**, scarcely. 1178 **cleenli**, purely; **delitable**, delightful; **take**, taken; **gleymed**, smeared. 1182 **withouten**, except for. 1183 **wite**, know. 1185 **loesynge**, losing. 1186 **saaf**, saved.

Book I

Chapter Forty-four

Hou everi man mai be saved bi the passioun of Crist, be he never so wrecchid, yif he aske it.

1190 And therfore yif thou thenke that y have heere bifore spoken over highe to thee, for thou mai not take it ne fulfille it as y have seid or schal seie, I wole fal doun to thee as lowe as thou wolt, as wel for my profight as for thyn. And than I seie thus, that be thou nevere so mykil a wrecche, have thou doon never so mykil synne, forsake thisilf and al thi werkes goode and badde, crie merci and aske oonli savacioun bi the vertu of His
1195 precious passion mekeli and trustili, and withoute doute thou schalt have it. And for this origynal synne and all othere that thou hast doon, thou schalt be saaf, as ankir incluse; and not oonli thou, but alle Cristene soulis whiche trusten upoun His passioun and meken hemself, knowelechynge her wrecchidnesse, askynge merci and forgyvenesse, by the fruit of His precious passioun oonli, lowynge hemsilf to the sacramentis of Holi
1200 Chirche. Though it be so that thei han ben encombrid with synne al here liyftyme and nevere hadden felynge of goostli savour or swetenesse or gostli knowynge of God, thei schullen in this feith and in here good wille, bi vertue of this precious passioun of oure Lord Jhesu Crist, be saf and come to the blisse of hevene. Al this knowist thou wel, but yit me liketh for to seie it. See here the endelees merci of oure Lord, how lowe He falleth
1205 to thee and to me and to alle synful caityves. Aske merci and have it. Thus seide the prophete in the persone of oure Lord: *Omnis enim quicunque invocaverit nomen domini, salvus erit* (Joel 2:32). Everi man, whatevere he be, calle the name of Jhesu, that is to seie aske savacion bi Jhesu and bi His passioun, he schal be saaf. This curtesie of oure Lord summe men taken wel, and ben savyd therbi, and summe in truste of merci
1210 and of this curtesie liyn stille in here synne, and wenen for to have it whanne hem list. And thanne mowe thei not, for thei aren taken or thei witen, and so thei dampnen hemself.

1192 profight, profit. **1195 trustili**, trustingly. **1196 ankir incluse**, enclosed anchorite. **1198 meken**, humble; **knowelechynge**, acknowledging. **1199 lowynge**, humbling. **1203 saf**, saved. **1205 caityves**, wretches. **1210 liyn**, lie. **1211 or**, before. **1212 hemself**, themselves.

But than seist thou: "Yif this be sooth, thanne wondre y greteli for that y fynde writen in summe hooli mennys sawes. Sume seyn, as I undirstonde, that he that cannot love
1215 this blissid name Jhesu, ne fynde ne fele in it goostli joie and delitableté with wondirful swettenesse in this lif here, fro the sovereyn joie and goostli swettenesse in the blisse of hevene he schal be aliene, and nevere schal he come therto. Sotheli thise wordes, whanne I hem rede, stoneth me and maketh me greteli aferd; for y hope, as thou seist, that many bi the merci of oure Lord schullen ben saaf bi kepynge of Hise comaundementis and by
1220 veri repentaunce for here yvel lif bifore doon, the whiche felid nevere goostli swetenesse ne inly savoure in the name of Jhesu or in the love of Jhesu. And forthi I mervaile me the more that thei seie contrarie hereto, as it semeth."

As unto this y mai seie as me thenketh, that there seiynge, yif it be wel undirstonde, is sooth, ne hit is not contrarie to that that y have seid. For this name Jhesu is not ellis
1225 for to seie upon Ynglisch but heelere or hele. Now every man that lyveth in this wrecchid lif is goostli sike, for there is no man that lyveth withoutin synne, the whiche is goostli sikenesse, as Seynt Johun seith of hymsilf and othere perfight men thus: *Si dixerimus quia peccatum non habemus, ipsi nos seducimus, et veritas in nobis non est* (1 John 1:8). Yif we seyn that we have noo synne, we bigile ouresilf and there is noo soothfastnes
1230 in us. And forthi he mai nevere fele ne come to the joie of hevene unto he be first maad hool of this goostli sikenesse. But this gostli heele mai noo man have that hath use of resoun but yif he desire it and love it and have delite thereinne, in as michel as he hopith for to gete it. Now the name of Jhesu is nothyng ellis but this goostli hele; wherfore it is sooth that thei seyn, that ther mai no man be saaf but yif he love and like in the name
1235 of Jhesu, for there mai no man be goostli hool but yif he love and desire goosteli heele. For right as yif a man were bodili sike, there were noon ertheli thynge so dere ne so nedeful to hym, ne so mykil schulde be desired of him as bodili heele, for though thou woldest geve hym alle the rychessis and worschipis of this world and nought make hym hool, yif thou myghtest, thou plesist hym not. Right soo it is to a man that is sike
1240 goostli and felith the peyne of goostli sikenesse. Nothinge is so dere, ne so nedeful, ne

1213 **But than,** From this point to the end of the chapter is the "Holy Name" section, omitted from several MSS; Gardner (1936, pp. 20–23) argues for its authenticity. See Textual Notes. 1214 **sawes,** sayings. 1215 **delitableté,** delightfulness. 1217 **aliene,** cast out; **Sotheli,** Truly. 1218 **stoneth,** astonishes; **aferd,** afraid. 1221 **inly,** inward. 1223 **undirstonde,** understood. 1225 **heelere or hele,** healer or health. 1227 **perfight,** perfect. 1231 **heele,** health.

so mykil coveited of hym, as is goostli heele; and that is Jhesu, withouten which alle the joies of hevene mai not like hym.

And this is the skile, as I hope, whi oure Lord whanne He took mankynde for oure savacion, He nolde not be callid bi noon name that bitokenyd His endelees beynge, or
1245 His myght, or His wisdom, or His rightwisenesse, but oonli bi that that bitokened the cause of His comynge and was savacion of mannys soule, which savacion was most dere and most nedeful to man. And this savacion bitokeneth this name Jhesu. Thanne bi this it semeth sooth that there schal no man be saaf, but yif he love Jhesu; for there may no man be saaf but yif he love savacion oonli, for to have it thorugh that blissid persone
1250 Jhesu bi the mekenesse of His manhede and by the merite of His passioun, whiche love he may have that lyveth and dieth in the lowest degré of charité. Also y mai seie, on anothir manere, that he that cannot love this blissid name Jhesu with goostli mirthe, ne enjoie in it with heveneli melodie here, he schal nevere have ne fele in hevene that fulhed of sovereyne joie the whiche he that myght in this liyf bi habundaunce of perfight
1255 charité enjoie in Jhesu schal fele and have, and so mai here seiynge ben undirstande.

Neverthelees he schal be saaf and have ful mede in the sight of God, yif he in this liyf be in the lowest degré of charité bi kepinge of Goddis comaundementis; for oure Lord seith Hymsilf thus: *In domo patris mei multe mansiones sunt* (John 14:2). In My Fadris hous aren many sere dwellynges. Summe are for parfite soules, the which in this liyf
1260 were fulfilled of grace of the Holi Gost and songen loovynge to God in contemplacion of Hym, with wondirful swettenesse and heveneli savour. Thise soules, for thei hadden moost charité, schullen have highest mede in the blisse of hevene, for thise are callid Goddis derlyngges. Othere soulis that are not disposid to contemplacion of God, ne hadden not the fulhed of charité as aposteles or martyres hadden in the bigynnynge of
1265 Hooli Chirche, schullen have the lower meede in the blisse of hevene, for thise are callid Goddis frendes. Thus calleth oure Lord in Holi Writ chosen soules, seiynge thus: *Comedite, amici, et inebriamini, carissimi* (Canticle 5:1). Mi freendes, ete yee, and my derlynges, be yee dronken. As yif oure Lord seid thus: Yee that aren My frendes, for yee kepid My comaundementis and sette My love bifore the love of the world, and loved Me more
1270 thanne ony erthli thyng, yee schullen be feed with goostli foode of the breed of liyf. But ye that aren My derlynges, that not oonli keped My comaundementis, but also of youre

1241 of, by. **1242 like**, please. **1243 skile**, reason. **1254 habundaunce**, abundance. **1259 sere**, various. **1260 loovynge**, praise. **1262 mede**, reward. **1263 derlyngges**, darlings.

owen fre wil fulfilleden My conceils, and over that ye loveden Me oonli and entierli with alle the myghtis of youre soule, and brenneden in My love with goostli delite, as diden principali the aposteles and martires and alle othere soules that myghten bi grace come to the gifte of perfeccioun: yee schullen be maad dronken with the highest and freschest wyn in My celere, that is, the sovereyne joie of love in the blisse of hevene.

1275

Chapter Forty-five

That a man schulde be besi for to recovere agen his worthynesse, and reforme in him the ymage of the Trinité.

Neverethelees though this be sooth of the endelees merci of God unto thee and to me and al mankynde, we schullen not therfore in trust of this be the more rekles wilfulli in oure lyvynge, but more bisi unto plese Hym, nameli now, syn we aren restorid agen in hope bi this passioun of oure Lord to the dignité and to the blisse whiche we hadden lorn by Adammys synne. And though we myghten nevere geete it here fulli, yit we schulde desire that we myght recovere here lyvand a figure and a likenesse of that dignité, that oure soule myght be reformed, as it were in a schadewe, bi grace to the ymage of the Trinité, whiche we hadden bi kynde and aftir schullen have fulli in blisse. For that is the lif that is veri contemplatif, unto bigynne here in that felynge of love and goosteli knowynge of God bi openyng of the goostli iye, whiche schal nevere be loste ne bi taken awey, but the same schal be fulfilled othirwise in the blisse of hevene.

1280

1285

1290
    This bihight oure Lord to Marie Mawdeleyn, whiche was contemplatif, and He seide thus of here: *Maria optimam partem elegit, que non auferetur ab ea* (Luke 10:42), that Marie hadde chosen the beste partie, that is the love of God in contemplacion, for it schal nevere be taken awey fro hire. I seie not that thou mai here lyvande recovere so hool ne so parfight clennesse, as innocence, knowynge and lovynge, as thou haddest first, ne as thou schalt have; ne thou may not eschape alle the wrecchidnessis ne the peynes of synne, ne thou lyvande in dedli fleisch may distroie and quenche al hooli the

1295

1276 celere, cellar. **1277 besi**, diligent. **1280 rekles**, careless. **1281 syn**, since. **1283 lorn**, lost. **1287 unto**, to. **1290 bihight**, promised; **Marie Mawdeleyn**, Mary Magdalene; for her as contemplative, see *Scale*, I.263. **1295 eschape**, escape. **1296 peynes**, punishments.

veyn fals love of thisilf, ne flee alle venial synnes, that thei ne wole — but yif thei ben stopped bi grete fervour of charité — alwey spryngyn oute of thyn herte, as watir renneth oute from a stynkinge welle. But I wolde yif thou myght not fulli quenche hit,

1300 that thou myghtest sumwhat sleke it and come to that clennesse as nygh as thou mai. For oure Lord bihighte the children of Israel whanne He ledde hem into the lond of biheste, and in figure of hem to alle Cristene men thus: *Omne quod calcaverit pes tuus tuum erit* (Deuteronomy 11:24). That is for to seie, as mykil as thou may trede upon with thi foot of verrey desire here, so mykil schalt thou have in the lond of biheste, that

1305 is in the blisse of hevene whanne thou comest thider.

Chapter Forty-six

Hou Jhesu schal be sought, desired, and founden.

Seke thanne that thou hast lost, that thou myght fynde it. Wel y woot, whoso myght oones have an inward sight a litil of that dignité and that goosteli fairenesse whiche a soule hadde bi kynde of the firste makynge and schal have bi grace, he schulde lothe

1310 and dispice in his herte alle the blisse, the likynge, and the fairnesse of al this world as stynk of carioun; and he schulde nevere have wil to doo othir dede nyght ne dai — savynge the freelté and the bare nede of the bodili kynde — but desire, morne, prai, and seke hou he myght come agen therto. Neverthelees, in as moche as thou hast not yit fulli seen what it is, for thi goostli yye is not yit openyd, I schal telle oon word for alle

1315 whiche thou schalt seke, desire, and fynde, for in that word is al that thou hast loste. This word is Jhesu. I mene not oonli this word Jhesu peynted upon the wal, or writen bi letres on the book, or fourmed bi lippes in soun of the mouthe, or feyned in the herte bi traveil of mynde; for on this maner wise may a man oute of charité fynde Hym. But I mene Jhesu Crist, that blissid persoone, God and man, son of Marie, that glorious

1320 virgyne, that is al goodnesse, endelees wisdom, love, and swettenesse, thi joie, thi worschipe, and thyn ai lastynge blisse, thi God, thi Lord, and thy savacioun.

Thanne yif it be so that thou felist grete desire in thyn herte to love and to plese Jhesu, either bi the mynde of this name Jhesu, or bi mynde or seynge of ony othir word, or praier, or in ony dede that thou doost, whiche desire is so mykil that hit putteth ought as

1299 renneth, runs. **1300 sleke**, slake. **1302 biheste**, promise. **1312 freelté**, frailty.

83

1325   it were bi strengthe alle othere thoughtes and desires of the world and of the fleisch, that thei moun not reste in thyn herte, thanne sekest thou wel Jhesu. And whanne thou felist this desire to God, to Jhesu Crist (al is oon) hoolpen and comfortid bi gostli myght thorugh light of Goddis grace so mykil that it is turnyd into love and into affeccioun, gosteli savour, and swettenesse, into light and knowynge, into soothfastnesse — so

1330   mykil that for the tyme the poynt of thi thought is sette upoun noon ertheli thynge, ne felith no stirynge of veynglorie, ne non othir yvel affeccioun (for thei moun not appere that tyme), but oonli is enclosid, rested, softed, anoynted, and comfortid thorugh gracious presence of oure Lord Jhesu Crist, thanne hast thou founden sumwhat of Jhesu. Not yit Hym fulli as he is, but a schadewe of Hym; for the betere that thou fyndest

1335   Hym, the more schalt thou desire Hym. Thanne bi what maner of praier or meditacioun or occupacion that thou mai have grettest desire to Hym, and have most felynge of Hym, bi that occupacion thou sekest Hym best and best fyndest Hym. Therfore yif it come to thy mynde as it were askand what hast thou lost and what sekest thou, lift up the mynde and the desire of thyn herte to thi Lord Jhesu Crist, that blissid maidenys

1340   sone, though thou be blynd and not mai see of His Godhede, and seie Hym hast thu lost, and Hym wolde thou have, and nothynge but Hym, noon othir joie, blisse in hevene ne in erthe, but Hym, to be with Hym wharso He is, and to see Hym and love Hym. And though it be so that thou fele a litil His goostli presence in devocion or in knowynge, or in ony othir gifte what it be, reste not therinne as though thou haddest fulli founden

1345   Jhesu and wolt no more seken aftir Hym, but ai be desirande aftir Jhesu more and more for to fynde Hym betere, as thou hadde right nought. For wite thou wel, what that thou felist of Hym, be it nevere so mykil, yhe, though thou were raveschid into the thridde hevene with Poule, yit haste thou not fulli founden Jhesu as He is in His joie. Knowe thou or fele thou never so mykil of Hym here in this liyf, He is yit above it. And therfore

1350   yif thou wolt fulli fynde Hym as He is in the blisse, cese nevere while thou lyvest of praiers and of goostli desyrynge.

Chapter Forty-seven

What profite is to have the desire of Jhesu.

1326 moun, are able to. **1327 hoolpen,** helped. **1342 wharso,** wherever. **1347 yhe,** yea.

Sotheli y hadde lever feele and have a sothfast desire and a clene love longynge in myn herte to my Lord Jhesu, though y myghte not seen of His Godhede with my goostli iye, thanne for to have withoutin this desire alle bodili penaunce of alle men lyvynge, alle visiouns or revelacions of angels apperynge, songes and sownes, savours or smelles, brennynges and ony likynges, bodili felande, and schortli for to seie, alle the joies of hevene and of erthe whiche y myght have withouten this desire to my Lord Jhesu. David the prophete felid as y seie, as I undirstonde, whanne he seide thus: *Quid enim michi est in celo, et a te quid volui super terram?* (Psalms 72:25). Lord, what thynge is to me in hevene, or what wolde y, withouten Thee above the erthe? As yif he seide thus: Lord Jhesu, what heveneli joie is likynge to me, withouten desire of Thee whiles y am in erthe, or withouten love of Thee whanne I come to hevene? As who seith, right noon. Thanne yif thou woldest fele onythynge of Hym bodili or goostli, coveite not but for to fele soothfasteli in thyn herte a desire of His grace and of His merciful presence that thee thenketh that thyn herte mai fynde noon othir reste in nothynge but in Hym. Thus coveitide David whanne he seide thus: *Concupivit anima mea desiderare iustificaciones tuas in omni tempore* (Psalms 118:20). Lord, my soule coveitide the desire of Thi rightwisenesse in every tyme. Seke thanne, as David dide, desire bi desire; and yif thou mai fele bi thi desire in thi praieres and in thy meditacions the homli and the merciful presence of thi Lord Jhesu Crist in thi mynde, bynde thyn herte feste therto, that thou falle not from Hym, and yif thou stumble, that thou myght fynde Hym soone agen. Seke thanne Jhesu, whom thou haste loste, as He sought thee. He wole be sought and He mai sumdel be founde, for He seith hymsilf: *Omnis qui querit, invenit* (Matthew 7:8). Every man that seketh schal fynde. The sekynge is traveilous, but the fyndynge is blisful. Doo therfore aftir the conceile of the wise man, yif thou wilt fynde Hym: *Si quisieris quasi pecuniam sapienciam, sicut thesaurum effoderis illam; tunc intelliges timorem domini, et scienciam invenies* (Proverbs 2:4–5). Yif thou seke wisdoom (which is Jhesu) as silver and gold, and delf deepe therafter, thou schalt fynde it. Thee bihoveth for to delve deepe in thyn herte, for thereinne He is hid, and cast ought clenli alle loves and likynges, sorwis and dreedis of alle ertheli thynges; and so schalt thou fynde wisdom, Jhesu.

1355
1360
1365
1370
1375
1380

1356 sownes, sounds. **1362 likynge,** pleasing. **1363 As who seith,** As one says. **1375 traveilous,** laborious. **1379 delf,** delve. **1380 ought,** out.

Chapter Forty-eight

Where and wherewith Jhesu schal be sought and founden.

Be thou like thanne to the woman of the Gospel, of the whiche oure Lord seith thus: *Que mulier habens dragmas decem, et si perdiderit unam, nonne accendit lucernam, et*

1385 *evertit domum suam et querit diligenter, donec invenerit illam? Et cum invenerit, convocat amicas suas, dicens, congratulamini michi, quia inveni dragmam, quam perdideram* (Luke 15:8–9). What woman is that whiche hath lost a dragme, that sche ne wole lightne a lanterne and caste hir hous upsodoun and seke it til sche fynde it? As who seith, noon. And whanne sche hath founden hit sche calleth hire frendis to hire, and

1390 seith to hem thus: "Makith mirthe with me and melodie, for I have founden the dragme that I had lost." This dragme is Jhesu, whiche thou hast lost; yif thou wilt fynde Hym, light up a lanterne, whiche is Goddis word, as David seith: *Lucerna pedibus meis verbum tuum* (Psalms 118:105). Lord, Thi word to my feet is a lanterne. Bi this lanterne schalt thou see where He is, and hou thou schalt fynde Hym; and yif thu wilt, thou mai

1395 with this light opyn anothir lanterne, that is the resoun of thi soule, for oure Lord seith: *Lucerna corporis tui est oculus tuus* (Matthew 6:22). The lanterne of thi bodi is thi bodili iye. Right so it mai be seid that the lanterne of thi soule is resoun, bi the whiche the soule mai see alle gosteli thinges. Bi this lanterne mai thou fynde Jhesu, and that is soth yif thou holde the lanterne up fro undirnethe the busschel, as oure Lord seith: *Nemo accendit*

1400 *lucernam et ponit eam sub modio, sed super candelabrum* (Matthew 5:15). There is no man that lighteth a lanterne for to sette it undir a busschel, but upon a candelstike; that is to seie, thi reson schal not be overleid with worldli bisinesse, ne veyn thoughtes and fleisschli affecciones, but ai upward above alle ertheli thynges, as mykil as thou may into biholdynge of Jhesu Crist; and yif thou doo soo, thou schalt thanne see bi Hym (for

1405 He is light) alle the mulle and the filthe and smale motes in thy hous, that is to seie, alle flesschli loves and dredis in thi soule. Not al, as David seith: *Delicta quis intelligit?* (Psalms 18:13). Who mai knowe alle his trespaces? As who seith, no man. And thou schalt cast oute of thyn herte alle siche synnes, and swepe thi soule clene with the besome of the drede of God, and with watir of thyn iyen wassch it; and so schalt thou

1387 dragme, drachma. **1388 upsodoun**, upside down. **1388–89 As who seith**, As one says. **1397 iye**, eye. **1405 mulle**, rubbish. **1409 besome**, broom; **iyen**, eyes.

1410   fynde thi dragme Jhesu. He is dragme, He is peny, and He is thyn heritage. This dragme wole not be founde so lightli as it mai be seid; for this werk is not of oon houre, ne of oon dai, but many daies and yeeris with mykil swete and swynke of the bodi and traveile of the soule. And yif thou cesist not, but sekest bisili, sorwe and seke depe, morne stille, and stoupe lowe til thyn iyen wateren for anguysche and for peyne for thou hast loste

1415   thi tresoure Jhesu; and at the laste, whanne that He wole, wel schalt thou fynde thi dragme Jhesu. And yif thou fynde as I have seide, that is, yif thou may in cleernesse and clennesse of conscience fele the hoomli and the peesful presence of Jhesu Crist mercifulli schewande Hym to the face of thi soule as a schadewe or a glymerynge, thou mai, yif thou wolt, calle thi frendes to thee for to make mirthe with thee, for thou hast founden

1420   thi dragme Jhesu.

Chapter Forty-nine

Where Jhesu is loste and founden thorugh His mercy.

Se now thanne the curtesie of Jhesu and the merci of Hym. Thou haste loste Hym, but where? Soothli in thyn hous, that is in thi soule. Yif thou haddest lost Hym oughte of thyn hous, that is to seie, yif thou haddest lost al the resoun of thy soule bi thi first

1425   synne, thi soule schulde nevere have founden Him agen; but He lefte to thee thi resoun, and so He is in thi soule and nevere schal be lost oute of hit. Neverthelees, thou art nevere the neer to Hym til thou have founden Him. He is in thee, though He be lost fro thee; but thou art not in Hym til thou have founden Hym. Thanne was this His merci, that He wold suffre Hym be loste onli where He mai be founden. It nedeth not to renne

1430   to Rome ne to Jerusalem for to seke Hym there, but turne thi thought into thyn owen soule, where He is hid — as the prophete seith, *Vere tu es deus absconditus* (Isaiah 45:15), Soothli Lord, thou art an hid God — and seke Hym there. Thus seith Hymsilf in the Gospel: *Simile est regnum celorum thesauro abscondito in agro; quem qui invenit homo, pre gaudio illius vadit, et vendit universa que habet, et emit agrum illum* (Mat-

1435   thew 13:44). The kyngedom of hevene is like to tresoure hid in a feld, whiche, whanne a man fyndeth, for joie of it he goth and selleth al that he hath, and bieth that ilke feeld.

1412 **swynke**, toil. 1413 **bisili**, diligently. 1418 **Hym**, Himself. 1423 **Soothli**, Truly. 1436 **bieth**, buys; **ilke**, same.

Jhesu is tresoure hid in thi soule; thanne yif yow fynde myght Hym in thi soule, and thi soule in Him, I am siker for joie of it thou woldest gyve alle the likynges of alle ertheli thinges for to have it. Jhesu slepeth in thyn herte gosteli, as He dide sumtyme whanne
1440 He was in the schip with Hese disciplis, but thei for drede of perisschynge wakeden Hym, and as tite He savyd hem from tempest. Doo thou so stire Him bi praiere and waken Hym with criynge of desire, and He schal ryse sone and helpe thee.

Chapter Fifty

What letteth a man to heere and see Jhesu withinne hymsilf.

Neverthelees, I hope betere that thou slepist to Hym and not He to thee; for He calleth
1445 thee wel ofte with His swete prevy vois and stireth thyn herte wel stilli, that thou schuldest leve alle othere jangelynge of vanitees in thi soule and oonli take keep to Him for to heere Him speke. Thus seith David of oure Lord: *Audi, filia, et vide, et inclina aurem tuam, et obliviscere populum tuum, et domum patris tui* (Psalms 44:11). Mi doughter, heere and see and bowe thyn ere to me, and forgete the folk of thy worldeli
1450 thoughtes and the hous of thi fleischli and kyndeli affeccions. Loo, here mai thou see how oure Lord calleth thee and alle othere whiche wolen herkene to Hym. What letteth thee thanne, that thou mai neither see Hym ne heere Him? Sotheli there is mykil dene and criynge in thyn herte of veyn thoughtes and fleischli desires, that thou mai neither heere Hym ne see Him; and therfore put awey unrestful dene and breke the love of
1455 synne and of vanité, and bringe into thyne herte love of vertues and ful charité, and thanne schalt thou here thi Lord speke unto thee. For as longe as He fyndeth not His ymage reformed in thee, He is straunge and fer fro thee.

1438 siker, certain. **1440 Hese**, His. **1441 as tite**, immediately. **1442 sone**, at once. **1443 letteth**, hinders. **1444 hope**, suppose. **1445 prevy**, secret; **stilli**, quietly. **1446 take keep**, pay attention. **1450 kyndeli**, natural. **1452 dene**, din. **1457 straunge**, estranged.

Chapter Fifty-one

That mekenesse and charité are the special lyveré of Jhesu, thorugh the whiche mannys soule is reformed to the liknes of Him.

1460 Forthi schape thee for to be araied in His likenes, that is in mekenesse and charité, whiche is His lyveré, and thanne wole He hoomli knowe thee and schewe to thee His privytee. Thus seide Himsilf to His disciplis: *Qui diligit me, diligetur a patre meo, et manifestabo ei meipsum* (John 14:21). Whoso loveth Me, schal be loved of My Fadir, and I schal schewe Mysilf unto Him. There is no vertu ne werk that thou mai doo mai
1465 make thee like to oure Lord, withouten mekenesse and charitee; for thise aren special Goddis lyveré. And that semeth wel in the Gospel, where oure Lord speketh of mekenesse thus: *Discite a me, quia mitis sum et humilis corde* (Matthew 11:29). Lereth of Me, He seith, not for to goo baarfoot ne for to goo into desert and faste fourti daies, ne for to cheese yow disciplis, but lerith of Me mekenesse, for I am mylde and meke of herte.
1470 Also of charitee He seith thus: *Hoc est preceptum meum: ut diligatis invicem sicut dilexi vos. Item: in hoc cognoscent homines quia discipuli mei estis, si dileccionem habueritis ad invicem* (John 13:34–35). This is My biddynge, that yee love you togedere, as I have loved you; for in that schal men knowe yow for My disciples. Not for ye worchen miraclis or casten out develis, or prechen or techen, but yif eche of you love other in
1475 charité. That charité is that thou coudest als wel love thyn even Cristene as thisilf.

Chapter Fifty-two

Hou a man schal see the grǒound of synne in hymsilf.

Now hast thow herd a litil what thi soule is, and what worschipe it hadde, and how he loste it; and also y have told thee that this worschipe mght bi grace and bisi travaile sumwhat be recovered agen in partie of felynge. Now schal I telle thee febli as y can
1480 hou thou schalt mow entre into thisilf, for to se the ground of synne and for to distroie it as mykil as thou may, and so schalt thou mowe recovere a partie of thi dignité. Thou

1458 lyveré, livery. **1461 hoomli**, familiarly. **1462 privytee**, mystery. **1467 Lereth of**, Learn from. **1472 togedere**, each other. **1480 mow**, be able to.

schalt cese for a tyme from alle bodili werkes, from al outeward besinesse as thou mai wel. Thanne schalt thou drawe into thisilf thi thought from thi bodili wittes, that thou take noo kepe what thou heerest or seest or felist, so that the poynt of thyn herte be not
1485 ficchid in hem. Aftir this drawe inner thi thought from al ymaginynge, yif thou mai, of ony bodili thyng, and from alle thoughtis of thi bodili dedis bifore doon, or of othere mennys dedis. This is a litil maistrie for to doo whanne thou hast devocioun; but thou schalt doo thus as I seie whanne thou hast no devocioun, for thanne is it mykil the hardere. And sette thyn entent and thi purpoos as thou woldest not seke, ne fele, ne
1490 finde, but upon thi lord Jhesu oonly, the grace and the presence, the techynge and the comfort of thi Lord Jhesu Crist. This is traveilous, for veyn thoughtis wolen alwei presen to thyn herte thikke, for to drawe thi thought doun to hem. But thou schalt with stable mynde of Jhesu Crist with besinesse in praieres agenstonde hem, and yif thou doo thus, thou schalt fynde sumwhat — not Jhesu whom thou sekest. What thanne?
1495 Sotheli, right nought but a merk ymage and a peynful of thyn owen soule, whiche hath neither light of knowynge ne felynge of love ne likynge. This ymage yif thou biholde it wittirly, is al bilappid with blake stynkande clothis of synne, as pride, envie, ire, accidie, glotonye, and leccherie.

Chapter Fifty-three

Unto what thinge is the ymage of synne like, and what it is in itsilf.

1500 This is not the ymage of Jhesu, but it is an ymage of synne; as Seynt Poul calleth hit, a bodi of synne and a bodi of deeth. This ymage and this blak schadewe thou berist aboughte with thee whereevere thou goost. Out of this springen many grete stremes of synne, and smale also. Right as out of the ymage of Jhesu, yif it were reformed in the beemes of goostli light, schulde steme up to hevene and brennynge desires, clene
1505 affecciouns, wise thoughtis, and alle honesté of vertues; right so out of this ymage

---

1485 **ficchid**, fixed. 1487 **maistrie**, feat of skill. 1489 **not**, nothing. 1491 **traveilous**, difficult. 1492 **presen**, press. 1493 **besinesse**, diligence; **agenstonde**, resist. 1495 **merk**, dark. 1497 **wittirly**, surely; **bilappid**, surrounded; **accidie**, sloth. 1497–98 **pride ... leccherie**, a list of the seven capital sins with the omission of avarice. 1500 **Seynt Poul calleth hit**, see Romans 6:6. 1504 **steme**, blaze (see Textual Notes).

springen stiryngis of pride, of envie, and sich othere, whiche casten thee doun from the honesté of man into a beestis likenesse. But peraventure thou bygynnest for to thenke unto what thynge this ymage schulde be like; and therfore that thou schuldest not longe studie thereaboughte, I telle thee it is like to no bodili thing. "What is it thanne?" seistow.

1510 Sothli it is not, and that may thou fynde yif thou wilt assaie as y have seid to thee. Drawe into thisilf thi thought from alle bodili thynges, and thanne schalt thou fynde right not whereinne thi soule mai reste. This nought is nothynge ellis but a lackynge of love and of light, as synne is not ellis but a wantynge of God.

Yif it so were that the ground of synne were mykil abatid and dried up in thee, and thi
1515 soule were clensid and reformyd lightli to the ymage of Jhesu, thanne yif thou drowgh into thisilf thyn herte thou schuldest not fynde nought, but thou schuldest fynde Jhesu — not oonli the nakid mynde of His name, but thou schuldest fynde light of undirstondynge bi Hym, and no merkenesse of unknowynge; thou schuldest fynde love and likynge of Hym, and noo peyne of bitternesse ne bitynge. But for thou art not yit
1520 reformed, therfore whanne thi soule cometh in fro al bodili thynge, and fyndeth not but merkenesse and hevynesse, hym thenketh an hundrid wynter til he be out agen bi sum bodili delite or veyn thought. And that is no wonder; for whoso come to his hous and founde nothynge therinne but stynkynge smoke and a flitynge wif, he wolde sone renne oute of it. Right so thi soule, whanne it fyndeth noo comfort in the silf but blak smoke
1525 of goostli blyndenesse and grete flitynge of fleischli thoughtes criynge upon thee that thou may bee in noo pees, soothli it is sone irke til it be oute agen. This merkenesse is that ilke nought the whiche y spak of and the ymage.

Chapter Fifty-four

Whoso wole fynde Jhesu, hym bihoveth abide and traveile in this goostli merkenesse of this ymage of synne.

1509 thereaboughte, thereabout. **1510 not**, nothing. **1512 not**, nothing. **1513 God**, see Textual Notes. **1515 lightli**, easily; **drowgh**, drew. **1518 merkenesse**, darkness. **1523 flitynge**, contentious; the aphorism in this sentence is a commonplace; see Proverbs 21:9, and Chaucer, The Wife of Bath's Prologue (*The Canterbury Tales*, III[D]278–80), where smoke is also mentioned. **1524 the silf**, the self; possibly to be construed as *theself*, thyself. **1526 irke**, irksome.

1530   Neverthelees, in this nought bihoveth thee to swynke and swete; that is to sai, thee bihoveth drawe in thi thought from alle bodili thynges as moche as thou may. And thanne, whanne thou fyndest right nout but sorwe and peyne and blyndenesse, yif thou wolt fynde Jhesu, the peyne of this nought bihoveth thee to suffre, and abide in this merkenesse and arise in thi thought agens this ilke merkenesse, bi fervent desire to God;

1535   not settynge the poynt of thi thought in that ilke nought, but in Jhesu whiche thou desirest, as thou woldest bere it doun, and goo thorugh it. Thou schalt grise and lothe this nought right as it were the devyl of helle, and thou schalt despice it and al tobreke it; for al withinne this nought is Jhesu hid in His joie, whom thou mai not fynde bi thi sekynge, but yif thou passe thorugh this merkenesse of this nought. This is that goosteli

1540   traveile that I spak of; and this travaile is a cause of al this writynge, for to stire thee therto yif thou feele grace. This nought that y speke of is the ymage of the firste Adam. Seynte Poul knewe it wel, for he seid thus of it: *Sicut portavimus ymaginem terreni hominis, ita portemus ymaginem iam et celestis hominis* (1 Corinthians 15:49). As we han here biforn born the ymage of an ertheli man (that is, the first Adam), right so that

1545   we myght now bere the ymage of the heveneli man, whiche is Jhesu, the secunde Adam. He baar this ymage wel often ful hevye, for it was so comberous to hym that he criede oute of it seiynge thus: *O quis me liberabit de corpore huius mortis?* (Romans 7:24). A, whoo schal delyvere me fro this bodi and ymage of deeth? And thanne he comforteth hymsilf and othere thus: *Gracia dei per Jesum Christum* (Romans 7:25), the

1550   grace of God bi Jhesu Crist.

    Now have y tolde thee a litil of this ymage, how it is nought. Neverthelees, yif it be feer fro thi knowynge hou it myght be sooth that y sai, that nought myght be an ymage, for nought is but nought; and so that thou mai lightli undirstande it, I schal telle thee more opynli of this ymage as me thenketh.

Chapter Fifty-five

1555   What propirli is the ymage of synne and what cometh thereof.

1530 swynke, toil. **1534 merkenesse,** darkness; **ilke,** same. **1536 bere it doun,** bring it down; **grise,** feel horror. **1537 despice,** despise; **tobreke,** break in pieces. **1552 feer,** far.

This ymage is a fals mysruled love unto thisilf. Oute of this love cometh al maner of synnes bi sevene ryveres, the whiche aren thise: pride, envie, ire, accedie, coveitise, glotony, and leccherie. Loo, this is sumwhat that thou may see and feele, that bi oon of thise ryveris renneth out al maner of synne and putteth thee out of charité yif it be deedli, or it letteth the savour of charité yif it be venial.

Now mai thou grope that this ymage is nought, but is moche of badde; for it is a grete springe of love unto thisilf with sich sevene ryveris as I have seid. But now seist thou, "How mai this be sooth? I have forsaken the world and am stokyn in an hous; I deele with no man. I flite not, ne I stryve not, I neither bie ne selle, ne have no wordeli bisynesse, but bi the merci of God y kepe me chaste. I withhalde me from delites; and over this I preie, y wake, y travaile bodili and goostli as y mai. How thanne schulde this ymage be thus moche in me as thou seist?"

As unto this I graunte and answere to thee that I hope that thou doost alle thise werkis and many mo therto, and yit mai hit be soth that I seie. Thou art besi up thi myght for to stoppe the ryveres withoute, but inhap the sprynge withinne thou levest al opyn. Thou art like to a man whiche hadde in his gardcyn a stinkynge welle with many ryveres fro it. He wente and stopped the ryveres and lefte the sprynge hool, and wende al hadde be siker. But the water spronge up atte the ground of the welle and stood stille, so moche that it corruptid al the fairnesse of the gardeyn, and yit ran there no watir out. Right so it mai be with thee, yif it be soo that thou hast bi grace stopped the ryveris of this ymage withouten. So moche it is wel, but bewaar of the sprynge withinne. Soothli, but yif thou stoppe and clense that as moche as thou mai, it wole corrumpe alle the floures of the gardyn of thi soule, schewe thei nevere so faire outeward in sighte of men. But now seist thou: "Wherbi schal I knowe that the ground is stoppid, yif y traveile aboute it?" As unto this y schal telle thee bi asai, hou thou schalt knowe this image yif it be in thee, and hou moche it is in thee, and therbi thou schalt knowe how moche it is stoppid in thee, and how litil also. And in as moche as pride is the principal ryvere, I schal telle thee therof first.

1560
1565
1570
1575
1580

1557 **sevene ryveres**, i.e., the seven capital sins; the list that follows is complete (compare *Scale,* I.1497–98). **1561 grope**, grasp. **1563 stokyn**, inserted. **1564 flite**, contend; **bie**, buy. **1568 hope**, suppose. **1572 wende**, supposed. **1573 siker**, secure. **1577 corrumpe**, corrupt. **1580 asai**, testing.

Chapter Fifty-six

What pride is and whanne it is synne.

1585 Pride is not ellis, as clerkes tellen, but love of thyn owen excellence, that is, of thyn owen worschipe. Thanne the more thou lovest and likest in thyn owen worschipe, the more is thi pride, and so the more is this ymage in thee. Yif thou fele in thyn herte a stirynge of pride, that thou art holier, wisere, betere, and more vertuous than an nothir is, that God hath geven thee grace for to serve Hym betere than othir doon, and thee

1590 thenketh alle othire binethe thee and thee above hem, or ony othir thought of thisilf whiche schewith to the sight of thi soule ony excellence, and an overpassynge of othir men or of women, and of this stirynge thou felist a love and a delite, and a veyn plesynge in thi silf that thou art so: this is a tokene that thou berist this blak ymage, which though it be prevei in mannys iye, he schewith him opynli in Goddis sight. But

1595 now seist thou, that thou mai not flee siche styrynges of pride. For ofte sithes thou felist hem agens thi wil, and therfore thou holdest hem no synne, or if thei be synne, thei are not but venial synne. As unto this I seie thus, that the felynge of thise stirynges of pride or of ony othir sich springen out, oither of the corrupcion of this foule ymage or bi incastynge of the enemye, it is no synne, in as moche as thou felist hem. And that is

1600 a grace and a privelege bi vertu of the passioun of Jhesu Crist grauntid to alle Cristene men baptizid in watir and in the Hooli Goost; for sothli to Jewes or Sarzynes, whiche trowen not in Crist, alle siche stirynges aren deedli synnes to hem. For Seynt Poul seith: *Omne, quod non est ex fide peccatum est* (Romans 14:23). Al that is doon withouten trouth in Crist is deedli synne. But we Cristene men have this privelegie of His merci,

1605 that sich felynges aren no synne, but thei are peyne of origynal synne. Neverthelees whanne bi necgligence of thisilf and blyndenesse of thisilf this felyng is receyved unwarli in thi thought and turned into love and a likynge, thanne is ther synne more or lasse aftir the mesure of the love sumtyme venyal and sumtyme deedli. Whanne it is venial and whanne deedli, fulli I cannot wel telle thee.

1591 overpassynge, surpassing. **1598 oither**, either. **1599 incastynge**, injection. **1601 Jewes or Sarzynes**, Jews or Saracens (Muslims); Clark (p. 178n251) describes Hilton's severe view of the status of the unbaptized as "ultra-Augustinian." **1604 trouth**, faith. **1605 peyne of**, punishment for.

Chapter Fifty-seven

1610 Whanne pride is deedli synne, and hou it is in fleischli lyvande men deedli synne.

Nevertheles, a litil schal I telle thee, as me thenketh. Whanne the stirynge of pride is receyved and turned into a likynge, so moche that the herte chesith hit for a ful reste and a ful delite, and seketh noon othir reste, but oonli likynge thereinne, thanne pride is deedli synne; for he maketh and cheseth this delite as his God, withouten agenstondynge

1615 of resoun and of wille, and therfore it is deedli synne. But now seist thou: "What fool is he that wole chese pride for his God? No man that lyveth wolde doo so." As unto this I seie y ne cannot, ne wole not, telle thee in special who doth so, ne who synneth so in pride deedli, but in general I schal seie thee ther is two maner of pride, oon is bodili pride, and anothir is gostli pride.

1620 Bodili pride is of fleischli lyvynge men; goostli pride is of ypocrites and heretikes. Thise thre synnen dedli in pride. I mene of siche a fleischli lyvynge man as Seynt Poul speketh of thus: *Si secundum carnem vixeritis, moriemini* (Romans 8:13). Yif ye lyven aftir youre fleisch, ye schal die. Thanne seie y thus, that a worldli man whiche lyveth and seketh principali the worschipe of himsilf, and cheseth the likynge of it as a reste of

1625 his herte and the ende of his blisse, he synneth deedli. But now seist thou: "Who wolde chese love of his worschipe instide of God?" As unto this I sai that he that loveth his worschipe, as for to seme betere and grettere of staat, richere and highere than anothir, and travaileth aboute it as moche as he mai, yif he love it so moche, that for the getynge of it, the kepyng of it, and the savynge of it, he breketh the comaundement of God, or

1630 breketh love or charité to his evene Cristene, or is redi and in ful wille for to breke it rathere thanne he schulde forbere his worschipe, or his name or his fame or his staat or of fulfillynge of his wil, soothli he synneth deedli, for he loveth his worschipe and chesith it more than the love of God and of his even Cristene. And yit nevertheleees this man that synneth thus deedli, he wolde seie with his mouth that he wolde not chese

1635 pride for his God; but he bigileth himsilf, for he chesith it bifore in his dede. Nevertheleees, anothir worldli man that loveth worschipe of hymsilf and pursueth thereaftir, yif he loveth it not so moche that noithir hc wold for the getynge or for the savynge of it doo a deedli synne or ellis breke charité to his even Cristene, he synneth not deedli but

1614 agenstondynge, resistance. **1620 ypocrites**, hypocrites. **1623 aftir**, according to. **1637 noithir**, neither.

venyali, more or lasse aftir the mesure of his love and his likynge, with othire
1640 circumstancis.

Chapter Fifty-eight

Hou pride is in heretikes deedli synne.

An heretike synneth deedli in pride, for he chesith his reste and his delite in his owen
opynyoun and in his owen seiynge, for he weneth it is sooth that opynyon or seiynge
whiche is agens God and Hooli Chirche. And therefore synneth he in pride deedli, for he
1645 loveth himsilf and his owen wil, and with so moche that though it be opynli agens
ordenaunce of Hooli Chirche, he wole not leve it, but reste thereinne, as in a ful
soothfastnesse, and so maketh he it his god. But he bigileth himsilf, for God and Holi
Chirche are so onyd and acordid togidere that whoso dooth agen that oon, he dooth
agen that othir and so he doth agens bothe. And therfore who that seith he loveth God
1650 and kepith his biddynge, and dispiceth Hooli Chirche, and setteth at nought the lawes
and the ordenaunce of it maad bi the heed and the sovereyn in governaunce of alle
Cristen men, he lieth. He chesith not God, but he cheseth the love of himsilf, whiche is
contrarie to the love of God, and so he synneth deedli. And in that, that he weneth most
for to plese God, he most displeseth him, for he is blynde and wole not see. Of this
1655 blyndenesse and of this fals restynge of heretikes in here owen felynge speketh the wise
man thus: *Est via que videtur homni recta; et novissima eius ducunt ad mortem* (Proverbs 14:12). There is a wai whiche semeth to a man rightful, and the laste ende of hit
bringith him to endelees deth. This wai speciali is called heresie, for othir fleischli synneres
that synnen deedli and lyen stille thereinne comonli supposen evere amys of hemsilf,
1660 and felen bitynge in conscience that thei goo not the right wai. But an heretik supposith
evere that he dooth wel and techeth wel, and so he weneth that his wai were the right
wai, and therfore felith he no bitynge of conscience ne mekenesse in herte. And sothli
but God sende hym mekenesse while he lyveth heere, of His merci, at the laste ende he

1642 **An heretike**, this chapter reflects the growing concern about heresy in Hilton's England; see Clark, p. 178n257. 1643 **weneth**, supposes. 1648 **onyd**, united. 1655 **restynge**,
remaining. 1661 **weneth**, supposes.

goth to helle, and neverthelees yit weneth he for to have doon weel and geten him the
1665 blisse of hevene for his techynge.

Chapter Fifty-nine

Hou pride is in ypocrites deedli synne.

The ypocrite also synneth deedli in pride. He is an ipocrite that cheseth veyn joie of
himsilf as the reste and ful delite of his herte, upon this manere wise: whanne a man
dooth many good dedes bodili and goostli, and aftir is yput to his mynde by suggestioun
1670 of the enemye a biholdynge of hymsilf and of his good dedes, how good, how holi he is,
how worthi in mennes doom, and hou high in Goddis sight above othere men, he
perceyveth this styrynge and resseyveth it wilfulli, for he weneth it be gode and of God
in as mykil as it is sooth, for he dooth alle thise good dedes betere thanne othere men.
And whanne it is receyved thus bi assent of his wil as good, thanne riseth therof a love
1675 and a delite in his herte of himsilf that he is so good and so hooli and so moche grace
hath, that it neer hande ravesschith his mynde out of alle othere thoughtis, bothe goostli
and fleischli, for the tyme, and settith it in this veyn joie of himsilf as in a reste of his
herte. This ravyschynge in goostli pride is delectable, and therfore he kepith it, holdeth
it, and norischith it as moche as he mai; for this love and this veyn delite he praieth, he
1680 waketh, he fasteth, he wereth the heire, and othere affliccions, and al this greveth hym
but litil. He looveth and thanketh God sumtyme with his mouth and sumtyme wringeth
out a teer of his iyen, and thanne hym thenketh al saaf inowgh. But soothli al this is for
love of hymsilf, whiche he cheseth and resseyveth it as it were love and joie in God.
And in that is al the synne. He cheseth not synne wilfulli as for synne, but he cheseth
1685 this delite that he deliteth inne, this joie, as for god, as the reste of his soule, withouten
displesynge or agenstondynge of wille, for he weneth it were joie in God. And it is not
so, and therfore he synneth deedli. Job seith thus of an ypocrite: *Gaudium ypocrite ad
instar puncti. Si ascendit in celum superbia eius, et caput eius nubes tetigerit, velut
sterquilinium in fine perdetur* (Job 20:5–6). The joie of an ypocrite is no more thanne a

---

1668 reste, goal. **1669 yput**, put. **1671 doom**, judgment. **1680 heire**, i.e., the hairshirt, the
traditional garment of the penitent. **1681 looveth**, praises. **1682 iyen**, eyes; **inowgh**, enough.
1685 god, good. **1686 agenstondynge**, resistance.

1690 poynt, for yif he stiye into hevene with risynge of his herte, and his hed touche the skies, at the laste ende he is cast oute as a dongeheep. The joie of an ypocrite is but a poynt, for though he worschipe himsilf nevere so moche and joie in hymsilf al his liftyme, and depeynte himsilf with alle hise good deedes in sight and lovynge of the world, at the laste it is not but sorwe and peyne. But now seist thou, there are fewe sich

1695 or ellis noon that is so blynd that wolde chese veyn joie in hymsilf as for the joie in God. As unto this I cannot seie, ne wole not yif I knew; but oo thynge I telle thee, there be many ypocrites, and neverthelees thei wene thei been none, and there ben many that dreden as ypocrites themself, and soothli thei ben none. Which is oon and whiche is othir, God knoweth and noon but He. Whoso wil mekeli drede, he schal not be bigiled,

1700 and whoso weneth to be siker he mai lightli falle; for Seynt Poul seith: *Qui existimat se aliquid esse, cum nichil sit, ipse se seducit* (Galatians 6:3). Whoso weneth hymsilf to be ought whanne he is right nought, he bigileth hymsilf.

Chapter Sixty

Hou stirynges of pride and veynglorie in good men are but venial synne.

Neverthelees, a man or a woman whiche disposeth hym to lif contemplatif, yif it be so

1705 that he forsake hymsilf as in his wille and offre hym hooli to God with a ful general wil that he wolde not synne in pride wityngeli, ne have no veyn joye in hymsilf wilfulli, but oonli in God, yif he coude and myght; and aftir this ful wille offred hym to God he felith manye stirynges of veynglorie and deliteth in hem for the tyme, for he perceyveth hit not; this likyng is but venyal synne. And nameli yif it be so that whanne he cometh to

1710 himsilf he perceyveth this veyn likynge, he reproveth hymsilf and agenstondeth this stirynge with displesynge of wille, and asketh merci and helpe of God, thanne the likynge that was bifore synne, oure Lord of His merci soone forgeveth it. And yit he schal have meede for his good travaile in the agenstondynge. And that is the curtesie of oure Lord to alle thoo that aren speciali Hise servauntis and more hoomli of His court, as

1715 alle thoo aren whiche for His love forsaketh in gode trewe wille alle worldli and fleischli

1690 **stiye**, ascend. **1693 depeynte**, depict; **lovynge**, praise. **1706 wityngeli**, consciously. **1711 displesynge**, displeasure.

synnes, and gif hem hooli, bodi and soule, unto His service up her myght and her knowynge, as ankeris enclosed and also trewe religious men, whiche principali for the love of God and savacioun of here soules entreden ony religion approvid bi Hooli Chirche. Or ellis yif it be so that they entre religion first for a wordli cause, as for here bodili
1720 sustenaunce or ony othir siche, yif thei repente hem and turne it into a goosteli cause, as for the service of God, thise, as longe as thei kepe this wille and pursue it as thei mai up here myght for freelté, thei are trewe religious. Also what man or woman that it be, in what degree he bee in Holi Chirche, preest, clerk, or lewed man, widue or wif or mayden, that wole for the love of God and salvacion of his soule forsake alle the
1725 worschippis and likynges of the world in his herte trewli and fulli bitwixe God and hym, and al wilfulle bisynesse of ertheli thynges unto bare nede, and offre his wille entierli for to be his servaunt up his myght, bi devoute praieres and hooli thoughtes with othere gode deedis that he mai doon bodili or goosteli, and kepeth this wille hool to God stidefastli — alle these aren special Goddis servauntis in Holi Chirche. And for this good wille and
1730 this good purpoos that thei have of the gift of God, thei schal encreese in grace and charité here lyvynge, and thei schal have for this special wille a special grace and a mede in the blisse of hevene bifore othere chosen soulis the whiche offrid not hooli here wille and here bodi to Goddis service, neithir opynli ne privelé, as thei diden. Alle thise, whiche y speke of and calle Goddis servauntes, and of His court more speciali, though
1735 thei bi frelté or bi unconnynge whanne thei feele sich stirynge of veynglorie, for the tyme delite therinne, and perceyve not it, for here resoun of here witte is letted bi the likynge that thei feele, that it mai not see the stirynge — thei synnen not deedli in this likynge of veineglorie. For that wille that they have sette general in here herte bifore unto plese God and for to forsake synne, yif thei knewe hit, kepith hem there in siche stirynges,
1740 and in alle othere that comen of freelté, that thei synnen not deedli, and schal kepe hem as longe as the ground of that wille is keped hool.

1716 gif hem, give themselves. **1716–17 up her myght and her knowynge**, according to their ability and knowledge. **1717 religious**, in religious orders. **1718 religion**, religious order. **1722 freelté**, frailty. **1723 lewed**, ignorant. **1735 frelté**, frailty; **unconnynge**, ignorance. **1736 letted**, hindered.

Chapter Sixty-one

Hou sere states in Holi Chirche schulle have sere medes in the blisse of hevene, and of two medes, sovereyn and secundarie.

And overe this I seie more, in comforte of thee and of alle othere havynge the staat of
1745   anker incloos, and also bi the grace of God in comfort of hem alle that entren ony religioun approved bi Holi Chirche, that alle thoo that bi the merci of oure Lord schal be savyd, thei schal have special mede and a singuler worschipe in the blisse of hevene for here staat of lyvynge, bifore othere soulis that hadden not that staat in Holi Chirche, though thei be nevere so hooli. Whiche worschipe is betere thanne al the worschipe of
1750   this world withouten ony comparison, for yif thou myghte see what it were, thou woldest not for al the worschipe of this world, though thou myghtest have it withoutin synne, chaunge thi staat either of ankir or of religious, ne leese that syngulere mede in the blisse of hevene, whiche is called accidental meede.

    Neverethelees, that othere men mystake not this that y seie, therfore I schal seie it
1755   more opynli. Thou schalt undirstonde that there are two meedis in the blisse of hevene, whiche oure Lord geveth to chosen soulis. The toon is sovereyn and principal, as is love and knowynge of Hym aftir the mesure of charité geven of God to a soule lyvynge in deedli fleisch. This meede is best and sovereyne, for it is God Himsilf; and it is comone to alle soulis that schul be saaf in what staat or gree that thei ben lyvynge in
1760   Hooli Chirche, more or lasse aftir the quantité and the mychilheed of here charité. For he that most loveth God in charité here in this liyf, what degree he be in, be he lewid or lerid, seculer or religious, he schal have most mede in the blisse of hevene, for he schal most love God and knowe Hym, and that is the sovereyne meede. And as for this meede, it schal falle that sum wordli man or woman, as a lord or a ladi, knyght or
1765   squyer, marchaunt or plowman, what degree he be in, man or woman, schal have more meede than sum prest or frere, monke or chanoun or ankir incloos. And whi? Soothli for he lovede more God in charité of His gifte. An nothir meede there is, that is secundarie,

1742 sere, various. **1745 anker incloos**, enclosed anchorite. **1747 special mede**, the doctrine of graduated heavenly rewards is found in Thomas Aquinas, *Summa Theologica* 1, q.12, a.6 (Clark, p.178n264). **1756 toon**, one. **1759 saaf**, saved; **gree**, rank. **1760 mychilheed**, greatness. **1761–62 lewid or lerid**, ignorant or learned; here: lay or clergy. **1762 seculer or religious**, living in the world or a member of a religious order. **1766 chanoun**, canon.

whiche oure Lord geveth for special good deedes that a man dooth wilfulli over that he
is bounden to doo. Of three deedis principali doctours of Holi Chirche maken mynde of,
1770 as of martirdom, prechynge, and maydenhed. Thise three werkes as for an excellence,
in as moche as thei passe alle othere, thei schullen have a special meede, whiche thei
calle auriole, and that is not ellis but a synguler worschipe and a special tokene ordeyned
of God in reward of that special deede, bifore othere men that diden not so, over the
sovereyne meede of the love of God whiche is comoun to hem and to alle othere. Right
1775 so is it of othere special gode dedis, the whiche yif thei be doo soothfastli aren speciali
acceptable in the sight of God, and in the doom of Hooli Chirche thei are excellente; as
are enclosynges of ankeris doon bi auctorité of Holi Chirche, also entrynges into ony
religioun approved, and the streightere that the religioun is, the more excellent is the
meede in the doom of Hooli Chirche. And also aftir thise and binethe thise, the takynge
1780 of the ordre of prest for cure of mennys soulis, and for to ministre the sacraments of
Holi Chirche, or ellis for singuler devocioun for to pleese God and profiten here even
Cristene bi the sacrifice of the precious bodi of oure Lord Jhesu Crist. Sothli thise aren
special deedis and excellent, opynli schewid in the doom of Hooli Chirche and in the
sight of oure Lord, whanne thei aren doon soothfasteli for God; and thei schal have a
1785 special meede, ech man in his degree, in the blisse of hevene. The staat of bischop and
of prelates is aboven alle thise deedes as for this accidental meede. That this is sooth it
semeth bi Holi Writte in the prophete Daniel, where he seith thus: *Tu autem, vade
prefinitum tempus, et requiesces, et stabis in sorte tua in fine dierum* (Daniel 12:13).
This is thus moche to seie: The angel whanne he hadde schewed to Daniel the pryvitees
1790 of God, he seide to hym thus: Go thou to the reste of thi bodili deeth, and thou schalt
stonde in thi soort as a prophete. And sothli as Daniel schal stonde as a prophete at the
day of doom, and have the worschipe and the excellence as a prophete over the sovereyne
blissid mede of the love and the sight of God, right soo schalt thou stonde in thy sorte
as an anker, and a religious in the sort of religioun, and so have othere excellent dedes,
1795 and so have a synguler worschip passynge othere men at the dai of doom.

1770 **maydenhed**, virginity. 1772 **auriole**, aureole, crown, halo; on this doctrine, see Clark, p.
179n266. **1778 religioun**, religious order; **streightere**, stricter. **1779 meede**, reward; **doom**,
judgment. **1789 pryvitees**, mysteries. **1791 soort**, lot.

Chapter Sixty-two

A schort stirynge to mekenesse and to charité.

Now bi this that I have seid, thou mai, yif thou wole thorugh it, conceyve comfort for thi degree of lyvynge and also maner of mekenesse. For though it so be that thou schalt have thus moche mede special for thi staat of lyvynge, yif thou be saaf, neverthelees it 1800 mai be that many a wif and many a wordli woman schal be neer God than thou, and more schal love God and betere schal knowe Him than thou, for al thi staat, and that oweth to be schame to thee but thou be besi to gete love and charité of the gifte of God as he or sche hath that dwelleth stille in the wordli besynesse. For yif thou mowe have as moche charité of the gifte of God as sche or he hath that dwellith in wordli besynesse, 1805 thou schalt have as moche of sovereyne meede as he or sche schal have. And thou schalt have over that, for that staat whiche thou hast taken, have singuler mede and a worschipe whiche he schal not have. Thanne yif thou wolt doo wel, forgete thi staat, as hit were right nought, for it is sooth, bi itsilf it is nought; and loke that al thi desire be and thi bisynesse be for to gete charité and mekenesse and othere goostli vertues, for 1810 therin liyth al.

Chapter Sixty-three

Hou a man schal knowe hou mykil pride is in hym.

I have nygh forgete this ymage, but now I turne agen therto. Yif thou wolt wite hou moche pride there is in thee, thou mai assaie thisilf thus. Loke now wiseli, and flatere not thisilf, yif lovynge, praisynge or worschip or fleischli favour of wordli men or of 1815 othere be likynge to thyn herte, and turneth it into veyn gladnesse, and holde thee wel apaied of thisilf, thenkynge stilli in thin herte that men schulde preise thi liyf, and rewarde thi speche more thanne anothir; also, on the contrarie wise, yif it be so that men reprove thee and sette thee at nought, holde thee but a fool or an ypocrite, or yif thei sclaundre

1803 besynesse, activity; **mowe**, are able. **1810 liyth**, lies. **1812 nygh**, almost. **1814 lovynge**, praise. **1815 likynge**, pleasing. **1816 apaied**, satisfied. **1818 sclaundre**, slander.

thee or speke yvel of thee falsli, or in ony othir wei that thei dispice thee or disese thee
1820 unskilfulli, and therfore thou felist in thyn herte anguisch hevynesse agens the persoones
and a greet risynge in thyn herte with agenstondynge for to suffre ony schame or
vilonye in sight of the world; yif it be thus with thee, this is a tokene that there is moche
pride in this merke ymage, seeme thou nevere so hooli in the sight of men. For though
thise stirynges be not but litil or venial, neverthelees thei schewe wel that ther is moche
1825 pride hid in the grounde of thyn herte, as a fox daareth in his den.

   Thise stirynges and many moo springen out of this image, so moche, that it mai
unnethis doo ony good deede but it schal be medeled with sum pride or sum veyn delite
in thisilf, and so with thi pride thou defoulest thy good dedes and makest hem wlatsum
in the sight of thi Lord. I scie not that thei aren lost for thei are medelid with this pride,
1830 but I seie that thei are not so plesaunt to thi Lord as thei schulde bee yif thei were symple
and rooted in mekenesse. And therfore yif thou wolt have mekenesse and clennesse of
herte for to come to the love of God, thee bihoveth not oonli flee reste of thyn herte in
veynglorie bi wilful assentynge to pride, and also the rekles likynge thereinne of freelté,
though it be agen thi wille, but also the feelynge of pride thou schalt flee and eschewe as
1835 moche as thu mai. But that may thu not doo but yif thou be ful quyk and redi aboughte
the kepynge of thyn herte, as I schal telle thee aftir.

Chapter Sixty-four

Of envie and ire and of here braunchis, and hou sumtyme instide of synne mannys
persoone is hated.

Turne this image upsodoun and loke wel thereinne, and thou schal fynde two membris
1840 of envie and ire fastned therto, with many branches spryngynge ought of hem, the
whiche letten the love and charité that thou schuldest have to thyn even Cristene. The
braunchis of envie and ire aren thise: haterede, yvel suspecioun, fals and unskilful demynge,

---

1819 **disese**, cause distress. 1820 **unskilfulli**, irrationally. 1821 **agenstondynge**, opposition.
1822 **vilonye**, villainy. 1823 **merke**, dark. 1825 **daareth**, lurks, is concealed. 1827 **unnethis**,
scarcely; **medeled**, mingled. 1828 **wlatsum**, disgusting. 1835 **aboughte**, about. 1841 **letten**,
hinder. 1842 **unskilful**, unreasonable; **demynge**, judging.

malencolie, risynge of herte agens hem that dispisen thee or speken yvel agens thee, a gladnesse of here disese, and a felnesse agens synful men that wole not doo as thee

1845 thenketh thei schulde doo, with gret desire of thyn herte undir colour of charité and rightwesnesse desirest that thei were wel ponysschid for here synne. This stirynge semeth good, neverthelees it is, yif thou ransake it wel, more fleischli agens the persoone thanne goostli agen the synne. Thou schalt love the man, be he nevere so synful, and thou schalt hate synne in everi man what that he bee. Manye aren bigiled in this, for thei

1850 sette the bittir instide of the swete, and taken myrkenesse instide of light, as the prophete telleth: *Ve vobis, qui dicitis malum bonum, et bonum malum; ponentes lucem tenebras et amarum dulce* (Isaiah 5:20). Woo bee to hem that seyn yvel is good and good is yvel, and setteth light as myrkenesse, and bittir instede of swete. Thus doon alle thoo that whanne thei schulden hate the synne of here even Cristene and love the persoone, thei

1855 hate the persoone instide of synne, and wene that thei hate the synne. Wherefore it is a craft bi hitsilf, whoso cowde doon it wel.

Chapter Sixty-five

That it is mykil maistrie sothfastli to love men in charité and hate here synne.

It is no maistrie for to wake and faste til thyn heed wirke and thi bodi waike, ne for to goo to Rome and to Jerusalem upon thi bare feet, ne for to stirte aboute and preche as

1860 thou woldest turne alle men bi thi prechynge; ne it is noo maistrie for to make chirches and chapeles, for to feede pore men and make hospitales. But it is a greet maistrie for a man to kunne love his even Cristene in charité, and viseli hate the synne of him and love the man. For though it be soo that alle thise deedis toforeseide aren goode in hemsilf, neverthelees thei aren comone to gode men and women and also to badde, for eche man

1865 mai doo hem yif he wolde and hadde wherof, and forthi for to doo that ech man mai doo, I holde no maistrie. But for to love his even Cristene in charité and hate his synne,

1844 **disese**, distress; **felnesse**, fierceness. 1847 **ransake**, examine. 1848–49 **love the man . . . hate synne**, an Augustinian idea, expressed in *De doctrina christiana*, 1.27–28, and elsewhere; see Clark, p. 180n294. 1853 **myrkenesse**, darkness. 1858 **maistrie**, feat of skill; **wirke**, ache; **waike**, weakens. 1859 **stirte**, start. 1860 **turne**, convert. 1862 **kunne**, know how to; **viseli**, wisely.

mai there no man doo but gode men oonli, whiche have it of the gift of God and not of her owene travaile, as Seynt Poule seith: *Caritas dei diffusa est in cordibus vestris per spiritum, qui datus est vobis* (Romans 5:5). Love and charité is sched and spred in youre hertis bi the Hooli Goost, whiche is gyven to you, and therfore it is the more precious and the more deynté for to come bi.

1870

Chapter Sixty-six

That for the same deedis outewarde sere men schal have seere medis.

Alle othere gode deedis withouten this maketh not a man good, ne worthi the blisse of hevene, but this aloone, and oonli it, maketh a man good and alle his good deedis medeful.

1875 Alle othere giftis of God and werkes of man are comoun to gode and to badde, but this gifte of charité is oonli to gode and chosen soulis.

A good man for the love of God he fasteth, he waketh, gooth on pilgrimage, and forsaketh the likynge of the world soothfasteli in his herte withoutin feynynge. Hee schal have his meede in the blisse of hevene. An ypocrite for veynglorie of himsilf dooth

1880 the same deedis and receyveth his meede heere. Also a verry prechour of Goddis word, fulfilled of charité and of mekenesse, sent of God, and of Holi Chirche resseyved, schal have a special mede, that is the auriol, for his prechynge. An ypocrite or an heretik, that nevere hadde mekenesse ne charité, ne aren not sent off God ne of Holi Chirche, thei have here mede heere. Also a gode man in wordli staat, for love of God maketh chirchis

1885 and chapeles, habbeies, hospitales, and othere good deedis of merci. He schal have his mede in the blisse of hevene, not for the deede in hitsilf, but for the good wil and the charité that he hadde of the gifte of God for to doo thoo gode deedes. Anothir man for vanité of himsilf and worschipe and praisynge of the world and his owene name dooth the same good deedis and hath his meede heere. The cause is, in al thise, that the ton

1890 hath charité and the tothir hath noon. Whiche is oon and whiche is othir, oure Lord knowith and noon but He.

1871 deynté, valuable. **1872 sere**, various; **medis**, rewards. **1874 medeful**, worthy of reward. **1881 resseyved**, received. **1882 auriol**, aureole. **1885 habbeies**, abbeys. **1889 ton**, one. **1890 tothir**, other.

Chapter Sixty-seven

That alle menys good deedis schal be appreved that hath likenes of good, save of the opyn heretik and the opyn cursid man.

And therfor we schulden love and worschipe alle men in oure hertis, and receyve alle
1895 heere dedes that have the likenes of godenesse, though the dooeres in Goddis sight be badde, save of the opyn heretike and the opyn cursid man. Of thise two speciali we schullen flee and eschewe the presence and the comonynge with hem, and we schulde reprove and refuse here deedes, seme thei nevere so goode, as longe as thei are rebel to God and to Holi Chirche. As yif a wordli cursid man make a chirche, or feede a pore
1900 man, thou mai sikirli holde it nought and deme it as it is. Also yif an opin heretike, whiche is rebel to Hooli Chirche, preche and teche, though he converte an hundrid thousand soulis, halde the dede as to himsilf right nought. For thise men aren opinli oute of charité, withouten whiche al is nought that a man doth; and therfore seie I it is a grete maistrie a man for to kunne love his even Cristene in charité. Al this seiynge mai opynli
1905 be proved bi Seynt Poulis wordis thus: *Si linguis hominum loquar, et angelorum, caritatem non habuero, nichil sum; et si habuero omnem fidem, ita ut montes transferam, caritatem non habeam, nichil sum. Et si noverim misteria omnia, nichil sum; et si distribuero omnes facultates meas in cibos pauperum, et tradidero corpus meum igni ut ardeam, caritatem non habuero, nichil michi prodest* (1 Corinthians 13:1–3). Seynt Poul in
1910 preisynge of charité seith thus: Yif I speke the langage of men and angelis also, and I have no charité, I am right nought. And yif I have so moche feith that y mai turne hillis and bere hem awey, and I have no charité, yit am I nought. And also yif I hadde knowynge of alle pryvitees, withouten charité I am nought. And yif I gyve al that y have to pore men, and my bodi to the fier to be brent, and y have no charité, it profiteth me
1915 nought. Heere it semeth wel bi Seynt Poulis wordis that a man mai doo alle bodily gode deedis withoute charité, and that charité is not ellis but for to love God and his even Cristen as himsilf.

1896 **cursid**, excommunicated. 1897 **comonynge**, association. 1898 **reprove**, condemn. 1900 **sikirli**, certainly. 1902 **halde**, consider. 1904 **maistrie**, difficulty; **kunne**, know how to. 1913 **pryvitees**, mysteries.

Chapter Sixty-eight

That no good deede mai make a man sikir withoute charité; and that charité is oonli had of the gifte of God to hem that are meke, and who is parfightli meke.

1920 How schulde thanne ony caytif lyvynge in erthe, what that he be, have delite or trust or sikirnesse in himsilf for aughte that he can doo or mai doo with alle his bodili myghtes and al his kyndeli reson, sethen al is not worth withouten love and charité to his even Cristene? And this charité mai not be geten bi no worchinge of hymsilf, for it is a free gift of God sent to a meke soule, as Seynt Poul seith. Who daar seie hardili, "I have

1925 charité," or "I am in charité"? Sothli no man mai seie it sikirli, but he that is perfightli and sothfastli meke. Othir men mai trowe and hope of hemsilf that thei ben in charité bi tokenes of charité, but he that is perfightli meke feleth it, and therfore mai he seie it. Thus meke was Seynte Poul, and therfore he seide thus of himsilf: *Quis me separabit a caritate dei? Tribulacio, an anguscia?* (Romans 8:35). Who schal departe me fro the

1930 charité of God? Tribulacion or anguisch? And he answerith hymsilf and seith, that there schal no creature putte me from the charité of God whiche I have in Crist Jhesu.

Many man dooth deedis of charité and hath no charité, as I have seide. For to re-prove a synner for his synne into his amendynge and in covenable tyme, it is a deede of charité, but for to hate the synnere instide of synne, it is agens charité. He that is verili

1935 meke can departe the toon from the tothir, and no man but he; for yif a man hadde alle morale vertues of al philosophie, also yif man hadde knowynge of cleergie and of al dyvynyté and is not sothfastli meke, he schal erre and stumble and take the toon for the tothir; but mekenesse is worthi to receyve a gifte of God, the whiche mai not be leered bi techynge of man. And therfor he that is meke can hate the synne and truli love the man.

1940 But now peraventure thou bigynnest for to dreede, for I seide that charité mai not be geten bi no werk of man that man mai doo. Hou thanne schal thou do? As unto this I seie that there is nothinge so harde for to gete as is charité; this is sooth, as with thyn owen traveile. Also, on the contrarie wise, there is no gift of God mai be hadde so lightli as charité, for oure Lord gyeveth noo gifte so freeli, ne so glaadli, ne so comonli as He

1918 sikir, secure. **1919 parfightli**, perfectly. **1920 caytif**, wretch. **1922 kyndeli**, natural. **1925 sikirli**, certainly. **1926 trowe**, believe. **1933 covenable**, suitable. **1936 knowynge**, knowledge. **1938 leered**, learned. **1941 do**, act. **1943 lightli**, easily.

1945 dooth charité. "Hou schal y have it?" seist thou thanne. Be meke and lowe in spirite and thou schalt have it; and what is lightere for to doo thanne for to be meke? Sotheli noo thynge. Thanne semeth it that there is nothynge that mai so lightli be had as charité, and therfore be not thou to moche adrad; be meke, and have it. Thus seide Seynt Jame the Apostil: *Deus superbis resistit, humilibus dat graciam* (James 4:6). Oure Lord, he seith,

1950 agenstondeth proude men, but to meke men He geveth grace. Whiche grace is propirli charité, for aftir the mesure of thi mekenesse so schal thu have charité.

Yif thou have mekenesse unperfightli, oonli in thi wille not in thyn affeccion, than schalt thou have unperfight charité. This is good, for it sufficeth to savacioun, as David seith: *Imperfectum meum viderunt oculi tui* (Psalms 138:16). Lord with thyn iyen of

1955 merci thou seest my unperfeccioun. But yif thou have mekenesse perfightli, than thou schalt have perfight charité, and that is the beste. The tothir bihoveth us to have yif we wolen be saaf, and this we schullen desire. Than yif thou aske me who is perfightli meke, thou schalt no more have at this tyme of me of mekenesse but this: he is meke that soothfastli knoweth and felith himsilf as he is.

Chapter Sixty-nine

1960 Hou a man schal wite hou moche ire and envie is hid in the ground of hys herte.

Now turne agen to this image, yif thou wole asaie hou moche ire and envie is hid in the ground of thyn herte that thou felist not. Loke wel and biholde thiself visili whanne siche stirynges of envie and ire agens thyn even Cristen spryngen out of thyn herte. The more arisynge that thou hast, and the more stired that thou art bi malencolie bittirnesse

1965 or wikkid wil agens hem, the more is this image in thee; for the more thou grucchist bi unpacience either agens God for tribulacion or sikenesse or for bodili disese sent of God, or agens thyn even Cristene, for ought that thei dooth agens thee, the lasse is the image of Jhesu reformed in thee.

1948 adrad, afraid. **1950 agenstondeth**, resists. **1952 unperfightli**, unperfectly. **1954 iyen**, eyes. **1957 saaf**, saved. **1962 visili**, wisely. **1965 grucchist**, complain.

Chapter Seventy

1970 Bi what tokenes thou schalt wite yif thou love thyn enemye and what ensample thou schalte take of Crist for to love Hym also.

I seye not that siche maner of grucchynges or fleischli angres aren deedli synnes; but I seie that thei letten clennesse of herte and pees of consciencie, that thou mai not have ful charité, bi the whiche thou schuldest come to lif contemplatif. For that ende is the cause of al my seiynge, that thou schuldest not oonli clense thyn herte from deedli
1975 synnes, but also of venyal, as moche as thou mai, that the ground of synne myght bi grace of Jhesu Crist be sumwhat quenchid in thee. For though it be so that thou feelist noon yvel wil agens thyn even Cristen for a tyme, yit art thou not sikir that the ground of irc is quenchid in thee, ne yit arte thou not lord of the vertu of charité. For suffre him touche thee a litil bi ony angrynesse or a schrewid word, and thou schalt feele anoon yif
1980 thyn herte be yit maad hool bi fulhede of charité. The more that thou art stirid and yvel willed agens the persone, the ferthere art thou from perfight charité of thyn even Cristene and the lasse that thou art stirid, the neer art thu to charité.

And yif thou be not stirid agen the persoone bi angir or bi feel cheer outeward, ne bi no privey hate in thyn herte for to dispice hym or deme hym or for to sette him at
1985 nought; but the more schame and velanye he doth to thee in word or in dede, the more pité and the more compassioun thou haste on hym, as thou woldst of a man that were oute of his mynde. And thee thenketh that thou cannot fynde in thyn herte for to hate hym, for love is so good in the silf, but praie for hym and helpe hym and desire his amendynge, not oonli with thi mouth as ypocrites doon, but with thyn herte in affeccioun
1990 and love. And thanne hast thou perfight charité to thyn even Cristene. This charité had Seynt Stevene perfightli whanne he preide for hem that stooned him to the deeth. This charité counceilide Crist to alle thoo that wolden be his perfite folwers whanne he seide thus: *Diligite inimicos vestros, benefacite hiis qui oderunt vos, orate pro persequentibus vos* (Matthew 5:44). Love youre enemyes and dooth good to hem that haten you; praieth
1995 for hem that pursue you. And therfore yif yee wolen folwe Crist, be like to Hym in this craft. Leere for to love thyne enemyes and synful men, for alle thise been thyn even Cristene. Looke and bithenke thee how goodli Crist was to Judas, hou benynge, hou

1975 ground, foundation. **1979 schrewid,** wicked. **1991 Seynt Stevene,** see Acts 7:54–60. **1995 pursue,** persecute. **1996 Leere,** Learn. **1997 benynge,** benign.

curteis, and how loweli to hym that He knewe dampnable. And neveretheles He chees him to His apostel, and sente him for to preche with othere apostelis. He gaaf hym powere to worche myracles, He schewed to him the same good chiere in worde and in deede as He dide to the tothire apposteles. He biwreied hym not, ne spak nevere yvel of hym; and yit though He hadde doon alle thise, He had seid nothynge but sooth. And overmore, whanne Judas toke Hym, He kissid hym and called hym His frend. And al this charité schewed Crist to Judas, whiche He knewe for dampnable, in no manere of flaterynge ne feynynge, but in soothfastnesse of good love and clene charité. For though it were so that Judas were unworthi for to have had ony gift of God or ony signe of love for his wikkiddenesse, neverthelees it was worthi and skilful that oure Lord schulde schewe as He is. He is love and goodnes to alle Hise creatures, as He was to Judas. Folwe aftir sumwhat if thou may, for though thu be stoken in an hous with thi bodi, neverthelees in thyn herte, where the stide of love is, thou schulde mow have part of siche love to thyn even Cristen as y speke of. Whooso weneth thanne hymsilf for to be a perfighte lovere and a folwer of Cristis techynge and His lyvynge (as sum man weneth that he is, in as mykil as he prechith and techith and is pore of wordli goodis as Crist was), and cannot folwe Crist in this love and in this charité for to love his evene Cristene, ecche man, good and badde, frendes and foos, withoutin feynynge or flateringe, dispisynge in his herte agens the man, angrynesse, and maliciousli reprovynge, sothli he bigileth hymsilf. For the ner that he weneth for to bee, the ferthere he is; for Crist seide Himsilf to hem that wolden be His folweres and His disciples thus: *Hoc est preceptum meum, ut diligatis invicem, sicut dilexi vos* (John 13:34). This is My biddynge, that ye love you togidre, as I lovede you. For yif ye love as I lovede, thanne are ye My disciplis.

But now, seist thou, how schal y love him that is badde als wel as him that is gode? As unto this I seie, that thou schalt love bothe in charité, but not for the same cause; as I schal telle thee hou thou schalt love thyne evene Cristene as thysilf. Now thou schalt love thysilf oonli in God, or ellis for God. In God thou loveste thisilf whanne thu art rightful bi grace and vertues; and thou lovest not thisilf, but oonli for that rightwisenesse and vertu that God gyveth thee. Thanne lovest thou thisilf in God, for thou lovest not thisilf but God; also for God thou lovest thisilf, as yif thou were in deedli synne and

2001 **biwreied**, revealed. 2003 **Judas**, see Matthew 26:47–50. 2009 **stoken**, inserted. 2010 **stide**, place; **mow**, be able to. 2011 **weneth**, suppose. 2013 **wordli**, worldly (frequently spelled thus). 2016 **reprovynge**, blaming. 2017 **ner**, nearer. 2020 **togidre**, each other. 2025 **rightful**, righteous.

woldest be maad rightful and vertuous; thanne lovest thou thisilf not as thou art, for thou art unrightful, but as thou woldest be. Right so schalt thou love thyn even Cristene.

2030 Yif thei ben goode and rightful, thou schalt love hem bi charité in God, oonli for thei ben goode and rightful; for thanne lovest thou God in hem, as goodnesse and rightwisenesse, more thanne hem yif thei ben badde and in deedli synne, as thyn enemyes that haten thee or othere of the whiche thou haste ful evidence that thei aren not in grace. Yit schalt thou love hem not as thei aren, ne as good men and rightful, for thei are badde and

2035 unrightful, but thou schalt love hem for God, that thei myght be gode and rightful. And so schalte thou nothynge hate in hem, but the thynge that is contrarie to rightwisenesse, and that is synne. This is as I undirstonde the techynge of Seynt Austyn, for to departe the love of the man fro the hate of the synne in the love of thyn evene Cristene. He that is sothfastli meke, or wolde be meke, can love his evene Cristene, and noon but he.

Chapter Seventy-one

2040 Hou a man schal knowe hou mochel coveytise is hid in hys herte.

Lifte up this image and loke wel al aboughte, and thou schalt mowe see covetise and love of erthely thynge occupie a greet partie of this ymage, though it seme litil. Thou haste forsaken the richesse and moche avere of this world, and art sperid in a dongoun; but hast thou forsaken the love of al this? I hope not yit; it is lasse maistrie for to forsake

2045 goodis of the world thanne for to forsake the love of hem. Peraventure thou hast not forsake coveitise, thou haste chaunged fro grete thyngis into smale, as from a pound to a peny and from a silveren pece into a dische of an halpeny. This is a symple chaunge; thou art no good marchant. Thise ensamples aren childisch; neverthelees thei bitoken more. Yif thou trowe not me, assaie thisilf yif thou have love and delite in the havynge

2050 and in the biholdynge of ony thynge that thou haste, swich as it is, with the whiche love thou feedist thyn herte for a tyme or yif thou have desire and yeerne for to have sum-thynge that thou haste not, with siche desire thyn herte is traveiled bi unskilful bisynesse, that the clene desire of vertues and of God mai not reste thereinne. This is a tokene that

2037 techynge of Seynt Austyn, *De doctrina christiana,* 1.27–28; see *Scale* I.1848–49 and gloss; **departe,** separate. **2043 avere,** possessions; **sperid,** locked. **2044 hope,** suppose; **maistrie,** difficulty. **2052 traveiled,** troubled; **unskilful,** irrational; **bisynesse,** activity.

2055 there is coveitise in this ymage, and yif thou wole assaie betere, loke yif onythinge that thou haste be taken awai from thee, bi maistrie or bi borwynge or bi ony othir wise, and thou mai not geten it agen, and forthi thou art disesid in thyn herte, and angrid and trobelid in thyn herte; bothe thee wanteth that thynge that thou wolde have and mai not gete it, and also agen hym that hath it thou art stired, for he myght restore it agen and wole not. This is a tokene that thou lovest wordli goodes, for thus doon wordli men.

2060 Whanne that heer good and her richesse is taken from hem, thei aren hevy, sori, and angry, and flite and stryve agens hem that han it, openli with word and bi deede; but thou doost alle thise in thyn herte pryveli, where God seeth. And yit arte thou in more defaute thanne a wordli man, for thou hast forsaken in likenesse the love of alle wordli thynges; but a wordli man hath not so, and therfore he is excusid though he stryve and

2065 pursue bi lawful weies for to have hem agen. But now seist thou, that thee bihoveth have thy necessaries of siche thinges as longeth to thee, as wel as a wordli man. I graunte wel therto, but thou schuldest not love hyt, ne noo likynge have in the biholdynge and in the kepynge of it, ne sorwe ne hevynesse fele in the leesynge or in the withdraw- ing of it; for, as Seynte Gregor seith, as moche sorwe as thou hast in the lesynge of a

2070 thynge, so moche love haddest thou in the kepynge. And therfore yif thyn herte were maad hool and thou hadde soothfastli felid a desire of goostli thynges, and hadde thereof a sighte of the leste goostli thynge that is, al the love and likyng of ony ertheli thynge thou schuldest sette it at nought, it schulde not cleve on thee. For to love and for to have more thanne thee nedeth skilfulli, it is a grete defaute. Also for to love that thing that

2075 thee nedith is defaute, but not so greet; but for to have and use that thee nedeth withoutin love of it is no defaute. Soothli manye that han the staat and the likenesse of povertee aren moche blyndid in this poynt and hyndred froo the love of God. But I accuse no man, ne no staat reprove, for in every astaat summe aren goode and sume aren othir. But oo thynge I seie to eche man and woman whiche hath take the staat of poverté

2080 wilfulli, whethir he be religious or seculer, or what degree he be inne: As longe as his affeccioun is bounden, festened, and as it were glewid with the love of ony othir ertheli thynge that he hath or ellis wolde have, he mai not have ne feele soothfastili the clene love and the cleer sight of goostli thyngis.

2055 **maistrie**, force. 2056 **disesid**, distressed. 2057 **thee wanteth**, is lacking to you. 2061 **flite**, contend. 2063 **defaute**, fault. 2065 **pursue**, follow. 2068 **leesynge**, losing. 2069 **Seynte Gregor seith**, see *Moralia*, 1.5.7 and 31.13.21 (Clark, p. 181n298). 2081 **glewid**, glued.

For as Seynt Austyn seith to oure Lord thus: "Lord, he loveth Thee but litil, that loveth
2085 ony thynge with Thee." For the more love and coveitise of ony ertheli thinge is in thee,
the lasse is the love of God in thyn herte. For though it be soo that this love of ertheli
thinge putte hem not oute of charité, but it be so moche that it strangle the love of God
and of here even Cristen, sothely it hyndreth hem and letteth thee from the fervour of
charité, and also from that special meede that thei schulde have in the blisse of hevene
2090 for perfight poverté. And that is a grete losse yif they myght see it; for whooso myght
knowe goosteli mede, how good, and how precious, and how worthi it is ay lastynge,
he wolde not for al ertheli joie, or al ertheli thynge, though he myght have it withouten
synne, lette ne leese the leeste meede of the blisse of hevene, whiche he myghte have yif
that he wolde. I speke ferthere thanne y can do, but I pray thee thorugh the grace of
2095 God, doo soo yif thou mai, or ony othir whoso wole; for that were a comfort to me,
that though y mai not have it in mysilf as I seie, that I myght have it in thee, or in ony
othir creature whiche hath receyved of oure Lord more plenté of His grace thanne y.
But see now thanne, hou coveitise in the nakid ground letteth a man or a woman so
moche from the goosteli felynge of the love of God, how moche more it letteth thanne
2100 and encombrith wordli men and women whiche, bi alle here wittes and bisynesse,
nyght and dai studie and travaile hou thei myght gete richesse and plenté of wordli
goodis. Thei kunne noon othir delite have but in wordli thynges, ne thei wole not, for
thei seke it not. I sei no more at this tyme of hem, for in this writynge y speke not to
hem; but this I seie, yif thei myght see and wold see what thei doo, thei schulde not
2105 doo so.

Chapter Seventy-two

Hou a man schal knowe whanne he synneth not in etynge and drynkynge and whanne
he synneth deedli and whan veniali.

Yit mai thou see more in thys image, though it be myrk; and that is fleischli love to thisilf
in glotonie, sleuthe, and leccherie. Thise fleischli likynges maken a man wel beestli, and

2084 **Seynt Austyn seith**, *Confessiones*, 10.29.40 (Clark, p. 181n302). 2093 **lette ne leese**,
prevent nor lose. 2108 **myrk**, dark. 2109 **sleuthe**, sloth.

2110 fer from inli savour of the love of God and from the cleer sight of goostli thingis. But
now seist thou, that y seie that thee bihoveth nedelynges ete and drynke and slepe, and
that mai thou not doo withoute likynge, therfore thee thenketh this likynge is no synne.

As unto this I answere, yif thou kepe in etynge and drynkynge and in othir nedeful
thinges to the bodi mesure, up thi nede as resoun asketh, and thou resseyvest no more
2115 thanne kynde asketh, and al this thou doost for thi goostli delite whiche thou felist in thi
soule, I graunte for sothe that thou thanne synnest right nought. For thanne can thou
wel ete and slepe, sothli and withoutin doute. I am ful fer from that knowynge, and
ferthere from the wirkynge; for to ete I have bi kynde, but for to kunne ete I mai not but
bi grace. Seynt Poul hadde bi grace this knowynge as he seide of himsilf thus: *Ubique*
2120 *et in omnibus institutus sum; et scio satiari, et esurire, habundare, et penuriam pati.*
Omnia possum in eo qui me confortat (Philippians 4:12–13). I am enformed and taught
in alle thinges, for I can hungre and can ete, I can with plenté and I can with poverté. I
mai al in Him that strengtheth me.

Seynt Austyn seid to oure Lord thus: "Lord, Thou hast taughte me that I schulde take
2125 mete as medicene." For honger is a sikenesse of kynde, and mete is medicyn therto and
therfore the likynge that cometh withal, in as moche as it is kyndeli and nedefulle, it is
no synne; but whanne it passith into luste and into wilful likynge, thanne it is synne. And
therfore, there lieth al the maistrie, for to kunne departe visili the nede fro the lust and
wilful likynge. Thei aren so knettid togedre, and that oon cometh so with the tothir,
2130 thanne it is hard to receyve that oon as the nede and reprove the tothir as wilful likynge
and luste, whiche ofte tyme cometh undir colour of nede. Yif a man wolde oonli take
mete and drynke as medicyn for sikenesse, he schulde kunne departe wel the luste from
the nede. Neverthelees, syn it is so that nede is the ground of this synne, and that neede
is no synne. For be a man nevere so hooli, hym bihoveth ete and drynke and slepe,
2135 therfore the lust and the likynge that cometh undir colour of this nede and passeth this
nede is the lasse synne.

For a man comonli synneth not deedli in glotonye, but he be cumbred with othere
deedli synnes bifore doon. Thanne mai he the lightliere synne deedli in this. For this is

---

2110 inli, inward. **2111 nedelynges**, necessarily. **2114 up**, according to. **2115 asketh**, requires. **2118 kynde**, nature. **2123 strengtheth**, strengthens. **2124 Seynt Austyn seid**,
Confessiones, 10.31.44 (Clark, p. 181n306). **2125 mete**, food. **2128 maistrie**, difficulty; **kunne
departe visili**, know how to separate wisely. **2129 likynge**, pleasure. **2137 cumbred**, encum-
bered.

sooth, he that chesith the luste and the likynge of his fleisch in delices and welfare of
2140   mete and drinke as a ful reste of his herte, nevere to have othir joie ne othir blisse, but to
lyve ay in siche lustis of his fleisch, yif he myght, hit is no doughte but that he synneth
deedli, for he loveth his fleisch more than God. But he that lieth in deedli synne as pride
or envie or siche othere, he is blynde and so bounden to the devel that for the tyme he
hath not the power clenli of his free wille; and therefore he mai not weel agenstonde
2145   fleischli likynges, but falleth doun wilfulli into hem, as a beest doth upoun a carioun.

And in as moche as he hath noo general wille bifore to God principali, bicause that he
is in deedli synne, therfore the lust of glotonye whiche he falleth inne is lightli to hym
deedli synne, for he maketh noon agenstondynge, general ne special. But anothir man or
woman whiche is in grace and in charité hath alwei a good general wille to God in hise
2150   soule, whethir he slepe or wake, ete or drinke, or what dede that he dooth, so that the
dede be not yvel in the silf; bi the whiche wille he chesith and desireth God aboven alle
thynges, and he hadde wel levere forbere al the likynge of this world thanne his God, for
the love of Him. This wille, though it be but general, it is of so greet vertu bi the grace
of oure Lord Jhesu, that though he falle bi freelté in luste and likynge of mete and
2155   drinke, or in siche othere sikenessis, othir in excesse of to moche etynge, or to often, or
to gredili, or to lustli and delicatli, or to soone in untyme, it saveth and kepith hym from
deedli synne. And this is soth, as longe as he is in charité bi othere good deedis and
kepith this general wille hool in al that he dooth; and nameli yit, yif he knowe amonge his
owen wrecchidnesse, and crieth God merci, and is in purpos speciali for to agenstonde
2160   alle siche lustis fleischli.

Oure Lord is good and merciful, and thise venyal synnes of glotonye He forgyveth
sone to a meke man; for the stirynges and the likynges of glotonye, in as moche as thei
ben hardest for to flee bicause of nede of the bodili kynde, amonge alle othere synnes
aren most excusable and lest perilous. And therfore thou schal not rise agens the ground
2165   of this synne as thou schalt agenes alle othere synnes. For the ground of this synne is
oonli nede, whiche mai not be eschewid but yif thou wolt doo wors and slee the nede,
as many foolis doo, whiche schulden slee the theef and spare the trewe man, that is to
seie thei schulde slee the unskilful lust and the wilful likynge, and spare and kepe the

2139 **likynge**, pleasure. 2140 **reste**, resting place. 2141 **doughte**, doubt. 2144 **agenstonde**,
resist. 2152 **levere forbere**, rather forgo. 2155 **to**$_{1,2}$, too. 2156 **in untyme**, at the wrong time.
2168 **unskilful**, irrational.

2170 bodili kynde. But agen alle othere synnes thou schalt arise for to distroie; not oonli the gret deedli and the grete venyal synnes, but also agens the ground of hem in as moche as thou mai.

See bi this skile, thou mai not lyve withoute mete and drinke; but thou mai lyve withoute leccherie yif thou wole, and nevere be but the betere. And therfore thou schalt not oonli flee the dede in the silf, whiche is deedli synne, and also the wilful likynge of
2175 it in thyn herte withoutin dede, whiche is venial, and sumtyme it is deedli; but also thou schalt arise agen the ground of it, for to distroie the risynge and the felynge and the fleischli stirynges.

Chapter Seventy-three

The ground of leccherie schulde be distroied with goostli travaile and not with bodili.

But this travaile agen the ground of leccherie nameli schal be goostli, as bi prayers and
2180 goostli vertues, and not bodili bi no bodili penaunce. For wite thou wel, though thou wake and faste and scourge thisilf and doo al that thou can, thou schal nevere have the clennesse and that chastité withoute the gifte and the grace of mekenesse. Thou schulde mowe rathere slee thisilf thanne thou schuldest slee fleischli stirynges and likynges of lustis of leccherie, oither in thi herte or in thi fleisch, bi ony bodili penaunce. But bi the
2185 grace of Jhesu in a meke soule, the ground mai be stoppid and distroied, and the springe mai be dried and that is veri chastité in bodi and soule.

And the same manere mai be seid of pride, coveitise, and siche othere; for thou myghttest lyve though thou were neither proud ne covetous, and therfore thou schalt distroie alle the felynges of hem as moche as thou myght. But in glotonye thou schal
2190 arise and smyte awey alle unskilful stirynges, and save the ground hool. And therfore he that riseth agens the feelynge of fleischli likynge in mete and drinke more fulli and more scharpli thanne agen the feelynge and the stirynge of pride, for thei seme faire and are not lightli reprevyd, or of envie, ire, coveitise, or leccherie, I seie that he is half blynd. For he seeth not yit goostli the unclennesse of pride and envie, how foul it is in Goddis

2172 **skile**, reason. 2180 **wite**, know. 2183 **mowe**, be able to. 2190 **unskilful**, irrational. 2191 **mete**, food. 2193 **lightli reprevyd**, easily rejected. 2194 **unclennesse**, impurity.

2195 sight. I hope yif a man myght see with his goostli iye hou foule pride and coveitise aren
in the sight of God, and hou contrarie to Him, he schulde more lothe the stirynge of
pride and the veyn delite of it; and also he schulde more agrise and arise agen an yvel wil
of envie or ire to his even Cristene, thanne agens many stirynges and likynges, oithir of
glotonye or leccherie. Nevertheles, alle men wenen not so, for comonli men aren more
2200 arwgh for to fele a stirynge of fleischli synne, and have for it more hevynesse, thanne
for grete likynges in veynglorie or othere goostli synnes. But thei aren not wise, for yif
thei wole undirstonde Holi Writ and doctours sawes thereof, schulde thei fynde as I
saie, whiche y ne mai ne wole not reherce now.

Chapter Seventy-four

That a man schulde be bisi for to putte awai alle stirynges of synne but more bisili
2205 goostli synnes than bodili.

I ne wole not excuse hem that fallen in likynges of glotonye and leccherie, that thei
synnen not; for I woot wel that alle the spices of hem aren synne more or lasse, aftir the
mesure of the lust and wilful likynges, with othere circumstaunces of hem. But I wolde
that thou knewe and chargid eche a synne as it is: more or lasse the more, as aren alle
2210 goostli synnes, the lasse as aren alle fleischli synnes. Yit schal thou neverthelees hate
and flee alle bodili and goostli synnes up thi myght; for wite thou wel, that fleischli
desires and unskilfulle likynges in mete or drinke, or ony likynges that longen to the bodi
passynge resonable nede, though thei be not ay grete synnes to hem that aren in charité,
neverthelees to a soule that desireth clennesse and goostli felynge of God, thei aren ful
2215 hevy and bittir, and moche for to eschewe. For the spirit mai not fele hys kyndeli savour
withinne of the gostli presence of Jhesu Crist til the fleisch have lost moche of his bestli
savoure withoute; and therfore yif thou wole come to clennesse in herte, thee byhoveth
agenstonde unskilful stirynges of fleiscli desires. But agen the ground of it that is nede,
as kyndeli honger whiche thou schal nedelynges fele and tente thertoo in tyme, and

2195 **goostli iye**, spiritual eye. 2197 **agrise**, be horrified. 2199 **wenen**, suppose. 2200 **arwgh**,
frightened. 2202 **sawes**, sayings. 2207 **spices**, species. 2211 **up thi myght**, according to your
ability. 2212 **unskilfulle likynges**, irrational pleasures. 2215 **kyndeli**, natural. 2218 **fleiscli**,
fleshly. 2219 **nedelynges**, by necessity; **tente**, tend.

117

2220 helpe thisilf agens it bi medicyn of mete as thou woldest helpe thisilf resonabli agens
bodili sikenesse, that thou myght ete and the more freli serve thi God bodili and goostli.

Chapter Seventy-five

That hunger and othere peynes of the bodi letteth moche goostly wirkynge.

For wite thou wel that what man or woman schal ben occupied in goostli thoughtes,
unskilful peyne of hungir wilfulli taken, or sikenesse in the stomac or in the heed or in
2225 ony othir partie of the bodie, for the defaute of thisilf bi to moche fastynge or in ony
othir wise, schal moche lette the spirit and moche hyndre him from the knowynge and
the biholdynge of goosteli thynges, but he have more grace. For though it be so that
bodili peyne, othir of penaunce othir of siknesse, or ellis bodili occupaccion, sumtyme
letteth not the fervour of love to God in devocioun but often encresith it. Sothli y hope
2230 that it letteth the fervour of lust in contemplacion, whiche mai not be had ne felid sadli,
but in gret reste of bodi and soule. Forthi doo thou skilfulli that longeth to thee and kepe
thi bodili kynde up resoun and suffre than til God sende what He wole, be it heele or
sikenesse. Take it generali and grucche not agens God wilfulli.

Chapter Seventy-six

What remedie a man schal use agenes defaute maad in etynge and drinkynge.

2235 Doo thanne as I seie thee: take thi mete, and ordeyne for it yif nede it be up resoun, and
take it gladli as for nede. But beware of lust that cometh with the nede; eschew to
moche as wel as to litil. And whanne thou hast doon, and it cometh to thi mynde bitynge
in conscience that thou hast eten to moche or to litil, and bigynnest to tarie and drawest
thee to over moche bittirnesse, lift up thi desire of thyn herte to thi good Lord Jhesu,
2240 and know thisilf for a wrecche and a beeste, and aske Him forgevenesse bi His merci.
And whanne thou hast doon thus, the schortliere the levere, leve of thanne and tarie no

2226 **lette**, hinder. 2231 **skilfulli**, reasonably; **longeth**, belongs. 2233 **grucche**, complain.
2235 **mete**, food. 2238 **tarie**, trouble. 2241 **levere**, better; **of**, off.

lengere withal, ne stryve not to moche as thou wolde distroie it uttirli, for it is not for to doo. Thou schal never brynge it so aboute. But redili ordeyne thee to sum othir occupacioun bodili or gostli, aftir thou felist thee disposid, that thou mighttest the more

2245 profite in othire vertues, as mekenesse and charité.

For wite thou wel, he that hath in his desire and in his travaile noon othir reward to noon othir thinge but to mekenesse and charité, ai cravynge aftir hem how he myght gete hem, he schal in that desire with worchynge folwynge aftir, profite more and waxe in alle other vertues, as in chastité, abstinence, and siche othire, though he have but litil

2250 reward to hem, more in a yeer thanne he schulde have withouten this desire profite in sevene yeer, though he stryve with glotonye and leccherie and siche othire contynueli and bete himsilf eche dai with scourgis from morwe til evesong tyme.

Chapter Seventy-seven

That thorwgh besi desire and travaile in mekenesse and charité, a man cometh sunnere to othere vertues to travaile in hemself.

2255 Gete to thee thanne mekenesse and charité, and yif thou wole traveile and swynke bisili for to have hem, thou schal mowe have inow for to doo in getynge of hem. Thei schal rule and mesure thee ful pryveli, hou thou schalt ete and drynke and socoure al thi bodili nede, that ther schal no man wite it but yif thou wole, and it schal not be in perplexité, ne in dwere, ne in angirnesse and hevynesse, but in a pees of glaad conscience with a

2260 sad restfulnesse. I speke forthere thanne I thought for to have spoken in this matier, but neverthelees doo, yif thou mai, as y sai, and I hope God schal make al wel.

Bi this thanne that I have seid mai thou sumdel see in this ymage of synne hou moche it letteth thee. The Gospel seith how Abraham spak to the riche man that was biried in helle on this wise: *Est chaos magnum inter nos et vos firmatum, ut hii qui volunt*

2265 *transire ad vos, non possunt, nec huc transmeare* (Luke 16:26). There is a gret chaos (that is a grete myrkenesse to sai) is bitwix us and yow, that we moun not come to you ne yee to us. This myrke image in thi soule and in myn also mai be callid a greet chaos,

---

2243 ordeyne, dispose. **2246 reward**, regard. **2253 sunnere**, sooner. **2256 inow**, enough. **2259 dwere**, doubt. **2260 sad**, resolute. **2262 sumdel**, somewhat. **2266 myrkenesse**, darkness.

for it letteth us that we moun not come to Abraham, whiche is Jhesu, and it letteth him that he wole not come to us.

Chapter Seventy-eight

2270   What cometh of the merkenese of the image of synne and what cometh bi the wyndowes thereof.

Lifte up this lanterne and see in this ymage fyve wyndowis bi the whiche synne cometh into thi soule, as the prophete seith: *Mors ingreditur per fenestras nostras* (Jeremiah 9:21). Deeth cometh in bi oure wyndowes. Thise wyndowes aren oure fyve wittes, bi
2275   the whiche oure soule gooth out from himsilf and sicheth his delite and his feedynge in ertheli thynges, agens his owen kynde: as bi the sight, for to se corious and faire thynges; bi the eere, for to heere wondres and newe tydynges; and so of the othere wittis. Bi unskilful usynge of thise wittes into vanyté wilfulli, the soule is moche letted from the goostli wittys withinne; therfore thee bihoveth stoppe the wyndowis and spere
2280   hem, but oonli whanne nede asketh for to open hem. And that were litil maistrie yif though myghttest oones see thi soule bi cleer undirstondynge, what it is, and hou faire it is in his owen kynde, ne were that it is overleid with a blaak cloude of this foule ymage.

Chapter Seventy-nine

That a soule for defaute of knowynge of hitsilf wendith out bi the fyve wittes for to sek liking outward.

2285   But now for thou knowest it not, therfore thou levest the inli sight of thisilf and sekest thi mete from withoutin as a beest unresonable. Thus seith oure Lord to a chosen soule in Hooli Writ: *Si ignoras te, o pulcra inter mulieres, egredere et abi post vestigia gregum sodalium tuorum, et pasce edos tuos* (Canticle 1:7). Thou faire amonge women, if thou knowe not thisilf, goo oute and walke aftir the steppis of the flok of thyne felawes and

2274 **wittes**, senses. 2275 **sicheth**, seeks. 2276 **kynde**, nature. 2278 **unskilful**, irrational. 2279 **spere**, lock. 2285 **inli**, inward. 2286 **mete**, food.

2290 feede thy kedis. And it is thus moche for to seie: Thou soule faire in kynde, maad to the
likenesse of God, freel as woman in thi bodi for thi first synne, bicause that thou
knowist not thisilf, that aungels foode schulde be thi delites withinne, therfore thou
goost out bi thi bodili wittes and sekest thi mete and thi likynge as a beest of the flook,
that is, as oon of the reproved; and therwith thou fedist thi thoughtes and thyn affecciouns,
2295 whiche aren unclene as kides.

Chapter Eighty

That a soule schulde not seke withoute, but aske withinne of Jhesu, al that it
nedeth.

This is a schame to thee for to do so. And therfore turne agen hom into thisilf, and holde
thee withinne and seke no more withouten, and nameli swynes mete; for yif thou algate
2300 be a beggere, aske and crave withinne of thi Lord Jhesu, for He is riche inow, curtais
and free inow, and gladliere wole gyve thanne thou wolt aske. And renne no more out as
a beest of the flook, as a wordli man or woman that hath no nothir delite but in his bodili
wittes. And yif thou do thus, thy Lord Jhesu wole gyve thee al that thee nedeth, for He
mai lede thee into His wyne seler and make thee to assaie of His wynes, for He hath
2305 many tonnes, whiche thee liketh best. Thus a chosen soule, joiynge in Holi Writ, seith to
oure Lord: *Introduxit me rex in cellam vinariam* (Canticle 2:4). A kynge ledde me into
his wyne seeler. And that is for to sai: In as moche as I forsook the dronkennesse of
flesschli lustes and wordli likynges, whiche aren bittere as wormode, forthi the kynge
of blisse, oure Lord Jhesu ledde me in; that is to saie, first into mysilf for to biholde and
2310 knowe mysilf, and aftir He ladde me into his seler, that is to seie, above mysilf bi
overpassynge oonli into Hym, and gaf me assaie of His wyne, that is to saie, a taast and
a liknesse of goostli swettenesse and heveneli joie. Thise aren not wordes of me, a
wrecchid caitif lyvynge in synne, but thei aren the wordes of the spouse of oure Lord in
Hooli Writte. And thise wordes I seie to thee, that thou myght drawe in thi soule fro
2315 withoutin and folwe aftir as as thou may.

2290 kedis, kids. **2291 freel**, frail. **2300 inow**, enough. **2301 renne**, run. **2304 seler**, cellar;
assaie, test. **2305 tonnes**, vessels. **2308 wormode**, wormwood. **2311 overpassynge**, passing
over.

Chapter Eighty-one

That the hoole of ymaginacion nedeth to be stopped, als wel as the wyndowes of the wittes.

But now seist thou, that thou doost soo. Thu seist thou hast no wordeli thinges, ne heerist, ne hast noon use of the bodili wittes more thanne nede asketh, and forthi thou
2320 art enclosid. As to this I seie: Yif thou doo thus, thanne hast thou stopped a grete wyndowe of this image. But yit art thou not siker, for thou hast not stopped the privey hoolis of this image in thyn herte. For though thou see not me with thi bodili iye, thou may see me with thi soule bi imaginacioun; and so mai thou doo of alle othere bodili thinges. Than yif thi soule be feed wilfulli bi imagynynge in vanitees of the world, in
2325 desirynge of wordeli thynge for a wilful comfort and delite, sothli though thi soule be withinne as for thi bodili wittes it is neverthelees ful feer withoute bi sich veyn ymaginacion.
   But now askist thou for it be ony gret synne, a soule for to occupie him in sich vanytees, eithir in wittis or in ymagynynge. As unto this I wolde thou schuldest nevere aske no man this questioun, for he that loveth God or wole love soothfastli, he askith
2330 not whethir this is gretter synne. For him schal thenke what thynge letteth hym fro the love of God is gret synne, and hym schal thenke no synne but that thynge that is not good and letteth him fro the love of God. What is synne but a wantynge and a forberynge of God? I seie not that it schal be peynful to hym as a deedli synne or a venial schulde be, ne I seie not but that hee knowe deedli from a venyal.

Chapter Eighty-two

2335 Whanne the use of the wittes and of the imaginacioun is deedli synne, and whanne venyal.

Neverethelees, sumdeel schal y seie to thi questioun, for thi desire draweth oute of myn herte more thanne I thought for to have seid in the bigynnynge. Oure Lord seith in the Goospel thus: *Homo quidam fecit cenam magnam et vocavit multos. Et misit servum*

2321 **siker**, certain. 2322 **hoolis**, holes. 2332 **wantynge**, lacking; **forberynge**, forgoing. 2333 **peynful**, punishable. 2337 **sumdeel**, somewhat.

2340   *suum dicere invitatis ut venirent. Primus dixit: Villam emi; rogo te, habe me excusatum.*
Secundus dixit: Iuga boum emi quinque, et eo probare ea. Et tercius dixit: Uxorem duxi,
et ideo non possum venire (Luke 14:16–20). A man made a gret sopeer and called many
therto, and sent his servaunt at sopeer tyme to hem that weren praied. The first excuside
hym that he myght not come, for he hadde bought a toun; the tothir also excuside hym

2345   that he myght not come, for he hadde bought fyve yokkes of oxsen and yeede for to
assaie hem; the thridde excusid hym for he hadde wedded a wif. I leve for to speke of
the firste and of the laste, and telle the myddel, of hym that boughte the oxen.

    Thise fyve yokkes of oxen bitoken the fyve wittes, whiche aren beesteli, as an oxe.
Now this man that was callid to the sopeer was not reproved for he boughte the oxen,

2350   but for he yeede for to assaie hem, and so he wolde not come. Right so y seie to thee,
for to have thy wittes and use hem in nede, it is no synne; but yif thou goo for to assaie
hem bi vcyn delite in creaturis, thanne it is synne. For yif thou chese that delite as a fynal
reste of thi soule and as a ful likynge, that thou kepist noon nother blisse have but sich
othir wordli vanyté, thanne it is deedli synne. For thou chesist it as thi God, and so schal

2355   thou be putte fro the sopeer. For the wise man forbeed us that we schulde not assaie
oure wittes so, whanne he seide thus: *Non eatis post concupiscentias vestras*
(Ecclesiasticus 18:30). Thou schalt not goo aftir thi lustes, ne wilfulli assaie thyn likynges.
A man or a woman that is encombred with deedli synnes schal not ascape deedli synne
in this, though he see it not; but I hope that it toucheth not thee. Neverethelees, yif thou

2360   bi freelté delite thee in thi wittes and in sich vanyté, but with that, thou kepist thee in
charité in othir sides, and thou chesist not that delite for a ful reste of thi soule, but thou
settest ai God bifore al thyng in thi desire, this synne is venyal, aftir the circumstaunces
more or lasse. Ne thou schalt not for thise venyal synnes be putte fro the sopeer in the
blisse of hevene, but thou schal wante the tastynge and the assaiynge of that delicat

2365   sopeer lyvynge in erthe, but yif thou be bisie with alle thi myghtes for to agenstonde
sich venyal synnes. For though it be soo that venial synnes breketh not charité, soothli
thei lette the fervour and the goostli felynge of charité.

2342 **sopeer**, supper. 2343 **praied**, invited. 2344 **toun**, farm. 2345 **yokkes**, yokes; **yeede**,
went. 2346 **assaie hem**, try them out. 2367 **lette**, obstruct.

Chapter Eighty-three

Hou an ankir schal have hir to hem that comen to hir.

But now seist thou that thou mai not kepe thee from heerynge of vanytees, for divers
2370 worldli men and othere that comen ofte tyme for to speke with thee, and telle thee
sumtyme talis of vanité. As unto this y seie thus, that comenynge with thyn evene
Cristene is not moche agens thee, but helpith thee sumtyme yif thou worche visili. For
thou mai assaie therbi the mesure of thi charité to thyn evene Cristene, whethir hit be
moche or litil. Thou art bounden, as eche man or woman is, to love thyn evene Cristene
2375 principali in thyn herte, and also in deede for to schewe hym tokenes of charité as
resoun asketh, up thi myght and up thi knowing.

Now syn it is so that thou owest not to goo oute of thyn hous for to seche occasioun
how thou myght profite thyn evene Cristene bi deedis of merci, for thou art inclose,
neverethelees thou art bounden for to love hem alle in thyn herte, and to hem that
2380 comen to thee for to schewe hem tokenes of love sothfastli. And therfore whoso wole
speke with thee, what that he be, or in what degree that he be, and thou knowe not what
he is, ne whi that he cometh, be soone redi with a good wille for to wite what his wille
is. Be not daungerous, ne suffre him stonde longe for to abide thee, but loke hou redi
and hou glaad thou wolde be yif an angel of hevene wolde come and speke with thee.
2385 Soo redi and so buxum be thou in wille for to speke with thyn even Cristene whanne he
cometh to thee. For thou wost not what he is, ne what he wolde, ne what nede he hath
to thee, ne thou of hym, til thou have assaied hym.

And though thou be in preiere or in devocioun, that thee thenketh looth for to breeke
of, for thee thenketh thou schuldest not leve God for mannys speche, me thenketh it is
2390 not so in this caas; for yif thou be wise, thou schal not leve God, but thou schal fynde
Hym and have Hym and see Him in thyn evene Cristene as wel as in praiere. Yif thou
coude wel love thyn evene Cristene, but schulde not hyndre thee for to speke with hem
discretli. Discrecioun schalt thou have upoun this manere as me thenketh. Whoso cometh
to thee, aske hym mekeli what he wole; and yif he come to telle his disese and to be

2368 **have hir**, conduct herself. 2372 **visili**, wisely. 2376 **up thi myght**, according to your
ability; **up thi knowing**, according to your knowledge. 2377 **syn**, since; **seche**, seek. 2383
daungerous, standoffish. 2385 **buxum**, obedient. 2389 **of**, off. 2394 **disese**, distress.

2395 comfortid of thi speche, heere him glaadli, and suffre him to seie what he wole for ese
of his owen herte. And whanne he hath doon, comforte hym goodli and charitabli, and
sone breke of. And thanne aftir, yif he wole falle into idel tales or vanytees, or of othere
mennys deedis, ansuere hym not but litil, ne feede not his speche; and he schal soone be
irke and sone take his leve.

2400   Yif it be anothir man that cometh to knowe thee, as a man of Holi Chirche, heere hym
loweli with reverence for his ordre, and yif his speche comforte thee, aske of hym,
and make thee not for to teche hym. For it falleth not to thee for to teche a preest, but
in nede. Yif his speche comforte thee not, answere but litil, and he wole soone goo his
wai. Yif it be anothir man that cometh for to gyve his almasse or ellis for to heere thee
2405 speke, or for to be knowen of thee, speke mekeli and goodli to him withal. Repreve no
man of his defautis; it falleth not to thee, but yif he be the more hoomli with thee, that
thou wite wel that he wole not take it agreef. And schorteli for to seie, as moche as thou
conceyvest that schulde profite thyn evene Cristene goostli, mai thou seie yif thou can
and he wil take it. And of alle thynges kepe silence as moche as thou mai, and thou schal
2410 have litil prees in schort tyme that schal lette thee. Thus thenketh me; doo betere yif
thou mai.

Chapter Eighty-four

Of the myrke image of synne and of the clothinge therof.

Bi this that y have seide mai thou see a litil the myrkenesse of this ymage; nought for y
have discreyed it to thee for fulli as it is, can y not. Neverthelees bi this litil mai thou see
2415 the more yif thou loke weel. But now seist thou: "Wherbi knowest thou that I bere siche
an ymage aboute with me as thou spekest of?" As unto this I answere: y mai take upoun
me a word of the prophete, and is this: *Inveni idolum michi* (Hosea 12:8) This is thus
mykil to seie, I have founden a fals ymage, that men calle a mawmet, in mysilf, wel
foule disfigured and forschapen with wrecchidnesse of alle thise synnes whiche I have
2420 spoken of, bi the whiche I am cast doun into many wrecchidnessis more thanne y can

2398 ansuere, answer. **2402 teche**, teach. **2404 almasse**, alms. **2406 hoomli**, familiar. **2407 agreef**, amiss. **2410 prees**, crowd. **2418 mawmet**, idol; from Mohammed, associated by medieval Christians with idolatry. **2419 forschapen**, deformed.

or mai seie; that me thenketh yvel fore and repente and crie merci. Bi this wrecchidnesse that y feele in mysilf, moche more than I have seide, mai I the betere telle thee of thyne image. For alle comen we of Adam and of Eve, cloothid with clothis of a beestis hide, as Hooli Writt seith of oure Lord thus: *Fecit dominus Ade et uxori eius tunicas pelliceas* (Genesis 3:21). Oure Lord maade to Adam and to his wif clothis of a beestis hide, in tokene that for synne he was forschapen like to a beest; with whiche beestli clothis we alle aren born, and umbilapped and disfigured from oure kyndeli schaap.

2425

Chapter Eighty-five

Whiche aren the lymes of the ymage of synne.

Thanne is this an uggli ymage for to loke upon. The heed is pride, for pride is principal and the firste synne, as the wise man seith: *Inicium omnis peccati superbia* (Ecclesiasticus 10:15). The bigynnynge of al maner synne is pride. The baak and the hyndre part of it is coveitise, as Seynt Poul seith: *Que retro sunt obliviscens, in anteriora me extendam* (Philippians 3:13). I schal forgete alle wordli thynges whiche aren bakward, and I schal strike me forward to endelees thynges. The brest, in whiche is the herte, is envie, for it is noo fleischli synne, but it is a develis synne, as the wise man seith: *Invidia diaboli mors intravit in orbem terrarum. Imitantur illum omnes qui ex parte eius sunt* (Wisdom 2:24–25). Bi envie of the devil deeth com into al the world; forthi al thoo that aren of his part folwen hym thereinne. The armes of it aren wraththe, in as moche as a man wreketh hym with his armes of his wraththe, agens Cristis forbedynge in the Gospel: *Si quis percusserit te in unam maxillam, prebe sibi et alteram* (Matthew 5:39). Yif a man smyte thee upon the ton cheke with his hond, thou schalt not smyte hym agen, but offre hym that othir cheke. The beli of this image is glotonye, as Seynt Poul seith: *Esca ventri, et venter escis; deus hunc et has destruet* (1 Corinthians 6:13). Mete serveth to the beli, and the beli serveth for to gete mete; but God schal distroie bothe the beli and the mete. That schal be in the laste ende, in the fulle reformynge of chosene, and in the demynge of the reproved. The membris of hit aren leccherie, of the whiche Seynt Poul seith thus: *Non exhibeatis membra vestra arma iniquitatis ad peccatum* (Romans 6:13). Yee schullen not gyve youre membres, speciali youre pryvé membres, to be armes to

2430

2435

2440

2445

2427 umbilapped, surrounded; **kyndeli**, natural. **2439 wreketh**, avenges. **2441 ton**, one.

synne. The feet of this ymage aren accidie, and therfore the wise man seith to the slowe
2450 for to stire him to goode werkis thus: *Discurre, festina, suscita amicum tuum* (Proverbs
6:3). That is to seie, renne quykli aboute to good werkes, and haste thee swithe, for the
tyme passeth; and reise up thi freend, whiche is Jhesu, bi devoute praier and meditacioun.

Chapter Eighty-six

Whereof the image of Jhesu is maad, and the ymage of synne and hou we aren passynge
forth by the image of synne.

2455 This is not the ymage of Jhesu, but it is likere an image of the devyl; for the ymage of
Jhesu is maad of vertues with mekenesse, parfite love, and charité. But this ymage is of
fals fleschli luste to thisilf, with alle thise membris festned therto. This ymage berist
thou aboute, and eche man, what that he be, until bi the grace of Jhesu it be sumdel
destroied and broken doun. Thus it semeth that David seith in the sautier: *Verumptamen*
2460 *in ymagine pertransit homo; sed et frustra conturbatur* (Psalms 38:7). This is for to
seie, though it so were that a man were maad in the bigynnynge to the ymage of God,
stable and stidefast, neveretheles bicause of synne he firste passith lyvynge in this
world, in this image of synne, bi the whiche he is unstable and trobiled in veyn. Also
Seynt Poule speketh of this ymage thus: *Sicut portavimus ymaginem terreni hominis, sic*
2465 *portemus ymaginem celestis hominis* (1 Corinthians 15:49). That is to seie, yif we wolen
come to the love of God, as we have bore bifore the ymage of the ertheli man, that is of
the first Adam, that is this ymage of synne, right so now that we myght bere the ymage
of the heveneli man Jhesu, whiche is the image of vertues.

What schalt thou thanne doo with this ymage of synne? Unto this I answere thee bi
2470 the word that the Jewes seiden to Pilat of Crist: *Tolle, tolle, crucifige eum!* (John
19:15). Take this bodi of synne and doo hym on the Cros, that is for to seie, breke doun
this image and slee the fals love of synne in thisilf. As Cristis bodi was slayn for oure
trespace, right so thee bihoveth, yif thou wole be like to Crist, slee thi bodili feelynge
and fleschli luste in thisilf. Thus seid Seynt Poul: *Qui autem Christi sunt, carnem suam*
2475 *crucifixerunt cum viciis et concupiscenciis* (Galatians 5:24). Ye that aren Cristis folweres

2449 accidie, sloth. **2451 swithe**, greatly. **2455 likere**, more similar to. **2458 sumdel**, somewhat. **2459 sautier**, psalter. **2471 doo**, put.

have crucified and slayn here fleisch, that is the image of synne, with alle the lustis and the unskilful likynges of it.

Slee thanne and breke doun pride and sette up mekenesse; also breke doun ire and envie and reise up love and charité to thyn even Cristene; also in stide of coveitise,
2480 poverté in spirite; in stide of accidie, fervour of devocioun with a glaad redynesse to alle good deedes; and in stide of glotonye and leccherie, sobirté and chastité in bodi and in soule. Thus counceileth Seynt Poul whanne he seid thus: *Deponentes veterem hominem cum suis actibus, qui corrumpitur secundum desideria erroris; et induite novum hominem, qui secundum deum creatus est in sanctitate et iusticia* (Ephesians 4:22, 24). Ye
2485 schal put doun the olde man, that is the ymage of the olde Adam with alle his membris, for he is roten in desires of errour, and ye schal schape you and clothe you in a newe man, whiche is the ymage of God, bi holynesse and rightwisenesse and fulheed of vertues. Who schal helpe thee to breke doun this ymage? Sothli thi Lorde Jhesu. In the vertue and in the name of Hym schal thou breke doun the mawmet of synne. Prai Hym
2490 bisili, and desire, and He schal helpe thee.

Chapter Eighty-seven

What profite cometh of the kepynge of the herte, and hou moche the soule is.

Gadere thanne thyn herte togidre and doo aftir the conceile of the wise man, whanne he seith thus: *Omni custodia serva cor tuum, quoniam ex ipso procedit vita* (Proverbs 4:23). With al thi bisinesse kepe thyn herte, for out of it cometh liyf; and that is soth
2495 whanne it is wel kepid, for thanne wise thoughtes, clene affeccions, and brennynge desires of vertues and of charité and of the blisse of hevene comen oute of it, and maketh the soule for to lyve a blissid lif. Also upoun the contrarie wise, yif it be not wel kepid, thanne as oure Lord seith in the Gospel: *De corde exeunt cogitaciones male, que coinquinant hominem* (Matthew 15:19–20). Badde thoughtes and unclene affeccions
2500 comen oute of the herte, the whiche filen a man, as oure Lord seith. Thei owthere bynemen the liyf of the soule bi deedli synne, or ellis thei feble the soule and maketh it seek, yef thei ben venial. For what is a man but hise thoughtes and his loves? Thise

2479 **stide**, place. 2481 **sobirté**, soberness. 2489 **mawmet**, idol. 2500 **filen**, defile. 2501 **bynemen**, destroy; **feble**, enfeeble. 2502 **seek**, sick.

maken a man oonli good or badde. As moche as thou lovest thi God and thyn even Cristene and knowest Hym, so moche is thi soule; and if thou litil love Hym, litil is thi

2505 soule; and yif thou nought love Hym, nout is thi soule. It is nought as for good, but it is moche as for synne. And yif thou wolt wite what thou lovest, loke whereupoun thou thenkest; for where thi love is, there is thyne iye; and where thy likynge is, there is most thyn herte thynkynge. Yif thou moche love God, thee liketh to thenke moche upon Hym. Rule wel thi thoughtes and thyne affeccions, and thanne art thou vertuous.

Chapter Eighty-eight

2510 Hou the ymage of synne schal be broken doun.

Bigyn thanne on, and breke this image. Whanne thou hast inwardli bithought thee of thisilf and of thi wrecchidnesse as I have seid — how proud, hou veyn, how envious, how malicious, how covetous, and how fleischli and how ful of corrupcioun; also of how litil knowynge, felynge, or savour thou hast in God; how wise, how quyk, and

2515 how moche savour thou hast in ertheli thynges; and schorteli that thee thenketh thee as ful of synne as the hide is ful of fleisch — be thou not adreed to moche, yif thee thenketh so of thisilf. And whanne thou hast don thus, lift up thi desire and thyn herte to thi Lord Jhesu Crist, and prey Hym of helpe. Crie to Him bi greet desire and sighynges, that He wole helpe thee to breke the charge of this veyn image, or elles that He wole

2520 breke it. Thenke also that sich a schame it is to thee to be feed with swynes mete of fleischli savouris, that schuldest feele a goostli savour of heveneli joie. Yif thou doo thus, thanne bigynnest thou for to arise agen the hool ground of synne in thee; and it mai so be that thou schal feele peyne and sorwe, for thou schalt undirstonde that there mai no soule lyve withoute greet peyne, but he have reste and delite in his creatour or in his

2525 creaturis.

Thanne whanne thou arisest agens thisilf bi a fervent disire to feele of thi Lord Jhesu, and for to drawe thi love from al bodili thinge, in so moche that thou art encombred of thisilf and thee thenketh that alle cratures risen agen thee and alle thynge whiche thou hadde delite in bifore turneth thee to peyne; and whanne thou forsakest thus thisilf and

2507 for where thi love is, there is thyne iye, Proverbial. See Whiting, L558. **2519 charge**, burden. **2528 cratures**, creatures.

2530 thou mai fynde no confort in God: nedelynges thi soule schal suffre peyne. Nevertheles, I hope whoso wolde suffre this peyne awhile, stidefastli clevynge upon that desire that he wolde have not but his Lord Jhesu, and falle not lightli therfro ne seeke no confort outward for a tyme, for it lasteth not longe, oure Lord is neer and soone schal eese thyn herte. For He wole helpe thee to bere thi bodi ful of corrupcioun, and He wole breke

2535 doun this image of love in thisilf; not al at oonys but litil and litil, til thou be sumdel reformed to His liknesse.

Chapter Eighty-nine

How a man schal have hym agens stirynges of pride and of alle othere vices.

Aftir sich an hool risynge agen thisilf, whanne it is passid thou schal the more sobirli and more esili rule thisilf and sette thee more saadli for to kepe thisilf and thi thoughtes

2540 in thyne affecciouns, for to knowe hem whethir thei ben good or badde. Thanne yif thou feele a stirynge of pride, or ony othir spice of it, be soone waar yif thou mai, and suffre hit not lightli passe awai, but take in thi mynde and rende it, breke it and dispice it, and doo al the schame that thou mai therto. Loke that thou spare it not, ne trowe it not, speke he nevere so faire, for it is fals though it seme sooth, as the prophete seith:

2545 *Popule meus, qui beatum te dicunt ipsi te decipiunt, et in errorem te ducunt* (Isaiah 3:12). This is to saie thus: Thou man of my peple, thei that seyn thou art blissid and holi, thei bigile thee and brynge thee into errour. And yif thou doo ofte thus bisili, thou schalt bi grace of Jhesu withinne schort tyme stoppe moche of the spryng of pride and moche abate the veyn delite therof, that thou schal unnethis fele it. And whanne thou felest it,

2550 it schal be so weyke, and as it were neerhande deed, that it schal not moche deere thee. And thanne schalt thou mow have a goostli sight of mekenesse, hou good and hou faire it is, and thou schalt desire it and love it for the goodnesse of itsilf, that thee schal like for to biholde as thou art, and yif nede be for to suffre gladli dispite and reprof for the love of rightwisenesse. Upon the self maner whanne thou feelist stirynges of ire, and

2555 malicious risynge of herte, or overmoche yvel wil agens thyn even Cristene for ony

2530 nedelynges, of necessity. **2541 spice**, species; **waar**, aware. **2542 lightli**, easily. **2547 bisili**, diligently. **2549 unnethis**, scarcely. **2550 neerhande**, almost. **2551 mow**, be able to. **2554 self**, same.

maner of cause, though it seme resonable and for charité, bewaar of it and be redi with thi thought for to refreyne it, that hit turne not into fleschli appetite. Agenstonde it, and folwe hit not neither in word ne in deede, as moche as thou mai, but as he riseth smyte him doun agen; and so schalt thou slee it with the swerd of drede of God, that it schal

2560 not dere thee. For wite thou wel in alle thise stirynges of pride, envie, veynglorie, or ony othir, that as sone that thou perceyvest it, and with displesynge of thi wille and of thi resoun thou agenstondist it, thou sleest it, though it so be that it cleve stille upon thyn herte agens thi wille, and wole not lightli passe awai. Drede it not; for it letteth thi soule from pees, but it defouleth not thi soule. Right so upon the same wise schalt thou doo

2565 agens alle yvele stirynges of covetise, accidie, glotonye, and leccherie, that thou schal be ay redi with thy reson and with thi wille for to reprove hem and despice hem.

Chapter Ninety

What thynge helpith most a mannys knowynge, and geteth him that hym wanteth, and distroieth synne in hym.

And thanne mai thou doo the more redili and betere, yif thou be besi for to sette thyn

2570 herte most upon oon thyng. And that thyng is not ellis but a gosteli desire to God for to love Him, for to knowe Hym, for to see Hym, for to have Him heer bi grace in a litil felynge, and in the blisse of hevene a ful beynge. This desire, yif thou kepe, it schal wele telle thee whiche is synne and whiche is noon, and whiche is good and whiche is bettere good. And if thou wilt festyn thi thought therto, it schal teche thee al that thee nedeth,

2575 and it schal gete thee al that thee wanteth. And therfore, whanne thou schal arise agens the ground of synne in general, or ellis agens ony special synne, hange faste upon this desire and sette the poynt of thi thought more upon God whom thou desirest thanne upon the synne whiche thou reprovest; for yif thou doo so, thanne feighteth God for thee and He schal destroie the synne in thee. Thou schalt moche sonnere come to thi

2580 purpos yif thou soo doo thanne yif thou lose this felynge and this meke desire to God principali, and wole sette thyn herte oonli agen stirynge of synne, as thou woldest destroie it by maistrie of thisilf. Thou schalt nevere brynge it so aboute.

2557 **Agenstonde**, Resist. 2561 **displesynge**, disapproval. 2572 **beynge**, being. 2579 **sonnere**, sooner. 2582 **maistrie**, power.

Chapter Ninety-one

Hou a man schal be schapen to the image of Jhesu, and Jhesu schapen in hym.

But doo as I have seid, and betere yif thou may, and I hope bi grace of Jhesu thou schal
2585 make the devel aschamed, and alle sich wickid stirynges thou schalt breke adoune, that
thei schal not moche dere thee. And upon this maner wise mai this image of synne be
broken doun and destroied in thee, bi the whiche thou art forschapen fro the kyndeli
schap of the ymage of Crist. And thanne schalt thou be schapin agen to the ymage of
Jhesu bi mekenesse and charité; and thanne schalt thou be ful schapen to the image of
2590 God, heere lyvynge bi a schadewe in contemplacion, and in the blis of hevene be ful
sothfastnesse.

Of this schapynge to the ful liknesse of Crist speketh Seynt Poul thus: *Filioli, quos*
iterum parturio, donec Christus formetur in vobis (Galatians 4:19). Mi dere children,
whiche y bere as a woman berith a child, unto Crist be agen schapen in you. Thou hast
2595 conceived Crist bi truthe, and He hath liyf in thee in as moche as thou hast a good wille
for to serve Hym and please Hym, but He is not yit ful schapen in thee, ne thou in Him
bi fulheed of charité. And therfore Seynt Poul baar me and thee and othere also with
traveile, as a woman bereth a child, unto the tyme that Crist hath His ful schap in us and
we in Hym.

2600 Whoso weneth for to come to the workyng and to the ful use of contemplacioun and
not bi this way, that is for to sai not bi fulheed of vertues, he cometh not in bi the dore,
and therfore as a theef he schal be caste out. I seie not but that a man bi gifte of God mai
have bi tymes a taastynge and a glymerynge of lif contemplatif, sum man in the
bigynnynge, but the saad feelynge of hit schal he not have. For Criste is the doore and
2605 porter, and withoute His leve and His lyveray mai there no man come in, as He seith
Hymsilf: *Nemo venit ad patrem nisi per me* (John 14:6). No man cometh to the Fadir but
bi Me. That is for to seie, no man mai come to the contemplacion of the Godheed but he
be first reformed bi fulhed of mekenesse and charitee to the liknesse of Jhesu in His
manhede.

2586 dere, harm. **2587 forschapen**, deformed; **kyndeli**, natural. **2589 schapen**, formed. **2590**
bi, by; **be**, by. **2604 saad**, serious. **2605 lyveray**, livery.

Chapter Ninety-two

2610 Hereinne is told the cause whi this writynge is maad, and hou sche schal have hire in the redynge that it was maad unto.

Lo, I have tolde thee a litil, as me thenketh, first of contemplacioun, what it is, and sithen of the weies that bi grace leden therto. Not for I have it in felynge and in worchynge as I have it in seiynge; nevertheles I wolde bi thise wordes, siche as thei aren, first stire 2615 myn owen necgligence for to doon betere than I have doon, and also my purpos is for to stire thee or ony othir man or woman that hath take the staat of contemplatif liyf for to traveile more bisili and more mekeli in that maner of lif bi siche simple wordes as God hath gyven me grace for to seie. And therfore yif ony word be thereinne that stireth or conforteth thyn herte more to the love of God, thanke God, for it is His gift and not of 2620 the word. And yif it conforteth thee nought, or ellis thou takest it not redeli, studie not to longe theraboute, but lei hit biside thee til anothir tyme, and gyve thee to praier or to othir occupacion. Take it as it wole come, and not al at onys.

Also thise wordes that I write, take hem not to streiteli, but there as thee thenketh bi good avysement that I speke to schorteli, oithir for lackynge of Ynglisch or wantynge 2625 of resoun, I prey thee mende it there nede is oonli. Also thise wordis that y write to thee longen not alle to oon man whiche hath actif lif, but to thee or to anothir whiche hath the staat of liyf comtemplatif.

The grace of oure Lord Jhesu Crist be with thee. Amen

2610 have hire, conduct herself. **2613 sithen**, afterwards; **worchynge**, doing. **2617 bisili**, diligently. **2623 streiteli**, strictly. **2624 oithir**, either.

The Scale of Perfection

Book II

Chapter One

This chapitle scheweth that a man is seid the image of God aftir the soule and not aftir
the bodi.

For as moche as thou coveitest greteli and askest it pur charité for to heere more of an
image the whiche y have bifore tymes in partie discried to thee, therfore I wole glaadli
5   with drede falle to thi desire; and helpynge the grace of oure Lord Jhesu Crist, in whom
I fulliche truste, y schal opene to thee a litil more of this image. And in the bigynnynge,
yif thou wole witen pleynli what I mene bi this image, I telle thee forsothe that y
undirstonde not ellis but thyn owen soule; for thi soule and my soule and everi resonable
soule is an image, and that a worthi image, for it is the ymage of God, as the apostel
10   seith: *Vir est ymago dei* (1 Corinthians 11:7). That is, man is the image of God and maad
to the image and to the liknesse of Him, not in bodili schap withoutin, but in the myghtes
of it withinne, as Holi Writ seith: *Formavit deus hominem ad similitudinem suam* (Genesis 1:27). That is, oure Lord God schoop in soule man to the ymage and the liknesse of
Him. This is the ymage that I have spoke of and schal speken of. This ymage, maad to
15   the liknesse of God in the first schapynge was wondirli faire and bright, fulle of brennynge
love and goostli light. But thorugh synne of the first man Adam it was disfigured and
forschapen into anothir liknesse, as y have bifore seid. For it fil from that gostli light and
that heveneli foode into that peynful myrkenesse and beestli lust of this wrecchid liyf,
exilid and flemed out fro the heritage of hevene that it schuld han had yif it hadde

1 **chapitle**, chapter; **seid**, said to be; **aftir**, according to. 3 **coveitest**, desire; **pur**, by. 4 **partie**,
part; **discried**, described. 5 **falle**, consent. 6 **fulliche**, completely. 7 **yif**, if; **wole**, will; **witen**,
know; **forsothe**, in truth. 11 **schap**, form; **myghtes**, powers. 13 **schoop**, formed. 15 **schapynge**,
forming; **wondirli**, wonderfully; **brennynge**, burning. 16 **goostli**, spiritual. 17 **forschapen**,
deformed. 18 **myrkenesse**, darkness. 19 **flemed**, driven; **han**, have.

20   stonden, into the wrecchidnesse of this erthe, and aftyrward into the prisoun of helle,
ther to have ben withouten eende. Fro the whiche prisoun to that heveneli heritage it
myght nevere have comen agen, but yif it hadde be reformed to the first schap and to
the first liknesse. But that reformynge myght not ben had by noon ertheli man, for
everiche man was in the sam meschief, and noon myght suffice to helpe hymsilf, and
25   so mykil lasse ony othir man. Therfore it nedide bi doon by Hym that is more thanne a
man, and that is oonli God; and that was skilful, that He schulde reforme and restoren
man to blisse yif he schulde be saaff, whiche of His eendeles goodnesse schoop him
thereto. Hou thanne hit myght be reformed, and hou it is reformed to the firste likenesse
bi Him that first formed it, bi the grace of God schal I telle thee, for that is the entente
30   of this writinge.

Chapter Two

Hou it nedide to mankynde that oonli thorugh the passioun of oure Lord it schulde be
restorid and reformed that was forsaken bi the first synne.

The rightwisenesse of God asketh that a trespaas doon be not forgyven but yif amendis
be maad for it, yif it mai be doon. Now is it sooth mankynde, that was hool in Adam the
35   first man, trespaced agens God so wondir grevousli whanne hit forfetide the special
biddynge of God and consentide to the fals conceile of the feend, that it deservide
rightwiseli for to have be departid from Him and dampned to helle withouten ende — so
fer forth, that stondinge the rightwisenesse of God, the trespaas myght not be forgeven
but yif amendis and ful satisfaccioun were first maad therfore. But this amendes myght
40   no man make that was man oonli and come out of Adam by kyndeli generacion, for this

20 stonden, stood. **24 sam meschief**, same misfortune. **25 mykil**, much; **nedide bi doon**, needed to be done. **26 skilful**, reasonable. **27 saaff**, saved; **schoop**, created. **31 schulde**, could. **33 rightwisenesse**, righteousness; **but yif**, unless. **34 sooth**, true; **hool**, whole. **35 agens**, against. **36 biddynge**, command; **conceile**, counsel; **feend**, i.e., devil (here and throughout). **37 rightwiseli**, justly; **departid**, separated. **37–38 so fer forth**, to the extent. **38 stondinge the rightwisenesse of God**, were the justice of God to stand. **39 but yif**, unless; **ful satisfaccioun**, the doctrine of the atonement in this chapter is based on Anselm, *Cur deus homo*, especially 1.20, 2.8–11; see Clark, p. 303n3. **40 kyndeli**, natural.

skile, for the trespas and the unworschipe was endeles gret, and therfore it passide mannys myght for to make amendis for it. And also for this skile: he that hath trespaced and schal make amendis, hym bihoveth gyve to hym that he trespacide unto al that he oweth though that he hadde not trespaced, and also over that, hym bihoveth gyve him

45   sumwhat that he oweth not, but oonli for that he trespacid. But oonly mankynde hadde not wherwith he myght paie God for his trespaas, over that he ought Hym. For what good dede that man myght doon in bodi or in soule, it was but his dette. For everi man oweth, as the Gospel seith, for to love God with al his herte and al his soule and alle his myghtes; and betere myght he not doo than this. And neverthelees this deede sufficed

50   not to the reformynge of mankynde, ne this myght not he doon but yif he hadde first be reformed. Than nedid it that yif mannys soule schulde be reformed and the trespaas maad good, that oure Lord God Hymsilf schulde reforme this image and make amendis for this trespaas, syn that no man myght. But that myght He not doo in His Godhede, for He myght not, ne ought not, make amendis bi suffrynge of peyne in His owen kynde.

55   Therfore it nedide that He schulde take the same mankynde that hadd trespaced, and bicome man; and that myght He not by the comon lawe of kyndeli generacion, for it was impossibile Goddis sone to be born of a touchid woman. Therfore He moste bicome man thorugh a gracious generacioun, bi wirkynge of the Holi Goost, of a clene gracious maiden, oure Ladi Seynt Marie. And so was it doon. For oure Lord Jhesu Crist, Goddis

60   sone, bicam man, and thorugh His precious deeth that He suffride made amendis to the Fadir of hevene for mannys gilt. And that myght He wel doon, for He was God, and He oughte not for Hymsilf, but for as mykil as He was man born of the same kynde that Adam was that first trespacede. And so, though He ought not for His owen persone, for Himsilf myght not synne, neverthelees He ought it of His free wille for the trespas of

65   mankynde, the whiche kynde He took for savacioun of man of His endeles merci. For sooth it is ther was nevere man that myght yelde to God onythinge of his owene that he ought not, but oonli this blissid man Jhesu Crist. For He myght paien thingis that He

41 **skile**, reason; **unworschipe**, dishonor; **passide**, surpassed. 42 **myght**, power; **skile**, reason. 43 **hym bihoveth gyve**, it is necessary for him to give. 44 **over**, beyond. 45 **sumwhat**, something; **but oonli**, only because. 46 **not**, nought; **ought**, owed. 48 **oweth**, is obliged. 50 **ne**, nor; **yif**, if. 51 **nedid it**, it was necessary. 53 **syn**, since. 54 **kynde**, nature. 56 **kyndeli**, natural. 57 **touchid**, touched (sexually). 58 **gracious**, through grace; **clene**, pure. 61 **mannys**, man's. 62 **oughte**, owed; **kynde**, nature. 65 **savacioun**, salvation. 66 **sooth**, truth. 67 **ought**, owed; **paien**, pay.

oughte not as for Himsilf, and that was not but o thynge: and that was for to gyve His preciouse liyf by wilfull takynge of deeth for love of sothfastnesse. This ought He nout.

70 As mykil good as He myght doo to the worschipe of God in His liyf, was al but dette. But for to take deeth for love of ryghtwisenesse, He was not bounden therto.

He was bounde to rightfulnesse, but He was not bounden to dyen. For deeth is oonli a peyne ordeyned of God to man for his owen synne; but oure Lorde Jhesu synned nevere, ne He myght not synnen, and therefore He oughte nought for to dien. And yit

75 wilfulli He diede, than paid He to God more thanne He oughte. And syn that was the beste manere deede and most worthi that evere was doon, therfor was it resonable that the synne of mankynde schulde be forgyven, in as mykil as mankynde had founden a man of the same kynde withoutin weem of synne, that is Jhesu, that myght make amendis for the trespaas doon and myght paien oure Lord God al that he oughte, and

80 overmore, that he oughte not. Thanne siththe oure Lord Jhesu, God and man, diede thus for savacion of mannys soule, it was rightful that synne schulde be forgyven and mannys soule, that was His image, schulde mow be reformyd and restorid to the first likenesse and to the blisse of hevene.

This passioun of oure Lord and this precious deeth is the ground of al the reformynge

85 of mannes soule, withouten whiche myght nevere mannys soule have be reformed to the liknes of Him, ne come to the blisse of hevene. But blissid mot He be in al His wirkynge. Now is it so, that thorugh vertu of His passioun the brennynge suerd of cherubyn that droof Adam ought of paradise is now put awei, and the eendeles gates of hevene aren opened to ilk man that wole entre in therto. For the persone of Jhesu is

90 bothe God and kynge, evene in blisse to the Fadir, and as man He is portour at the gate redi to receyve ilke a soule that wole be reformed heere in this liyf to His liknesse. For now mai ilke a soule, yif that he wole, be reformed to the liknesse of God, sith that the trespaas is forgeven and the amendis bee maad thorugh Jhesu for the first gilt. Neverethelees, though this be sooth, alle soules have not the profite ne the fruit of His

95 precious passioun, ne aren reformed to the liknes of Hym.

68 o, one. **69 liyf**, life; **sothfastnesse**, truth; **ought He nout**, owed He not. **70 worschipe**, honor. **73 peyne**, punishment. **74 oughte**, was obliged. **75 oughte**, owed; **syn**, since. **76 manere**, kind of. **77 mykil**, much. **78 weem**, blemish. **80 overmore**, moreover; **siththe**, since. **82 mow be**, be able to be. **86 mot**, may. **87 wirkynge**, working; **brennynge suerd**, burning sword. **88 droof**, drove; **ought**, out. **89 wole**, will. **90 evene**, equal. **91 ilke a**, each. **92 yif**, if; **sith**, since. **94 sooth**, true; **profite**, benefit.

Chapter Three

That Jewes and paynymes and also fals Cristene men are not reformed effectuali thorugh vertu of this passioun for here owen defaute.

Two maner of men aren not reformed bi vertu of His passioun. Oon is of hem that troweth it not; anothir is of hem that loven it not. Jewes and paynemes han not the
100   benefeetes of this passioun, for thei trowen it not. Jewes trowen not that Jhesu man, the sone of the Virgine Marie, is Goddis sone of hevene. Also paynemes trowen not that the sovereyn wisdom of God wolde bicome sone of man, and in manhede suffre the peynes of deeth. And therfore the Jewes holden the prechynge of the Croos of the passioun of Crist not but sclaundre and blasfemye, and the paynemys holden it but
105   fantom and folie. But trewe Cristen men holden it the sovereyne wisdom of God and His grete myght. Thus Seynt Poul seide: *Predicamus vobis Christum crucifixum, Iudeis quidem scandalum, gentibus autem stulticiam: ipsis autem vocatis Iudeis, atque Grecis, Christum dei virtutem* (1 Corinthians 1:23–24). That is: We prechen to you that we trowen, that Jhesu Crist crucified, the sone of Marie, is Goddis sone, sovereyne vertu
110   and wisdom of God. The whiche Jhesu to Jewes and to paynemys that trowen not in Hym is but sclaundre and folie. And therfore thise men bi there untrouthe putten hemsilf fro the reformynge of her owen soule, and stondynge there untrouthe, schullen thei never be saaf ne come to blisse of hevene. For sooth it is, fro the bigynnynge of the world unto the laste ende, was there nevere man saaf, ne schal be saaf, but yif he hadde
115   or have trouth general or special in Jhesu Crist, other comende or comen. For right as alle chosen soulis that weren bifore the incarnacioun undir the Eelde Testament hadden trouthe in Crist, that He schulde come and reforme mannys soule, eithir openli, as patriarkes and prophetes and othire holi men hadden, or elles priveli and generali, as children and othere simple and imperfight soulis hadden that knowen not speciali the
120   pryvetees of the incarnacioun, right so alle the chosen soulis undir the Newe Testament

96 **paynymes**, pagans. 97 **here**, their; **defaute**, fault. 99 **troweth**, believes; **paynemes**, pagans. 100 **benefeetes**, benefits. 104 **sclaundre**, scandal. 105 **fantom**, phantom; **folie**, folly. 109 **trowen**, believe. 111 **untrouthe**, unbelief. 112 **fro**, from; **her**, their; **stondynge there untrouthe**, their unbelief continuing. 113 **saaf**, saved; **sooth**, true. 114 **but yif**, unless. 115 **comende**, coming; **comen**, having come. 116 **Eelde**, Old. 117 **trouthe**, belief. 118 **priveli**, secretly. 119 **imperfight**, imperfect. 120 **pryvetees**, mysteries.

han trowed in Crist that He is comen, oithir openli and felyngeli, as gosteli men and wise men han, or ellis generali, as children that dien cristened and othere symple and lewed soulis han that aren norischid in the bosom of Holi Chirche. Syn this is sooth, thanne thynketh me that thise men gretli and grevousli erren that seyn that Jewis and Sarcenys
125 and paynemes, bi kepynge of hire owen lawe, mown be maad saaf, though thei trowen not in Jhesu Crist as Holi Chirche troweth and as Cristen men doon, in as mykil as thei wene that her owen trouth is good and siker and sufficient to here savacion, and in that trouthe thei doon, as hit semeth, many good deedes of rightwisenesse, and peraventure yif thei knewen that Cristen feith were betere than here is, thei wolde take it and leve
130 here owen, that thei therfore schulde be saaf. Nai, it is not ynowgh so. For Crist, God and man, is bothe wei and eende, and He is mediatour atwix God and man, and withouten Him mai no soule be reconsiled ne come to blisse of hevene. And therfore thei that trowen in Hym that He is not bothe God and man mowen nevere be saaf ne come to blisse. Othere men also, that loven not Crist ne His passioun, aren not reformed in hire
135 soule to the liknesse of Hym; and thise men aren fals Cristen men, the whiche are out of charité and leven and dien in deedli synne. Thise men trowen wel, as it semeth, that Jhesu is Goddis sone, and that His passioun sufficeth to savacioun of mannys soule, and thei trowen also alle the articles of the feith, but it is an unschapli trouthe, and a deed, for thei loven Him nought, ne thei chese not the fruit of His passioun, but thei
140 liggen stille in here synne, and in here fals love of this world unto here laste eende. And so be thei not reformed to the liknes of God, but goon to peynes of helle eendelesli, as Jewes and Sarcenes doon, and into mykil more pyne thanne thei, in as mykil as thei

121 han trowed, have believed; **felyngeli**, in feeling; **gosteli**, spiritual. **122 han**, have; **lewed**, ignorant. **124 thynketh me**, it seems to me; **Sarcenys**, Saracens. **125 mown be**, are able to be. **126 mykil**, much. **127 wene**, suppose; **siker**, certain. **128 rightwisenesse**, righteousness; **peraventure**, perhaps. **129 here**, theirs. **130 schulde be saaf**, the salvation of the heathen was a topic of lively interest in the later Middle Ages; for Langland's more generous view, see *Piers Plowman*, B.11.62–69; Cindy L. Vitto, *The Virtuous Pagan in Middle English Literature*; George H. Russell, "The Salvation of the Heathen: The Exploration of a Theme in *Piers Plowman*," *Journal of the Warburg and Courtauld Institutes,* 29 (1966), 101–16; and Clark, pp. 303–04 (nns 7 and 8); **ynowgh**, enough. **131 atwix**, between. **133 mowen**, can. **136 leven**, live. **138 unschapli**, misshapen. **139 nought**, not. **140 liggen stille**, lie constantly. **142 pyne**, pain.

hadden the trouthe and kepte it not; for that was more trespace than yif thei nevere
hadde had it.

145   Thanne yif thou wolt wite whiche soules aren reformede heere in this liyf to the image
of God thorugh vertu of His passioun, sothli oonli tho that trowen in Him and loven
Hym. In the whiche soulis the ymage of God, that was thorugh synne forschapen as it
were into a foule beestis liknesse, is restored and reformed unto the first schap, and into
the worthynesse and worschipe that hit hadde in the bigynnynge, withoutin whiche
150   reformyng in feith schal nevere soule be saaf ne come to blisse.

Chapter Four

Of two maner reformynge of this image, oon in fulnesse and othir in partie.

Now, seist thou, "Hou mai this be sooth that the image of God, the whiche is mannys
soule, myghte be reformed here in this liyf to His liknesse in ony creature?" It semeth
nai, it myght not ben. For if it were reformed, thanne schulde hit have stable mynde,
155   cleer sight, and clene brennynge love in God and in goostli thinges ai lastandli, as it had
in the bigynnynge. But that is in no creature, as thou trowest, lyvynge in this liyf. For as
agentis thisilf, thou canst wel sai thou thenkest thee ful feer therefroo. Thi mynde and
thi resoun, and the love of thy soule aren so mykil sette in bihaldynge and in the love of
ertheli thynges, that of goostli thinges thou felist right litil. Thou feelist no reformynge in
160   thisilf, but art soo umbilapped with this blak image of synne, for aught that thou maist
doon, that upon what side thou turnest thee thou feelist thisilf defouled and spotted with
fleischli stirynges of this foule ymage. Othir chaungynge feelist thou noon fro fleischliheed
into goostlinesse, neither in the privei myghtis of thi soule withinne, ne in bodili feelynge
withoute. Wherfore thou thenkest that it myght not be that this image myght be re-
165   formed; or ellis yif it myght be reformed, thanne askest thou hou it myght be reformed.
    To this y answere and seie thus. There is two maner of reformynge of the ymage of
God, the whiche is mannys soule. Oon is in fulnesse, anothir is in partie. Reformynge in

145 wite, know. **147 forschapen**, deformed. **153 ony**, any. **155 brennynge**, burning; **goostli**,
spiritual; **ai lastandli**, everlastingly. **157 agentis**, concerning; **feer**, far. **158 bihaldynge**, be-
holding. **160 umbilapped**, surrounded. **162 fleischliheed**, state of being fleshly. **163
goostlinesse**, state of being spiritual; **privei**, secret. **167 partie**, part.

fulnes mai not be had in this lif, but it is delaied aftir this lif to the blisse of hevene, where mannys soule schal fulli be reformed; not to that staat that it hadde atte the firste
170 bigynnynge bi kynde, or myght have hadde thorugh grace yif it hadde stonde hool, but it schal be restored to mykil more blisse and mykil more highere joie thorugh the mykil merci and eendeles goodnesse of God thanne it schulde have had yif it nevere had fallen. For thanne schal the soule resseyven the hoole and the fulfillyng of God in alle myghtis of it, withouten medlere of ony othir affeccioun; and it schal seen mankynde in
175 the persoone of Jhesu above the kynde of angelis ooned to the Godhede. For than schal Jhesu, bothe God and man, ben al in al, and oonli He and noon othir thanne He, as the prophete seith: *Dominus solus exaltabitur in die illa* (Isaiah 2:11). That is, oure Lord Jhesu in that dai that is the ai lastande dai schal be highed oonli, and noon but He. And also the bodi of man schal thanne be glorified, for it schal receyve fulli the riche dowarie
180 of undeedlinesse with al that longeth therto. This schal a soule han with the bodi, and mykil more thanne I can seyn; but that schal ben in the blisse of hevene, and not in this lif.

For though it be soo that the passioun of oure Lord bi cause of this ful reformynge of mannys soule, neverthelees it was not His wille for to graunte this ful reformynge anoon aftir His passioun to alle chosen soulis that were lyvande in tyme of His passioun,
185 but He delaied it unto the laste day, and for this skile. Sooth it is that oure Lord Jhesu of His merci hath ordayned a certayn nombre of soulis to savacion, the whiche nombre was not fulfilled in tyme of His passioun, and therfore hit nedide that bi the lengthe of tyme thorugh kyndeli generacion of men it schulde be fulfilled. Thanne yif it hadde so ben that as tite aftir the deeth of oure Lord, everi soule that wolde have trowed in Hym
190 schulde anoon sodeynli have ben blissid and be ful reformed withoutyn ony othir abidynge, there wolde noo creature that lyvede thanne that he ne wolde have resseyved the feith, for to have ben maad blissid. And thanne schulde generacioun have ceesid, and so schuld wee that been now lyvynge, chosen soules, and othere soulis that comen aftir us, not have ben born, and so schulde oure Lord have failid of his noumbre.

170 **stonde hool**, stood whole. 173 **resseyven**, receive. 174 **myghtis**, powers; **medlere**, mingling. 175 **kynde**, nature. 176 **ben**, be. 178 **ai lastande**, everlasting; **highed**, exalted. 179 **dowarie**, dowry. 180 **undeedlinesse**, immortality; **longeth**, belongs. 182 **bi cause**, because. 184 **anoon**, at once; **lyvande**, living. 185 **skile**, reason. 187 **hit nedide**, it was necessary. 188 **kyndeli**, natural; **it schulde be fulfilled**, the doctrine of the chosen in these paragraphs is based on Anselm, *De concordia*, q. 3, c. 9; see Clark, p. 304n13. 189 **as tite**, immediately. 190 **abidynge**, waiting. 191 **resseyved**, received.

195   But that may not ben. And therfore oure Lord purveyede for us mykel betere, in that that He delaiede the ful reformynge of mannys soule unto the laste eende, as Seynt Poule seith: *Deo pro nobis melius providente, ne sine nobis consummarentur* (Hebrews 11:40). That is, oure Lord purveied betere for us in delaiynge of the ful reformynge thanne yif He hadde grauntid it thanne, for this skile: that the chosen soules heere bifore schulden
200   not maken an ende withoutin us that comen aftir. And anothir skile is this: for syn that a man in his first formyng of God was sette in his free wil and hadde free chesynge whethir he wolde have fulli God or noon, it was therfore resonable that syn that he wolde not chese God thanne, but wrecchidli fle from Hym, yif he schulde aftirward be reformed, that he schulde be sette ageyn in the same free cheesynge that he was first inne, wethir he wolde
205   have the profite of his reformynge or noo. And this mai be a skile why mannys soule was not fulli reformed anoon aftir the passioun of oure Lord Jhesu Crist.

Chapter Five

That the reformyng in partie is on two maneres. Oon in feyth, anothir in feith and in felynge.

Anothir reformynge of this image is in partie, and this reformynge mai be had in this lyf;
210   and but yif it be had in this liyf, it schal nevere be had, ne the soule schal nevere be saaf. But this reformyng is on two maneres. Oon is in feith oonli, anothir is in feith and in felynge. The firste, that is the reformyng in feith, sufficeth to savacioun; the secunde is worthi to have passande mede in the blisse of hevene. The firste mai be had lightli and in schort tyme. The secunde mai not soo, but thorugh lengthe of tyme and mykil gosteli
215   traveile. The firste mai be had with the feelynge of the ymage of synne, for though a man fele nothynge in himsilf but alle stirynges of synne and fleischli desires, yit he mai, not withstondynge al that felynge, yif he wilfulli assente not therto, ben reformed in feith to the liknesse of God. But the secunde reformynge putteth out the likynge and the feelynge of fleischli stirynges and worldly desires, and suffreth noon sich spottis abiden
220   in this image. The firste reformynge is oonli of bigynnynge and profitynge soulis, and of

195 **purveyede**, provided. 199 **skile**, reason. 201 **chesynge**, choosing. 203 **fle**, flee. 206 **anoon**, immediately. 209 **partie**, part. 210 **saaf**, saved. 213 **passande mede**, surpassing reward. 220 **profitynge**, proficient.

actif men. The secunde is of perfight soulis and of contemplatif men. For bi the firste reformynge the ymage of synne is not distroied, but it is left as it were al hool in felynge. But the secunde reformynge destroieth olde feelynges of this image of synne, and bringeth into the soule newe gracious feelynges thorugh wirkynge of the Holi Gost. The

225 first is good, and the secunde is betere, but the thridde, that is in the blisse of hevene, that is alderbest. First bigynne we to speken of that toon and siththen of the tothir, and so schul we comen to the thridde.

Chapter Six

That thorugh the sacrament of baptym that is groundid in the passioun of Crist this image is reformed fro the original synne.

230 Two maner of synne maken a soule to lese the schap and the liknesse of God. That oon is callid original, that is the first synne. That othir is callid actuel synne, that is wilfulli doon. Thise two synnes putten a soule fro the blisse of hevene and dampnen it to the eendeles pyne of helle, but yif it be thorugh grace of God reformed to His liknesse, or it passe hens out of this lif. Neveretheles, two remedies there aren agens thise two synnes,

235 bi the whiche a forschapen soule mai be restored ageyn. Oon is the sacrament of baptym agens the origynal synne; anothir is the sacrament of penaunce agens the actuel synne. The soule of a childe that is born and is uncristened, bicause of the origynal synne hath no liknesse of God; he is not but an image of the feend and a brond of helle. But as soone as it is cristened, it is reformed to the ymage of God, and thorugh vertu of feith of Holi

240 Chirche sodeynli is turned fro the liknes of the feend and maad like to an angel of hevene. Also the same falleth to a Jewe or in a Sarceyn, whiche or thei be cristened aren not but manciples of helle, but whanne thei forsaken ther errour and fallen mekeli

221 actif, active; **perfight**, perfect. **226 alderbest**, best of all; **toon**, one; **tothir**, other. **227 the thridde**, the threefold division of stages of the spiritual life as *bigynnynge, profitynge, perfight* ("beginning, proficient, perfect") is conventional; see Gregory, *Moralia*, 24.11.28 (Clark, p. 304n17). **228 baptym**, baptism. **231 actuel**, actual, i.e., sins actively committed, as opposed to inherited original sin. **233 pyne**, pain; **or**, before. **235 forschapen**, deformed; **baptym**, baptism. **238 brond**, firebrand. **241 falleth**, happens; **or$_2$**, before. **242 manciples**, stewards; **ther**, their (see Textual Notes).

245 to the trouthe in Crist, and receyven the baptym of water in the Holi Goost, soothli withouten ony taryyinge thei aren reformed to the liknesse of God — so fulli, as Hooli Chirche troweth, that yif thei myghten as swithe aftir baptym passen ought of this world, thei schulden streite fleen to hevene withoutyn ony more lettynge, hadde thei doo nevere so moche synne bifore in tyme of here untrouthe, and nevere schulde thei feele of the peyne of helle ne of purgatorie. And that pryvylege schulen thei have bi the merite of the passioun of Crist.

Chapter Seven

250 That thorugh the sacrament of penaunce that stondeth in contricion and in confessioun and in satisfaccioun this image is reformed fro actuel synne.

Also what Cristen man or woman that hath loste the liknesse of God thorugh deedli synne, brekynge Goddis comaundementis, yif he thorugh the touchynge of grace soothfastli forsake his synne with sorwe and contricioun of herte, and be in ful wil for

255 to amende hym and turne hym to God and to good lyvynge, and in this wil he receyveth the sacrament of penaunce, yif that he mai, or ellis yif that he may not, he is in ful wille therto — sotheli y seie that this mannys soule or womannys, that was forschapen first to the liknesse of the devel thorugh deedli synne, is now bi the sacrament of penaunce restored and schapen ageyn to the image of oure Lord God. This is a greet curtesie of

260 oure Lord, and an endeles merci, that so lightli forgyveth al manere synne, and so sodeynli geveth plenté of grace to a synful soule that asketh merci of Hym. He abideth no grete penaunce-doynge ne peynful fleischli suffrynge, or He forgyve it, but He asketh a lothynge of synne and a ful forsakynge of it in wille of the soule for love of Hym, and a turnynge of the herte to Hym. This asketh He, for thus gyveth he. And thanne, whanne

265 He seeth this, withouten ony delaiynge He forgyveth the synne and reformeth the soule to His liknesse. The synne is forgyven, that the soule schal not be dampned. Neverthelees, the peyne dettid for the synne is not yit fulli forgeven but yif contricion and love be the

244 **taryyinge**, delay. 245 **troweth**, believes; **as swithe**, immediately; **ought**, out. 246 **streite**, straightaway; **lettynge**, hindrance. 247 **untrouthe**, unbelief. 259 **curtesie**, graciousness. 260 **lightli**, easily. 261 **geveth**, gives; **plenté**, fullness; **abideth**, waits for. 262 **or**, before. 267 **dettid**, owed; **forgeven**, forgiven.

more. And therfore schal he goon and schewen hym and schryven him to his gosteli
fadir, and receyven penaunce enjoyned for his trespace and gladli fulfille it, soo that
270   bothe the synne and the peyne mai be doon away, or he passe hens. And that is the
skileful ordenaunce of Holi Chirche for gret profite of mannes soule, that though the
synne be forgeven thorugh veri contricioun, neverthelees in fulfillynge of mekenesse
and in makynge hool satisfaccioun, he schal yif he mai schewe to his prest plener
confessioun. For that is his tokene and his warant of forgevenesse agens alle his enemyes,
275   and that is nedeful for to have.

     For yif a man had forfeted his lif agens a kynge of this erthe, it were not inow to hym
as ful sikernesse for to have oonli forgyvenesse of the kynge, but yif he have a chartre,
the whiche mai be his tokene and his warant agens alle othere men. Right so mai it be
seid goostli, yif a man have forfeted agens the kyng of hevene his lif thorugh deedli
280   synne, it is not ynow to hym to ful sikirnesse for to have forgyvenesse of God oonli bi
contricion atwix God and hym, but yif he have a chartre maad bi Holi Chirche, yif he
may come therto. And that is the sacrament of penaunce, the whiche is his chartre and
his tokene of forgevenesse. For sith he forfeteth bothe agens God and Holi Chirche, it
is skilful that he have forgevenesse for that oon and a warant for that othir. And this is
285   a skile whi that confession is nedeful.

     Anothir skile is this, that syn the reformynge of the soule stondeth in feith oonli, not
in felynge, therfore a fleschli man that is rude and boistous and cannot demen lightli, but
outeward of bodily thinges, schuld not mowe han trowed that his synnes hadden ben
forgeven, but yif he had sum bodili tokene. And that is confessioun, thorugh the whiche
290   tokene he is maad as siker of forgevenesse, yif he doo that in him is. This is the trouthe
of Hooli Chirche, as I undirstonde.

     Also anothir skile is this. Though the ground of forgevenesse stonde not principali in
confessioun, but in contricion of herte and forthenking of synne, neverethelees I hope
that there is many a soule that schulde nevere have feelid veri contricioun, ne had ful
295   forsakynge of synne, yif confession had not ben. For it falleth ofte sithes that in tyme of

---

268 schewen hym, reveal himself; **schryven him**, confess himself. **271 skileful**, reasonable. **272 veri**, true. **273 plener**, full. **276 agens**, to; **inow**, enough. **277 sikernesse**, security; **chartre**, charter; that is, the legal document recording an official action or an agreement. **284 skilful**, reasonable. **287 rude**, rough; **boistous**, crude; **lightli**, easily. **288 mowe**, be able to. **290 siker**, certain. **293 forthenking**, repenting; **hope**, suppose. **294 feelid**, felt. **295 ofte sithes**, often.

schrifte grace of conpunccioun cometh to a soule that bifore nevere feelid grace, but ai was coold and drie, and feer from feelynge of grace. And forthi, syn schrift was so profitable to the more part of Cristene men, Holi Chirche ordeyned it for more sikirnesse generali to alle Cristene men, that everiche man or woman schulde oones in the yeer atte

300   the leste be schriven of alle here synnes that comen to ther mynde to ther goostli fadir, though thei han had never so mykil contricion bifore tyme.

Neverthelees, I hope wel that yif al men had ben as bisi aboughte the kepynge of hemself in feelynge of al maner synne, and had come to as grete knowynge and felynge of God as sum man is, that Holi Chirche schulde nevere have ordeynede the tokene of

305   confessioun as for a needful bond, for hit had not nedid. But for alle men aren not so perfighte, and peraventure mykil of the more partie of Cristene men is unperfight, therfore Holi Chirche ordeyned confessioun in wei of general bond to alle Cristene men that wole knowen Hooli Chirche as her moder and wolen ben buxum to hir biddinge. Yif this be sooth, as I hope it is, thanne erreth he greteli that generali seith that confessioun of

310   synne for to schewe to a prest is neither nedeful to a synnere ne bihoveful, and no man is bounden therto. For bi that that I have seid, it is bothe nedeful and spedful to alle soulis that in this wrecchid lif aren defouled thorugh synne, and nameli to thoo that aren thorugh deedli synne forschapen from the liknesse of God; the whiche mow not be reformed to His liknes, but bi the sacrament of penaunce, that principali standeth in

315   contricioun and sorwe of herte, and secundarili in schrift of mouth folwande aftir, yif it mai be had. Upoun this manere, bi the sacrament of penaunce, is a synful soule reformed to the ymage of God and to His likenesse.

Chapter Eight

Hou in the sacrament of baptym and of penaunce thorugh a privei unperceivable wirkynge of the Hooli Goost this image is reformed though it be not seen ne feelid.

297 schrift, confession. **298 more**, greater. **302 aboughte**, about. **306 perfighte**, perfect; **peraventure**, perhaps. **308 buxum**, obedient. **309 hope**, expect. **310 schewe**, reveal; **nedeful**, necessary; **bihoveful**, obligatory; **neither nedeful . . . ne bihoveful**, Hilton's sharp rejection of the Wycliffite position on confession is notable; see Clark, p. 305n27. **311 spedful**, advantageous. **312 thoo**, those. **313 mow**, can. **314 standeth**, consists.

320 But this reformynge stondeth in feith and not in feelynge; for right as the propirtee of
feith is for to trowen that thou seest not, right soo it is for to trowen that thou feelist
not. But he that is reformed in his soule bi the sacrament of penaunce to the image of
God, he feeleth noo chaungynge in himsilf, neithir in his bodili kynde withoutin, ne in
the privé substaunce of his soule withinne, othir than he dide. For he is as he was unto

325 his feelynge, and he feelith the same stirynges of synne and the same corrupcioun of his
fleisch in passions and worldli desires risynge in his herte as he dide biforn. And yit
neverthelees schal he trowe that he is thorugh grace reformed to the likenesse of God,
though he neithir feele it ne see it. He mai feele wel sorwe for his synne, and a turnynge
of his wil fro synne to clennesse of lyvynge, yif that he hath grace and take good keep

330 of himsilf. But he mai neithir seen ne feele the reformynge of his soule, hou it is wondirfulli
and unperceyvabli chaunged from filthe of the feend to the faireheed of an angel thorugh
a privei gracious wirkinge of oure Lord God. That mai he not seen, but he schal trowe
it; and yif he trowe it, thanne is his soule reformed in feith. For right as Holi Chirche
troweth bi the sacrament of baptym soothfastli resseyved, a Jewe or a Sarasyn or a

335 child born is reformed in soule to the liknesse of God thorugh a privé unperceyvable
wirkynge of the Hooli Goost, not agenstondynge alle the fleschli stirynges of his bodi of
synne, the whiche he schal feelen aftir his baptym as wel as he dide bifore; right so bi
the sacrament of penaunce mekeli and truli resseyved, a fals Cristen man that hath ben
encombrid with deedli synne al his liyftyme is reformed in his soule withinne

340 unperceyvabli, outtaken oonli a turnynge of his wille thorugh a privé myght and a
gracious wirkynge of the Holi Gost, that sodaynli wirketh and in tyme of a moment or
a twynkelynge of an iye righteth a froward soule, and turneth it from goostli filthe to
fairenesse unseable, and of a servaunt of the feend maketh a sone of joie, and of the
prisoner of helle maketh a partener of heveneli heritage, not agenstondande al the fleisschli

345 feelynge of this synneful image that is the bodili kynde.

For thou schalt undirstonde that the sacrament of baptym or of penaunce is not of
that vertu for to lette and destroie uttirli alle the stirynges of fleischli lustes and peynful
passiouns, that a man schulde nevere feele no manere risynge ne stirynge of hem no

---

320 stondeth, consists. **324 privé**, secret. **329 clennesse**, purity; **keep**, care. **331 faireheed**,
fairness. **332 wirkinge**, working. **336 agenstondynge**, despite. **340 outtaken**, except. **342
froward**, unruly. **343 unseable**, invisible. **344 partener**, partner (see Textual Notes). **347
vertu**, power; **lette**, prevent.

tyme. For if it were so, thanne were a soule fulli reformed here to the worschipe of the

350 first makynge; but that mai not be fulli in this lif. But it is of that vertu that it clenseth the soule from alle the synnes bifor doon; and yif it be departed from the bodi, saveth it from dampnacioun; and yif it duelle in the bodi, it geveth the soule grace for to agenstonde the stirynges of synne. And it kepith it in grace also, that no maner stirynge of lust or of passioun that it felith in the fleisch, be it nevere so grevous, schal dere it, ne departen it

355 from God, as longe as it wilfulli senteth not therto. Thus Seynt Poul menede whanne he seide thus: *Nichil dampnacionis est hiis qui sunt in Christo, qui non secundum carnem ambulant, etc.* (Romans 8:1). That is: Thise soules that aren reformed to the ymage of God in feith, thorugh the sacrament of baptym or of penaunce, schal not be dampned for feelynges of this ymage of synne, yif it so be that thei goo not aftir the stirynges of

360 the flesch bi fulfillynge of deede.

Chapter Nine

That we schul trowe stidefasteli reformynge of this image, yif oure conscience wittenesse us a ful forsakynge of synne and a trewe turnynge of oure wil to good lyvynge.

Of this reformynge in feith speketh Seynt Poul thus: *Iustus autem ex fide vivit* (Hebrews 10:38). The rightwise man lyveth in feith. That is, he that is maad rightful bi

365 baptym or penaunce, he lyveth in feith, the whiche sufficeth to savacion and to heveneli pees, as Seynt Poul seith: *Iustificati ex fide, pacem habemus ad deum* (Romans 6:1). This is, we that aren righted and reformed thorugh feith in Crist han pees and acord maad atwixe God and us, not agenstondynge the vicious feelinges of oure bodi of synne.

370 For though this reformynge be privei and mai not wel be feelid here in this liyf, neverthelees whoso troweth it stidefasteli and schape his werkes bisili for to acorde to his trouthe, and that he turne not ageyn to deedli synne, sothli whanne the houre of deeth cometh and the soule is departed from this bodili liyf, thanne schal he fynde it

349 **worschipe**, honored status. 352 **duelle**, dwell; **agenstonde**, resist. 354 **dere**, harm; **departen**, separate. 355 **senteth**, consents; **menede**, meant. 364 **rightwise**, righteous; **rightful**, just. 367 **righted**, justified. 368 **agenstondynge**, withstanding. 372 **trouthe**, faith.

sooth that I seie now. Thus Seynt Joon seide in confort of chosen soulis that lyven here in feith undir the feelynge of this peynful image: *Karissimi, et nunc sumus filii dei; sed non apparuit quid erimus. Scimus autem quoniam cum apparuerit, tunc apparebimus cum eo, similes ei in gloria* (1 John 3:2). That is: Mi dere frendis, we aren right now whiles that we lyven here the soones of God, for we aren reformed bi feith in Criste to His liknesse; but it schewith not yit what we aren, but it is al privei. Neverthelees we knowen wel that whanne oure Lord schal schewe Him atte the laste dai, thanne schal we appere with Hym like to Hym in endeles joie.

Yif thou wolt witen thanne yif thi soule be reformed to the image of God or noo, bi that that I have seid thou maist have an entré. Ransake thyn owen conscience and loke what thi wille is, for thereinne stondeth al. Yif it be turned from al deedli synne, that thou woldest for nothynge wityngeli and wilfulli breke the comaundement of God, and for that thou hast mysdoon here bifore agens his biddynge, thou haste beschreven mekeli, with ful herte to leve it and with sorwe that thou dedest it, I seie thanne sikirli that thi soule is reformed in feith to the likenesse of God.

Chapter Ten

That alle the soules that lyven mekeli in the trouthe of Holi Chirche and han here trouthe quykened with love and charité aren reformid bi this sacrament, though it so be that thei mown not fele the special gift of devocion or of goostli feelynge.

In this reformynge that is oonli in feith, the most parte of chosen soules leden heer liyf, that setten her wil stedefast for to fleen alle manere deedli synnes, and for to kepen hemsilf in love and charité to here evene Cristen and for to kepe the comaundement of God aftir hir kunnynge. And whanne it so is, that wikked stirynges and yvel willis risen in here hertis, of pride or of envie, of ire or of leccherie, or of ony othir heved synne,

---

374 Joon, John. **383 entré**, entrance; **Ransake**, Examine. **385 wityngeli**, consciously. **386 mysdoon**, misdone; **beschreven**, confessed. **387 sikirli**, certainly. **391 mown**, can. **394 evene**, fellow. **395 aftir hir kunnynge**, according to their knowledge. **396 heved**, chief, capital; the reference is to what are commonly called the seven deadly sins; in addition to the four sins mentioned here, the seven capital sins include sloth, gluttony, and avarice.

thei agenstonden hem and striven agens hem bi displesynge of wille, so that thei folwe not in deede thise wikkid willis. And neverthelees, yif it so be that thei falle lightli as it were agens here wille, thorugh freelté of unkunnynge, as tite here conscience greveth

400 hem and pyneth hem so grevousli that thei mown have noo reeste til thei ben schryven and may have forgyvenesse. Sothli alle thise soules that thus lyven, as y hope, aren reformed in feith to the image of God. And yif thei lasten in this reformynge, or be founden thereinne in the hour of deeth, thei schullen be saaf and come to the ful reformynge in the blis of hevene, though it be soo that thei nevere myghten have goosteli

405 felynge ne inli savour ne special grace of devocioun in al her liyftime. For ellis yif thou sai that no soule schal be saaf but yif it were reformed into goostli felynge, that it myght feele devocioun and gosteli savour in God, as some soulys doon thorugh special grace, thanne schulden fewe soulis be saaf in reward of the multitude of othere.

Nai, it is not likli for to trowe that, that for thoo soulis that aren oonli devoute, and bi

410 grace comen to goosteli feelynge, and for no mo, oure Lord Jhesu schulde have taken mankynde and suffrid hard passioun of deeth. It had bee but a litil purchace to Hym for to have come fro so feer to so neer, and fro so high to so lowgh, for so fewe soulis. Nai, His merci is spreed largere than so. Neverthelees, on the contrarie wise, yif thou trowe that the passioun of oure Lord is so precious and the merci of God is so mochil that ther

415 schal no soule be dampned, and nameli of no Cristen man, doo he nevere so ille, as summe foolis wenen, sotheli thei erren gretli. Therfore goo in the mene and helde thee in the myddis, and trowe as Holi Chirche troweth. And that is that the moste synful man that lyveth in erthe, yif he turne his wil thorwgh grace from deedli synne with soothfast repentaunce to the servyce of God, he is reformed in his soule, and yif he die in that

420 estate he schal be saaf. Thus behight oure Lord bi His profete, seiande thus: *In quacunque hora conversus fuerit peccator et ingemuerit, vita vivet et non morietur* (Ezekiel 18:21). That is: In what tyme that it be that the synful man is turned from synne to God and he have sorwe therfore, he schal lyven and he schal not dien endelesli. Also on that othir side, whoso liggeth in deedli synne, and wole not leve it ne amende hym therof, ne

397 **agenstonden**, resist; **displesynge**, displeasure. 399 **freelté**, frailty; **unkunnynge**, ignorance; **as tite**, immediately. 400 **pyneth**, pains; **mown**, can; **schryven**, confessed. 403 **saaf**, saved. 405 **inli**, inner. 408 **reward**, regard. 409 **it is not likli**, Hilton's stress on the availability of salvation to all, not just the perfect or contemplatives, is notable, as is the emphasis on orthodox belief. 411 **purchace**, attainment. 412 **lowgh**, low. 414 **mochil**, great. 416 **wenen**, suppose. 420 **behight**, promised.

425 receyve the sacrament of penaunce, and though he receyve it he taketh it not soothfastli
for the love of God, that is for love of vertu and clennesse, but oonli for drede of
schame of the world, or ellis for drede oonli of the peynes of helle — he is not reformed
to the likenesse of God. And yif he die in that plight he schal not be saaf. His trouthe
schal not save hym, for his trouthe is a deed trouthe and lakketh love, and therfore hit
430 serveth him of nought.

But thei that han trouthe quykened with love and charité aren reformed to the liknesse
of God, though it be but the leste degré of charité, as aren symple soulis, the whiche
feelen not the gifte of special devocion ne gostli knowynge of God, as some gosteli men
doon, but trowen generali as Holi Chirche troweth, and witen not fulli what that is, for
435 it nedeth not to hem. And in that trouthe thei kepen hem in love and charité to here even
Cristen as mykil as thei moun, and fleen alle deedli synnes aftir her connynge, and doon
the dedes of merci to here even Cristene. Alle thise longen to the blisse of hevene, for it
is writen in the Apocalipsis thus: *Qui timetis deum, pusilli et magni, laudate eum* (Revelations 19:5). This is: Ye that dreden God, bothe grete and smale, thanketh Him.
440 Bi grete aren undirstonde soulis that aren profitande in grace, or ellis in love perfight
of God, the whiche aren reformed in goosteli feelynge. Bi the smale aren undirstanden
soulis unperfite, of worldli men and women and othere, that han but a childisch knowynge
of God and ful litil feelynge of Hym, but aren brought forth in the bosom of Holi
Chirche and norischid with the sacrament as children aren fed with mylk. Alle thise
445 schullen thanke God and loven Hym for savacioun of here soules bi His endelees merci.
For Holy Chirche, that is moder of alle thise and hath tendir love to alle hir childrin
goostli, praieth and asketh for hem alle tendirli of hir spouse (that is, Jhesu), and geteth
hem heele of soule thorugh vertu of His passioun, and nameli for hem that counen not
speken hemself bi goostli praiere for here owen nede.
450 Thus I fynde in the Gospel that the woman of Chanane askide of oure Lord heele to
hir doughter that was traveiled with a feend, and oure Lord maad daunger bicause sche
was an aliene. Neverthelees, she ceeside not for to crien til oure Lord hadde grauntid to

426 **clennesse**, purity. 428 **trouthe**, belief. 434 **witen**, know. 436 **moun**, are able; **aftir her
connynge**, according to their knowledge. 437 **longen**, belong. 440 **profitande**, advancing.
442 **unperfite**, imperfect. 444 **fed with mylk**, a common image for spiritual beginners derived
from 1 Corinthians 3:1–2; used also in *Scale* Book I, chapter 9, Book II, chapter 31. 448 **heele**,
health; **counen**, can. 451 **traveiled with**, troubled by; **maad daunger**, made difficulty, was
reluctant. 452 **ceeside**, ceased.

hire hire askynge and seide to hire thus: "A, woman, mykil is thi trouthe; be it doon to thee right as thou wolt." And in the same hour was hir doughter maad hool. This
455 woman bitokeneth Holi Chirche, that asketh helpe of oure Lord for symple unconnynge soules, that aren traveilid with temptacioun of the world and kunnen not speken perfightli to God bi fervour of devocioun ne brennande love in contemplacion; and though it seme that oure Lorde make daunger first bicause that thei aren as hit were alienes fro Hym, neverthelees for the grete trouthe and the desert of Holi Chirche he graunteth hire al that
460 sche wole. And so aren thise simple soulis, that trowen stidefasteli as Holi Chirche troweth, and putteth hem fulli in the merci of God and meken hem undir the sacraments and lawes of Holi Chirche, maad saaf thorugh the praier and the trouthe of hir goostli modir, that is Holi Chirche.

Chapter Eleven

That soules reformed neden ai for to fighten and stryven agen stirynges of synne whiles thei
465 lyven heer, and hou a soule mai witen whanne he assenteth to ille stirynges and whanne not.

This reformynge in feith mai lighteli be geten, but it mai not so lighteli be holden. And therfore what man or woman that is reformed to the liknesse of God in trouthe, mykil traveile and bisynesse hem bihoveth to have, yif thei wolen kepe this image hool and clene, that it falle not doun ageyn thorugh weikeynesse of wille to the ymage of synne.
470 He mai not be idel ne rekles, for the ymage of synne is so neer festned to hym, and so contynueli preseth upon hym bi divers stirynges of synne, that but yif he be right waar he schal ful lightli thorugh asent falle ageyn therto. And therfore hym nedeth ay be stryvynge and fightynge ageyn wikked stirynges of this ymage of synne, and that he make noon acord therwith, ne take noo frendschipe with it, for to be buxum to his
475 unskilfulle biddynges, for yif he do, he bigileth hymsilf. But sothli yif he stryve with hem, hym nedeth not mykil to drede of assentynge, for strif breketh pees and fals acord. It is good that a man have pees with al thynge, outetaken with the feend and with

453 trouthe, faith. 455 unconnynge, ignorant. 457 brennande, burning. 459 desert, merit. 461 meken, humble. 465 witen, know. 466 geten, obtained; holden, kept. 468 traveile, trouble; bisynesse, activity; hem bihoveth, they must. 469 weikeynesse, weakness. 471 waar, aware. 474 buxum, obedient. 475 unskilfulle, irrational. 477 outetaken, except.

this image of synne, for ageyns hem it nedeth ai feighten in his thought and in his werk until he hath geten over hem the maistrie. And that schal nevere ben fulli in this lif, as longe as he berith and felith this ymage. I sei not but that a soule mai thorugh grace have the hyghere hand over this ymage, so fer forth that it schal not folwen ne senten to the unskilful stirynges of it. But for to ben so clene delivered fro this ymage, that hit schulde feele no suggestioun ne jangelynge of noo fleschli affeccion, ne of veyne thought noo tyme, may no man have in this lyf.

480

I hope that a soule that is reformed in feelynge by ravyschynge of love into contemplacion of God mai be so feer fro the sensualité and fro the veyn imaginacion, and soo feer drawen oute and departid from the fleischli feelynge for a tyme, that it schal not feelen but good; but that lasteth not alwai. And therfore seie I that every man bihoveth strive ageyns this ymage of synne, and nameli he that is onli reformed in feith, that so lightly mai be disseyved therwith. In the persone of the whiche men Seynt Poul seith thus: *Caro concupiscit adversus spiritum et spiritus adversus carnem* (Galatians 5:17). That is, a soule reformed to the liknesse of God fighteth ageyn the fleschli stirynges of this image of synne, and also this ymage of synne striveth ageyn the wille of the spirite. This maner of fightynge in this duble ymage Seynt Poul knew weel whanne he seide thus: *Inveni legem in membris meis, repugnantem legi mentis mee, et captivum me ducentem in legem peccati* (Romans 7:23). That is: I have founden two lawes in mysilf, o lawe in my soule withinne, and anothir lawe in my fleschli lymes withoute fightynge ageyns hit, that often ledeth me as a wrecchid prisoner into the lawe of synne. Bi thise two lawes in a soule I understond this double image: bi the lawe of the spirit I undirstonde the resoun of the soule whanne it is reformed to the image of God; bi the lawe of the flessch I undirstonde the sensualité, whiche I calle the ymage of synne. In thise two lawes a soule reformed ledeth his lif, as Seynt Poul seith: *Mente enim servio legi dei, carne vero servio legi peccati* (Romans 7:25). In my soule, that is, in my wil and in my resoun, I serve to the lawe of God; but in my flesch, that is, in the feelynge of my fleschli appetite, I serve to the lawe of synne. Neverthelees, that a soule reformed schulde not dispeiren, though he serve to the lawe of synne bi feelynge of the vicious sensualité ageynes the wille of the spirite bicause of corrupcion of his bodili kynde, Seynt Poul excuseth it, seiande thus of his owen persoone: *Non enim quod volo bonum*

485

490

495

500

505

478 **werk**, deed. 481 **so fer forth**, to the extent; **senten**, consent. 482 **unskilful**, irrational. 483 **jangelynge**, disruption. 486 **feer**, far. 497 **lymes**, limbs. 500 **resoun**, reason. 506 **dispeiren**, dispair. 508 **seiande**, saying.

The Scale of Perfection

hoc ago; sed malum quod odi, hoc facio. Si autem malum quod odi facio, iam non ego
510 *operor illud, sed quod habitat in me, peccatum* (Romans 7:19–20). I do not that good
that I wolde doon, that is, I wolde feele noon fleschli stiringe, and that do y not; but I
doo the yvel that I hate, that is, the synful stirynges of my flesch. I hate and yit I feele
hem. Neverethelees, syn it is so that y hate wikkid stirynges of my flesch, and yit y fele
hem and ofte delite in hem agens my wille, thei schal not be arected agens me for
515 dampnacion, as yif y hadde doon hem. And whi? For the corrupcion of this image of
synne dooth hem, and not I.

Loo, here Seynt Poul in his owen persone conforteth alle soulis that aren thorugh
grace reformed in feith, that thei schuld not to mykil drede the berthene of this ymage
with the unskilful stirynges thereof, bi so that thei sente not wilfulli therto. Neverethelees
520 in this poynt many soulis that aren reformed in trouthe aren ofte sithis mykil tormentid
and trobelid in veyn. As thus: whanne thei han feelid fleschli stirynges of pride, of envie,
of covetise, or of leccherie, or of ony othir heed synne, thei witen not sumtyme whethir
thei sentiden to hem or noo. And that is no grete wondir, for in tyme of temptacion a
freel mannes thought is so trobled and so overleid that he hath no cleer light ne fredom
525 of himself, but is taken often with likynge unwarli, and goth forth with it a grete while
or thanne he perceyve it. And therfore fallen summe of hem in doute and in dwere
whethir thei synneden or not in the tyme of temptacion.

As anemptis this poynt I seie as me thenketh, that a soule mai have assaiynge on this
manere whethir he assenteth or noo. Yif it so be that a man be stired to ony maner of
530 synne, and the likynge is so grete in his flesschli felynge that it trobleth his resoun and
as it were thorugh maistrie occupieth the affeccioun of the soule; neverthelees he kepith
hym, that he folweth not in dede, ne he wolde not though he myght, but it is rathere to
hym peyneful for to feelen the likynge of that synne, and fayn he wolde putten hit awai
yif he myght; and thanne whanne the stirynge is overpassid he is glaad and wil paied
535 that he is delyvered of it and that he feelith no more of it — bi this assai mai he witen that
were the likynge nevere so grete in the fleschli feelynge, that he assentide not, ne synnede
not, nameli deedliche.

514 **arected**, accounted. 518 **berthene**, burden. 519 **unskilful**, irrational; **bi so**, as long as.
520 **trouthe**, faith; **ofte sithis**, often. 522 **heed**, capital; see the list in chapter 10, above; **witen**,
know. 523 **sentiden**, consented. 524 **freel**, frail. 526 **or thanne**, before; **dwere**, doubt. 528
anemptis, concerning. 531 **affeccioun**, emotion, feeling. 534 **wil paied**, well satisfied.

154

Book II

Neverthelees, a remedie there is that is sikir and certayn to siche a symple soule that
is marred in itsilf and cannot helpin itsilf: that he be not to bold in himsilf, uttirli wenande
540   that siche fleschli stirynges with likynges aren no synnes, for he myght so fallen into
recchelesnesse and into a fals sikernesse, ne also that he be not to dredful ne to symple
in witte, for to demen hem alle as deedli synnes, or elles as grete venyal, for neithir is
sooth. But that he holde hem alle as synne and wrecchidnesse of hymsilf, and that he
have sorwe for hem, and that he be not to bisi for to deme them neithir deedli ne venyal.
545   But yif his conscience be gretli greved, that he hasteli goo and schewe to his confessour
in general or in special siche stirynges, and nameli that ilke stirynge that bigynneth
fastne roote in the herte and most often occupieth it, for to drawen it doun to synne and
wordli vanité. And whanne he is thus schryven of thise in general or in special, trowe
thanne stidefastli that thei aren forgyven, and dispute no more aboughte hem that aren
550   passid and forgyven, whethir thei weren deedli or venial, but that he be more besi for to
kepen him betere agens hem that aren comynge. And yif he doo thus, thanne mai he
come to reste in conscience.

But thanne are some so fleschli and so unkunnynge that thei wolden feele or seen or
heren the forgifnesse of hire synnes, as openli as thei moun feelen or seen a bodili
555   thyng; and for as mykil as thei feelyn it not, so thei fallen often in siche dweris and
doutes of hemsilf and nevere moun come to reste. And in that be thei not wise, for feith
goth bifore felynge. Oure Lord seide to a man that was in the palsie whanne He heelid
hym thus: *Confide fili, remittuntur tibi peccata tua* (Matthew 9:2). That is: Sone, trowe
stidefasteli thy synnes aren forgeven thee. He seide not to him, see or feele how thi
560   synnes aren forgeve thee, forgifnesse of synne is doon goostli and unseabli thorugh
grace of the Holi Goost, but bileve it. Right upon the same wise, every man that wole
come to reste in conscience, him bihoveth first yif he doo that in him is trowen withouten
goostli feelynge forgifnesse of his synnes; and yyf he first trowe it, he mai aftirward
thorugh grace feele it and undirstonde it, that it is so. Thus seide the apostil: *Nisi credederis,*
565   *non intelligetis* (compare Isaiah 7:9) But yif ye first trowen, ye moun not undirstonde.

538 sikir, certain. **539 to**, too; **wenande**, supposing. **541 recchelesnesse**, carelessness;
sikirnesse, security. **542 witte**, intelligence. **544 bisi**, concerned. **545 schewe**, show. **549**
aboughte, about. **550 besi**, active. **553 unkunnynge**, ignorant. **554 moun**, are able to. **555**
dweris, doubts. **560 unseabli**, invisibly. **561 wise**, manner. **562–63 yif he doo . . . synnes**, to do
what is in him to believe, without spiritual feeling, in the forgiveness of his sins. **565 moun**,
may.

Trouthe goth bifore and undirstondinge come aftir. The whiche undirstondynge, that I calle the sight of God yif it be gracious, a soule mai not have but thorugh grete clennesse, as oure Lord seith: *Beati mundo corde, quoniam ipsi deum videbunt* (Matthew 5:8). Blissed ben clene of herte, for thei schul see God — not with heer fleschli iye, but with 570 the innere iye, that is, undirstondynge clensid and illumined thorugh grace of the Holi Gost for to seen soothfastnesse. The whiche clennesse a soule mai not feele but it have stable trouthe goynge bifore, as the apostil seith: *Fide mundans corda eorum* (Acts 15:9). That is, oure Lord clenseth the hertis of His chosen thorwgh feith. Therefore it is nedeful that a soule trowe first the reformynge of himsilf maad thorugh the sacrament 575 of penaunce, though he see it not, and that he dispose him fulli for to lyven rightwiseli and vertuousli as his trouthe asketh, so that he mai aftir that come to the sight and to the reformynge in feelynge.

Chapter Twelve

That this image is bothe fair and foule whilis it is in this lif, though it be reformed; and of dyversité of felyng priveli had atwixe thise soulis that aren reformede and othere that 580 aren nought reformed.

Fair is mannys soule, and foule is a mannys soule. Fair in as mykil as it is reformed in trouthe to the liknesse of God, but it is foule in as mykil as it is yit medelid with fleschli felynges and unskilful stirynges of this ymage of synne. Foule withouten as it were a beest, faire withinne like to an angel. Foule in feelynge of the sensualité, fair in trouthe 585 of the resoun. Foule for the fleschli appetite, faire for the good wil. Thus fair and thus foule is a chosen soule, seiynge Holi Writ thus: *Nigra sum, sed formosa, filie Ierusalem sicut tabernacula cedar et sicut pelles Salomonis* (Canticle 1:4). I am blak, but I am fair and schapli, yee doughteris of Jerusalem, as the tabernaculis of cedar and as the skynnes of Salomoun. That is: Yee angelis of hevene, that aren doughteres of the highe Jerusa- 590 lem, wondreth not on me, ne dispice me not for my blak schadwe, for though I be blak

567 gracious, of grace; **clennesse**, purity. **569 clene**, pure; **iye**, eye. **571 soothfastnesse**, truth. **582 medelid**, mingled. **583 unskilful**, irrational. **589 That is**, Hilton's exposition of the Canticle in this chapter is indebted to Bernard, *Sermons on the Song of Songs*, 25–27; see Clark, p. 306nn57–59. **590 dispice**, despise.

withoute bicause of my fleschli kynde, as is a tabernacle of cedar, nevertheles I am ful fair withinne as is the skyn of Salomon, for y am reformed to the likenesse of God. Bi cedar is undirstonde myrkenesse, and that is the devyl. Bi tabernacle of cedar is undirstonde a reprevid soule, the whiche is a tabernacule of the devyl. Bi Salomon, that bitokeneth

595   peseble, is undirstonden oure Lord, for He is pees and pesible. Bi the skyn of Salomon is undirstonden a blissid aungel, in whom oure Lord woneth and is hid, as lif is hid withinne the skyn of a quyk bodi, and therfore is an angel likened to a skyn.

Thanne mai a chosen soule with meke trust in God and gladnesse in herte seie thus: Though I be blak bicause of my bodi of synne, as is a reprevid soule that is the taber-

600   nacle of the feend, neverthelees I am withinne wel faire thorugh trouthe and good wille, like to an angil of hevene. For so seith he in anothir place: *Nolite considerare me quia fusca sum, quoniam decoloravit me sol* (Canticle 1:5). That is: Biholdeth me not for y am swart, for the sunne hath defaded me. The sunne maketh a skyn swart onli withoute and not withinne, and it bitokeneth this fleschli liyf. Therfore seith a chosen soule thus:

605   "Repreve me not for y am swart, for the swartenesse that y have is al withouten, of touchynge and of berynge this ymage of synne. But it is nothinge withinne." And therfore soothli, though it be so that a chosen soule reformed in feithe dwelle in this bodi of synne, and feele the same fleischli stirynges and use the same bodili werkes as doth a tabernacle of cedar, so fer forth that in mannes dome ther schulde no difference be

610   bitwixe that oon and that tothir — neverthelees withinne in here soules is there ful grete diversité, and in the sight of God is there ful grete twynnynge. But the knowynge of this, whiche is oon and which is othir, is oonli kept to God, for it passeth mannys doom and mannys feelynge. And therfore we schal no man demen as ille for that thinge that mai be usid bothe yvel and weel. A soule that is not reformed is taken so fulli with the

615   love of this world, and so mykil overleid with the likynge of his flesche in al his sensualité, that he cheseth it as a ful reste of his herte; and in his privei menynge hee wolde not ellis have, but that he myght ay be siker therof. He feleth noo licour of grace stirynge hym to lothe this fleschli liyf ne for to desiren heveneli blisse.

And therfore I mai seie that he bereth not this ymage of synne, but he is born of it, as

620   a man that were sike and so weike that he myght not beren hymsilf, and therfore is leid

---

593 myrkenesse, darkness. **594 reprevid**, condemned. **595 peseble**, peaceable. **596 woneth**, dwells. **597 quyk**, living. **603 swart**, dark; **defaded**, faded. **609 so fer forth**, to the extent. **611 twynnynge**, separation. **612 doom**, judgment. **616 cheseth**, chooses. **617 siker**, certain.

in a bed and born in a liter. Right so siche a synful soule is so weike and so unmyghti for lakkynge of grace, that it mai neither stiren hand ne foot for to doon ony good dede, ne foragenstonde bi displesynge of wille the leeste stirynge of synne whanne it cometh, but it falleth doun therto as dooth a beest upon a carion. But a soule that is thorugh grace

625   reformed, though he use his fleischeli wittis and feele fleischli likynges, neverthelees he lotheth hem in his herte, for he nolde for nothinge fulli resten in hem. But he feelith the reste in hem as the bityng of an eddre, and he hadde lyvere han his reste and the love of his herte in God, yif that he coude; and sumtyme desireth therto, and often irketh of the likynge of this liyf for love of the liyf ai lastande.

630   This soule is not bore in this image of synne as a sike man, though he feele it; but he bereth it. For thorugh grace he is maad myghti and stronge for to suffren and beren his bodi with alle the stirynges of it, withouten hurtynge or defoulynge of himsilf; and that is in as mykil as he loveth hem not, ne folweth hem not, ne senteth not to hem, the whiche aren deedli synne, as anothir dooth. This was bodili fulfilled in the Gospel of a

635   man that was in the palsie and was so feble that he myght not goon, and therfore was he leid and born in a lighter and brought to oure Lord, and whanne oure Lord sigh hym in myschief, of His goodnesse He seide to hym thus: *Surge et tolle grabatum tuum, et vade in domum tuam* (Mark 2:11). That is: Rise up and take thi bed and goo into thi hous. And so he dide, and was hool. And sothli right as this man baar upon his bak whanne

640   he was made hool the bed that bifore baar hym, right so it mai be seide goosteli, that a soule reformed in feith bereth this image of synne, in the whiche he was born in biforn.

And therfore be not adred to mykil of thi blakkenesse that thou haste of berynge of this ymage of synne. But agens the schame and the discomfort that thou haste of the biholdynge of it, and also agens the upbreidynge that thou feelist in thyn herte of thi

645   goostli enemyes, whanne thei seyn to thee thus: "Where is thi Lord Jhesu? What feelist thou? Where is the fairhede that thou spekest of? What feelist thou ought but blyndenesse of synne? Where is the image of God that thou seist is reformed in thee?" Comforte thee thanne bi trouthe stilli, as I have bifore seid; and yif thou doo soo, thou schalt bi this trouthe destroien alle temptaciones of thyne enemyes. Thus seith the apostle: *Accipe*

650   *scutum fidei, in quo tela hostis nequissima poteris extinguere* (Ephesians 6:16). That is:

---

621 liter, litter; **weike**, weak. **623 foragenstonde**, resist; **displesynge**, disapproval. **627 eddre**, adder. **628 irketh**, wearies. **629 ai lastande**, everlasting. **633 senteth**, consents. **636 lighter**, litter; **sigh**, saw. **637 myschief**, misfortune. **646 fairhede**, fairness. **648 stilli**, constantly.

Take to thee a schelde of stidefast trouth, thorugh the whiche thou schalt moun quenche alle the brennynge daartes of thyn enemye.

Chapter Thirteen

Of thre maner of men, of the whiche summe aren not reformed, and summe ben reformed oonli in feythe, and summe in feithe and in feelynge.

655   Bi this that I have bifore seid maist thou seen that aftir diverse parties of the soule aren dyvers staatis of men. Summe aren not reformed to the liknesse of God, and summe aren reformed oonli in feith, and summe aren reformed in feith and in felynge.

     For thou schalt undirstonde that a soule hath two parties. The toon is called the sensualité; that is the fleschli feelynge bi the fyve outeward wittes, the whiche is comoun to man and to beest. Up the whiche sensualité, whanne it is unskilfulli and unordynateli

660   rulid, is maad the image of synne, as I have bifore seid, for than is the sensualité synne, whanne it is not rulid aftir resoun. That tothir partie is callid reson, and that is departid on two — the overe partie and the nethere partie. The overe is likned to a man, for it schulde be maister and sovereyne, and that is propirli the ymage of God, for bi that

665   oonli the soule knoweth God and loveth God. And the nethere is likned to a woman, for it schulde be buxum to the overe partie of resoun, as a woman is buxum to man. And that liyth in knowynge and rulynge of ertheli thinges, for to use hem discreteli aftir nede and for to refuse hem whanne it is no nede; and for to have ai with it thyn iye upward to the overe partie of resoun, with drede and with reverence for to folwe it.

670   Now mai y seie that a soule that lyveth aftir likynges and lustis of the flesch, as it were an unskilfull beest, and neither hath knowynge of God ne desire to vertues ne good lyvynge, but is al blynded in pride, freten in envye, overleid with coveitise, and defoulid with leccherie and othere grete synnes, it is not reformed to the ymage of God. For it lieth and resteth fulli in the ymage of synne, that is the sensualité. Anothir soule

651 trouth, faith; **moun**, be able to. **655 aftir**, corresponding to; **parties**, parts. **658 two parties**, the definition of the soul that follows is based on Augustine, *De trinitate*, 12.3–14, as elaborated by medieval theologians; see Clark, p. 307n65. **659 wittes**, senses. **660 Up**, Of; **unskilfulli**, irrationally. **662 tothir**, other. **663 overe**, upper; **nethere**, lower. **666 buxum₁**, obedient. **668 iye**, eye. **672 freten**, eaten.

675 that dredeth God and agenstondeth deedli stirynges of the sensualité and folweth hem
not, but lyveth resonabli in rulynge and governaunce of wordli thinges, and setteth his
entent and his wille for to plesen God bi his outeward werkes, is reformed to the
liknesse of God in feith, and though he feele the same stirynges of synne as that othir
dide, it schal not dere hym, for he resteth not in hem as that tothir dooth. But anothir
680 soule that fleeth thorugh grace alle deedli steringes of sensualité and venyalis also, so fer
forth that he felith hem not, it is reformed in feelynge. For he folweth the over partie of
resoun in bihaldynge of God and of heveneli thinges, as I schal telle thee aftir.

Chapter Fourteen

Hou men thorough synne forschapen hemsilf into seere bestis liknesse and thise aren
callid the loveres of this world.

685 A wrecchid man is he thanne that knoweth not the worthinesse of his soule, ne wole not
knowe it — hou it is the moste worthi creature that evere God made, outaken an angil
whom it is like to, high aboven alle othir bodili kynde, to the whiche nothinge mai
sufficen as ful reste but oonli God. And therfore he schulde noo thinge loven and liken
but oonli God, ne coveiten ne seken but hou he myght be reformed to His liknesse. But
690 for he knoweth not this, therfore he seketh and coveiteth his reste and his likynge
outeward in bodili creaturis werse thanne himsilf is. Unkyndeli he dooth, and unresonabli
he werketh, that loveth not the sovereyne good and ai lastande liyf that is God unsought
and unloved, unknowen and unworschipid, and cheseth his reste and his blisse in a
passynge delite of an ertheli thinge. Neverthelees thus don alle the loveres of this world,
695 that han her blisse and her joie in this wrecchid liyf.
      Summe han it in pride and veynglorie of hemsilf, that whanne thei have loste the drede
of God thei traveilen and studien nyght and dai hou thei myght come to worschipe and
praisynge of the world, and maken no force hou so be thei myghten comen therto and
overpassen alle othere men oither in clergie or in crafte, in name or in fame, in richesse

675 agenstondeth, resists. **679 dere,** harm. **680 venyalis,** venial sins (in contrast to deadly
sins). **683 forschapen,** deform; **seere,** various. **686 outaken,** except. **692 ai lastande,** everlasting. **698 maken no force,** take no care. **699 oither,** either; **in clergie or in crafte,** in learning or
in a skill.

700   or in reverence, in sovereynté and in maistirschipe, in high estate and in lordeschipe. Sum men han heer delite and here reste in richesse and in outeragious aver of ertheli godes, and setten her hertis so fulli for to getin it that thei seken not ellis but hou thei myghten comen therto. Summe han heer likynge in fleschli lustes of glotonye and leccherie and othir bodili unclennesse, and summe in oo thynge and summe in anothir.

705   And thus wrecchidli thise that doon thus forschapen hemsilf fro the worthinesse of man and turnen hem into dyvers beestis liknesse.

      The proude man is turned into a lion for pride, for he wolde be dred and worschipid of alle men, and that noo man ageynstonde the fulfillynge of his fleschli wille, in word ne deede; and yif ony man wole letten his proud wille, he wexeth fel and wrooth, and

710   wole be vengid of him as a lion vengeth him on a litil beest. This man that doth thus is now no man, for he dooth unresonabli ageen the kynde of man, and so he is turned and transformed into a lioun. Envious and angri men aren turned into houndes thorugh wraththe and envye, that berken agen hir even Cristene, and biten hem bi wikkid and malicious wordes, and greven hem that not trespaceden with wrongeful deedis, harmynge

715   hem in bodi and in soule agens Goddis biddynge. Summe men aren forschapen into assis, that aren slowe to the service of God, and unwillid for to doon ony good deede to here evene Cristene. Thei aren redi inow for to renne to Rome for wordli profite or for ertheli worschipe, or for plesance of an ertheli man, but for goostli mede, for helpe of heer owen soules, or for worschip of God, thei aren soone irke. Thei wole not therof,

720   and yif thei ought doon thei goon but a paas and yit with a froward wille. Summe aren turned into swyne, for thei aren so blynde in witte and so beestli in maneres, that thei han no drede of God, but folwen oonli the lustes and the likynges of heer flesch, and han no rewarde to honesté of man, for to rulen hemself aftir the biddynge of resoun, for to restreyne the unskilful stirynges of the fleschli kynde; but as soone as ony fleschli

725   styrynge of synne cometh, thei aren redi for to falle therto, and folwe it as a swyn doth. Summe men are turnyd into wolves that lyven bi raveyn, as a fals covetous man dooth that thorugh maistrie and overledynge robbeth his even Cristene of here wordli goodes. Summe into foxis, as fals men and disceyvable that lyven in treccherie and in gile.

701 aver, possession. **706 beestis liknesse**, the association of the seven deadly sins with animals is a commonplace in the Middle Ages; compare Spenser, *The Faerie Queene*, 1.4.18– 37. **709 letten**, obstruct; **fel**, fierce. **711 ageen**, against. **717 inow**, enough. **718 mede**, reward. **719 heer**, their; **irke**, wearied. **720 paas**, pace. **721 witte**, intelligence. **723 rewarde**, regard. **726 wolwes**, wolves; **raveyn**, rapine. **727 maistrie**, force; **overledynge**, deceit; **wordli**, worldly.

730 Alle thise and many othere moo, that lyven not in drede of God but breken His commaundementis, forschapen hemsilf from the liknesse of God and maken hem like unto beestis. Yhe, and worse than beestis, for thei aren like unto the feend of helle. And therfore sothli, thise that lyven thus, yif that thei ben not reformed whanne the hour of deeth cometh and the soules of hem aren departed from the bodies, than schal her iyen ben openyd that is now stoppid with synne, and thanne schal thei feelen and fynden the

735 peyne of here wikkidnesse that thei lyveden inne here. And for as mykil as the image of God was not reformed thorugh the sacrament of penaunce in hem, neithir in feith ne in feelynge heere in this lif, thei schullen ben acursid, kest oute from the blissid face of oure Creatour, and thei schal be dampned with the devel into the depnesse of helle, there fore to ben ai withouten ende. Thus seith Seynt Johan in the Apocalips: *Timidis, et*

740 *incredulis, execratis, et homicidis, fornicatoribus, veneficis et ydololatris et omnibus mendacibus, pars illorum erit in stangno ardenti igne et sulphure* (Revelations 21:8). That is, to proude men and mystrowande, to cursid and to mansleers, to lecchouris and to covetous, to poysoneris, worschiperis of maumetis, and to alle fals lieres, dool schal ben with the devyl in the pitte of helle brennynge with fier and bremston. Yif the loveris

745 of this world wolden often thenke on this, hou al this world schal passen and drawen to an· ende, and hou alle wikkid love schal ben hard ponysched, thei schulde withinne schort tyme lothe worldli lust that thei now moste liken. And thei schulde liften up here herte for to love God, and besili seken and traveilen hou thei myghten be reformed to His liknes or thei passiden hens.

Chapter Fifteen

750 Hou loveris of this world unable hemsilf on seere wise to the reformynge of here owen soulis.

But now seyn summe of hem thus: "I wolde fayne love God, and ben a good man and forsake the love of the world yif that I myght; but y have no grace therto. Yif I hadde

---

731 Yhe, Yea. **733 iyen,** eyes. **737 kest,** cast. **739 fore to ben,** to be. **742 mansleers,** murderers. **743 maumetis,** idols; see the gloss to *Scale*, I.2418; **dool,** sorrow. **749 or,** before. **750 seere wise,** various ways.

162

755 the same grace that a good man hath, y schuld doo as he dooth; but for I have not, therfore y may not, and so it is not me to witen, but I am excusid." Unto thise men y seie thus: Sooth it is as thei seyn, that they have no grace and therfore thei liggen stille in here synne and moun not risen oute. But that availeth hem right nought, it excuseth hem not agens God, for it is heer owene defaute. Thei unablen hemsilf bi dyvers weies so mykil, that the light of grace mai not schynen to hem ne resten in here hertes. For
760 summe aren so froward that thei wolen noo grace han, ne thei wolen no good men ben; for thei witen wel yif thei schulden be good men, hem bihoveth nedes forberen and leven the grete likynge and the luste of this world that thei han in ertheli thinges. And that wolen thei not, for thei thenken it so swete that thei wolde not forgoon it. And also thei moste take werkes of penaunce, as fastynge, wakynge, praiynge, and othere good-
765 deedes-doynge in chastizynge of here fleisch, and in withdrawynge of her fleischly wille; and that moun thei not doon, for it is maad so scharpe and so pyneful to hire thenkynge that thei ugglen and lothen for to thenken therupon, and so cowardeli and wrecchidli dwellen thei stille in there synne.

Some wolden have grace, as it semeth, and thei bigynnen for to ablen hem therto; but
770 here wille is wondir weik, for as soone as ony stirynge of synne cometh, though it be contrarie to the biddynge of God, thei fallen as tite therto, for thei aren so bounden thorugh custum bi often fallinge and ofte assentynge to synne bifore, that hem thenketh it impossible for to agenstonde it, and so feyned hardenesse of performynge weiken her wille and smyten it doon agen. Summe also feelen stirynge of grace, as whanne thei han
775 bitynge of conscience for here yvele lyvynge, and that thei schulden leve it. But that is pyneful to hem and so hevy, that thei wole not suffren it ne abide with it, but thei fleen therefro and forgeten it yif thei moun, so fer forth that thei seken likyng and comfort outeward in fleschli creaturis, so that thei schuld not feelen this bitynge of conscience withinne her soule.
780 And overmore summe men aren so blynde and so beesteli that thei wenen that there is noon othir liyf but this, ne that there is no soule of man othir than of a beest, but that the soule of man dieth with the bodi as doth the soule of a beeste. And therfore thei seyn, "Ete we and drynke we, and make we merie heere, for of this be we siker. We

755 **witen,** know. 756 **liggen,** lie. 757 **moun,** can. 758 **defaute,** fault. 760 **froward,** contrary. 761 **hem bihoveth,** they must. 767 **ugglen,** abhor. 769 **ablen,** enable. 771 **as tite,** immediately. 772 **hem thenketh,** it seems to them. 776 **hevy,** distressing. 777 **so fer forth,** to the extent. 780 **overmore,** moreover; **wenen,** suppose. 783 **siker,** certain.

785 seen noon othir hevene." Sotheli summe aren siche wrecchis that seyn thus in her hertis, though thei seyn it not with her mouth. Of the whiche men the prophete seith thus: *Dixit insipiens in corde suo, non est deus* (Psalms 13:1). That is, the unwise man seide in his herte, ther is no God. This unwise man is everi wrecchid man that liketh and loveth synne and cheseth the love of this worlde as reste of his soule. He seith there is no God; not with his mouth, for he wole speken of Him sum tyme whanne he fareth wel

790 fleischli, as it were in reverence, whanne he seith, "Blissid be God," summe in dispite whanne he is angry agens God or his even Cristene, and swerith bi His blissid bodi or ony of His membris. But he seith in his thought that there is no God, and that is eithir for that he weneth that there is noon othir liyf than this or ellis yif he wene that there is anothir liyf.

795 Neverthelees he weneth that God seth not his synne, or that He wole not ponyssche it so harde as Holi Writ seith, or that He wole forgyve hym his synne though that he flee it not, or ellis that there schal no Cristen man be dampned doo he nevere so ille, or ellis yif he faste oure Ladi faste, or seie everi dai a certeyn orisoun, or heere everi dai two massis or thre, or do a certeyn bodili dede as it were in the worschipe of God, he schal

800 nevere goo to helle, doo he nevere so mykil synne, though he forsake it not. This man seith in his herte that there is no God, but he is unwise as the prophete seith. For he schal feelen and fynden in peyne that He is God whom he forgaat and sette not bi in welthe of this world, as the prophete seith: *Sola vexacio dabit intellectum* (Isaiah 28:19). That is, oonli peyne schal geve undirstondynge; for he that knoweth not this heere,

805 schal wel knowen it whanne he is in peyne.

Chapter Sixteen

A litil conceile hou loveres of this world schullen doon yif thei wolen be reformed in heer soules bifore that thei passen hennys.

784 **noon othir hevene**, the ideas in this paragraph were associated in the Middle Ages with the pagan philosophy known as Epicureanism; **Sotheli**, Truly. 793 **weneth**, supposes. 796 **forgyve**, forgive. 798 **oure Ladi faste**, the regular Saturday fast in honor of the Virgin; **orisoun**, prayer.

Thise men, though that thei witen weel that thei ben oute of grace and in deedli synne, thei han no care ne sorwe ne thought therfore. But thei maken fleschli merthe and wordli solas as mykil as thei mowen, and the ferthere that thei ben from grace, the more mirthe thei maken. And perchance some hoolden hem wel paied that thei have no grace, so that thei mowen more fulli and freli folwe the likynge of fleschli lustes, as though God were on slepe and might not seen hem. And this is oon of the moste defaute. And so bi her owen frowardenesse thei stoppe the light of grace from her owen soule that it may not resten thereinne; the whiche grace, in as mykil as in it is, schyneth to alle gosteli creatures, redi for to entren in there it is resseyved, as the sunne schyneth over alle bodili creatures there it is not letted. Thus seith Seynt Johan in the Gospel: *Lux in tenebris lucet, et tenebre eam non comprehenderunt* (John 1:5). That is, the light of grace schyneth in merkenesse, that is, to mennys hertis that aren merke thorugh synne, but the merkenesse taketh it not. That is, thise blynde hertis receyven not that gracious light ne han not the profite of hit. But right as a blynde man is al umbilappid with light of the sunne whan he stondeth therinne and yit seeth he it not, ne hath no profite therof for to goon therbi, right so goostli a soule blyndid with deedli synne is al unbilappid with this goostli light, and yit is he nevere the betere. For he is blynde and wole not seen ne knowen his blyndenesse, and that is oon of the moste lettynge of grace, that a wikkid man wole not be aknowe his owen blyndenesse for pride of himself; or ellis yif he knowe it, he chargeth it not but maketh myrthe and game as he were over al siker.

Therfore unto alle thise men that aren thus blyndid and bounden with the fals love of this world and aren so foule forschapen from the fairehede of man, I seie and conceile that thei thenken on her soule, and that thei able hem to grace as mykil as thei mowen, and that mowen thei doon upon this wise, yif thei wolen. Whanne that thei feelen hem oute of grace and overleid with deedli synne, thanne that thei thenke what meschief and peril is to hem for to ben oute of grace and be departid from God as thei be, for there is nothynge that holdeth hem from the pitte of helle that thei ne schulden as tite fallen therinne, but oo baare sengle threed of this bodili lif wherby thei hangen, that lightliere mai be lost thanne a sengle threed mai be broken on two. For were the breeth stoppid in

808 witen, know. **809 merthe**, happiness. **810 solas**, delight. **811 paied**, satisfied. **813 moste defaute**, greatest faults. **814 frowardenesse**, perversity. **817 letted**, prevented. **819 merke**, dark. **821 umbilappid**, surrounded. **825 moste lettynge**, greatest obstructions. **826 aknowe**, aware of. **827 chargeth**, accounts; **siker**, secure. **830 mowen**, are able. **831 upon this wise**, in this manner. **834 as tite**, immediately. **835 lightliere**, more easily.

the bodi, and that mai lightli falle, her soule schulde passe forth and anoon ben in helle withouten ende. And yif thei wolden thenken thus, thei schulden quaken and schaken for drede of the rightwise domes of God and of the harde ponyschynge of synne; and
840 thei schulden morne and sorwe for here synne and for thei han no grace.

And thanne schulde thei crien and praien that thei myghten have grace, and yif thei doon thus, thanne schulde grace fallen in hem, and putten oute myrkenesse and hardenesse of herte and weikenesse of wille, and geven hem myght and strengthe for to forsake the fals love of this world as mykil as is deedli synne. For ther is noo soule so
845 feer from God thorugh wikkidnesse of wille in deedli synne, I oughtake noon in this bodi of synne, that he ne mai thorugh grace be rightted and reformed to clennesse of good lyvynge, yif he wil bowen his wil to God with mekenesse for to amenden his liyf, and herteli aske grace and forgyvenesse of Hym, and excusen oure Lord and fulli accusen himself. For Hooli Writ seith: *Nolo mortem peccatoris, sed magis ut convertatur et vivat*
850 (Ezekiel 33:11). That is, oure Lord seith: "I wil not the deeth of a synnere, but I wole more that he be turned to me and lyve." For oure Lord woleth that the moste froward man that lyveth forschapen thorugh synne, yif he turne his wille and aske grace, that he be reformed to His likenesse.

Chapter Seventeen

That reformynge in feith and in feelynge mai not sodeynli be geten, but thorugh grace
855 and mochil traveile bodili and goostli.

This reformynge is in feithe, as I have bifore seid, that lighteli mai be had, but aftir this cometh reformynge in feith and in feelynge, that mai not lightli be geten, but thorugh longe traveile and mykil bisynesse. For reformynge in feith is comone to alle chosen soulis, though thei ben but in the lowest degree of charité, but reformynge in felynge is
860 speciali of thise soulis that mowen come to the staat of perfeccioun, and that mai not sodeynli be had. But aftir grete plenté of grace and mykil goostli traveile a soule mai come therto; and that is whanne it is firste heeled of goostli sikenesse, and whanne alle

837 **anoon,** at once. 840 **for₂,** because. 843 **weikenesse,** weakness. 845 **oughtake,** except. 856 **lighteli,** easily. 861 **plenté,** plenty.

bittir passions and fleschli lustis and othere oolde feelynges aren brente oute of the herte with fier of desire, and newe gracious feelynges aren brought in with brennynge love and goostli light. Than neigheth a soule to perfeccion and to reformynge in feelyngc.

For soth it is, right as a man that is brought neigh to the deeth thorugh bodili sikenesse, though he resseyve a medicyn bi the whiche he is restorid and sikir of his liyſ, he mai not for it as tite risen up and goon to werke as an hool man mai for the feblenesse of his bodi holdeth hym doun, that hym bihoveth to abiden a good while, and kepen hym with medicynes, and dioten hym with mesure aftir the techynge of a leche til he mai fulli recovere bodili heele. Right so goostli: he that is brought to goostli deeth thorugh deedli synne, though he thorugh medicyne of the sacrament of penaunce be restorid to lif, that he schal not be dampned, neverthelees he is not as tite hool of alle his passiouns and of his flesschli desires, ne able to contemplacion. But him bihoveth abiden a grete while and taken good kepe of himsilf, and rulen him so that he myght recovere ful heele of soule. For he schal langure a grete while or thanne he be fulli hool. Neverthelees, yif that he take medicynes of a good leche and use hem in tyme with mesure and descrecion, he schal mykil the sunnere be restorid and reformyd to his goostly strengthe and come to the reformyng in feelynge.

For reformynge in feith is the lowest staat of alle chosen soulis, for binethe that myght he not wel ben, but reformynge in feelynge is the highest staat in this liyf that the soule mai come to. But fro the loweste to the higheste mai not a soule sodeynli stirte, ne more than a man that wole clymbe upon an high laddre and setteth his foot upon the lowest stele mai atte the nexte fleen up to the higheste; but hym bihoveth bi processe gon oon aftir anothir, til he mai come to the overeste. Right so it is goostli: no man is maad sodeynli sovereyne in grace, but thorugh longe exercise and sligh wirkynge a soule mai come therto, nameli whanne he helpeth and techeth a wrecchid soule in whom al grace liggeth. For withoute special helpe and inli techynge of hym mai no soule come therto.

---

863 brente, burnt. **868 as tite**, immediately. **869 hym bihoveth**, he must. **870 dioten**, feed; **leche**, physician. **878 sunnere**, sooner. **882 stirte**, start. **883 laddre**, as Clark notes (p. 308n82), this is the only reference to the ladder metaphor, despite the title *Scale* (i.e., "Ladder") *of Perfection*. **884 stele**, rung. **888 liggeth**, lies; **inli**, inward.

Chapter Eighteen

890 On encheson whi so fewe soulis as in regarde of the multitude of othere comen to this reformynge in feith and in feelynge.

But now seist thou, syn oure Lord is so curtais of His goodnesse, and of His gracious giftes so free, wondir it is thanne that so fewe soules, as it semeth in reward of the multitude of othere, moun come to the reformyng in feelynge. Hit semeth that He were
895 daungerous, and that is not soth; or that He took no reward of His creaturis, the whiche bi takynge of feith aren bicomen His servauntis. Unto this I mai ansuere and seyn as me thenketh, that oon chesoun is this. Many men that aren reformed in feith setten not here herte for to profite in grace, ne for to seken noon higher staat of good lyvynge thorugh besi traveile in praiynge and thenkynge and othere bodili and goostli workynge; but hem
900 thenketh it hem inowgh for to kepe hem from deedli synne, for to stande stille in that plight as thei aren inne. For thei seyn that it is yinowgh to hem for to ben saaf and have the leeste degree in hevene; thei wolen coveiten no more.

Thus perchaunce doon summe of the chosen soules that lyven in the world actif liyf, and that is litil wondir of hem, for thei aren so occupied with wordli besynesse that
905 neden to be doon, that thei moun not fulli setten here herte to profiten in goosteli wirkynge. And neverthelees it is perilous to hem, for thei fallen often and al dai, and aren now up and now doon, and mowe not comen to stablenesse of good lyvynge. Neverthelees they aren sumwhat excusable, of here staat of lyvynge. But othere men and women that aren free fro worldli besynes yif thei wolen, and moun han here nedeful sustenaunce withoute
910 grete bodili bisynesse, as speciali religious men and women moun that bynden hemsilf to the staat of perfeccioun bi takynge of religioun, and othere men also in seculere staat that han mochil resoun and grete kyndeli witte, and myghten yif thei wolde disposen hem therto come to mychil grace — thise men are more for to blamen, for thei stondeth stille as thei weren idel, and wolen nought profite in grace, ne no ferthere seken for to
915 comen to the love and to the knowynge of God.

890 **On encheson**, One reason; **in regarde of**, in respect to. 892 **curtais**, courteous. 893 **in reward of**, in regard to. 895 **daungerous**, niggardly; **reward**, regard. 897 **chesoun**, reason. 898 **profite**, advance. 900 **inowgh**, enough. 901 **yinowgh**, enough; **saaf**, saved. 905 **profiten**, advance. 908 **of**, because of. 910 **religious**, members of a religious order. 911 **takynge of religioun**, entering a religious order.

Book II

For soothli it is perilous to a soule that is reformed oonli in feith, and wole no more seken ne profiten ne geven to bodili and goosteli traveile, for he mai so lighteli leese that he hath and fallen to deedli synne. For a soule mai not stonde stille alwei in oo staat while that he is in the flesch, for it is eithir profetynge in grace or ellis peirynge in synne. For it fareth bi hym as it dooth yif a man were drawen oute of a foule pit, and whanne he were uppe, he wolde no ferther goon thanne the pittis brinke. Soothli he were a mykil fool, for a litil puff of wynde or an unware styringe of himsilf schulde caste him doun ageyn werse than he was bifore. Neverthelees yif he flee from the brinke as feer as he mai, and goo forthe on the erthe, thanne, though there come a grete storm, he is more siker, for he fallith not agen into the pitte.

Right so goostli: he that is drawen oute of the pitte of synne thorugh reformynge of feith, and whanne he is oute of deedli synne hym thenketh hym siker inowgh, and therfore he wole not profiten but wole holden him stille as he is bi the pittis brynke as neer as he mai. Sothli he is not wise, for at the leeste temptacion of the enemy or of his flesch he falleth into synne agen. But nevertheles yif he flee fro the pytte, that is, yif he sette his herte fulli for to come to more grace and for to travaile bisili hou he mai come therto, and gyve him hertcli to praiynge, thenkynge, and othere good-werkes-doynge, thanne though grete temptacions risen agennys him, he fallith not lightli to deedli synne agen.

And soothli it is wonder to me, that syn grace is so good and so profitable, whi a man whanne he hath but a litil therof, yhe, so litil that he myght noo lasse have, that he wole seyn, "Hoo! I wil no more of this, for I have ynowgh." Whanne I see a wordli man, though he have of wordli good moche more thanne hym nedeth, yit he wole nevere seyn, "Hoo! y have inowgh, I wole no more of this." But he wole ai coveite more and more, and travailen alle hise wittes and his myghtes, and nevere wole stynten of his covetise til he mai have more. Mikil more thanne schulde a chosen soule coveiten goostli good, for that is ai lastande and maketh a soule blissid, and he nevere schuld ceese of his yernynge, yif he dide wel, gete what he gete myghte. For he that most coveiteth, moste schal have; and soothli yif he dide thus, he schulde profiten and wexen in grace greteli.

920

925

930

935

940

945

919 **profetynge**, advancing; **peirynge**, growing worse. **923 feer**, far. **925 siker**, secure. **929 the enemy**, i.e., the devil (this is Hilton's regular usage). **936 yhe**, yea. **940 stynten**, stop.

Chapter Nineteen

Anothir encheson of the same, and hou wilful bodili custum undiscreteli rewarded and usid, sumtyme hyndren soulis fro felinge of more grace.

Anothir enchesoun is this. Sum men that aren reformed in feith in the bigynnynge of here turnynge to God setten hemsilf in a certeyn manere of doynge, whethir it be bodili
950   or goostli, and thenken for to kepen ai that manere of forth werkynge, and not for to chaungen it for noon othir that cometh thorugh grace, though it were betere. For thei wenen that that doynge schulde be beste for hem alweie for to holden; and therfore thei resten hem therinne, and thorugh custum thei bynden hem so therto, that whan thei han fulfillid it thei thenken hem wondir weel esid, for thei wene that thei han doon a grete
955   thynge to God. And perchaunce yif it falle that thei ben lettid from here custom, though it be for a skileful cause, thei ben hevy and angri and han trobelynge of conscience, as yif thei hadde doon a grete dedli synne. Thise men hyndren hemsilf sumwhat fro feelynge of more grace, for thei setten here perfeccion in a bodili werk, and so thei maken an ende in the myddis of the weie, where noon eende is.

960   For whi, bodili costoms that men usen first in hire bigynnynge are goode, but thei aren but meenes and weies, ledande a soule to perfeccion; and therfore he that setteth his perfeccioun in a bodili werke, or in ony goostli werk that he feleth in the bigynnynge of his turnynge to God, that he wole no ferthere seken, but ai reste therinne, he hyndreth himsilf greteli. For it is a sympil craft that apprentice is alwei alike wise inne, and that
965   can on the first dai as mykil of it as he can twenti yeer aftir; or ellis yif the crafte be good and sotiel, he is of a dul witte or ellis of an yvel wille, that profiteth not therinne. But thanne is it sooth that of alle craaftis that aren, the service of God is moste sovereyn and moste sotil, the highest, the hardeste for to come to the perfeccioun of it, and also it is moste profitable and moste of wynnynge to him that mai soothfasteli performe it. And
970   therfore it semeth that the prentis of it that is ai like ferforth in the leernynge, othir he is dul-witted or ellis ille-willid.

---

946 **encheson**, reason. 952 **wenen**, suppose. 954 **esid**, at ease. 955 **lettid**, prevented. 956 **hevy**, doleful. 961 **ledande**, leading. 964 **apprentice**, an apprentice. 966 **sotiel**, difficult; **profiteth**, advances. **968 sotil**, intricate, difficult. **970 prentis**, apprentice.

I repreve not thise customes that men usen in the staat of bigynnynge, whethir thei
ben bodili or goostli, for y seie that thei aren ful goode and spedeful to hem for to usen.
But y wolde that thei heelden hem not but as a wei and an entré towarde goosteli
975 feelinge, and that thei usiden them a covenable mene, until a betere come, and that thei
in usynge of it coveitide aftir betere; and thanne yif a betere come that were more
goostli and more drawande in the thought from fleischlinesse and from the sensualité
and veyn ymaginacioun, and that schuld be lettid bicause of othir wilful custum, that
thei leve thanne here custom, whanne it mai be left withoute sclaundre or disese of
980 othere, and folwe that thei feelen. But yif neither lette othir, thanne that thei use bothe yif
that thei mai. I mene not of costoms nedeful thorugh bond of lawe, or of rule, or of
penaunce, but of othere wilfulli taken. Thus techeth the prophete in the sautier, seiynge
thus: *Etenim benediccionem dabit legislator, ibunt de virtute in virtutem, et videbitur
deus deorum in Syon* (Psalms 83:8). Sothli the bringere of the lawe schal geve his
985 blissynge, thei schulen goon fro vertu to vertu, and God of goddis schal be seyn in
Syon. The bringere of the lawe, that is oure Lord Jhesu Crist, schal gyve His blissynge,
that is, schal gyve His giftes of grace to His chosen soules, callende hem from synne
and rightynge hem bi gode werkes to His liknesse; thorugh whiche grace thei schullen
profiten and wexen from vertu to vertu until thei comen to Syon; that is until thei come
990 to contemplacion, in the whiche thei schullen see God of goddis; that is, thei schullen
see wel that ther is non but oon God, and thei schulen see that there is not but God.

Chapter Twenty

Hou that withouten moche bodili and goostli bisynesse and withoute moche grace of
mekenes of soulis mowen not be reformed in feelinge ne be kept in it whan thei mai
come therto.

995 Now, seist thou, syn it so is that reformynge in feith is so lowgh and so perilous for to
reste inne, bicause of drede of fallynge agen to deedli synne, and reformynge in feelynge
is so high and so siker, whoso myghte come therto — thanne coveitest thou for to wite

972 **repreve**, blame. 973 **spedeful**, advantageous. 974 **entré**, entrance. 975 **covenable mene**,
suitable manner. 977 **drawande**, drawing. 979 **disese**, discomfort. 980 **lette**, hinder. 982 **sautier**,
psalter. 985 **seyn**, seen. 995 **lowgh**, low.

what manere of traveile were most spedeful for to usen, bi the whiche a man myghte profiten inne and come therto, or yif there were ony certeyn traveile or special deede bi
1000   the whiche a man myght come to that grace and to that reformynge in feelynge. As unto this I seie thus: Thou wost weel what man or woman wole dispose him for to come to clennesse of herte and to feelynge of grace, hem bihoveth have mykil traveile, and grete fightynge in wille and in werk lastyngeli agens the wikkid stirynges of alle the heed synnes, not oonli agens pride or envie, but agens alle othere, with alle the spices that
1005   comen oute of hem, as I have seid heer biforn in the firste partie of this writynge. For whi, passions and fleschli desires letten the clennesse in herte and pees in conscience. And hem bihoveth also traveile for to geten alle vertues; not oonli chastité and abstinence, but also pacience and myldenesse, charité and mekenesse, and alle the othere. And this mai not be doon bi oo maner of werk, but bi diversis werkes and
1010   manye, aftir dyverse disposyngis of men, as now praiynge, now thenkynge, now wirkynge sum gode deede, now assaiynge hemself in dyverse weies; in hungir and in thurste, in coolde and suffrynge of schame and dispite yif nede be, and in othere bodili disesis for love of vertu and soothfastnesse.

    This knowest thou wel, for this redist thou in every book that techeth of good lyvynge.
1015   Thus seith also everi man that wole stire mannys soule to the love of God. And so it semeth that there is no special traveile ne certeyn dede thorugh the whiche oonli a soule myghte come to that grace, but principali thorugh grace of oure Lord Jhesu Crist, and bi many deedis and grete in al that he mai doon, and yit al is litil ynowgh. And o skile mai be this. For sithen oure Lord Jhesu Hymsilf is special maister of this craafte, and also
1020   special leche of goostli sikenesse, for withouten Him al is nought; therefore it is resonable that aftir He stireth and techeth, so a man folwe and wirke. But he is a sympil maister that cannot kenne his disciple while he is in leernynge but ai oon lesson, and he is an unwise leche that bi oon medicyn wole heele alle soris. Therfore oure Lord Jhesu, that is so wise and so good, for to schewe His wisedom and His godenesse He techeth sundri
1025   lessounes to His disciplis, aftir that they profiten in here lyvynge, and gyveth to sundri soulis sundri medicynes aftir the felynge of hire sikenesse. And also anothir skille is this: yif that there were oon certayn deede bi whiche a soule myghte come to perfighte love of God, thanne schulde a man wene that he myght come therto bi his owen werke and

998 **spedeful**, advantageous. 1003 **heed**, capital. 1004 **spices**, species. 1006 **clennesse**, purity. 1008 **myldenesse**, gentleness. 1010 **disposyngis**, dispositions. 1018 **skile**, reason. 1019 **sithen**, since. 1020 **leche**, physician. 1022 **kenne**, teach.

172

thorugh his owen traveile, as a marchaunt cometh to his mede bi his owen traveile oonli,
1030 and bi his werke. Nai, it is not soo goostli of the love of God. For he that wole serve
God wiseli and come to perfite love of Hym, he schal coveiten for to han noon othir
mede than Him oonli. But thanne, for to have Hym mai no creature deserve oonli thorugh
his owene travaile, for though a man myghte travelen bodili and gosteli as mykil as alle
creatures that evere were myghten, he myghte not deserven oonli bi his werkes for to
1035 have God for his mede. For He is sovereyn blisse and eendelees goodnesse, and passith
withoute comparisoun alle mennys desertis; and therfore He mai not be getin bi noo
mannys special werk, as bodili meede mai. For He is free and geveth Himsilf where He
wole and whanne He wole, neithir for this werke ne for that, ne this tyme ne aftir this
tyme; for though a soule werke al that he can and mai al his liyftyme, perfighte love of
1040 Jhesu schal he nevere have, til oure Lord Jhesu wole freeli gyven it. Neverethelees oon
that othir side y scie also, that I hope that He geveth it not, but yif a man wirke and
traveile al that he may and can, yhe til hym thenketh that he mai no more, or ellis be in
ful wille therto yif that he myghte.

And soo it semeth that neithir grace oonli withouten ful wirkynge of a soule that in it
1045 is, ne wirkynge aloone withouten grace, bryngeth not a soule to reformynge in feelynge,
the whiche reformynge stondeth in perfite love and charité. But that oon joyned with
that othir — that is, grace joined to werke — bryngeth into a soule the blissid feelynge
of perfite love, the whiche grace may not resten fulli but on a meke soule that is ful of
dreede of God. Therefore I seie that he that hath not mekenesse, ne dooth not his
1050 bisynesse, mai not come to this reformynge in feelynge. He hath not ful mekenesse that
cannot felen of himsilf soothfasteli as he is, as thus: he that dooth al the good deedes
that he can, as in fastynge, wakynge, werynge of the heire and alle othere suffrynge of
bodili penaunce, or dooth alle the outeward werkes of merci to his evene Cristene, or
ellis inward as praiynge, wepynge, sighhynge, and thenkynge: yif he reste ai in hem,
1055 and lene so mykil to hem, and rewarde hem so greteli in his owene sight that he presumeth
in his owen desertes, and thenketh himsilf ai riche and good and holi and vertuous —
sothli as longe as he feelith thus, he is not meke inow. Ne though he seie or thenke that
al that he dooth is of Goddis grace and not of hymsilf, he is not yit meke inow, for he
mai not yit make himsilf nakid from al his good deedes, ne make hymsilf pore soothfastli

---

1029 mede, reward. **1041 hope**, expect. **1042 yhe**, yea; **hym thenketh**, it seems to him. **1046 stondeth**, consists. **1050 bisynesse**, activity. **1052 heire**, hairshirt, the traditional garment of the penitent. **1055 rewarde**, regard.

1060   in spirit, ne feelen himsilf nought, as he is. And soothli, until a soule can felabli thorugh grace noughten himsilf, and baaren himsilf from al the good that he doth thorugh biholdynge of soothfastnesse of Jhesu God, he is not perfighteli meke.

    For what is mekenesse but sothfastenesse? Sothli, not ellis. And therfore he that thorugh grace may see Jhesu, hou He dooth al, and hymsilf dooth right nought but

1065   suffreth Hym werken in hym what Him list, he is meke. But this is ful harde and as it were impossible and unresonable to a man that wirketh al bi mannys resoun and seeth no ferthere, for to doon many gode dedes and thanne for to arette hem alle to Jhesu, and setten hymself at not. Neverthelees whoso myght have a gosteli sight of soothfastenes, he schulde thenke it ful true and ful resonable to doon so. And soothli he that hath this

1070   sight he schal nevere doo the lasse, but he schal be stired for to traveile bodili and goostli mykil the more and with mykil the betere wil. And this mai be o cause whi that summe men peraventure swynken and sweten and pynen here wrecchid bodi with outeragious penaunce al here liyftyme, and aren ai seiynge orisons and sautiers and biddynge many othere bedis, and yit mowen thei nout come to that goostli feelynge of

1075   the love of God, as it semeth sum men doon in schortere tyme with lasse peyne, for thei han not that mekenesse that y speke of.

    Also on that othir side I seie, he that dooth not his bisynesse mai not come to the felynge of grace. He dooth not his bisynesse that thenketh thus: Whereto schulde I traveile? Wherto schulde I praie or thenken, fasten or waken, or ony bodili penaunce

1080   doon for to come to siche grace, syn it mai not be geten ne had, but oonli of the free gift of Jhesu? Therfore I wole umbiden in fleischlihede right as I am, and right not doon of siche werkis bodili ne gosteli until he geve it. For yif he wole gyve it, he asketh no wirkynge of me. Whatso that I doo, and hou litil that y doo, I schal have it. And yif he wole not gyve it, traveile I nevere so faste for it, I gete it nevere the more. He that seith

1085   thus mai not come to this reformynge, for he draweth himsilf wilfulli to ydelnesse of fleschlihede, and unablith hym to the gifte of grace, in as mykil as he putteth from him bothe inward werkynge that stondeth in lastynge desire and in longynge to Jhesu, and outeward werkynge bi traveile of his bodi in goode outeward deedes. So mai he not have it.

1060 felabli, in the senses, palpably. **1061 noughten**, make nothing. **1062 perfighteli**, perfectly. **1067 arette**, account. **1068 not**, nought. **1072 swynken**, work. **1073 orisons**, prayers; **sautiers**, psalters. **1074 biddynge**, praying; **bedis**, prayers. **1077 bisynesse**, activity. **1081 umbiden**, remain; **fleischlihede**, fleshliness. **1086 unablith**, disables.

1090   Therfore I seie that he that hath not trewe mekenesse ne ful herteli bisynes mai not come to the reformynge in feelynge. For withoute bisynesse — either inward oonli bi grete fervour and lastinge desire and bisi praiere and thought in God, or ellis bothe inward and outewarde — mai he not come to this goosteli reformyng of this image.

Chapter Twenty-one

That a man that wil come to Jerusalem, that is undirstonde to the cité of pees, the which
1095   is contemplacion, muste hoolde him lowe in mekenesse and in feith, and suffir disese bothe bodili and gosteli.

Neverthelees, for thou coveitest to have sum maner wirkynge bi the whiche thou myghtest the rathere neighen to that reformynge, I schal seie thee as me thenketh bi the grace of oure Lord Jhesu, the schorteste and the redieste helpe that I knowe in this wirkynge. And hou
1100   that schal be, I schal telle thee bi ensample of a good pilgrine, upon this wise.
      There was a man that wolde goon to Jerusalem, and for that he knewe not the weie, he come to anothir man that he hopid coude the weie thider, and askid whethir he myghte not come to that cité. That othir man seide to him that he myght not come thidir withoute grete disese and grete traveile, for the wei is longe and the perilis aren grete for
1105   theves and robberes, and many othere lettyngis ther ben that fallen to a man in the goynge. And also there are many sundri weies, as it semeth, ledynge thedirward, but men al dai are slayn and spoiled and mowen not come to that place that thei coveiten. Neverthelees, there is o weie, the which weie whoso wolde take it and hoolde it, he wolde undirtake that he schulde come to the cité of Jerusalem, and he schulde nevere
1110   lesen his liyf ne be slayn, ne dien for defaughte. He schulde ofte be robbid and yvel beten, and suffre mykil disese in the goynge, but he schulde have his liyf saaf.

1090 **herteli**, hearty. 1095 **disese**, discomfort. 1098 **rathere neighen**, sooner approach. 1100 **ensample**, example; **pilgrine**, pilgrim; **wise**, manner. 1102 **coude**, knew. 1103 **to that cité**, Clark suggests (p. 309n102) that Hilton follows a specific source for his exposition of the commonplace of the Christian life as a pilgrimage to the heavenly Jerusalem, namely Bernard, *Sermo in quadrigesima* 6. 1104 **disese**, discomfort; **for₂,** because of. 1105 **lettyngis**, obstacles. 1107 **spoiled**, despoiled. 1110 **lesen**, lose; **defaughte**, fault. 1111 **disese**, discomfort.

Thanne seith the pilgrime: "Bi so y mai ascape and have my liyf saaf and come to that place that I coveite, I charge not what myschief I suffre in the goynge; and therfore seie me what thou wolt, and soothli I bihote thee for to doon theraftir." That othir man
1115 ansuerith and seith thus: "Loo, I sette thee in the right weie." This is the weie, and that thou kepe this lernynge that I kenne thee. Whatsoo thou herest or seest or feelist that schulde lette thee in thi weie, abide not with it wilfulli, tarie not for it restfulli, biholde it not, like it not, drede it not; but ai go forth in thi weie, and thenke that thou woldest not ellis but bee at Jerusalem. For that thou coveitest, that thou desirest, and not ellis but
1120 that. And yif men robben thee and spoilen thee, scorne thee, beten thee, and despice thee, stryve not ageyn yif thou wolt have thi liyf, but holde thee with the harm that thou hast and goo forth as nought were, that thou take no more harm. And also yif men wolen tarie thee with tales and fage thee with leesynges for to drawe thee to myrthis and to leve thi pilgrimages, make deef eere and ansuere not agen, seie not elles but that thou
1125 woldest ben at Jerusalem. And yif men profre thee giftis and wole make thee riche with wordli goodes, tende not to hem; thenke ai on Jerusalem. And yif thou wolte holden this weie and doon as I have seide, I undirtake thi liyf thou schalte not be slayn, but thou schalt come to that place ther thu coveitest.

Goosteli to oure purpos, Jerusalem is as mykil for to say as sight of pees, and it
1130 bitokeneth contemplacion in perfighte love of God. For contemplacion is not ellis but a sight of Jhesu, the whiche is veri pees. Than yif thou coveite for to come to this blissid sight of veri pees and be a trewe pilgrim to Jerusalemward, though it be so that I were nevere there, neverthelees as ferforth as I can I schal sette thee in the weie thedirward. The bigynnynge of the high weie in the whiche thou schalt goon is reformynge in feith,
1135 groundid mekeli in the feith and in the lawes of Holi Chirche, as I have seid bifore. For truste sikirli, though thou have synned here bifore, yif thou be now reformed bi the sacrament of penaunce aftir the lawe of Holi Chirche, that thou arte in the right weie. Now thanne, syn thou art in the siker weie, yif thou wilt spede in thy goynge and make good jornés, thee bihoveth holden thise two thinges often in thi mynde, mekenesse and
1140 love. That is, I am nought, I have nought, I coveite nought, but oon. Thou schalt have

1112 **ascape**, escape. 1114 **bihote**, promise. 1116 **kenne**, teach. 1117 **lette**, obstruct. 1120 **spoilen**, despoil; **despice**, despise. 1123 **tarie**, trouble; **fage**, deceive; **leesynges**, deceptions. 1132 **veri**, true; **to Jerusalemward**, toward Jerusalem. 1133 **as ferforth**, to the extent. 1136 **sikirli**, certainly. 1138 **spede**, thrive. 1139 **jornés**, journeys.

the menynge of thise wordes in thyn entente and in habite of thi soule lastanli, though thou have not thise wordes speciali formed ai in thi thought, for that nedeth nought. Mekenesse seith, I am nought, I have nought. Love seith, I coveite nought but oon, and that is Jhesu.

1145   Thise two strynges, wel festened with mynde of Jhesu, maken good acord in the harpe of thi soule, whanne thei ben craftli touchid with the fyngir of resoun, for the lowere thou smytest upon that on, the highere souneth that tothir. The lasse thou felist that thou art or that thu hast of thisilf thorugh mekenesse, the more thou coveiteste for to have of Jhesu in desire of love. I mene not oonli of that mekenesse, the whiche a

1150 soule feelith in sight of his owen synne or frieltees or wrecchidnesse of this liyf, or of the worthinesse of his evene Cristene. For though this mekenes be soothfast and medicynable, neverthelees it is boistous and fleschli as in regard, not clene ne softe ne loveli. But I mene also this mekenesse that the soule feeleth thorugh grace, in sight and biholdinge of the endelees beynge and the wondirful goodnesse of Jhesu; and yif thou

1155 mowe not seen it yit with thi goostili iye that thou trowe it. For thorugh sight of His beynge, either in ful feith or in feelynge, thou schalt holden thisilf not oonli as the moste wrecche that is, but also as nought in substance of thi soule, though thou haddest doo nevere synne. And that is loveli mekenesse, for in reward of Jhesu that is soothfastli al, thou art right nought. And also that thou thenke that thou haste right nought, but arte as

1160 a vessel that stondeth ai tome or voide as nought were thereinne, as of thisilf. For doo thou nevere so manye good deedes outeward or inward, until thou have and feele that thou hast the love of Jhesu, thou hast right nought. For with that precious licour oonli, mai thi soule be fulfilled, and with noon othir. And for as mykil as that thynge aloone is so precious and so worthi, therfore what thou haste or what thou doost, holde it as

1165 right nought as for to resten inne, withoute the sight and the love of Jhesu. Keste it al bihynde thee and forgete it, that thou myghtest have that that is beste of alle.

    Right as a trewe pilgrym goynge to Jerusalem leveth bihynde him hous and lond, wif and childe, and maketh hemsilf pore and bare from al that he hath, that he myght goo lightli withoute lettynge: right so yif thou wolt ben a goostli pilgrim, thou schalt make

1170 thisilf nakid from al that thou haste, that are bothe gode dedes and badde, and casten alle bihynde thee, that thou be so pore in thyn owen feelynge that ther be nothing of thyn

1141 **lastanli,** lastingly. 1146 **craftli,** skillfully. 1150 **frieltees,** frailties. 1152 **medicynable,** medicinal; **boistous,** unruly; **regard,** aspect. 1160 **tome,** empty. 1165 **Keste,** Cast. 1169 **lettynge,** hindrance.

owen wirkynge that thou wolt lene upoun restandeli, but ai desirynge more grace of love and ai sekynge the goosteli presence of Jhesu. And yif thou doo thus, thanne schalt thou sette in thin herte fully and hooly that thou woldest ben at Jerusalem, and at noon

1175 othir place but there. And that is, thou schalt setten in thyn herte fulli and hooli, that thou woldeste nothynge have but the love of Jhesu and the goostli sight of Him as He wole schewen Him; for to that oonli thou art maad and bought, and that is thi bigynnynge and thyn ende, thi joie and thi blisse. And therfore, whatsoevere that thou have, be thou nevere so riche in othere dedis bodili and goostli, but yif thou have that, and knowe and

1180 feele that thou haste it, holde that thou hast right nought. Prente wel this resoun in the menynge of thyn herte, and cleve sadli therto; and hit schal save thee from alle perilis in thy goynge, that thou schalt not perischen, and it schal save thee fro theves and robbours, the whiche I calle unclene spiritis, that though thei spoile thee and bete thee thorugh dyvers temptaciouns thi liyf schal be ai saaf. And schorteli yif thou kepe it as I schal seie

1185 thee, thow schalt ascape alle periles and myschevys and come to the cité of Jerusalem withinne schort tyme.

Now thou art in the weie and knoweste what the place highte and whidir thou schalt drawe to. Bigyn than for to goon forth in thy jorné. Thi forthgoynge is not ellis but goostli werkes, and bodili also whanne that it nedeth, whiche thou schalte usen with

1190 discrecioun upon this wise. What werk that it be that thou schuldest doon, aftir the degree or staate asketh that thou stondest inne, bodili or goostli, yif it helpe this gracious desire that thou hast for to love Jhesu, and make it more hool and more esi, and more myghti to alle vertues and to al goodnesse, that werke holde I best; be it praiynge, be it thenkynge, be it redynge, be it wirkynge; and as longe as that werk strengtheth moste

1195 thyn herte and thi wille to the love of Jhesu, and ferthest draweth thyn affeccion and thi thought from wordli vanité, it is good for to use it. And yif it be so, that thorugh use savour of that lasseth, and thee thenketh anothir werk savoureth thee more, and thou feelist more grace in anothir, take anothir and leef that. For though the desire and the yernynge of thyn herte to Jhesu schulde ai be unchaungeable, neverthelees thi goostli

1200 werkes that thou schalt usen in praiynge or in thenkynge for to feeden and norischen

1174 **thin**, your. 1177 **schewen Him**, reveal Himself. 1180 **Prente**, Print. 1185 **ascape**, escape; **myschevys**, misfortunes. 1187 **highte**, is called. 1188 **jorné**, journey. 1190 **upon this wise**, in this manner. 1190–91 **aftir the degree . . . goostli**, such phrases imply that Hilton intended his work for a wider audience than enclosed anchoresses; see Clark, p. 310n113. 1192 **esi**, comforting. 1196 **wordli**, worldly.

this desire mowen be dyvers, and moun ben wel chaungid aftir that thou feelist thee disposed thorugh grace and appliynge of thyn owen herte.

For it farith bi werkes and by disire, as it dooth bi stikkes and bi a fier. For the mo stikkis are leid to the fier, the grettere is the flawme and the hattere is the fier. Right so
1205 the more dyverse goostli werkynge that a man hath in his thought for to kepen hool his desire, the myghtiere and the more brennande schal be his desire to God. And therfore loke wisely what werk thou canst best doon, and that moste helpeth thee for to save hool this desire to Jhesu (yif thou be free, and arte not bounden but undir the comoun lawe), and that do. Bynde thee not to wilful customs unchaungeabli, that schulde lette
1210 the fredom of thyn herte for to love Jhesu yif grace wole visite thee speciali. For I schal telle thee whiche customs aren ai goode and nedeful to be kepte. Loo, siche a custom is ai good for to ben holden that stondeth in getynge of vertu and lettynge of synne, and that custom schulde nevere be left, for thou schalt ai be meke and pacient, sobre and chaste, yif thou wel doo, and so of alle othere vertues. But the custom of anothir thynge
1215 that letteth a betere is for to leven whanne tyme is, there a man mai. As thus, yif a man have in custom for to seyn thus many bedes, or for to thenken oonli this manere thought and thus longe tyme, or for to waken or knelen thus longe, or ony othir bodili deede, this custom is for to leeve sum tyme whan resonable cause letteth, or ellis yif more grace come on othir side.

Chapter Twenty-two

1220 Of a general remedie agens wikkid stirynges and peynful taryynges that fallen in here hertis of the fleisch, the world, and the feend, and hou a stidefast desire to Jhesu mayntened and strenthed with devout praiere and bisi thenkynge on Him is a sovereyn remedye.

Now art thou in the weie, and thou wost hou thou schalt goon. Now beware of enemyes
1225 that wolen be bisie for to lette thee yif thei mowen, for al here entente is for to putten oute of thyn herte that desire and that longynge that thou hast to the love of Jhesu, and

1201 **mowen**, can; **moun**, can. 1209 **lette**, hinder. 1216 **bedes**, prayers. 1220 **taryynges**, troubles. 1225 **lette**, prevent.

179

for to dryve thee hoom ageyn to love of worldli vanyté. For ther is nothynge that greveth hem so mykil. Thise enemyes aren principali fleschli desires and veyne dredes, that risen oute of thi herte thorugh corrupcioun of thi fleschli kynde, and wolde lette the
1230 desire of the love of Jhesu, that thei myghten fulli and restefulli occupien thyn herte — these aren thi nexte enemyes. Also othere enemyes there aren, as unclene spirites that aren bisi with sleightes and wiles for to disseyven thee. But o remedie schal thou have that I seide bifore — whatso it be that thei seyn, trowe hem not, but holde forth thy weie, and oonli desire the love of Jhesu. Ansuere ai thus: I am nought, I have nought, I
1235 coveite not, but oonli for to love Jhesu.

Yif thyne enemyes seyn to thee first thus, bi stirynges in thyn herte, that thou arte not schryven aright, or there is sum olde synne hid in thin herte that thou knowest not, ne were not schryven of, and therfore thou mostist turne hoom agen and leve thi desire, and goo first and schryve thee betere: trowe not this seiynge, for it is fals, for thou arte
1240 schryven. Truste sikirli that thou art in the weie, and thee nedeth no more ransakynge of schrifte for that that is passid. Hold forthe thi wey and thenke on Jerusalem. Also yif thei seyn that thou arte not worthi for to have the love of God, wherto schalt thou coveite that thou myght not have, ne arte not worthi therto, trowe hem not, but goo forth, and seie thus: "Not for I am worthi, but for I am unworthi, therfore wolde I love
1245 God. For yif I hadde it, that schulde make worthi me. And syn I was maad therto, though I schuld nevere have it, yit wole I coveite it, and therfore wole I praien and thenken that I myght geten it." And thanne yif thyn enemyes seen that thou bigynnest to wexen bold and wel willed to thi werk, thei bigynne to wexe aferd of thee.

Neverthelees, thei wolen not ceesen of tariynge whanne thei mowen as longe as thou
1250 art goynge in the weie, what with drede and manassynge on that toon side, what with flaterynge and fals plesynge on that othir side, for to doo thee breke thi purpos and turnen hoom agen. Thei wolen seie thus: "Yif thou holde forth this desire to Jhesu so fulli traveilynge as thou bigynnest, thou schal falle in sikenesse, or in fantasies, or into frenesies, as thou seest that sum men doon, or thou schalt fallen in poverté and bodily
1255 myschef, and no man schal wille helpe thee; or thou myght falle into privei temptacions of the feend, that thou schalt not conne helpe thisilf inne. For it is wondir perilous ony

1231 **nexte**, closest. 1233 **trowe**, believe. 1248 **aferd**, afraid. 1249 **tariynge**, troubling. 1250 **manassynge**, menacing; **toon**, one. 1254 **frenesies**, frenzies. 1255 **myschef**, misfortune; **schal wille**, will want to.

man to gyve him fulli to the love of God, and leve al the world, and nothynge coveiteyng but oonli Him and the love of Him, for so many periles mowen falle that a man knoweth not of. And therfore turne hoom agen and leef this desire, for thou schalt never brynge

1260   it to a good ende, and doo as othere wordli men doon." Thus seyn thyn enemyes, but trowe hem not, but holde ai forth thi desire, and seie not ellis but that thou woldest have Jhesu, and ben at Jerusalem. And yif thei perceyve thanne thi wille so strenthid that thou wolt not spare for synne ne for sikenesse, for fantasye, ne frenesie, for doughtes ne for dredes, ne for gosteli temptacions, for myschef ne for poverté, for liyf ne for deeth; but

1265   ai forth thou wolte with oo thynge, and no thinge but oon, and makest deef eere to hem whatsoevere thei seyn as though thou herdest hem not, and holdest forth stilli in thyn praieres and in thi othere goostli werkes withouten stintinge, and thou dost with discrecion aftir conceil of thi sovereyne or thi goostli fadir; thanne bigynne thei for to be wrooth and to goon a litil neer thee. Thei bigynne for to robbe thee and bete thee and doo thee

1270   al the schame that thei mowen. And that is, whanne thei make that alle thi deedes that thou doost, be thei nevere so weel doon, aren demed of othere men as ille and turnyd into wers partie. And whatsoevere it be that thou woldest have doon in helpe of thi bodi or of thi soule, it schal be lettid and hyndrid bi othere men, so that thou schalt be put fro thi wille in alle thinges that thou skilfuli coveitest. And al this thei doon that thou schuldest

1275   be stired to ire or malencolie or yvel wil agens thyn even Cristene.

     But agens alle thise diseses and alle othere that mowen fallen, use this remedie. Take Jhesu in thy mynde, angre thee not with hem, tarie not with hem, but oonly on thi lesson. That is, thou arte not, thou hast not, thou maist not leesen of ertheli good, thou coveitest nought but the love of Jhesu, and holde forth thi weie to Jerusalem, with thyn

1280   occupacion. And neverthelees yif thou be taried sum tyme thorugh frielté of thisilf with sich diseses that fallen to thi bodili liyf thorugh yvel wil of man or malice of the feend, as soone as thou maist come agen to thisilf, and leve of the thenkynge of that disese and goo forth to thi werk. Abide not to longe with hem for drede of thyn enemyes.

1258 mowen, can. **1263 doughtes**, doubts. **1268 wrooth**, angry. **1269 neer**, nearer to. **1270 mowen**, can. **1271 ille**, evil. **1272 wers**, worse; **partie**, part. **1276 diseses**, discomforts. **1277 tarie**, trouble. **1278 not**$_{1,2}$, nought. **1280 occupacion**, attention; **frielté**, frailty. **1281 diseses**, discomforts.

Chapter Twenty-three

1285 Hou thou that art thus in this weie and wolt not be put out bi no diseses; thyne enemyes wolen than forgen thee and sette thee bifore alle thi good deedes and commende thee of hem and hou than thou schalt putte hem awey.

And aftir this, whanne thyne enemyes seen that thou art so wel-willed, that thou art not angri ne hevy ne wrooth, ne mykil stired agen no creature for ought that thei mowen doon or speken agens thee, but settest thyn herte fulli for to suffren al that mai falle,
1290 eese and uneese, praisynge or lackyng, and that thou wolt charge nothinge with thi, that thou myghtest kepe thi thought and thi desire hool to the love of God, thanne are thei mykil abasched. But thanne wolen thei assaie thee with flaterie and plesynge, and that is whanne thei brengen to the sight of thi soule alle thi good deedis and thi vertues, and beeren upon thee that alle men preisen thee and speken of thyn holinesse and hou alle
1295 men loven thee and worschipen thee for thi hooli lyvynge. This doon thyn enemyes that thou schuldest thenke here seiynge sooth, and han delite in this veyn joie and reste thee therinne. But yif thou doo wel, thou schalt holden al siche veyn jangelynge as falsheed and flaterie of thyn enemye, that profreth thee venym to drynken tempred with hony. Therfore refuse it and seie thou wolt not therof, but thou woldest ben at Jerusalem.
1300 Siche lettynges thou schalt felen or elles othere like, what of thi flesch, what of the world, what of the feend, mo than I mai reherce now. For a man as longe as he suffrith his thought wilfulli rennen al aboughte the world in biholdinge of sundri thynges, he perceyveth fewe lettynges. But as soone as he draweth al his thought and his yernynge unto oo thynge oonli, for to have that, for to see that, and for to knowe that, and loven
1305 that, and that is oonli Jhesu, than schal he wel feelyn manye peynful lettynges, for every thought that he feleth and is not that that he coveiteth is lettynge to him. Therfore I have tolde thee of summe speciali, as for exsample. And overmore I seie generali, that what stirynge that thou feelist of thi fleische or of the feend, plesant or peynful, bittir or swete, likynge or dredeful, gladsum or sorweful, that wolde drawe doun thi thought
1310 and thi desire from the love of Jhesu to wordli vanité and lette uttirli thi goostli covetise

1285 forgen thee, scheme against you. **1289 suffren**, endure. **1290 charge nothinge with thi**, concern yourself about nothing. **1294 beeren upon thee**, emphasize to you. **1297 jangelynge**, jangling. **1300 lettynges**, hindrances. **1309 gladsum**, joyous.

that thou hast to the love of Him, and that thyne herte schuld be occupied with that stirynge restandli: sette it at nought, receyve it not wilfulli, tarie not therewith to longe.

But yif it bee of a wordli thynge that bihoveth nedes to be doon unto thisilf or to thyn evene Cristene, spede thee soone of it, and brynge it to an ende that it hange not on thyn herte. Yif it be anothir thynge that nedeth not, or ellis it toucheth not thee, drede it not, like it not, but smyte it out of thyn herte redili. And seie thus: "I am nought; I have nought; nought I seke ne coveite but the love of Jhesu." Knyt thi thought to this desire, and strengthe it with praier and with othir goostli werk that thou forgete it not, and it schal leede thee in the right weie and save thee from alle periles, that though thou feele hem thou schal not perischen; and I hope that it schal brynge thee to the perfight love of oure Lord Jhesu.

Neverthelees on that othir side I saide also, what werk or what stirynge it be that mai helpe thi desire, strenthe it and norische it, and make thi thought ferthest from the love and mynde of the world, more hool and more brennande to the love of Jhesu, whethir it be praiynge or thenkynge, stillenes or spekynge, reedynge or heerynge, oonlynes or comonynge, goynge or sittynge — kepe it for the tyme and wirke thereinne as longe as savour lasteth, bi so that thou take therwith mete and drynke and slepe as a pilgrym dooth, and kepe discrecion in thi wirkynge aftir conceile or ordenaunce of thi sovereyne. For have he nevere soo grete haste in his goynge, yit he wole in tyme ete and drynken and slepen. Do thou so. For though it lette oon tyme, it schal fortherene thee anothir tyme.

Chapter Twenty-four

Hou a soule whan it is hid thorugh grace fro the vyle noise and besynesse of the world is a gode nyght and a lighti merkenesse, for thane may it freli praien and thenken on Jhesu.

Yyf thou wilte witen thane what this desire is, sotheli it is Jhesu. For He maketh this desire in thee and He geveth thee it. He it is that desireth in thee and He it is that is desired. He is al and He dooth al, yif thou myght seen Hym. Thou doost nought, but suffrist Hym

---

1312 restandli, constantly. **1314 spede**, hasten. **1325 oonlynes**, solitude. **1326 comonynge**, community; **goynge**, walking. **1330 fortherene**, advance. **1334 witen**, know.

werken in thi soule and assentest to Hym with grete gladenesse of herte that He voucheth saaf for to doo so in thee. Thou art not ellis but a resonable instrument whereinne that He werketh. And therfore whanne thou feelist thi thought bi touchynge of His grace bi
1340 taken up with this desire to Jhesu with a myghti devoute wille for to plesen Him and loven Him, thynke thanne that thou haste Jhesu; for He it is that desireth. Biholde Him wel, He goth bifore thee, not in bodili liknesse, but unseabli bi privei hid presence of His goostli myght; therfore see Hym gostly yif thou myght, or ellis trowe Him and folwe Him whidirso He goth; for Hee schal leede thee in the righte weie to Jerusalem, that is,
1345 the sight of pees in contemplacioun. Thus praiede the prophete to the Fadir of hevene, seiynge thus: *Emitte lucem tuam et veritatem tuam ipsa me deduxerunt, et adduxerunt in montem sanctum tuum, et in tabernacula tua* (Psalms 42:3). That is: Fader of hevene, sende oute Thi light and Thi soothfastenesse, that is, Thi sone Jhesu; and He schal lede me bi desire in me into Thi hooli hille and into Thi tabernaculis, that is, to the feelynge of
1350 perfighte love and heighte in contemplacioun.

Of this desire speketh the prophete thus: *Memoriale tuum domine in desiderio anime mee. Anima mea desideravit te in nocte, sed et spiritus meus in precordiis meis* (Isaiah 26:8–9). That is: Lord Jhesu, the mynde of Thee is printed in desire of my soule, for my soule hath desired Thee in the nyght and my spirite hath coveited Thee in al my thenkynge.
1355 And whi the prophete seith that he desired God al in the nyght, and what he meneth therbi, schal I telle thee. Thou woste weel that the nyght is a tymeful space atwixe to daies; for whanne oo dai is ended, anothir cometh not as tite, but first cometh nyght and departeth the daies, sumtyme longe and sumtyme schort, and thanne aftir that cometh anothir dai. The prophete menede not oonli of this maner nyght, but he menede of the
1360 goostli nyght. Thou schal undirstande that there ben two daies or two lightes; the first is fals light, the secunde is a trewe light. The fals light is the love of this worlde, that a man hath of himsilf of corrupcion of his fleisch; the trewe light is the perfight love of Jhesu feelid thorugh grace in a mannys soule. The love of the world is a fals light, for it passeth awei and lesteth not, and so it performeth not that it highte. This light byhighte
1365 the feend to Adam, whanne he stired hym to synne, and seide thus: *Aperientur oculi vestri et eritis sicut dii* (Genesis 3:5). That is: Youre iyen schullen ben opened and ye schullen ben as goddis. And he seide soth there; for whanne Adam hadde synned,

1342 unseabli, invisibly. **1356 tymeful**, temporal, durational; **atwixe to**, between two. **1357 as tite**, immediately. **1359 menede**, meant. **1364 highte**, promised; **byhighte**, promised.

anoon his innere iye was spered and goostli light withdrawen, and the utterere yyen were opened, and he felte and sigh a newe light of fleschli knowynge and wordli love
1370   that he sigh not bifore. And so sigh he a newe dai, but this was an ille dai; for this dai was it that Job wariede whanne he seide thus: *Pereat dies in qua natus sum* (Job 3:3). That is: Perische mote the dai in whiche I was born. He wariede not the dai rennynge in the yeere that God maade, but he wariede this dai that man maade, that is, the concupiscence and the love of the world in the whiche he was born, though he feelte it
1375   not thanne. This dai and this light he askide of God that it schulde perischen and no lengere lasten.

   But the love of Jhesu is a trewe dai and a blissed light, for God is bothe love and light, and He is ai lastynge, thus Seynt Johan seith: *Qui diligit deum manet in lumine* (1 John 2:10). That is: He that loveth God duelleth al in light. Than what man that perceyveth
1380   and seeth the love of this world fals and failande, and forthi he wole forsake it and seke the love of God; he mai not as tite feele the love of Hym, but him bihoveth a while abiden in the nyght, for he mai not sodeynli come from that oon light to that othir, that is, fro the love of the world to the perfite love of God. This nyght is not ellis but a foreberynge and a withdrawynge of the affeccioun and the thought of the soule from ertheli thynges,
1385   bi gret desire and yernynge for to seen and felen and loven Jhesu and gosteli thinges. This is the nyght; for right as the nyghte is myrke and an hidynge of alle bodili creatures and a restynge of alle bodili deedes, right so a man that setteth him fulli for to thenken on Jhesu, and desiren oonli the love of Him, is besi for to hiden his thought from veyn biholdynge and his affeccion from fleischli likynge of alle fleschli creatures, so that his
1390   thought be maad free, not ficched, ne his affeccion bounden, ne trobeled in nothinge lowere ne werse thanne hymsilf. And yif he mai doo soo, thanne is it nyght with him, for thanne is he in myrkenesse.

   But this is a good nyght and a lighti merkenesse, for it is a stoppynge ought of fals love of the world, and it is a neighynge to the trewe dai. And sotheli the merkere that the
1395   nyght is, the nerrere is the trewe light of the love of Jhesu; for the more that a soule mai thorugh longynge to God be hid fro noise and deene of fleschli affecciones, werldli desires, and unclene thoughtes, the nerrere is it for to feelen the light of the love of Hym,

1368 spered, closed; **utterere yyen,** outer eyes. **1369 sigh,** saw. **1371 wariede,** cursed. **1372 mote,** may; **rennynge,** current. **1381 as tite,** immediately; **him bihoveth,** he must. **1383 foreberynge,** withholding. **1386 myrke,** dark. **1390 ficched,** fixed. **1393 ought,** out. **1394 merkere,** darker. **1396 deene,** din.

for it is evene at it. Thus semede that the prophete menede whanne he seide thus: *Cum in tenebris sedeo, dominus mea lux est* (Micah 7:8). Whanne I sitte in myrkenesse oure
1400 Lorde is my light; that is, whanne my soule is hid from alle stirynges of synne as it were in sleep, thanne is oure Lord Jhesu my light, for thanne neigheth He of his grace for to schewe me of His light. Neverthelees this nyght is sumtyme peynful and sumtyme it is esi and confortable. It is peynful firste whanne a man is mykil foule and is nought thorugh grace usid for to ben often in this myrkenesse, but wolde fayne have it, and
1405 therfore he setteth his thought and his desire to Godward as mykil as he may, that he wolde not feelen ne thenken but oonli on Hym.

And bicause that he may not lightli have it, therfore it is peynful. For the custom and the hoomlynesse that he hath had bifore with synne of the world, and fleschli affecciones and ertheli thynges, and his fleschli deedes, presen so upon him and ai smyten in bi
1410 maistrie and drawen doun alle the soule to hem, that he mai not wel ben hid from hem as soone as he wolde ben. And therfore is this merkenesse peyneful to hym, and nameli whanne grace toucheth him nought abondauntli. Neverthelees, yif it be so with thee, be not to hevy ne strive not to mykil, as yif thou woldest thorough maistrie putten hem ought of thi thought; for thou may not doon soo. But abide grace, suffre esili, and breek
1415 not thisilf to mochil and slili yif thou maist drawe thi desire and thi goostli biholdynge to Jhesu, as yif thou woldest not charge hem.

For wite thou wel, whanne thou woldest desire Jhesu and oonli thenken on Him, and thou mai not freli for presynge in of swilk wordli thoughtes, sothli thou art outeward of the fals dai, and thou art entred into this myrkenesse. But thi merkenesse is not restefulle,
1420 bicause of disuse and unconnynge and unclennesse of thiself. And therfore use it often, and it schal bi processe thorugh feelynge of grace be more esi and more restful to thee. And that is whanne thi soule thorugh feling of grace is maad so free and so myghti and so gadred into hitsilf, that it lesteth to thenke on right nought, and that it mai withoute lettynge of ony bodili thynge thenke on right nought: than is it in a good myrkenesse.
1425 This nought I mene thus: that a soule mai thorugh grace be gadred into itsilf and stonde stille in itsilf freli and hooli, and not be dryven agens his wil ne drawen doun bi

1398 **menede**, meant. 1403 **esi**, easy. 1405 **to Godward**, toward God. 1408 **hoomlynesse**, familiarity. 1409 **presen**, press; **in**, inward. 1410 **maistrie**, force. 1411 **merkenesse**, darkness. 1415 **to mochil**, too much; **slili**, cleverly. 1416 **charge**, be concerned about. 1417 **wite**, know. 1418 **freli**, freely; **presynge**, pressing; **swilk**, such. 1420 **unconnynge**, ignorance; **unclennesse**, impurity. 1421 **esi**, comfortable. 1423 **lesteth**, desires. 1424 **nought**, nothing.

maistrie for to thenken or liken or loven with chesinge of affeccioun ony synne, or veynli or ertheli thynge. Than thenketh the soule nought, for thanne thenketh it on no ertheli thynge clevandeli. This is a riche nought. This nought and this nyght is a grete eese for a soule that desireth the love of Jhesu. It is in eese as for thought of ertheli thynge, but not as for Jhesu; for though the soule thenke not of ony ertheli thynge, neverethelees it is ful bisi for to thenken on Him.

What thinge thanne maketh this merkenesse? Sothli not ellis but a gracious desire for to have the love of Jhesu. For that desire and that longynge that it hath that tyme to the love of Jhesu, for to seen Hym and han Hym, dryveth oute of the herte alle wordli vanytees and fleschli affecciones, and gadreth the soule into itsilf and occupieth it oonli for to thenke hou it myght come to the love of Him, and so bryngeth into this riche nought. And sothli it is not al myrke ne nought whanne it thenketh thus; for though it bee myrke trom fals light, it is not al merke fro the trewe light. For Jhesu that is bothe love and light is in this merkenesse, whethir it be peynful or resteful. He is in the soule as travailande in desire and longynge to light; but he is not yit as restande in love, ne as schewende his light. And therfore it is called nyght and merkenesse, in as mykil as the soule is hid fro the fals light of this woorld and hath not yit fulli felynge of trewe light, but is in abidynge of the blissid love of God that it desireth.

Thanne yif thou wolt wite whanne thou arte in this syker merkenesse and whanne not, thou myght assaie thus, and seke no ferthere but thus. Whanne thou feelist thyn entente and thi wille fulli sette for to desiren thus God and thenke oonli on Hym, thou maight as it were first examyne thisilf in thi thought, whethir thou coveite for to have onythynge of this liyf for love of itsilf, or for to have the use of ony of thi bodili wittes in ony creature. And thanne yif thyne iye bigynne and ansuere thus, I wolde see right nought; and aftir that thyn eere, I wolde heere right nought; and thi mouthe, I wolde savoure right nought, I wold speke right nought of erthli thynge; and thi nose, I wolde smelle right nought; and thi bodi, y wolde feele right nought; and aftir, yif thyn herte seith, I wolde thenke right nought that is of ertheli thynge, ne of bodili deede, ne I wolde have affeccioun fastned fleschli in no creature, but oonli to God and to Godward, yif that y coude. And whanne thei ansuere alle thus to thee, and that is doon ful redili yif grace touche thee, thanne art thou entred sumwhat into merkenesse.

1427 maistrie, force; **chesinge**, choosing. **1429 clevandeli**, in a clinging way. **1430 eese**₁, comfort. **1441 travailande**, laboring. **1450 iye**, eye. **1455 to Godward**, toward God. **1456 coude**, was able to.

For though thou feele and perceyve glyntynges and proferynges of veyn thoughtes and presynge in of fleschli affeccions, neverthelees thou art in this profitable myrkenesse, 1460 bi so that thi thought be not ficchid on hem. For siche veyn ymaginacions that fallen in the herte unaviseli troblen this merkenesse and pyne the soule sumwhat, bicause that it wolde ben hid from hem and mai not. But thei doon not awai the profite of this myrkenesse, for the soule schal bi that weie come to reestful myrkenesse. And thanne is this myrkenesse restful, whanne the soule is hid for the tyme fro the pyneful feelynge of alle 1465 siche veyn thoughtes, and oonli is rested in desire and longynge to Jhesu with a goosteli biholdynge of Hym, as it schal be seid aftir. But it lasteth but a while hool; neverthelees though it be but a schort tyme, it is ful profitable.

Chapter Twenty-five

Hou that desire of Jhesu sothfastli feelid in this lightli myrkenesse sleeth alle stirynges of synne, and ableth the soule for to perceyve goostli lightnynges for the goostli Jerusa- 1470 lem, that is Jhesu.

Thanne sithen this merkenesse and this nyght is so good and so restful, though it be schorte, that stondeth oonli in desire and longynge to the love of Jhesu with a blynde thynkyngc of Him hou good thanne and hou blissid is it for to feelen His love and for to be illumyned of His blissid unseable light for to seen soothfastenesse, the whiche light 1475 a soule resseyveth whanne the nyght passeth and the dai springeth. This I hope was the nyght that the prophete menede whanne he seide: "My soule hath desired thee in the nyght" (Isaiah 26:9), as I bifore seide. It is mykil betere for to ben hid in the myrke nyght fro biholdynge of the world, though it were peyneful, than for to ben oute in the fals likynge of this world that semeth so schynande and so comfortable to hem that are 1480 blynded in knowynge of gosteli light. For whanne thou art in this merkenesse thou art mykil neer Jerusalem than whanne thou art in myddis of that fals light.

1458 **proferynges**, offerings. 1460 **ficchid**, fixed. 1461 **unaviseli**, unprompted. 1465 **siche**, such. 1469 **lightnynges**, illuminations. 1471 **sithen**, since. 1472 **stondeth**, consists. 1474 **unseable**, invisible. 1476 **menede**, meant. 1477 **myrke**, dark. 1479 **schynande**, shining. 1481 **neer**, nearer.

Therfore applie thyn herte fulli to the stirynge of grace, and use thee for to wonen in this myrknesse, and bi often assaiynge to be hoomli thereinne, and it schal soone be maad resteful to thee and the trewe light of goosteli knowynge schal spryngen to thee;

1485 not al at oonys, but pryveli bi litil and litil, as the prophete seith: *Habitantibus in regione umbre mortis, lux orta est eis* (Isaiah 9:2). To hem that wonen in the contré of the schadwe of deeth, light was sprongen. That is, light of grace was sprongen and schal sprynge to hem that can wonen in the schadwe of deeth, that is, in this merkenesse that is like to deeth. For as deeth sleeth a lyvynge bodi and al fleschli feelynge of it, right so

1490 desire to love Jhesu felt in this myrkenesse sleeth alle synnes, alle fleschli affeccions and unclene thoughtes for the tyme, and thanne neigheste thou faste to Jerusalem. Thou art not yit at it, but bi smale sodeyn lightnynges that gliteren oute thorugh smale cranés fro the cité schalt thou mowen see it from feer, or thou come therto. For wite thou wel, though thi soule be in this resteful myrkenesse withoute troblynge of wordli

1495 vanyté, it is not yit there it schulde be; it is not yit clothid al in light, ne turned al into the fier of love; but it feeleth wel that there is sumwhat aboven itsilf that it knoweth not ne hath not yit, but it wolde have it, and brennandli yerneth it. And that is not ellis but the sight of Jerusalem withoutforth, the whiche Jerusalem is like to a cité that the prophete Ezechiel sawgh in his visions.

1500 He seith that he sawgh a cité sette upon an hil heldande to the thought, that to his sight was no more whanne it was meten on lengthe and in brede than a rodde that was sixe cubites and a palme on lengthe; but as soone as he was brought into that cité and lokide aboughte him, thanne thoughte him that it was wondir moche, for he seigh many halles and chambris bothe open and privey. He sai bothe gates and porchis, uttirwarde and

1505 innerward, and mychil more biggynge than y seie now, on lengthe and on brede many hundrid cubitis. Thanne was this wondir to hym, hou this cité withinne was so longe and so large, that was so litil to his sight whanne he was withoute. This cité bitokeneth the perfight love of God, set in the liyf of contemplacioun the whiche unto the iye of a

1482 **wonen**, dwell. 1483 **hoomli**, familiar. 1491 **neigheste**, approach. 1492 **lightnynges**, illuminations. 1493 **cranés**, crannies. 1495 **there**, where. 1499 **Ezechiel**, see Ezekiel 40; the following exposition is from Gregory, *Homilia in Ezech.* 2.5.1 (Clark, p. 312n147). 1500 **heldande**, inclining; **thought**, see Textual Notes for a better reading. 1501 **meten**, measured; **brede**, breadth; **rodde**, rod, i.e., the measuring reed of Ezekiel 40:5. 1502 **cubites**, the biblical cubit is thought approximately equal to 18 inches; the palm, about four inches. 1503 **seigh**, saw. 1504 **uttirwarde**, outside. 1505 **biggynge**, buildings. 1508 **iye**, eye.

1510 soule that is withoute the feelynge of it, and traveileth in desire toward it, semeth sumwhat, but it semeth but a litil thinge, no more thanne a reed, that is, sixe cubitis and a palme on lengthe. Bi sixe cubites is undirstande perfeccioun of mannys werk, bi this palme a litil touchinge of contemplacioun. He seeth wel there is siche a thinge, that passeth the dissert of wirkynge of man a litil, as the palme passeth overe the sixe cubites, but he seeth not withinne what that is. Neveretheles yif he may come withinne the cité of 1515 contemplacioun, thanne seeth he moche more thanne he sawe fyrste.

Chapter Twenty-six

Hou a soule mai knowe fals illuminacions feyned bi the feend fro the trewe light of knowing that cometh oute of Jhesu; and bi what tokenes.

But now beware of the myddai feend, that feyneth light as it come oute of Jerusalem and it is not soo. For the feend seeth that oure Lord Jhesu scheweth to Hise loveris light 1520 of sothfastenesse; therfore in disceyvynge of hem that aren unwise he scheweth a light that is not trewe undir colour of trewe light, and so disceyveth hem. Neverthelees, hou a soule mai knowe the light of sothfastnes, whanne it schyneth fro God, and whanne it is feyned of the enemye, schal I seie thee as me thenketh bi ensaumple of the firmament.

Sumtyme in the firmament scheweth a light from the sunne and semeth the sunne and 1525 is not, and sumtyme scheweth the trewe sunne treuli. A knowynge of that oon from that othir is this. The feynede sunne schewith him not but atwixe tweyne blake reyny cloudes: than, bicause that the sunne is ney, there schyneth oute a lite from the cloudes as it were the sunne, and is noon. But the trewe sonne scheweth hym whanne the firmament is cleer or mykil clered from blake cloudes. Now to oure purpos. Sum men, 1530 as it semeth, forsaken the love of this world and wolden come to the love of God and to the light of undirstondynge of Him, but thei wole not come thorugh this myrkenesse that I have spoken of bifore. Thei wolen not knowe hemsilf truli ne mekeli, what thei

1510 **reed**, the unit (six cubits and a palm) measured by the *rodde*, above. **1513 dissert**, merit. **1518 myddai feend**, midday devil; see Psalms 90:6. See John Block Friedman, *Orpheus in the Middle Ages* (Cambridge, MA: Harvard University Press, 1970), pp. 188–89, for discussions of the midday fiend in the Middle English *Sir Orfeo* and elsewhere. **1523 of**, by; **enemye**, the devil. **1528 noon**, none.

han ben, ne what thei aren yit thorugh synne, ne hou nought thei aren in hire owen kynde anemptis God. Thei aren not bisi for to entre into hemsilf, alle othere thinges left,

1535 and fleen alle wikked stirynges of synne that risen in here hertis, of pride, of envie, ire, and othere synnes, thorugh lastende desire to Jhesu, in prayynge and in thenkynge, in silence and in wepynge, and in othere bodili exercise and goosteli exercise as devoute and holi men han doon. But as tite as thei han forsaken the world as it were outeward in liknesse, or ellis soone aftir, thei wenen that thei aren holi and able for to have the goosteli

1540 undirstondynge of the Gospeel and of Holi Writ. And nameli yif thei mowen fulfille litteralli the commaundementis of God and kepe hem from bodili synnes, thanne thei wenen that thei loven God perfiteli; and therfore thei wolen as tite prechen and techen alle othere men, as though thei hadden receyved grace of undirstondynge and perfeccioun of charité thorugh special grace and gifte of the Holi Gooste. And also thei aren mykil

1545 the more stired therto, for as myche as thei feelen sumtyme moche knowinge, as it were sodeynli gyven to hem withoute grete studie bifore-goynge, and also mykil fervour of love, as it semeth, for to preche truthe and rightwisenesse to here evene Cristene.

Therfore thei holden it as a grace of God, that visiteth hem with His blissed light bifore othere soulis. Neverethelees yif thei wolen loken wel aboute hem, thei schullen wel

1550 seen that this light of knowynge and the heete that thei feelen cometh nought of the trewe sunne, that is oure Lord Jhesu; but it cometh fro the myddai feend that feyneth light and likneth him to the sunne. And therfore schal he be knowen bi the ensample bifore seid.

Light of knowynge that is feyned bi the feend to a myrke soule is ai schewed bitwixe two blake reyny cloudis. The overe cloude is presumpcioun in an highinge of himsilf;

1555 the nethere cloude is doon-puttynge and a lowynge of his evene Cristen. Than what light of knowynge or feelynge of fervour that it be that schyneth to a soule, with presumpcion and highynge of itsilf and disdeyn of his evene Cristene the silf tyme felt, it is not the light of grace geven of the Holi Goste, though the knowynge in itsilf were sothfast; but it is either of the feend yif it come sodeynli or ellis of a mannys owen witte

1560 yif it come thorugh studie. And so mai it wel be knowen that this feyned light of knowynge is not the light of the trewe sunne.

1534 kynde, nature; **anemptis**, in respect to; **bisi**, active; **hemsilf**, themselves. **1538 as tite as**, as soon as. **1539 wenen**, suppose. **1542 as tite**, immediately. **1546 bifore-goynge**, preceding. **1554 overe**, upper; **highinge**, exaltation. **1555 doon**, down; **lowynge**, humiliating.

For thei that han this knowynge on this manere aren ful of goostli pride and seen it
not. Thei aren so blynt with this feyned light that thei holden the highenesse of here
owen herte and unbuxumnesse to the lawis of Hooli Chirche, as it were perfite mekenesse
1565   to the Gospel and to the lawes of God. And thei wenen that the folwynge of here owen
wille were fredom of spirit, and therfore thei bigynne to reyne as blake cloudis watir of
erroures and heresies, for the wordes that thei reynen bi prechynge sounen al to
backebitynge, to stryvynge, and to discord-makynge, reprevynge of states and of
persones; and yit thei seyn that al this is charité and zele of rightwisenesse. But it is not
1570   sooth, for Seynt Jame the apostil seith thus: *Ubi enim zelus et contencio, ibi inconstancia*
et omne opus pravum. Non est hec sapiencia desursum descendens a patre luminum, sed
terrena animalis et diabolica (James 3:16, 15). That is: Wherso that envie is and flitynge,
ther is unstabilnesse and al yvel werk. And therfore that knowynge that bryngeth forth
siche synnes cometh not fro the fadir of lightes, that is God, but it is ertheli, beestli and
1575   feendli.

    And so bi thise tokenes, that aren pride, presumpcion, unbuxumnesse, indignacioun,
bac-bitynge, and othere siche synnes (for thise folwen aftir the fendes), thus may the
fendes light be knowen from the trewe. For the trewe sunne scheweth him not bi
spicial visitacioun for to gyve light of undirstondynge or perfite charité to a soule, but
1580   yif the firmament be first maad bright fro blake cloudis; that is, but yif the conscience
be maad clene thorugh fier of brennynge desire to Jhesu in this merkenesse, the whiche
fier wasteth and brenneth alle wikked stirynges of pride, veynglorie, ire, envie, and alle
othere synnes in the soule, as the prophete seith: *Ignis ante ipsum precedet, et inflammabit*
in circuitu inimicos eius (Psalms 96:3). Fier schal goo bifore him; that is, desire of love
1585   schal goo bifore Jhesu in mannys soule and it schal brennen alle his enemyes, that is, it
schal waste alle synnes. For but yif a soule be first smyten doun fro the heighte of itsilf
bi drede, and be wel examyned and brent in this fier of desire, and as it were purified
from al goostli filthe bi longe tyme in devoute praieres and othere goostli exercises, it is
not able to suffre the schynynges of goostli light, ne for to receyven the precious licour
1590   of the perfite love of Jhesu. But whanne it is thus purified and maad sutil thorugh this

1563 blynt, blinded. **1564 unbuxumnesse to the lawis of Hooli Chirche**, disobedience to the
laws of Holy Church; possibly a reference to Lollardy; see Clark, p. 313n153. **1565 wenen**,
suppose. **1567 sounen**, tend. **1568 states**, conditions. **1572 flitynge**, contention. **1576
unbuxumnesse**, disobedience. **1590 sutil**, rarefied.

fier, than mai it receyve the gracious light of undirstandynge and the perfeccion of love, that is the trewe sunne. Thus seith Hooli Writ: *Vobis qui timetis domini orietur sol iusticie* (Malachi 4:2). The trewe sunne of rightwisenesse, that is, oure Lord Jhesu, schal springe to yow that dreden Him; that is, to meke soulis that meke hemself undir

1595 her even Cristene bi knowynge of here owen wrecchidnesse, and casten hemsilf doun undir God bi noghtynge of hemsilf in here owen substaunce thorugh reverente drede and goostli biholding of Him lastandli, for that is perfight mekenesse.

Unto thise soulis the trewe sunne schal risen, and illumynen here resoun in knowynge of soothfastnesse and kyndele here affeccioun in brennynge of love: and than schal thei

1600 bothe brennen and schynen. Thei schullen thorugh vertu of this heveneli sunne brennen in perfite love, and schynen in knowynge of God and goostli thynges, for than ben thei reformid in felinge. Therfore he that wole not be desceyved, I hope it is good to hym to drawe doun himsilt and hiden him in this merkenes, first fro entermetynge of othere men, as I have before seid, and forgete al the world yif he mai; and folwe Jhesu with

1605 lastyng desire offrid in praiere and thenkynge of Him. And thanne I trowe that the light that cometh aftir this myrkenesse is siker and sothfast, and that it schyneth out of the cité of Jerusalem fro the trewe sonne to a soule that traveileth in myrkenesse and crieth aftir light, for to wissen it the weie and comforten it in traveile. For I hope aftir trewe myrkenes bifore cometh nevere feyned light. That is, yif a man treuli and fulli sette hym

1610 for to forsake the love of the world, and mai thorugh grace come to feelynge and knowynge of himsilf and holden mekeli in that feelynge, he schal not be disceyved with noon erroures, ne heresies, ne ypocrisies, ne fantasies, for alle thise comen into a soule bi the gate of pride. Thanne yif pride be stopped oute, ther schal noon sich resten in a soule, and though thei come and profren hem, thei schul not entre. For the grace that

1615 the soule feeleth in this meke merkenesse schal teche the soule soothfastenesse, and schewe to it that alle siche proferynges aren of the enemye.

1596 **noghtynge**, rendering as nothing. 1597 **lastandli**, constantly; **perfight**, perfect. 1603 **entermetynge of**, busying oneself with. 1606 **siker**, certain; **sothfast**, true. 1608 **wissen**, guide. 1614 **profren hem**, offer themselves.

Chapter Twenty-seven

Hou grete profite it is to a soule for to be brought thorugh grace into this lighti merkenes, and hou a man nedeth to dispose him yif he wole come therto and hou it is oonli the gate and the entré to contemplacioun.

1620 Ther are manye devoute soules that thorugh grace comen into this myrkenesse and feelen the knowynge of hemself, and yit witen thei not fulli what it is; and that unkunnynge in partie hyndreth hem. Thei feelen wel often her thought and her affeccioun drawen oute and departid from the mynde of ertheli thynges, and brought into grete reste of delitable softenesse withoute peynful trobelyng of veyn thoughtes or of her bodili wittes;
1625 and they feelen that tyme so grete fredom of spirit that thei thenken on Jhesu pesibli and offren here praiers and here psalmes myghtili savourli and sweteli to Him as longe as frielté of the bodeli kynde mai suffre it. Thei witen weel that this feelynge is good, but thei witen not what it is. Therfore to alle siche soules I seie as me thenketh, that this maner of feelinge, though it be but schort and but seldom, is soothfastli this myrkenesse
1630 that I speke of; for it is a feelynge of hemself first, and a risynge above hemsilf thorugh brennande desire to the sight of Jhesu; or ellis yif I schal seie more sooth, this gracious felynge is a gosteli sight of Jhesu. And yif thei mowen kepe hem in that reste, and brynge thorugh grace into custum so that thei myghten lightli and freli have it whan hem lust, and holden hem thereinne, thei schulde nevere be overcome bi temptacion of the
1635 feend ne of the flesch, ne bi errour ne heresie; for thei are set in the gate of contemplacion, able and redi for to receyve the perfighte love of Jhesu. Therfore he that hath it, it is good that he knowe it mekeli, kepe it tendirli, and pursue it ferventli; that no creature lette hym uttirli fro it that he ne folw it whan he mai, and that he forgete and sette at nought al thynge that schuld put him fro this, yif he be free of himsilf and mai goo
1640 where he wole withouten sclaundir or disese of his evene Cristen. For me thenketh he mai not come to this reste lightli, but yif he have grete plenté of grace and sette himself for to folwe aftir the stirynge of grace; and that oweth he for to doon, for grace wolde ai be free, and nameli fro synne and fro wordli bisynesse, and from alle othere thinges that letten the werkynge of it, though thei be no synne.

1617 lighti, lightened. **1625 pesibli,** peacefully. **1627 frielté,** frailty. **1638 folw,** follow. **1640 sclaundir,** slander; **disese,** discomfort. **1644 letten,** hinder.

1645 Neverthelees, anothere soule that hath not yit receyved this fulnesse of grace, yif he desire to come to this goostli knowinge of Jhesu, as moche as in him is, him bihoveth to ablen himsilf to it, and putten awei alle lettynges that stoppen grace as moche as he mai. Him bihoveth lerne for to dye to the world and forsake the love of it truli. First pride, bodili and gostcli, that he desire after no worschipe of the world ne praisinge,

1650 name ne fame, staat ne degré, maistrie ne lordeschipe, wordli connynge ne wordli crafte, benefices ne richesse, precious clothinge ne wordli aray, ne nothinge wherthorugh he schulde ben worschiped above othere men. He schal coveiten noon of al this, but yif thei ben put on him; he schal take hem with drede, so that he be bothe pore outewarde and inwarde, or ellis fulli inwarde in herte; and that he coveite for to be forgeten of the

1655 worlde, that men rewarde him no more, be he nevere so riche or so connynge, than the porest man that lyveth. Also that he suffre not his herte resten in biholdynge of hise owen good dedes or of his vertues, wenynge that he dooth betere than anothir for he forsaketh the world and othere doo not so, and therfore lete wel bi himsilf.

Also him bihoveth leven alle risynges of herte and yvel willes of ire and envie agens

1660 his evene Cristene, and that he disese no man, ne angre hem unskilfulli in worde ne in dede, ne gyve ony man matier wherthorugh he myghte skilfulli ben angred or stired; so that he myght be free from every man, that no man have to doone with him ne he with ony man. Also that he forsake covetise, that he coveite right nought of ertheli good, but oonli aske his bodili sustenaunce as him nedeth, and holde him paid whan God stireth

1665 othere men for to gyve him. And that he putte no manere truste in avere of ertheli good, ne in helpe or favour of ony wordli frend, but principali and fulli in God, for yif he doo otherwise he byndeth hymsilf to the world, and he mai not therfore be free for to thenken on God. And also glotonye and leccherie, and othere fleschli unclennesse uttirli him bihoveth to leven, that the affeccion be not bounden to no woman by flesschli love

1670 or fleschli hoomlynesse. For it is no doute that siche blynd love that is sumtyme atwixe man and woman, and semeth good and honeste for as moche as thei wolden not synnen in deede, in the sight of God it is ful unclene and grete synne. For it is a gret synne that

---

1646–47 him behoveth to ablen, he must enable. **1647 lettynges,** hindrances. **1650 staat ne degré,** condition nor rank; **connynge,** knowledge. **1652 coveiten,** desire. **1657 wenynge,** supposing. **1658 lete,** esteem. **1660 disese,** discomfort; **unskilfulli,** unreasonably. **1661 matier,** matter. **1664 paid,** satisfied. **1665 avere,** possession.

a man schal suffre his affeccion, that schuld be festened to Jhesu, and to alle vertues and to al goostli clennesse, for to be bounden with ony fleschli love of ony creature 1675 wilfulli; nameli yif it be so mykil that it bereth doun his thought and maketh it unrestful, that he mai no savour have in God. Thus I holde it wilfulli that a man doth it and seith it is no synne, or ellis it is so blent with it that he wole not seen it. And also coveite no delices of metes and drynkes oonli for lust of his flesch, but holde him paied with sich mete as he mai esili have withoute grete bisynes; nameli if he be hool, what mete it be 1680 that wole doon awai the hungir and kepe the bodi in comoun strengthe unto the service of God; and than he grucchith not, strive not, angre not for his mete, though he be not served sumtyme as the flesch wolde.

Alle thise synnes and alle othire him bihoveth forsake uttirli in his wille and in his dedes whanne he mai, and alle othere thynges that letten him, so that he mai dispose him 1685 for to thenken freli on Jhesu. For as longe as thise lettyngis and siche othere hangen upon hym he mai not dien to the world, ne come into the myrkenesse of knowynge of himsilf; and therfore that he myght come therto him bihoveth for to doon al this as Seynt Poul dide, seiynge thus of himsilf: *Michi mundus crucifixus est, et ego mundo* (Galatians 6:14). The world is slayn and crucified to me, and I to the world. That is, he 1690 that forsaketh the love of the world in worschipes and richesses, and in alle worldli thyngis bifore seid for love of God, and loveth it not, ne desireth it not, ne pursueth it not, but is weel paied that he hath right nought of it, ne wolde have it though he myght — sotheli to him the world is deed, for he hath no savour ne delite therinne. Also yif the world sette him at nought and hath no rewarde to him, doth him no favour, ne worschip, 1695 setteth no price bi hym, but forgeteth him as a deed man, thanne is he deed to the world. And in this plight was Seynt Poule sette perfightli, and so bihoveth to anothir man in partie that wolde folwen and come to the perfite love of God. For he may not lyven to God fulli, until he die first unto the world.

This dyynge to the world is this myrkenesse, and it is the gate of contemplacioun and 1700 to reformynge in feelynge, and noon othir than this. Ther mowen ben many dyverse weies and seere werkes ledynge dyvers soules to contemplacion; for aftir sundri disposynges of men, and aftir sundri statis, as are religious and seculeres, that thei aren inne, aren divers exercises in wirkynge. Nevertheles, ther is no gate but oon; for what

1677 **blent**, blinded. 1678 **delices**, delights; **metes**, foods; **paied**, satisfied. 1679 **bisynes**, activity. 1681 **grucchith**, complains. 1687 **him bihoveth for to**, he must. 1692 **paied**, satisfied. 1693 **deed**, dead. 1694 **rewarde**, regard. 1701 **seere**, various. 1702 **disposynges**, dispositions.

exercise it be that a soule have, but yif he mai come bi that exercise to this knowynge
1705 and to a meke feeling of himsilf, and that is that he be mortified and deed to the world
as in his love, and that he mai feele himsilf sette sumtyme in this reestful myrkenesse bi
the whiche he mai be hid fro vanitee of the world and seen himsilf what he is, soothli he
is not yit comen to the reformynge in feelynge, ne hath not yit fulli contemplacion. He
is ful feer therfro. And yif he wole come bi ony othir gate, he is but a theef and a brekere
1710 of the wal, and therfore he is unworthi he schal be caste oute. But he that can brynge
himsilf firste to nought thorugh grace of mekenesse and dien on this maner, he is in the
gate, for he is deed to the world and he lyveth to God. Of the whiche Seynt Poul
speketh thus: *Mortui enim estis, et vita vestra abscondita est cum Christo in deo*
(Colossians 3:3). Ye are deede, that is, ye that for the love of God forsaken al the love
1715 of the world aren dede to the worlde, but youre liyf is hid with Crist in God. That is, ye
that leven goostcli in love of God, but that lif is hid from worldli men as Crist lyveth and
is hid in His Godhede fro the love and the sight of fleschli loveris.

This gate oure Lord Himsilf schewed in the Gospel whanne He seid thus: *Omnis qui
reliquerit patrem aut matrem, fratrem aut sororem propter me, centuplum accipiet, et
1720 vitam eternam possidebit* (Matthew 19:29). Every man that forsaketh for My love fadir
or modir, suster or brother, or ony ertheli good, he schal have an hondredfoold in this
liyf and afterward the blisse of hevene. This hundredfolde that a soule schal have yif he
forsake the worlde is not ellis but the profight of this lighti merkenesse, that I calle the
gate of contemplacioun. For he that is in this myrkenesse and is hid thorugh grace from
1725 wordli vanité, he coveiteth not of wordli good, he seketh it not, he is not taried withal,
he loketh not thereaftir, he loveth it not, and therfore hath he an hundredfoold more than
the kynge hath or than he hath that most coveiteth of ertheli good. For he that nought
coveiteth but Jhesu hath an hondredfoold, for he hath more reste, more pees in herte,
more verey love and delite in soule in o dai, thanne he hath that most coveiteth of the
1730 world and hath al the welthe of it undir his wille in al his liyftyme.

This is thanne a good myrkenesse and a riche nought, that bringeth a soule to so
mykil goostli eese and so stille softenes. I trowe that the prophete David menede of this
nought whanne he seide thus: *Ad nichilum redactus sum, et nescivi* (Psalms 72:22).
That is: I was broute to nought, and I wiste nought. That is, the grace of oure Lord
1735 Jhesu sent into myn herte hath slayn in me and brent to nought al the love of the world,

1709 feer, far. **1725 taried**, troubled. **1729 verey**, true. **1731 nought**, nothing. **1732 eese**,
comfort; **menede**, meant.

and y wiste not how. For thorugh no wirkynge of mysilf ne bi myn owen witte I have it not, but of the grace of oure Lord Jhesu Crist. And therfore, me thenketh, he that wole have the light of grace and fulsumli feele the love of Jhesu in his soule, hym bihoveth forsaken al the fals light of wordli love, and abiden in this merkenesse. And

1740 neverthelees yif he be adred first for to wone therinne, turne not ageen to love of the world, but suffre awhile and putte al his hope and his truste in Jhesu, and he schal not longe be withoute goosteli light. Thus biddeth the prophete: *Qui ambulat in tenebris, et non est lumen ei, speret in domino, et innitatur super deum suum* (Isaiah 50:10). Whoso gooth in myrkenesse and hath no light, that is, whoso wole hiden him fro love of the

1745 world and mai not redili feele the light of goostli love, despeire not, ne turne not ageen to the world but hope in oure Lord, and lene upon Hym, that is, truste in God and cleve sadli to Him bi desire and mekeli abide awhile, and he schal have light. For it fareth bi it as it dooth bi a man that hadde ben in the sunne a gret while, and aftir that come sodeynli into a merk hous there no sunne schyneth. He schuld first be as he were blynd

1750 and seen right nought; but yif he wole abide awhile he schal mowe soone seen aboute him, first grete thingis and aftirward smale, and sithen al that is in the hous. Right so goostli: he that forsaketh the love of the world and cometh to himsilf into his owen conscience, it is myrk first sumwhat and blynd to his sight. But yif he stande stille and holde forth with bisi praiere and often thenkenge the same wille to the love of Jhesu, he

1755 schal mowen seen aftirward grete thynges and smale, also that he first knewe not. Thus semede it that the prophete bihighte, seiynge thus: *Orietur in tenebris lux tua, et tenebre tue erunt sicut meridies. Et requiem dabit tibi dominus deus tuus, et implebit animam tuam splendoribus* (Isaiah 58:10–11). Light schal springen to thee in merkenesse. That is, thou that forsakest soothfastli the light of al worldeli love and hideste thi thought in

1760 this myrkenesse, light of blissid love and goosteli knowynge of God schal springe to thee. And thi merkenesse schal be as myddai. That is, thi mirkenesse of travailande desire and thi blynd trust in God that thou haste firste schal turne into cleer knowynge and into sikernesse of love. And thi Lord God schal geve reste to thee. That is, thi fleschli desires and thi peynful dredis and doutis, and wikked spirites that han contynueli

1765 bifore traveiled thee, alle thise schullen weiken and leesen moche of here myght; and thu schalt be maad soo stronge that thei schal not deren thee, for thou schalt be hid in reeste from hem. And thanne schal oure Lord Jhesu Crist fulfille thi soule with

1738 fulsumli, copiously. **1740 adred**, afraid; **wone**, dwell. **1747 sadli**, firmly. **1756 bihighte**, promised. **1765 weiken**, weaken; **leesen**, lose. **1766 deren**, harm.

schynyngges. That is, whanne thou arte brought into this goostli reste, thanne schalt thou more esily tende to God, and not ellis doon but love Him. And thanne schal He bi
1770 beemys of goostli light fulfille alle the myghtes of thi soule. Have thou no wonder, though I calle the forsakynge of wordli love myrkenesse, for the prophete calleth it soo, seiynge to a soule thus: *Intra in tenebras tuas, filia Caldeorum* (Isaiah 47:5). Goo into thi myrkenesse, thou doughter of Caldee. That is, thou soule, thou arte as a doughter of Caldee for love of the world, forsake it and goo into thi myrkenesse.

Chapter Twenty-eight

1775 That in reformynge of a soule the wirkynge of oure Lord is departed in foure tymes, that aren callynge, rightynge, magnifyyng, and glorifyynge.

Lo I have seid a litil yif thou coveite for to be reformed in feelynge, how thou schalt dispose thee toward thi forthgoynge. Nevertheless, I seie not that thou maight doon thus of thisilf, for I wot wel that oure Lord Jhesu bringeth al this to the ende, whereso
1780 He wole. For He oonli thorugh His grace stireth a soule, and bryngeth it into this myrkenesse first, and sithen into light, as the prophete seith: *Sicut tenebre eius, ita et lumen eius* (Psalms 138:12). That is, right as the light of knowynge and the feelynge of goosteli love is of God, right so the myrkenesse (that is, the forsakynge of wordli love) is of Hym. For He dooth al; He formeth and He reformeth. He formeth oonli bi Hymsilf,
1785 but He reformeth us with us; for grace goven, and appliynge of oure wille to grace, werketh al this. And upon what maner wise He dooth that, Seynt Poul reherseth thus: *Quos deus prescivit fieri conformes ymaginis filii eius, hos vocavit; et quos vocavit, hos iustificavit; quos iustificavit, hos magnificavit; quos magnificavit, hos glorificavit* (Romans 8:29–30). Thise that God knew bifore, that schulde be maad schapli to the
1790 image of His Sone, thise He callide, and thise He righted, thise He magnified, and thise He glorified.

    Though alle thise wordes mowen be seid of alle chosen soulis in the lowest degree of charité, that aren oonli reformed in feith, nevertheless thei mowen ben undirstonde more speciali of these soulis that are reformed in feelynge, unto the whiche oure Lord

1778 forthgoynge, way forward, progress. **1779 of**, by. **1785 goven**, given. **1789 schapli**, conforming. **1790 righted**, justified. **1793 mowen ben**, can be.

1795 Jhesu schewith moche plenté of grace, and dooth moche more bisynesse aboughte hem. For thei aren His owen soones speciali, that beren the ful schap and the liknesse of His sone Jhesu. In the whiche wordis Seynt Poul departeth the wirkynge of oure Lord into foure tymes. First is the tyme of callynge of a soule from wordli vanytee, and that tyme is often esi and comfortable. For in the bigynnyng of turnynge siche a man that is

1800 disposid to mykil grace is so quykli and so felandeli inspired and feelith ofte so grete suettenesse in devocion, and he hath so manye teeris in conpunccion, that he thenketh him sumtyme as he were half in hevene. But this softnesse passeth awei aftir for a while; and thanne cometh the secunde tyme, that is tyme of rightynge. That is traveilous; for whanne he bigynneth for to goo forth myghtili in the weie of rightwisenesse and

1805 settith his wille fulli agens alle synnes withouten and withinne, and streccheth out his desire to vertues and to the love of Jhesu, than feeleth he mykil lettynge and hardenesse, bothe withinne himsilf, of frowardnesse of his owen wille, and fro withoute, of temptacions of his enemye, that he is often in ful grete torment.

And that is no wondir, for he hath ben so longe croked to the fals love of the world,

1810 that he mai not be maad right and evene withoute grete beykynge and bowynge, right as a croked staaf mai not be maad evene, but yif it be cast and beyked in the fier. Therfore oure Lord Jhesu, seynge weel what thynge is bihofful to a froward soule, suffrith it to be taried and traveiled with sundri temptacions, and for to be wel examyned thorugh goostli tribulacions til al the ruste of unclennesse myght be brent ought of it.

1815 And that schal be bothe withinne, of dredis and doughtis and perplexitees, that it schal neerhande fallen into dispeir; for it schal seemen as it were forsaken of God and left al in the handis of the feend, outaken a litil privei trust that it schal have in the goodnesse of God and his merci. For that privei trust oure Lord Jhesu leveth in siche a soule, goo he nevere so feer fro it, bi the whiche the soule is ai born up from dispeire and saved

1820 from goostli myschief. And also withouten itsilf schal it be mortfied and pyned in sensualité. Eithir bi dyvers sikenesse or bi feleable turmentis of the feend, or ellis thorugh

---

1795 bisynesse, activity; **aboughte**, about. **1803 rightynge**, justification; **traveilous**, difficult. **1806 lettynge**, hindrance. **1807 frowardnesse**, perversity. **1809 croked**, crooked. **1810 right**, straight; **beykynge and bowynge**, smelting and bonding. **1812 bihofful**, necessary; **froward**, perverse. **1813 taried**, troubled. **1814 brent ought**, refined (burnt). The use of metallurgic metaphors for the refining of the soul are well suited to a penitenital, purgatorial religion. See II.2278–82, below. **1815 dredis and doughtis**, fears and doubts. **1816 neerhande**, almost. **1817 outaken**, except for. **1820 mortfied**, made dead; **pyned**, tormented. **1821 feleable**, palpable.

a privé myght of God, the seli soule bi feelynge and berynge of the wrecchid bodi schal so be pyned, for it schal not wite where ne how that it schulde not mowen suffre for to ben in the bodi, ne were that oure Lord Jhesu kepith it therinne.

1825   And yit neverthelees hadde the soule levere for to ben in al this pyne thanne for to be blyndid agen with the fals love of this world. For that was helle to siche a soule; but the suffrynge of this manere pyne is not but purgatorie, and therfore he suffreth it gladli, and he wolde not putte it awai though he myght, for it is so profitable. Al this dooth oure Lord in grete profite of the soule, for to dryve it out fro the reste in fleschli feelynge,

1830   and departen it fro luste of the sensualité, that it myght receyve goostli light. For aftir this, whanne the soule is thus mortified and brought from worldli love into this myrkenesse, that it hath no more savour ne delite of wordli likynge than of a stree, but he thenketh it bittir as wormood; than cometh the thridde tyme of magnyfiynge. And that is whanne the soule is reformed in felynge in partie, and receyveth the gifte of

1835   perfeccioun and the grace of contemplacioun and that is a tyme of grete reste. And aftir this cometh the ferthe tyme, of glorifiynge; that is whanne the soule schal be fulli reformed in the blisse of hevene. For thise soulis that aren callid from synne and thus righted or ellis on othir manere likli, dyversli assaiande bothe thorugh fier and watir, and aftirward aren thus magnyfied, schullen be glorificd. For oure Lord schal gyve hem fulli

1840   that thei coveitide, and more thanne thei coude coveiten. For He schal receyve up hem above othere chosen soulis to the evenehede of Cherubyn and Seraphyn, syn thei passiden alle othere in knowynge and love of God heere in this liyf.

Therfore he that wole come to this magnyfyynge drede not the rightynge, for that is the weie. For oure Lord seide bi His prophete a word of grete comfort to alle siche

1845   soules that aren examyned thorugh fier of tribulacions, thus: *Puer meus non timere, si transieris per ignem, flamma non nocebit te* (Isaiah 43:2). That is: Mi childe, yif thou passe thorugh fier, drede not, for the flamme schal not dere thee. It schal clense the soule from al fleschli filthe and make it able for to receyve goosteli fier of the love of God. And that nedeth for to be doon first. For as I have bifor seid, it mai not ellis be

1850   reformed in feelynge.

1822 seli, innocent. **1823 wite**, know. **1825 levere**, rather; **pyne**, pain. **1830 departen**, separate. **1832 stree**, straw. **1833 wormood**, wormwood. **1838 assaiande**, testing. **1841 evenehede**, equality; **passiden**, surpassed. **1847 dere**, harm.

Chapter Twenty-nine

Hou it falleth sumtyme that soulis bigynnynge and profitynge in grace han more fervour of love as bi outeward tokenes than sum men han that are perfite and neverthelees yit is it not so.

But now seiest thou: "Hou mai this be sooth?" For there are many soulis newli turned
1855   that have manye goosteli feelynges. Sum han grete conpuncciouns of here synnes, and sum men han grete devocions and fervoures in praiere, and han ofte sundri touchynges of goostli light in undirstondynge; and summe han othere manere feelynges of comfortable heete or grete suettenesse. And neverthelees this soule come nevere fulli in this resteful myrkenesse that y speke of, with fervent desire and lastende thought in God.
1860   Than askist thou whethir thise soules be reformed in feelynge or not? It semeth yhis, in as mykil as thei han siche grete goosteli feelynges that othere men that stonden oonli in feith feelen not of.

   Unto this I may seien, as me thenketh, that this goostli feelynges, whethir thei stonde in conpuccion or devocioun, or in goostli imaginacion, aren not the goosteli felynges
1865   whiche a soule schal have and fele in the grace of contemplacioun. I seie not but that thei aren soothfaste and graciousli goven of God, but thise soulis that feelen sich aren not yit reformed in feelynge, ne thei han not yit the gifte of perfeccioun ne goosteli the brennynge love of Jhesu, as thei mai come to. And neverthelees often it semeth othirwise, that siche soulis felten more of love of God than othere that han the gifte of perfeccion,
1870   in as mykil as the feelynge scheweth more outeward bi fervour of bodili tokenes, in wepynge and sighhinge, praiynge, knelynge, and spekynge, and othere bodili stirynge, so fer forth that it semeth to anothir man that thei weren ai raveschid in love. And though me thenketh it not so, wele y woot that these maner felynges and fervours of devocion and conpuccioun that thise men feelen aren gracious giftes of God sent into
1875   chosen soulis, for to drawen hem oute of worldeli love and fleschli luste that han be longe tym rooted in here herte, fro the whiche love thei schulde not ben drawen ought but bi siche feleable stirynges of grete fervoures.

   Neverthelees, that the fervour is so moche in outward schewynge it is not oonli for mykilnesse of love that thei han, but it is for litilnesse and weikenesse of hire soulis, that

---

1857–58 comfortable, comforting. **1858 suettenesse**, sweetness. **1860 yhis**, yes. **1863 stonde**, consist. **1864 conpuccion**, compunction. **1872 so fer forth**, to the extent. **1873 woot**, know.

1880 mowen not beeren a litil touchynge of God. For it is yit as it were fleschli, festened to the flesch, and nevere was yit departed fro it thorugh goostli mortifiynge; and therfore the leeste touchynge of love and the leeste sparcle of goosteli light sent from hevene into siche a soule is so moche, so comfortable, so swete and so delitable, over al the likynge that evere it felte bifore in fleschli love of erthcli thynge, that it is overtaken with

1885 it; and also it is so newe and so sodeyn and so uncouth that it mai not suffren for to beren it, but bersteth and schewith it out bi wepynge, sobbynge, and othere bodili stirynge. Right as a costret that is olde, and resseyveth newe wyne that is fresch and myghti, the costret bolneth out and it is in poynt for to cleven and bresten, until the wyne hath boiled and spourged out al the unclennesse. But as sone as the wyne is fyned

1890 and clered, than stant it stille, and the costreet hool. Right so a soule that is olde thorugh synne, whanne it receyveth a litil of the love of God, that is so fresch and so myghti that the bodi is in poynt for to cleven and bresten, ne were that God kepith it hool. But yit it bersteth out at the iyen bi wepynge and atte the mouth bi spekynge, and that is more for weikenesse and feblenesse of soule than for mykilnesse of love. For aftirward, whan

1895 the love hath boiled out al the unclennesse of the soule bi sich grete fervours, than is the love cleer and stondeth stille and thanne is bothe the bodi and the soule mochil more in pees, and yit hath the selve soule moche more love thanne it hadde bifore, though it schewid lasse outeward. For it is now al hol in reste withinne, and not but litil in outeward schewynge of fervour.

1900 And therfore I seie that thise soulis that feelen sich grete bodili fervours, though thei ben in mochil grace, aren not yit reformed in feelynge, but thei aren greteli disposyd toward. For I trowe siche a man, nameli that hath ben greteli defouled in synne, schal not come to reformynge in feelinge, but yif he be brent first and purified with sich grete conpuncciouns goyng bifore. Anothir soule that nevere was mykil defoulid with love of

1905 the world, but hath ai be kepid fro grete synnes in innocence, mai lightliere and more pryveli, withoute grete fervour schewed outeward, come to this reformynge. Thanne is this sooth, as I hope, that siche confortes and fervours that a soule feeleth in the staat of biginnynge or of profitynge aren as it were his goostli foode sent fro hevene, for to

---

1885 uncouth, unknown. **1887 costret**, cask; **newe wyne**, see the parable of the wineskins, Matthew 9:17. **1888 bolneth**, swells; **bresten**, burst. **1889 spourged**, fermented; **unclennesse**, impurity. **1894 mykilnesse**, greatness. **1897 selve**, same. **1905 kepid**, kept. **1907 hope**, suppose. **1908 profitynge**, proficiency.

strengthen him in his traveile. Right as a pilgrym that traveileth al dai metelees and
1910 drynkeles, and is neerhande overcomen with werynesse, falleth at the laste to a good
inne, and there hath he mete and drynk and is wel refreschyd for that tyme: right so
goosteli a devoute soule that wole forsake the love of the world, and wolde fayn love
God and setteth alle his besines therto, praieth and traveileth al dai gosteli and bodili, and
sumtyme feelith no savour ne comfort in devocion. Thanne oure Lord havynge pité
1915 over al His creatures, that it schulde not perischen for defaute, ne turne into hevynesse
or grucchynge, sendeth it amonge His goostli foode, and comforteth it in devocioun as
He vouchith saaf. And whanne the soule feeleth ony gosteli comfort, thanne he hooldeth
him weel apaied of al his traveile and al his disese that he hadde on the day, whanne he
fareth wel at even bi feelyng of ony grace.
1920   The selve wise falleth it of othere soulis that aren profitande and fer forth in grace.
Thei feelen ofte sithes gracious touchynges of the Holi Goost in here soulis, bothe in
undirstondynge and sightte of goosteli thingis, and in affeccioun of love. But yit ben thei
not reformed in felynge, ne thei are not yit perfight. For whi, alle such feelynges comen
to hem in that staat as it were unwarli, for thei comen or they witen it, and goon from
1925 hem or thei witen it, and thei cannot come thereto agen, ne thei knowen not where thei
schullen seken it ne where they schullen fynde it. For thei han yit noon hoomlynesse
with hem, but sodeynli goon and sodeynli comen. Thei are not yit maad lordes of
hemsilf bi stabilnesse of thought and lastynge desire to Jhesu, ne the iye of here soule is
not yit opened to behooldynge of goostli thynges, but they neighen faste toward. And
1930 therfore thei are not yit reformed in feelynge, ne thei han not yit the ful gifte of
contemplacion.

Chapter Thirty

On what manere a man schal have the knowing of his owen soule and hou a man schal
setten his love in Jhesu God and man, oo persone and neverthelees yit is the love that is
caused of biholdynge of Him as God and man worthiere and betere than that that is
1935 causid of Him oonli as man.

1910 **neerhande**, nearly. 1913 **besines**, activity. 1915 **defaute**, defect; **hevynesse**, gloom.
1916 **grucchynge**, complaining. 1918 **apaied**, satisfied; **disese**, discomfort. 1920 **profitande**,
proficient. 1924 **or they witen**, before they know. 1929 **neighen**, approach.

Hit nedeth to a soule that wolde have knowynge of goostli thynges, for to have first knowynge of itsilf. For it mai not have knowynge first of a kynde aboven itsilf but yif it have a knowynge of itsilf; and that is whanne the soule is so gadred into itsilf, and departed from biholdynge of alle ertheli thynges and fro the use of the bodili wittes, that

1940 it feelith itsilf as it is in the owen kynde withoute a bodi. Thanne yif thou coveite for to knowen and seen thi soule what it is, thou schalt not torne thi thought to thi bodi for to seken and feelen it, as it were hid withinne in thi fleschli herte as thyn herte is hid and hoolden withinne thi bodi. Yif thou seke so, thou schalt nevere fynde it in itsilf. The more thou sekest for to fynden and feelen it, as thou woldest feelen a bodili thynge, the

1945 ferthere thou art therfroo. For thi soule is no bodi, but a lyf unseable; not hid ne hoolden in thi bodi as a lasse thynge is hid and hoolden withinne a more, but it is holdande and quykenande thi bodi, mykil more thanne the bodi is of myght and vertu.

Than yif thou wolte fynden it, withdrawe thy thought from al bodili thynge outeward and fro mynde of thyn owen bodi also, and from alle thy fyve wittes as mykil as thou

1950 maist; and thenke on the kynde of a resonable soule goostli, as thou woldest thenken for to knowen ony vertu, as soothfastnesse or mekenesse or ony vertu. Right so thenke that a soule is a liyf, undeedli and unseable, that hath myght in itsilf for to seen and knowen the sovereyn soothfastnesse, and for to love the sovereyn goodnesse that is God. Whan thou seest this, than thu felist sumwhat of thisilf. Seke thisilf in noon othir

1955 place; but the more fulli and the more cleerli that thou maight thenken on the kynde and the worthynesse of a resonable soule, what it is, and what is the kyndeli werkynge of it, the betere thou seest thisilf.

It is ful hard for a soule that is rude and mykil in the flesch for to have sight and knowynge of itsilf thus, for whanne it wolde thenke on itsilf or of angil, or of God, it

1960 falleth as tite into ymaginacion of a bodili schap, and it weneth bi that for to have the sight of itsilf, and so of God and othere goostli thinges. And that mai not ben; for alle goostli thinges are seen and knowen bi undirstondyng of the soule and not bi ymagynacioun. Right as a soule seeth bi undirstondynge that the vertu of rightwisenesse is for to yelden to ilke a thynge that it oweth for to han, ryght so on siche a manere bi

1965 undirstondynge mai the soule seen itsilf.

1937 kynde, nature. **1938 soule**, for the commonplace ideas following, see Augustine, *De quantitate animae*, 13.22 (Clark, p. 315n194). **1945 unseable**, invisible. **1946 holdande**, maintaining. **1947 quykenande**, giving life to. **1949 wittes**, senses. **1952 undeedli**, immortal. **1960 as tite**, immediately.

Neverthelees, I seie not that thi soule schal reste stille in this knowynge, but it schal be this seken highere knowynge aboven itsilf, and that is the kynde of God. For thi soule is but a myroure, in the whiche thou schalt seen God goostli. And therfore thou schalt first fynden thi myrour and kepen it bright and clene from fleschli filthe and wordli

1970   vanyté, and holden it wel up from the erthe, that thou mai seen it, and oure Lord therinne also. For to this ende travelen alle chosen soulis in this liyf, in here menynge and in here entente, though thei have not speciali the feelynge of this. And for that is it as I have seid bifore, that many soulis bigynnynge and profitynge han gret fervour and mykil suettenesse in devocion, and as it semeth brenne al in love, and yit han thei not

1975   perfight love, ne goosteli knowynge of God. For wite thou wel, feele a soule nevere so mykil fervour, so mykil that him thenketh the bodi mai not bere it, or though he melte al into wepynge, as longe as his thenkynge and his biholdynge of God is al in imaginacion and not in undirstondynge, he come not yit to perfight love ne to contemplacion.

For thou schalte undirstonde that the love of God is on three maner wise and al is

1980   good, but ilke is betere than othir. The first cometh oonli with feith, withouten gracious imaginacioun or goostli knowynge of God. This love is in the leste soule that is re- formed in feith, in the lowest degree of charité; and it is good, for it sufficeth to savacioun. The secunde love is that a soule feeleth thorugh feith and by imaginacion of Jhesu in His manhede. This love is betere than the firste, whan the imaginacioun is stired bi grace,

1985   and for whi, the gostli iye is opened in bihooldynge of oure Lordis manhede. The thridde love is that a soule feeleth thorugh gosteli sight of the Godhede in the manhede as it may been sen heere. This is the beste and the moste worthi, and that is perfight love. This love a soule feeleth not til it be reformed in feelynge. Soules bygynnande and profitande han not this love, for thei kunne not thenke on Jhesu ne love Him Godli, but as it were

1990   al manli and fleschli aftir the condicions and the liknes of man. And upon that reward thei schapin al her werkynge, in here thoughtis and in here affeccions. Thei dreden Him as man, and worschipen Hym and loven Hym principali in manli ymaginacioun, and goon no ferthere. As thus: yif thei have doon amys and trespaced agens God, thei thenken thanne that God is wrooth with hem as a man schulde be yif thei hadden

1995   trespaced agens hym, and therfore thei falle doun as it were to the foot of oure Lord with sorwe of herte and crien merci. And whanne thei han don thus thei han a good

1966 be, by. **1967 kynde**, nature. **1971 travelen**, labor. **1974 suettenesse**, sweetness. **1975 perfight**, perfect. **1980 ilke**, each. **1985 for whi**, because. **1990 reward**, regard. **1991 schapin**, shape. **1994 wrooth**, angry.

trust that oure Lord of His merci wole forgyve hem here trespas. This manere of doynge is right good, but it is not goostli as it myght ben.

Also whanne thei wole worschipe God thei presenten hemself in here thought as it were in bodili liknes bifore the face of oure Lord and ymagynen a wondirful light there oure Lord Jhesu is, and thanne thei reverencen Hym, worschipen and dreden Hym, and fulli putten hem in His merci for to don with hem what He wole. And also whanne thei wolen loven God, thei biholden Him as a man, not yit as God in man, eithir in His passioun or in sum othir thynge of His manhede. And in that biholdynge thei feelen ther hertis moche stired to love of God. This maner of werkynge is gracious, but it is moche lasse lowere than is the wirkynge of undirstondynge; that is whann a soule graciousli biholdeth God in man. For in oure Lord Jhesu aren to kyndes, the manhede and the Godhede ooned togidere. For mankynde was taken up in the persoone of Jhesu and is ooned to the Godhede. Than right as the Godhede is more sovereyne and more worthi than is the manhede, right so the goostli biholdynge of the Godhede in Jhesu man is more worthi, more goosteli, and more medful than biholdynge of the manhede aloone, whethir he biholde the manhede as deedli or as glorified. And right so bi the same skile the love that the soule felith in thenkynge and bihooldynge of the Godhede in man, whan it is graciouseli schewid, is worthiere, goostliere, and more medful than the fervour of devocion that the soule feelith bi imaginacion oonli of the manhede, schewe it nevere so mykil outeward. For in reward of that, this is but manli; for oure Lord scheweth Him not in ymaginacion as He is, ne that He is, for the soule myght not that tyme for freelté of fleschlihede suffren Him so.

Neverthelees unto sich soulis that kunne not thenken on the Godhede goostli, that thei schulde not erren in here devocion, but that thei schulden ben conforted and strengthed thorugh sum manere inward bihooldynge of Jhesu, for to forsake synne and the love of the worlde — therfore oure Lord Jhesu tempereth His unseable light of His Godhede, and clothid it undir bodili liknesse of His manhede, and scheweth it to the innere iye of the soule and fedeth it with the love of His precious flesch goostli, the whiche love is of so greet myght that it sleeth al wikked love in the soule and strengthed it for to suffre bodili penaunce and othir bodili disese in tyme of neede for love of Jhesu. And this is the schadwynge of oure Lord Jhesu overe a chosen soule. In the whiche schadwynge the

2000 there, where. 2006 whann, when. 2007 to, two. 2008 ooned, united. 2010 manhede, humanity. 2012 deedli, mortal; skile, reason. 2014 medful, worthy of reward. 2016 reward, regard. 2022 unseable, invisible. 2025 strengthed, strengthened.

soule is kept fro brennynge of wordli love, for right as a schadwe is maad of a light and
a bodi, right so this goostli schadwe is maad of the blissid unseable light of the Godhede,
2030 and of the manhede ooned therto, and is schewed to a devoute soule. Of the whiche
schadwe the prophete seith thus: *Spiritus ante faciem nostram Christus dominus: sub
umbra eius vivemus inter gentes* (Lamentations 4:20). Oure Lord Crist bifore oure face
is a spirit; undir His schadwe we schullen lyve amonge folkes. That is, oure Lord Jhesu
in His Godhede is a spiret, that mai not be seen of us lyvand in flesch as He is in His
2035 blissid light. Therfore we schulle lyven undir the schadwe of His blissid manhede as longe
as we aren heere. But though this be sooth that this love in ymaginacion bi good, neverthelees
a soule schulde desiren for to have goostli love in undirstondynge of the Godhede, for that
is the ende and the ful blisse of the soule, and alle othere bodili biholdynges aren but
meenes ledynge a soule to it. I seie not that we schulden departe God fro man in Jhesu,
2040 but we schullen love Jhesu bothe God and man — God in man, and man in God; goostli,
not fleschli.

Thus kennede oure Lord Marie Magdaleyn, that schulde be contemplatif, whanne He
seide to hire thus: *Noli me tangere, nondum enim ascendi ad patrem meum* (John 20:17).
Touche me not, I am not yit stied up to my Fader. That is for to seie, Marie Magdelene
2045 lovede brennandeli oure Lord Jhesu bifore the tyme of His passioun, but here love was
moche bodili and litil goostli. Sche trowed wel that He was God, but sche lovyd Him litil
as God, for sche coude not thanne, and therfore sche suffride al hire affeccioun and
hire thought fallen in Him as He was in forme of man. And oure Lord blamede here not
thanne, but praiside it moche. But aftir whanne He was risen from deeth and He apperde
2050 to hire, sche wolde have worschipide Him with sich maner of love as sche dide bifore;
and thanne oure Lord forbede hire and seide thus, "Touche me not." That is, sette not
the restynge ne the love of thyn herte in that forme of man that thou seest with thi
fleschli iye oonli, for to resten therinne; for in that forme I am not stied up to My Fadir.
That is, I am not evene to the Fadir, for in forme of man I am lasse than He. Touche me
2055 not so, but sette thi thought and thi love into that forme in the whiche I am evene to the
Fader (that is, the forme of the Godheede), and love Me, and knowe Me, and worschipe

2030 **ooned**, united. 2036 **bi**, be. 2039 **departe**, separate. 2042 **kennede**, taught; **contemplatif**,
on Mary Magdalene as a contemplative, see *Scale*, Book I, chapter 11; the classic expression
of the idea is in Gregory, *Homiliae in Ezech.* 2.2.7–12 (PL 76:952–55). 2044 **stied**, ascended.
2046 **trowed**, believed. 2047 **suffride**, allowed. 2053 **stied**, ascended. 2054 **evene**, equal.

Me as a God and man godli, not as man manli. So schalt thou touche Me, for syn I am bothe God and man, and al the cause whi y schal be worschiped and loved is for I am God, and for y took the kynde of man; and therfore make Me a God in thyne herte, and in thi love, and worschipe Me in thyn undirstondynge as Jhesu God in man, sovereyn soothfastnesse, and as sovereyne goodenesse and blissid liyf, for that am I. Thus kennede oure Lord hire as I undirstonde, and also alle othere soulis that aren disposid to contemplacioun and able therto, that thei schulden doon so.

Neverthelees, othere soulis that aren not sotel in kynde, ne are not yit maad goostli thorough grace, it is good to hem that thei kepe forth here owen wirkynge in imaginacion with manli affeccions, until more grace come freeli to hem. It is not sikir to a man for to leven a good werk uttirli until he see and feele a betere. Upon the same wise it mai be seide of othir manere feelynges that aren like to bodili thynges, as heeryng of delitable songe, or feelynge of comfortable heete in the bodi, or seynge of light, or swettenesse of bodili savour. Thise aren not goosteli feelynges, for goostli feelynges aren felt in the myghtis of the soule, principali in undirstondynge and in love and litil in imaginacioun; but thise feelynges aren in imaginacion, and therfore thei aren not goostli feelynges, but whan thei are best and moste trewe yit aren thei but outeward tokenes of inli grace that is feelt in the myghttis of the soule. This mai be openli prived bi Holi Writ seiynge thus: *Apparuerunt apostolis dispertite lingue tanquam ignis, seditque super singulos eorum spiritus sanctus* (Acts 2:3). The Holi Gooste apperide to the apostelis in the dai of Pentacost in liknesse of brennynge tunges, and enflawmede alle here hertis and satte upon ilke of hem. Now sooth it is the Holi Gost, that is God Himsilf unseable, was not that fier ne the tunges that weren seen, ne the brennyng that was feelt bodili, but He was unseabli feelt in the myghtis of hire soulis, for He lightned here resoun and kyndelide here affeccioun thorough His blisside presence so cleerli and so brennandeli, that thei hadden sodeynli the goostli knowynge of soothfastenesse and the perfeccion of love, as oure Lord bihighte hem, seyynge thus: *Spiritus sanctus docebit vos omnem veritatem* (John 16:13). The Holi Goost schal teche you al soothfastnesse. Thanne was that fier and that brennynge not ellis but a bodili tokene, outeward schewid in wittenessynge of that grace that was inwardeli feelt. And as it was in hem, so is it in othere soulis that aren visited and

---

2061 kennede, taught. **2064 sotel**, refined. **2066 manli**, human. **2068 delitable**, delightful. **2069 swettenesse**, sweetness. **2073 inli**, internal. **2074 prived**, proved. **2080 lightned**, illuminated (ignited). **2082 bihighte**, promised.

lightned withinne of the Holi Goste, and han with that siche outward feelynges in comfort and wittenessynge of the inward grace. But that grace is not, as I hope, in alle soulis
that aren perfite, but there oure Lord wole. Othere soules unperfite that han siche feelynges
2090   outewarde and han not yit receyved the inward grace, it is not good to hem for to resten
in siche feelynges to mykil, but in as mykil as thei helpen the soule to more stablenesse
of thought in God and to more love. For summe mowen ben trewe and summe mowen
be feyned, as I have seide bifore.

Chapter Thirty-one

Hou this maner of spekyng reformynge of a soule in feelynge and in what wise it is
2095   reformed is founden in Seynt Poulis wordis.

Now I have seide to thee a litil of reformynge in feith, and also I have touched thee a litil
of the forthgoynge from that reformynge to the highere reformynge that is in feelynge.
Not in that entente as I wolde bi thise wordes setten Goddis werkinge undir a lawe of
my spekynge, as for to seyn, thus wirketh God in a soule and noon othirwise. Nay, I
2100   meene not soo: but y seie aftir my symple feelynge that oure Lord Jhesu werkith thus in
summe creatures as I hope. And I hope wel that He werketh otherewise also, that
passith my witte and my feelynge. Neverthelees, wheer he werke thus or othirwise, bi
sundry menys, in lengere tyme or in schorter tyme, with mykil traveile or litil traveile,
yif al come to oon eende, that is to perfite love of Hym, than is it gode inowgh. For yif
2105   He wole geven a soule on o day the ful grace of contemplacion and withouten ony
travaile, as He weel mai, as good it is to that soule as yif he had ben examyned, pyned
and mortified, and purified twenti wyntir tyme. And therfore upon this manere wise
take thou my seiynge, as I have seid; and namely as I thenke for to seyn. For now bi the
grace of oure Lord Jhesu schal y speke a litil as me thenketh more openli of reformynge
2110   in feelynge — what it is and how it is maad, and whiche aren goostli feelynges that a
soule receyveth.
      Neverthelees first, that thou take not this maner of spekynge of reformynge of a soule
in feelynge as feynynge or fantasie, therfore I schal grounden it in Seynt Poules wordis,

2088 hope, believe. **2101 hope₁,** suppose. **2102 wheer,** whether.

where he seith thus: *Nolite conformari huic seculo, sed reformamini in novitate*
2115 *sensus vestri* (Romans 12:2). That is: Ye that aren thorugh grace reformed in feith,
conforme yow not henneforward to maneres of the world, in pride, in covetise, and in
othere synnes; but be ye reformed in newehede of youre feelynge. Loo, heere thou
maist see that Seynt Poul speketh of reformynge in feelynge; and what that newe
feelynge is he expounneth in anothir place thus: *Ut impleamini in agnicione voluntatis*
2120 *eius, in omni intellectu et sapiencia spirituali* (Colossians 1:9). That is: We praien God
that ye mowen ben fulfilled in knowynge of Goddis wille, in al undirstondyng and in al
maner goostli wisdom; that is, in reformynge in feelynge. For thou schalt undirstonde
that the soule hath two manere of feelynges: on withoute of the fyve bodili wittes,
anothir withinne of the goostli wittes, the whiche aren propirli the myghtis of the soule,
2125 mynde, reson, and wille. Whanne thorugh grace thise myghtes aren fulfilled in al
undirstondinge of the wille of God and in goostli wisdom, than hath the soule newe
gracious feelynges. That this is sooth, he schewith in anothir place thus: *Renovamini*
spiritu mentis vestre, et induite novum hominem, qui secundum deum creatus est in
iusticia, sanctitate, et in veritate (Ephesians 4:23–24). Be yee now renued in the spirit
2130 of youre soule; that is, ye schullen ben reformed not in bodili feelynge ne in imaginacion,
but in the overe partie of youre resoun. And clothe yow in a newe man, that is schapen
aftir God in rightwisenesse, holinesse, and soothfastnesse. That is, your reson, that is
propirli the ymage of God thorugh grace of the Holi Goost, schal be clothid in a newe
light of soothfastenesse, holynesse, and rightwisenesse and thanne is it reformed in
2135 feelynge. For whanne the soule hath perfight knowynge of God, than is it reformed.
Thus seith Seynt Poul: *Exspoliantes veterem hominem cum actibus suis; induite novum,*
qui renovatur in agnicione dei, secundum ymaginem eius qui creavit eum (Colossians
3:9–10). Spoile yousilf of the oolde man with alle his deedis; that is, casteth fro yow the
love of the world with alle wordli maneris. And clothe you in a newe man; that is, ye
2140 schullen be renewed in the knowynge of God aftir the liknesse of Hym that made yow.

Bi thise wordes maist thou undirstonden that Seynt Poul wold have mennys soulis
reformed in partie knowynge of God, for that is the newe feelynge that he speketh of
generali. And therfore upon his word I schal seyn more pleynli of this reformynge, as
God geveth me grace. For ther is two maner of knowynge of God. On is had principali
2145 in imaginacion, and litil in undirstondynge. This knowynge is in chosen soulis bigynnynge

2117 newehede, newness. **2131 overe partie**, upper part. **2138 Spoile**, Despoil.

and profitynge in grace, that knowen God and loven Hym al manli not goostli, with manli affeccions and with bodili liknesse, as I have bifore seid. This knowynge is good, and it is likned to mylk bi the whiche thei aren tendirli norischid as children, til thei ben able for to come to the fadris boord and taken of his hande hool breed. And that othir

2150 knowynge is principaly felt in undirstondynge, whanne it is comforted and illumyned bi the Hooli Goost, and litil in imagynacion. For the undirstondynge is ladi, and ymaginacion is a maiden, servande to the undirstondynge whanne nede is. This knowynge is oolde breed, mete for perfite soulis, and it is reformynge in feelynge.

Chapter Thirty-two

Hou grace openeth the innere iye of a soule into goostli biholdynge of Jhesu, and hou

2155 there is thre maner of knowynge of Jhesu bi example of thre men stondynge in the sunne, on blynd, anothir hath his iyen sperid, and the thridde forth lokynge.

A soule that is callid fro the love of the world, and aftir that it is righted and assaied, mortefied and purified, as I have bifore seid, oure Lord Jhesu of His merciful goodnesse reformeth it in feelynge whanne He vucheth saaf. He openeth the innere iye of the soule

2160 whanne He lightneth the reson thorugh touchynge and schynynge of His blyssid light, for to seen Hym and knowe Hym; not al fulli at oones, but litil and litil bi dyverse tymes, as the soule mai suffre Hym. He seeth Hym not what He is, for that mai no creature doon in hevene ne in erthe; ne he seth Him not as He is, for that sight is oonli in the blisse of hevene. But he seth Him that He is: an unchaungeable beynge, a sovereyn myght, sovereyn

2165 soothfastnesse, and sovereyne goodnesse, a blissid lyf, and an eendelees blisse. This seeth the soule, and moche more that cometh withal; not blyndli and savourli, as dooth a clerk that seeth Him be clergie oonli thorugh myght of his naked resoun, but that othir seeth Hym in undirstondynge that is comforted and lightned by the gifte of the Hooli Goost with a wondirful reverence and a privei brennande love, with goostli savour and

2170 heveneli delite, more cleerli and more fulli than mai be writen or seid.

2156 on, one; **sperid**, closed. **2157 righted**, justified. **2160 lightneth**, illuminates. **2167 be clergie**, by learning.

This sight, though it be schortli and litil, is so worthi and so myghti that it draweth and ravescheth al the affeccion of the soule therto from biholdynge and the mynde of al ertheli thynge, for to reste therinne everemore yif that it myghte. And of this maner sight and knowynge the soule groundeth al his inward wirkynge in alle the affeccions.

2175 For thanne it dredeth God in man as soothfastnesse, wondreth Him as myght, loveth Him as goodnesse. This sight and this knowynge of Jhesu, with the blissid love that cometh oute of it, mai be called the reformynge of a soule in feith and in feelynge that I speke of. It is in feith, for it is myrk yit as in reward of that ful knowynge that schal ben in hevene. For than schullen we seen Hym not oonli that He is, but even as He is; as

2180 Seynt Joon seith: *Tunc videbimus eum sicuti est* (1 John 3:2). That is: Thanne schulle we seen Him as He is. Neverthelees, it is in feelynge also, as in reward of that blynde knowynge that a soule hath stondynge oonli in feith. For this soule knoweth sumwhat of the kynde of Jhesu God thorugh this gracious sight, but that othir knoweth it not, but oonli troweth it, this is sooth.

2185 Neverthelees, that thou mowe the betere conceyve that I meene, I schal schewe thee thre manere reformynge of a soule bi ensample of three men stondynge in light of the sunne. Of the whiche three, oon is blynd, and anothir mai seen but he hath hise iyen spered, the thridde loketh forth ful sight.

The blynde man hath no maner knowynge that he is in the sunne, but he troweth it yif

2190 a trewe man telle hym; and he bitokeneth a soule that is oonli reformed in feith, that troweth in God as Holi Chirche techeth, and woot not what. This sufficeth as for savacion. The tothir seeth a light of the sunne, but he seeth it not cleerli what it is, ne as it is, for the liddes of his iyen letteth him that he mai not, but he seeth thorugh the liddes of his iyen a glymerynge of a greet light. And he bitokeneth a soule that is reformed in

2195 feith and in feelynge, and so is contemplatif. For he seeth sumwhat of the Godhede of Jhesu thorugh grace; not cleerli ne fulli, for the iyen liddes, that is his bodili kynde, is yit a wal atwixe his kynde and the kynde of Jhesu, and letteth him fro the cleer sight of Him. But he seeth thorugh this wal, aftir that grace toucheth him more or lasse, that Jhesu is God and that Jhesu is sovereyne goodnesse, and sovereyne beynge, and a

2200 blissid liyf, and that al othir goodnesse cometh of Him. This seeth the soule bi grace, not agenstondynge alle the bodili kynde; and the more clene and sotil that the soule ys maad,

2178 **myrk**, dark; **reward of**, regard to. 2184 **this**, that this. 2188 **spered**, closed. 2190 **trewe**, true. 2192 **tothir**, other. 2193 **letteth**, hinder. 2196 **kynde**, nature. 2197 **atwixe**, between. 2199 **beynge**, being. 2201 **agenstondynge**, withstanding; **clene**, pure; **sotil**, subtle.

the more it is departid from fleschlihede, the scharpere sight it hath and the myghtiere love of the Godhede of Jhesu. This sight is so myghti that though no man lyvand wolde trowe in Jhesu, ne love Him, he wolde trowe nevere the lesse ne love Him the lasse; for

2205 he seeth it so soothfastli thorugh grace that he mai not untrowe it.

The thridde man, that hath ful sight of the sunne, he troweth it not for he seeth it fulli; bitokeneth a ful blissid soule that withouten ony wal of bodi or synne seeth openli the face of Jhesu in the blisse of hevene. There is no feith, and therfore he is fulli reformed in feelynge.

2210 There is no staat above the secunde reformynge that a soule mai come to heere in this liyf; for this is the staat of perfeccion, in the weie to heveneward. Nevertheles alle the soulis that aren in this staat are not alle ilike ferforth. For summe have it litil, and schortli and seldom; and summe lengere, clerere and oftennere; and summe han it clerest and lengest, aftir the habundynge of grace; and yit alle thise han the gifte of contemplacioun.

2215 For the soule hath not perfighte sight of Jhesu al at onys, but first a litil, and aftir that it profiteth and cometh to more feelynge, and as longe as it is in this lyf it mai wexen more in the knowynge and in this love of Jhesu. And sothli I woot not what were more leef to siche a soule that hath a litil felt of it, than uttirli alle othire thynges left and sette hem at nought, and oonli tende therto for to have clerere sight and clennere love of Jhesu, in

2220 whom is al the blissid Trynyté.

This manere of knowynge of Jhesu, as I undirstonde, is the openynge of hevene to the iye of a clene soule, of the whiche holi men speken of in here writynge. Not as summe wenen, that the openynge of hevene is yif a soule myght seen bi imaginacion thorugh the skyes above the firmament, hou oure Lord Jhesu sitteth in His majesté in a

2225 bodili light as mykil as an hundred sunnes. Nai, it is not soo: ne though he see nevere so highe on that manere, sothli he seeth not the goostly hevene. The hiere he stiyeth above the sonne bi sich imagynacion for to see Jhesu God, the lowere he falleth bynethe the sunne. Neverthelees this maner sight is suffrable to symple soulis, that kunne no betere seke Hym that is unseable.

2212 ilike ferforth, alike advanced. **2217 leef**, preferred. **2219 clennere**, purer. **2223 wenen**, suppose. **2226 hiere**, higher; **stiyeth**, climbs. **2228 suffrable**, permissable; **kunne**, know how to.

Chapter Thirty-three

2230 Hou Jhesu is hevene to the soule; and hou a soule schal seke Jhesu above itself and
withinne itsilf; and whi Jhesu is callid fier and light.

What is hevene to a resonable soule? Sothli, not ellis but Jhesu God. For yif that be
hevene oonli that is above a thynge, than is God oonli hevene to mannys soule. For He
is oonli above the kynde of a soule. Thanne yif a soule mai thorugh grace have knowynge
2235 of that blissid kynde of Jhesu, sothli he seeth hevene, for he seeth God.

   Therfore ther are many men that erren in undirstondynge of summe wordes that aren
seid of God, for thei undirstonden hem not goostli. Hooli Writte seith that a soule that
wole fynde God schal liften upward the innere iye and seke God above itsilf. Thanne
summe that wolde doon aftir this seiynge undirstonden this word "aboven hemsilf," as
2240 for higher settynge in stide and for worthiere of place, as oon element or oon planete is
above anothir in settynge and in worthinesse of bodili place; but it is not so goostli. For
a soule is above a bodili thynge not bi settynge of stide, but bi sutilté and worthinesse of
kynde. Right so, in the selve wise, God is above alle bodili and goostli creaturis, not bi
settynge of stide, but thorough sutilté and worthinesse of His unchaungeable blissid
2245 kynde. And therfore he that wole wisili seke God and fynden Him, he schal not renne
oute with his thought as yif he wolde clymbe above the sunne and persen the firmament, and imagyne the majesté as it were a light of an hundred sonnes. But he schal
rathere drawe doun the sunne and al the firmament, and forgeten it and casten it binethen
hym ther as he is, and setten al this and al bodili thinge also at nought, and thenken
2250 thanne yif he can goostli, bothe of himsilf and of God also. And yif he doo thus, thanne
seeth the soule aboven himsilf and thanne seeth it hevene.

   Upon this self manere schal this word "withinne" be undirstonden. It is comonli seid
that a soule schal see oure Lord withynne al thynge and withinne itsilf. Sooth it is that
oure Lord is withinne alle creatures, not on that manere as a kirnel is hid withinne the
2255 schale of a note, or as a litil bodili thinge is hid and holden withinne anothir mykil. But He
is withinne alle creatures as hooldynge and kepynge hem in here beynge, thorough sutilté
and thorough myght of His blissid kynde and clennesse unseable. For right as a thyng

---

2240 stide, place. **2242 sutilté**, subtlety. **2244 stide**, place. **2246 persen**, pierce. **2255 schale**,
shell; **note**, nut. **2256 beynge**, being.

that is most precious and moste clene is leid innerest, right so bi that liknesse it is seid the kynde of God (that is most precious and most clene and most goostli, feerthest

2260 from bodilihede) is hid withinne alle thynges. And therfore he that wole seke God withinne, he schal forgete first al bodili thynge (for al that is withouten) and his owen bodi; and he schal forgeten the thenkynge of his owen soule and thenken on that unmaad kynde that is Jhesu, that made him, quykeneth him, and holdeth him, and gyveth hym resoun and mynde and love; the whiche is withinne hym thorugh His privei myght and

2265 sovereyne sotilté. Upon this manere schal the soule doo whanne grace touchith hym, ellis it wole but litil availe to seken Jhesu and fynde Him withinne itsilf and withinne alle cretures, as me thenketh.

Also it is seide in Holi Writ that God is light. So seith Seynt Joon: *Deus lux est* (1 John 1:5). That is, God is light. The light schal not ben undirstonden as for bodili light, but it

2270 is undirstonden thus: God is light, that is, God is truthe and soothfastnesse, for sothfastnesse is gostli light. Than he that most graciousli knoweth soothfastnesse, beest seeth God. And nevertheleees it is likned to bodili light for this skile. Right as the sunne schewith to the bodili iye itsilf and al bodili thynge bright, right so soothfastnesse, that is God, scheweth to the reson of the soule itsilf first, and bi itsilf alle othere goostli

2275 thynge that nedeth to be knowen of a soule. Thus seith the prophete: *Domine, in lumine tuo videbimus lumen* (Psalms 35:10). Lord, we schullen see light bi Thi light. That is, we schullen seen Thee, that art soothfastnesse, bi Thisilf.

On the selve wise it is seid that God is fier: *Deus noster ignis consumens est* (Hebrews 12:29). That is: Oure Lord is fier wastande. That is for to seyn, God is not fier elementarie,

2280 that heteth a bodi and brenneth it, but God is love and charité. For as fier wasteth al bodili thinge that mai be wasted, right so the love of God wasteth and brenneth al synne oute of the soule and maketh it clene, as fier maketh clene al manere metal. Thise wordis, and alle othere that aren spoken of oure Lord in hooli writynge bi bodili liknesse, moste nedis ben undirstonden goostli, ellis there is no savour in hem. Nevertheleees, the

2285 cause whi siche maner wordis aren seid of oure Lord in Holi Writ is this. For we aren so fleschli that we conne not of God, ne undirstonde of Hym, but yif we bi siche wordes first ben entred in. Neverthelees, whanne the innere iye is opened thorugh grace for to han a litil sight of Jhesu, thanne schal the soule turne lightli inowgh alle sich wordes of bodili thyngis into goostli undirstondynge.

2263 quykeneth, gives life to. **2271 beest**, best. **2272 skile**, reason. **2273 soothfastnesse**, truth. **2278 selve wise**, same manner. **2286 conne not**, know nothing. **2288 inowgh**, enough.

2290   This goostli oopenynge of the innere iye into knowynge of the Godhede y calle reformynge in feith and in feelynge. For thanne the soule sumwhat feelith in undirstondinge of that thynge that it hadde bifore oonli in nakyd trowing. And that is bigynnynge of contemplacion, of the whiche Seynt Poul seith thus: *Non contemplantibus nobis que videntur, sed que non videntur; quia que videntur, temporalia sunt, que autem non*

2295 *videntur, eterna sunt* (2 Corinthians 4:18). That is: Oure contemplacion is not in thinges that are seen, but it is in thinges unseable. For thynges that are seen aren passynge, but thinges unseable aren ai lastande. To the whiche sight every soule schulde desire for to come, bothe heere in partie, and in the blisse of hevene fulli. For in that sight and in that knowynge of Jhesu is fulli the blisse of a resonable soule, and endelees liyf. Thus seith

2300 oure Lord: *Hec est autem vita eterna: ut cognoscant te verum deum, et quem misisti Jesum Cristum* (John 17:3). That is: Fadir, this is endelees liyf; that Thi chosen soulis knowe Thee and Thi Sone Jhesu Crist whom Thou hast sent, oon soothfast God.

Chapter Thirty-four

Of two maner of love formed, what it meeneth, and unformed; and hou we aren biholden for to love Jhesu moche for oure makynge, but moche more for oure biynge, but most

2305 for oure ful savynge whanne He geveth the Holi Goost to us and maketh us saaf thorugh love.

But now, wondrist thou, syn this knowynge of God is the blisse and the ende of a soule, whi thanne have I seid heere bifore that the soule schal not ellis coveiten but oonli the love of God; but I spak nothynge of this sight, that a soule schulde coveite this?

2310   Unto this I mai seyn thus: that the sight of Jhesu is ful blis of a soule, and that is not oonli for the sight, but it is also for the blissid love that cometh oute of the sight. Neverthelees, for love cometh oute of knowynge and not knowynge of love, therfore it is seid that in syght principali of God with love is the blisse of a soule, and the more He is knowen the betere He is loved. But for as mykil as to this knowynge, or to this love

2315 that cometh of it, mai not the soule come withoute love; therfor seide I that thou schuldest oonli coveiten love. For love is cause whi a soule cometh to this sight and to

2292 trowing, belief. **2304 biynge,** being.

217

this knowynge; and that love is not the love that a soule hath in itsilf to God, but the love that God hath to a symple soule that can right nought loven Him is cause whi this soule cometh to this knowynge and to this love that cometh of it. And on what manere that is,
2320 I schal telle thee more openly.

Holi writeres seyn, and sooth it is, that there is two maneres of goostli love. On is callid unformed, anothir is called formed. Love unformed is God Himsilf, the thridde persoone in Trinyté; that is, the Holi Goost. He is love unformed and unmaad, as Seynt Joon seith thus: *Deus dileccio est* (1 John 4:8). God is love, that is, the Holi Goost. Love
2325 formed is the affeccion of a soule, maad bi the Holi Goost of the sight and the knowynge of soothfastenesse (that is God oonli) stired and sette in Hym. This love is callid formed, for it is maad bi the Hooli Goost. This love is not God in Himsilf, for it is maad, but it is the love of the soule, felt of the sight of Jhesu and sterid to Hym oonli. Now maist thou see that love formed is not cause whi a soule cometh to goostli sight of Jhesu, as sum
2330 men wolden thenke, that thei wolde love God so brennandli as it were bi there owen myght, that thei were worthi for to have the more goostly knowing of Hym. Nai, it is not so. But love unformed, that is, God Himsilf, is cause of al this knowynge. For a blynde wrecchid soule is so feer from the cleer knowynge and the blissid feelynge of His love thorugh synne and freelté of the bodili kynde, that it myght nevere come to it, ne were
2335 the endelees mekenesse of the love of God. But thanne bicause that He loveth us so moche, therfor He geveth us his love, that is, the Hooli Goost. He is bothe the gifte and the gyvere, and maketh us thanne bi that gifte for to knowen Him and loven Him. Loo, this is the love that I spaak of, that thou schuldest oonli coveiten and desiren this unformed love that is the Hooli Goost. For sothli a lasse thynge or a lasse gift than He is
2340 mai not availe us for to bringen us to the blissid sight of Jhesu. And therefore schullen we fulli desiren and asken of Jhesu oonli this gift of love, that He wolde for the mykilnesse of His blissid love touchen oure hertis with His unseable light to the knowynge of Him, and departen with us of His blissid love, that as He loveth us that we myght love Him agen. Thus seith Seynt Joon: *Nos diligamus deum, quoniam ipse prior dilexit nos* (1
2345 John 4:19). That is: Love we now God, for He first loved us. He loved us mykil whanne He maade us to His liknesse, but He loved us more whanne He boughte us with His precious blood thorugh wilful takynge of deth in His manhede fro the power of the

2321 Holi writeres seyn, Clark (p. 317n235) suggests Augustine, *De trinitate*, 15.18.32 and 15.19.37, as well as Bernard and William of St. Thierry. **2333 feer**, far. **2343 departen**, share. **2347 manhede**, humanity.

feend and from the peyne of helle. But He loveth most us whan He geveth us the gifte of the Holi Goost, that is love, bi whiche we knowen Him and loven Hym, and are maad

2350 siker that we aren His sones chosen to savacion. For this love aren we more bounden to Him than for ony othir love that evere He schewed for us, either in oure makynge or in oure biynge. For though He hadde made us and bought us, but yif He save us withal, what profite is it ellis to us oure makynge or oure biynge? Sothli right noon.

Therfore the moste tokene of love schewed to us, as me thenketh, is this: that He

2355 geveth Himsilf in His Godhede to oure soulis. He gaf Himsilf in His manhede first to us for oure raunsom, whanne He offride Himsilf to the Fader of hevene upon the autier of the Cros. This was a fair gifte, and a grete tokene of love. But whanne He gyveth Himsilf in His Godhede goostli to oure soulis for oure savacion, and maketh us for to knowen Him and loven Hym, thanne loveth He us fulli. For thanne gyveth He Himsilf to us, and more

2360 myght He nought gyven us, ne lasse myght not sufficen to us. And for this skile it is seid that the rightynge of a synful soule thorugh forgifnesse of synnes is arrected and approprid principali to the wirkynge of the Holi Goost; for the Hooli Goost is love, and in the rightynge of a soule oure Lord Jhesu scheweth to the soule most of His love, for He doth awai al synne and oneth it to Hym. And that is the beste thynge that He mai

2365 doon to a soule, and therfore it is approperid to the Hooli Goost.

The makynge of a soule is approprid to the Fadir as for sovereigne myght and powere that he schewith in makynge of it. The biynge is arectid and approprid to the Sone, as for the sovereyne witte and wisdom that he schewid in his manhede; for he overcam the feend principali thorugh wisdom and not thorwgh strenthe. But the rightynge and

2370 the ful savynge of a soule bi forgyvnesse of synnes is approprid to the thridde persone, that is, the Hooli Goost. For therin schewith Jhesu most love unto a mannys soule, and for that thynge schal He most sovereynli be loved agen of us. His makynge is comyn to us and to alle unresonable creaturis. For as He mad us of nought, so He made hem; and therfore is this werk grettest of myght, but it is not most of love. Also the biynge is

2375 comone to us and to alle resonable soulis, as to Jewes and to Sarsenes and to fals Cristene men. For He died for alle soulis ilike and boughte hem, yif thei wolen han the profite therof; and also it sufficeth for the biynge of alle, though it so be that alle han it not. And this wirkynge was moste of wisdom, and not most of love. But the rightynge

2350 **siker**, secure. 2352 **biynge**, buying, i.e., redemption. 2356 **autier**, altar. 2360 **skile**, reason. 2361 **arrected**, accounted. 2362 **approprid**, appropriated. 2364 **oneth it**, conjoins it (the soul). 2368 **witte**, intelligence. 2374 **biynge**, redemption. 2375 **Sarsenes**, Saracens. 2377 **biynge**, redemption. 2378 **rightynge**, justification.

and the halewinge of oure soulis thorugh the gifte of the Holi Goost, that is oonli the
2380   wirkynge of love; and that is not comone, but it is a special gifte oonli to chosen soulis.
And sothli that is the wirkynge of most love to us that aren His chosen children.

    This is the love of God that I speke of, which thou schalt coveiten and desiren; for
this love is God Himsilf and the Holi Goost. This love unformed, whan it is geven to us,
it wirketh in oure soulis al that good is, and al that longeth to goodnesse. This love
2385   loveth us er than we loven Him. For it clenseth us first of oure synnes, and maketh us
for to loven Him, and maketh oure wille stronge for to agenstonden alle synnes, and it
stireth us for to assaien ouresilf thorugh diverse exercises bothe bodili and goostli in alle
vertues. It stireth us also for to forsake the love and the likynge of the world; it sleeth in
us alle wikkid stirynges of synnes and flesschli affeccions and wordli dredis; it kepit us
2390   from alle malicious temptacions of the fend; and it dryveth us from bisynesse and from
vanité of the world, and fro conversacioun of wordli loveris. Al this dooth the love of
God unformed, whanne He geveth Himsilf to us. We doon right nought but suffre Him,
and assente to Him, for that is the moste that we doon, that we assente wilfulli to His
gracious werkynge in us. And yit is not that wille of us, but of His makynge, so that me
2395   thenketh He dooth in us al that is wel doon, and yit we seen it nought. And not oonli
dooth He thus, but aftir this love dooth more. For He openeth the iye of the soule and
scheweth to the soule the sight of Jhesu wondirfulli, and the knowynge of Hym, as the
soule mai suffre it thus bi litil and bi litil; and bi that sight He ravescheth al the affeccion
of the soule to Him.

2400   And thanne bigynneth the soule for to knowen Him goostli, and brennandli for to love
Him; than seeth the soule sumwhat of the kynde of the blisside Godhede of Jhesu, hou
He is al and He werketh al and that alle good dedis that aren doon and good thoughtis
aren oonli of Him. For He is al sovereyn myght and al sovereyn soothfastnesse and al
sovereyn goodnesse; and therfor everiche good dede is doon oonli of Him and bi Him,
2405   and He schal oonli have the worschipe and the thanke for alle good deedis, and nothyng
but He. For though wrecchid men stelen His worschipe from Him heere for awhile,
neverthelees atte laste ende schal soothfastnesse schewe wel that Jhesu dede al and that
man dide right nought of himsilf; and thanne schullen theves of Goddis good that aren
nought acordid with Him heere in this lif for here trespace be demed to the deeth, and

2379 **halewinge**, making holy. 2386 **agenstonden**, resist. 2391 **conversacioun**, manner of
living; **wordli loveris**, lovers of the world.

2410 Jhesu schal fulli be worschipid and thanked of alle blissid creaturis for His gracious wirkynge.

    This love is not ellis but Jhesu Himsilf, that for love wirketh al this in mannys soule and reformeth it in feelynge to His liknesse, as I have bifore seid, and sumwhat as I schal seyn. This love bringeth into the soule the fulhede of alle vertues, and maketh hem
2415 alle clene and trewe, softe and esi, and turneth hem alle into love and in likynge; and on what manere wise he dooth that, I schal telle thee a litil aftirward. This love draweth the soule from fleschlihede into goostlinesse, from erthli feelyng into heveneli savour, and from veyn bihooldyng of wordli thinges into contemplacion of goostli creaturis and of Goddis privetees.

Chapter Thirty-five

2420 Hou sum soulis loven Jhesu bi bodili fervours, and bi ther owen affeccions that aren stired bi grace and bi resoun; and sum loven Jhesu more restfulli, bi gostli affeccions onli, stired inward thorugh grace of the Hooli Gost.

Thanne mai I seyn that he that hath most of this love heere in this lif most pleseth God, and most cleer sight schal have of Him in the blisse of hevene: for he hath the most gifte
2425 of love here in erthe.

    This love mai not be had bi a mannys traveile owen, as sum men wenen. It is freeli had of the gracious gifte of Jhesu, aftir moche bodili and goostli traveile goynge bifore. For there aren summe loveres of God that maken hemsilf for to love God as it were bi here owen myght; for thei streynen hemsilf thorugh grete violence, and panten so strongli
2430 that thei bersten al into bodili fervours as yif thei wolden drawe doun God from hevene to hem, and thei seien in her hertis and with her mouth, "A, Lord, I love Thee, and I wole love Thee. I wolde for Thi love suffre deeth." And in this maner wirkynge thei feelen grete fervour and mykil grace. And sooth it is, as me thenketh, this wirkynge is good and meedful, yif it be wel temprid with mekenesse and with discrecion. But
2435 neverthelees thise men loven not the gifte of love on that manere as I speke of, ne thei asken it not so. For a soule that hath the gifte of love thorugh gracious bihooldynge of

2414 fulhede, fullness. **2426 wenen**, suppose. **2434 meedful**, worthy of reward.

Jhesu as I meene, or ellis yif he have it not yit but wolde have it, he is not bisi for to streyne itsilf over his myght, as it were bodili strenth, for to han it bi bodili fervours and so for to feelen of the love of Jhesu. But him thenketh that he is right not, and that he can doo right not of hymsilf, but as it were a deed thynge oonli hangynge and born up bi the merci of God. He seeth wel that Jhesu is al and doth al, and therfore asketh he not ellis but the gifte of His love. For syn the soule seeth that his owen love is nought, therfore it wold have His love, for that is inowgh. Therfore praieth he, and that desireth he, that the love of God wolde touche him with his blissid light, that he myght seen a litil of Him bi schewynge of His gracious presence, for thanne schulde he love Him; and so bi this weie cometh the gifte of love, that is God, into a soule.

    The more that the soule noughteth itsilf thorugh grace bi sight of this sothfastnesse — sumtyme withoutin ony fervour schewed outeward — and the lasse it thenketh it loveth or seeth God, the nerrere neigheth it to perseyve the gifte of the blissid love. For thanne is love maister, and wirketh in the soule and maketh it for to forgeten himsilf, and for to seen and biholden oonli hou love dooth. And thanne is the soule more suffrynge than doynge, and that is clene love. Thus Seynt Poul mened whanne he seide thus: *Quicumque spiritu dei aguntur, hii sunt filii dei* (Romans 8:14). Alle thise that aren wrought with the spirit of God aren Goddis soones. That is, thise soulis that aren maad so meke and so buxum to God that thei wirke not with hemsilf, but suffren the Holi Goost ai stiren hem and wirke in hem feelynges of love with a ful swete acord to His stirynge, thise aren special Goddis sones, most like unto Him.

    Othere soulis that kunne not loven thus, but traveilen hemsilf bi here owen affeccions and stiren hemsilf thorugh thenkynge of God and bodili exercise for to drawen out of hem bi maistrie the feelynge of love, fervours and othere bodili signes, loven not so goostli. Thei doon wel and medefulli, bi so that thei wolen knowe mekeli that here wirkynge is not kindeli the gracious feelynge of love, but it is manli doon bi a soule at the biddyng of resoun. And neverthelees thorugh the goodenesse of God, bicause that soule doth that in it is, thise manli affeccions of the soule stired into God bi mannys wirkynge aren turned into goostli affeccions, and aren maad medful as yyf thei hadde be doon goostli in the first bigynnynge. And this is a greet curteisie of oure Lord, schewed unto a meke soule, that turneth alle thise manli affeccions of kyndeli love into

2437 **bisi**, busy. 2449 **neigheth**, approaches. 2455 **buxum**, obedient. 2458 **kunne**, know how to. 2460 **maistrie**, force. 2461 **medefulli**, in a manner worthy of reward. 2465 **medful**, worthy of reward; **yyf**, if.

affeccioun and into the mede of his owen love, as yif he hadde wrought hem alle fulli bi himsilf. And so thise affeccions so turned moun ben called affeccions of goostli love
2470 thorugh purchace, not thorugh kyndeli bryngynge forth of the Holi Goost. I seye not that a soule mai wirken siche manli affeccions oonli of itsilf withouten grace, for I woot weel that Seynt Poul seith that we moun right nought doon ne thenken that good is of ouresilf withouten grace. *Non quod sumus sufficientes cogitare aliquid ex nobis, sed sufficiencia nostra ex deo est* (2 Corinthians 3:5). That is: We that loven God wenen not
2475 that we sufficen for to love and thenken good of ouresilf onli, but oure sufficience is of God. For God wirketh in us al, bothe good wil and good werk, as Seynt Poul seith: *Deus est qui operatur in nobis et velle et perficere pro bona voluntate* (Philippians 2:13). That is: God that wirketh in us bothe wil and fillynge of good wille. But I seie that siche affecciouns aren of God, maad bi the mene of a soule aftir the general grace that
2480 He gyveth to alle Hise chosen soulis; not of special grace maad goostli bi touchinge of His gracious presence, as He werketh in His perfite loveris, as I have bifore seid. For in unperfite loveres of God love werketh al ferli, bi the affeccions of man; but in perfite loveres, love werketh veryli, bi his owen goostli affecciouns, and sleeth for the tyme in a soule alle othere affecciouns bothe fleschli and kyndeli and manli. And that is propirli
2485 the wirkynge of love bi himsilf. This love mai be had a litil in partie heere in a clene soule, thorugh goostli sight of Jhesu; but in the blisse of hevene it is fulfillid bi cleer sight of Jhesu in His Godhede, for there schal noon affeccion be left in a soule, but al godli and goostli.

Chapter Thirty-six

That the gifte of love amonge alle the giftes of Jhesu is worthiest and most profitable;
2490 and hou Jhesu doth al that is wel don in His chosen onli for love. And hou love maketh the usynge of alle vertues and alle good dedis, light and esy.

Aske thou thanne of God nothinge but this gifte of love, that is, the Holi Goost. For amonge alle the giftes that oure Lord geveth ther is noon so good ne so profitable, so worthi ne excellent, as this is. For there is no gifte of God that is bothe gifte and the

2469 moun, may. **2482 ferli**, from a distance. **2483 veryli**, truly.

2495 gyvere, but this gifte of love; and therfore it is the beste and the worthieste. The gift of
profesie, the gifte of myracles-werkynge, the gift of grete kunnynge and conceilynge,
and the gifte of grete fastynge or of grete penaunce-doynge, or ony othir siche, aren
grete giftes of the Holi Goost, but thei aren not the Holi Goost, for a repreved soule and
a dampnable myght have alle thise giftes as fulli as a chosen soule.

2500   And therfore al thise manere of giftis aren not moche to be desired, ne greteli for to
chargen. But the gifte of love is the Hooli Goost, God Himsilf; and Him mai no soule have
and be dampned with Him, for that gifte oonli saveth it fro dampnacion, and maketh it
Goddis sone, partenere of heveneli heritage. And that love, as I have bifore seid, is not
the affeccioun of love that is formed in a soule, but it is the Holi Goost Himsilf, that is

2505 love unformed, that saveth a soule. For He gyveth Himsilf to a soule first, or the soule
loveth Him; and He formeth affeccion in the soule and maketh the soule oonli for to
loven Him oonli for Himsilf. And not oonli that, but also bi this gifte the soule loveth itsilf
and alle his evene Cristene as himsilf, onli for God; and this is the gifte of love that
maketh schedynge atwixe chosen soulis and the repreved. And this maketh ful pees

2510 atwixe God and a soule and oneth alle blissid creatures holli in God; for it maketh Jhesu
to loven us, and us Him also, and eche of us for to loven othir in Him.

Coveite this gifte of love principali, as I have seid. For yif He wole of His grace gyve
it on that manere wise, it schal openen and lightnen the resoun of thi soule for to seen
sothfastnesse, that is, Jhesu and goostli thynges. And it schal stire thyn affeccions holli

2515 and fulli for to loven Him and it schal werken in thi soule oonli as He wole, and thou
schalt biholden Him reverentli with softnesse of love and seen hou He dooth. This biddeth
He bi His prophete that we schulde doo, seiynge thus: *Vacate, et videte quoniam ego sum
deus* (Psalms 45:11). Ceese yee, and seeth that I am God. That is, ye that aren reformed
in feelynge and han youre innere iye opened into sight of goostli thinges, ceese yee sum

2520 tyme of outeward wirkynge, and seeth that I am God. That is, "Seeth onli hou I, Jhesu,
God doo; bihalde yee Me, for I doo al. I am love, and for love I doo al that I do, and ye
do nought. That this is sooth y schal schewe yow, for there is no good deede doon in
yow ne good thought felt in yow, but yif it be doon thorugh Me, that is, thorwgh myght,
wisdom and love, that is mightili, wittili, and loveli, ellis it is it no good deede. Now is it

2525 sooth that I, Jhesu, am bothe myght, wisdom, and blissid love, and ye nought; for y am

2496 **kunnynge**, knowledge. 2498 **repreved**, condemned. 2501 **chargen**, value. 2503 **partenere**,
partner; see Textual Notes. 2509 **schedynge**, separation. 2510 **oneth**, unites. 2513 **lightnen**,
illuminate. 2524 **loveli**, lovingly.

God. Than mowe yee wel seen that y oonli doo alle youre good deedes, and youre good thoughtes, and good loves in yow, and ye don right nought. And yit neverthelees are thise good deedis called your, not for yee wirken hem principali, but for I geve hem to yow for love that y have to you. And therefore, syn I am Jhesu, and for love do al this, ceese ye thanne of bihaldynge of youresilf and setteth youresilf at nought, and looketh on Me and seth that I am God, for y doo al this." This is sumwhat of the menynge of the vers of David bifore seide.

2530

See thanne and bihoolde what love werketh in a chosen soule that He reformeth in feelynge to His liknesse, whanne the reson is lightned a litil to the goostli knowinge of Jhesu and to the feelynge of His love. Thanne bringeth love into the soule the fulheed of vertues, and turneth hem alle into likynge and softenesse as it were withoute wirkynge of the soule; for the soule striveth not mykil for the getynge of hem as it dide bifore, but it hath hem esili and felith hem restfulli, oonli thorugh the gifte of love that is the Holi Goste. And that is a wel greet comfort to the soule and a gladnesse unspecable, whanne it feeleth sodeynli, and woot nevere hou, that vertu of mekenesse and pacience, sobirnesse and sadnesse, chastité and clennesse, lovereden to his even Cristene, and alle othir vertues, the whiche weren sumtyme travelous, pyneful, and hard to him for to kepen, aren now turned into softenesse and likynge, and into wondirful lightnesse — so fer forth that hym thenketh it no maistrie ne hardenesse for to kepen ony vertu, but it is most likynge to him for to kepen it. And al this maketh love.

2535

2540

2545

Othere men that stonden in the comoun weie of charité, and aren not yit so fer forth in grace, but wirken undir the biddynge of resoun, striven and fighten al dai agens synnes for the getynge of vertues, and sumtyme ben aboven and sumtyme binethen, as wrasteleres aren. Thise men don ful wel. Thei han alle vertues oonli in resoun and in wille, not in savour ne in love, for thei fighten hemsilf as it were bi here owen myghtes for hem. And therfore mowe they not have ful rest ne fulli the highere hand. Neverthelees thei schullen han moche meede, but thei aren not yit meke inowgh. Thei han not yit put hemsilf al fulli in Goddis hand, for thei seen Him not yit.

2550

But a soule that hath goostli sight of Jhesu taketh no grete keep of strivynge for vertues, it is not bisi abouten hem speciali; but it setteth al her bysynesse for to kepe that sight and that bihaldynge of Jhesu that it hath, for to halde the mynde stabeli therto, and

2555

2534 lightned, illuminated. **2535 fulheed**, fullness. **2539 unspecable**, unspeakable. **2541 sadnesse**, resolve; **clennesse**, purity; **lovereden**, love. **2551 highere**, upper. **2556 stabeli**, steadily.

bynde the love oonli to it that it falle not fro it, and forgeteth alle othere thynges as mykil as it mai. And whanne it dooth thus, than is Jhesu soothfastli maister in the soule and the soule is fulli buxum to Him and thanne fighteth Jhesu for the soule agens alle synnes, and umbischadueth it with His blissid presence, and geteth it alle vertues; and the soule is so comforted, and soo born up with the soft feelynge of love that it hath of the sight of Jhesu, that it feeleth no grete disese outward. And thus sleeth love generali alle synnes in a soule, and reformeth it in newe feelynge of vertues.

2560

Chapter Thirty-seven

Hou love, thoru a gracious biholding of Jhesu, sleth alle stirynges of pride and maketh the soule perfiteli meke; for it maketh the soule for to lese savour and delite in al ertheli worschip.

2565

Neverthelees, hou love sleeth synnes and reformeth vertues in a soule more speciali schal y seyn; and firste of pride, and of mekenesse that is contrarie therto. Thou schalte undirstonden that there is two maner of mekenesse. Oon is had bi wirkynge of resoun. Anothir is feelt bi special gifte of love. But bothe aren of love. But that oon love wirketh bi resoun of the soule; that othir wirketh bi himsilf. The firste is imperfight, that othir is perfight.

2570

The first mekenesse a man feelith of bihaldynge of his owen synnes and of his owen wrecchidnesse, thorugh which biholdynge he thenketh himsilf unworthi for to have ony gifte or grace or ony meede of God; but he thenketh it inowgh that He wolde of His grete merci graunte hym forgevenesse of hise synnes. And also he thenketh hym bicause of his owene synnes that he is wers than the moste synnere that lyveth, and that everi man doth betere than he. And so bi siche biholdynge casteth himsilf doun in his thoughtis undir alle men; and he is bisie for to agenstonde the stirynges of pride as mykil as he mai, bothe bodili pride and goostli, and disposeth himsilf, so that he assenteth not to the feelynges of pride. And yif his herte be taken sumtyme with it, that it be defouled with veyn joie or worschipe or of connynge or of preisynge or of ony othir thinge, as sone as

2575

2580

2559 buxum, obedient. **2560 umbischadueth**, overshadows. **2562 disese**, discomfort. **2564 sleth**, slays. **2579 agenstonde**, resist. **2582 connynge**, knowledge; **preisynge**, praising.

he mai perceyve it, he is yvel paid with himsilf, and hath sorwe for it in herte, and asketh forgyvnesse for it of God and schewith him to his confessour; and he accusith

2585 himsilf mekeli, and receyveth his penaunce. This is good mekenesse, but it is not yit perfite, for it is of soulis that are bigynnende and profitende in grace, causid of bihooldynge of synnes. Love werketh this mekenesse bi resoun of the soule.

Parfite mekenesse a soule feeleth of the sight and the goostli knowynge of Jhesu. For whanne the Holi Goost lightneth the reson into the sight of soothfastenesse, hou Jhesu

2590 is al and that He dooth al, the soule hath so grete love, and so grete joie in that goostli sight, for it is soothfaste that it forgeteth itsilf and fulli leneth to Jhesu with al the love that it hath for to biholden Hym. It taketh no kepe of the unworthinesse of itsilf ne of synnes biforc doon. But setteth at nought itsilf with alle the synnes and alle the good deedis that evere he dide, as yif there were nothinge but Jhesu. Thus meke was David

2595 whanne he seide thus: *Et substancia mea tanquam nichillum ante te* (Psalms 38:6). That is: Lord Jhesu, the sight of Thi blissid unmaad substance and Thyn endelees beynge scheweth wel unto me that my substance and the beynge of my soule that is chaungeable is as nought agens Thee. Also anemptis his even Cristene he hath no reward to hem, ne demyng of hem, whethir thei ben betere or werse thanne himsilf is. For he hooldeth

2600 himsilf and alle othere men as it were evene, ilike nought of hemself anemptis God; and that is sooth, for al the goodnesse that is doon in himsilf or in hem is onli of God, whom he biholdeth as al. And therfore setteth he alle othere creatures at nought, as he dooth himsilf. Thus meke was the prophete whanne he seide thus: *Omnes gentes quasi non sint, sic sunt coram eo, et quasi nichillum et inane ita reputati sunt* (Isaiah 40:17). Alle

2605 men aren biforc oure Lord as nought and as veyn and nought thei aren acconttid to Him. That is, anemptis the eendelees beynge and the unchaungeable kynde of God mankynde is as nought. For of nought it is maad, and into nought it schulde turnen, but yif he kepide it in the beynge that made it of nought. This is soothfastnesse, and this schulde make a soule meke yif it myght see thorugh grace this soothfastenesse. Therefore

2610 whanne love openeth the innere iye of a soule for to seen this soothfastnesse with othere circumstaunces that cometh withal, thanne bigynneth the soule for to be soothfasteli meke. For thanne bi the sight of God it feelith and seeth itsilf as it is; and thanne

---

2583 yvel paid, ill-satisfied. **2591 leneth**, inclines. **2596 unmaad**, uncreated. **2598 agens**, in comparison with; **anemptis**, in respect to; **reward**, regard. **2600 evene**, equal; **ilike**, alike. **2605 acconttid**, accounted. **2606 kynde**, nature. **2608 beynge**, being.

forsaketh the soule the bihooldynge and the lenynge to itsilf, and fulli fallith to the biholdynge of Hym. And whanne it dooth so, thanne setteth the soule right nought bi al

2615 the joie and alle the worschipe of this world; for the joie of wordli worschipe is so litil and so nought in regarde of that joie and that love that it feeleth in the goostli sight of Jhesu and knowynge of soothfastnesse, that though he myght have it withouten ony synne, he wolde not of it. Ne though men wolde worschipen him, preisen hym, favoren hym, and sette hym at greet staat, it liketh hym right nought, ne though he hadde the

2620 kunynge of alle the sevene artis of clergie, and of alle craftes undir sunne, or hadde powere for to wirke alle maner miraclis, he hath no more deynté of al this, ne more savoure of hem, thanne for to gnawen upon a drie stikke. He hadde wel levere forgeten al this and for to ben alone out of the sight of the world, than for to thenken on hem and be worschiped of alle men. For the herte of a trewe lovere of Jhesu is maad so mykil

2625 and so large thorugh a litil sight of Him and a litil feelynge of His goostli love, that al the likynge and al the joie of al erthe mai not sufficen for to fillen oon corner of it. And thanne semeth it wel that thise wrecchid wordli lovers that aren, as it were, ravysched in love of here owen worschipe, and pursuen aftir it for to han it and with al the myght and al the witte that thei han, thei have no savoure in this mekenesse, thei aren wondir

2630 fer therfro. But the lovere of Jhesu hath this mekenesse lastandeli, and that not with hevynesse and stryvynge for it, but with likynge and goostli gladnesse, the whiche gladnesse it hath, not for it forsaketh al the worschipe of this world, for that were a proude mekenesse that longeth to an ypocrite, but for he hath a sight and a goostli knowynge of soothfastnesse and of worthinesse of Jhesu thorugh gifte of the Hooli

2635 Goost.

That reverent sight and that loveli bihaldynge of Jhesu conforteth the soule so wondirfulli and berith it up so myghtili and so softli, that it mai not liken ne fulli resten in noon ertheli joie, ne it wole not. He maketh no fors whethir men lakken him or preisen hym, worschipen him or despicen hym as fore hymsilf. He setteth it not at herte neithir

2640 for to be wel paied yif men despicen him, as for more mekenesse, ne for to be yvel paied that men schulde worschipe hym or praise him. He hadde wel levere forgete bothe that oon and that othir, and oonli thenken on Jhesu, and gete mekenesse bi that weie;

2613 **lenynge**, inclination. 2618 **not**, nothing. 2619 **liketh**, pleases. 2620 **kunynge**, knowledge; **sevene artis of clergie**, i.e., the seven liberal arts. 2621 **deynté**, value. 2622 **levere**, rather. 2631 **hevynesse**, gloominess. 2638 **maketh no fors**, has no concern; **lakken**, blame; **preisen**, praise. 2639 **despicen**, despise; **as fore hymsilf**, as far as he is concerned. 2640 **paied**, satisfied. 2641 **levere**, rather.

and this is mykil the sikerere weie, whoso myght come therto. Thus dide David whanne he seide thus: *Oculi mei semper ad dominum, quoniam ipse evellet de laqueo pedes meos* (Psalms 24:15). That is, myn iyen aren ai upon Jhesu my Lord, for whi He schal kepe my feet from the snaris of synne. For whanne he dooth so, thanne forsaketh he uttirli hymself and undircasteth hym hooli to Jhesu. And thanne is he in a siker warde, for the schelde of sothfastenesse, that he biholdeth, kepeth hym so wel that He schal not ben hurte thorugh no stirynge of pride as longe as he holdeth hym withinne the schelde.

As the prophete seith: *Scuto circumdabit te veritas eius; non timebis a timore nocturno* (Psalms 90:5). Sothfastnesse of God schal umbiclippe thee with a scheeld, and that is yif thou, alle othere thynges lefte, oonli biholde Hym. For thanne schalt thou not dreden for the nyghtes drede, that is, thou schalt not drede the spirit of pride, whethir he come by nyght or bi dai, as the next vers seith thus: *A sagitta volante in die* (Psalms 90:6). Pride cometh bi nyght for to assaile a soule, whanne it is despiced and repreved of othere men, that it schulde bi that falle into hevynesse and into sorwe. It cometh also as an arwe fleynge in the dai, whanne a man is worschipid and preysed of alle men, whethir it be for wordli doynge or for goostli, that he schulde have veyne joie in hymsilf and fals gladdenesse restyngli in a passynge thynge. This is a scharp arwe and a perilous arwe; it fleeth swifteli, it striketh softeli, but it woundeth deedli.

But the lovere of Jhesu, that stabli biholdeth Hym bi devoute praieres and bisili thenkynge on Hym, is so umbilapped with the siker schelde of soothfastnesse that he dredeth not, for this arwe mai not entren into the soule; ne though it come, it hurteth not, but glenteth away and passeth forth. And thus is the soule maad meke, as I undirstonde, bi wirkynge of the Holi Gost, that is, the gifte of love; for he openeth the iye of the soule for to seen and to loven Jhesu, and he kepith the soule in that sight restfulli and sikirly, and he sleeth alle the stirynges of pride wondir priveli and softeli, and the soule woot nevere how, and he also bringeth in bi that wai soothfasteli and loveli the vertu of mekenesse. Al this dooth love, but not in alle hise loveres ilikeful. For sum men han this grace but schorteli and litil, as it were yit in the bygynnynge of it, and a litil assaiynge towarde it, for her

---

2643 sikerere, more certain. **2647 undircasteth**, casts beneath; **siker**, secure; **warde**, guardianship. **2650 schelde**, shield. **2652 umbiclippe**, embrace. **2656 despiced**, despised; **repreved**, condemned. **2658 fleynge**, flying. **2660 restyngli**, continuously. **2662 stabli**, steadily. **2663 umbilapped**, surrounded. **2664 glenteth**, glances. **2670 ilikeful**, to the same extent.

conscience is not yit fulli clensid thorugh grace. And sum men han it more fulli, for thei han clerere sight of Jhesu, and thei feele more of His love. And sum men han it most fulli, for thei han the ful gifte of contemplacion. Nevertheles he that leste hath on this

2675 manere as I have seid, sothli he hath the gifte of perfite mekenesse, for he hath the gifte of perfighte love.

Chapter Thirty-eight

Hou love sleeth alle stirynges of ire and envie softeli, and reformeth in the soule the vertues of pees and pacience and of perfite charité to his even Cristene, as he deede speciali in the apostelis and martyres.

2680 Love wirketh wiseli and softeli in a soule there he wole, for he sleeth myghtili ire and envie and alle passions of angrinesse and malincolie in it, and brengeth into a soule vertues of pacience and myldenesse, pesiblité and lovereden to his even Cristene. It is ful gret maistrie and grete hardenesse to a man that stondeth oonli in the wirkynge of his owen resoun for to kepen pacience, oonli reste and softnesse in herte, and charité

2685 anemptis his even Cristen yif thei disese him unskilfulli and doon hym wrong, that he ne schal doon sumwhat agens hem thorugh stirynge of ire or of malencolie, either in spekyng or in wirkynge or in bothe. And neverthelees, though a man be stired or trobeled in himsilf and be maad unrestful, bi so that it be not to mykil, passende over the boundis of resoun, and that he kepe his hand and his tunge and be redi for to forgyve trespace

2690 whanne merci is askid, yit this man hath the vertu of pacience, though it be but weikeli and nakidli; for as mykil as he wolde have it, and travayleth bisili in refreynynge of his unskilfulle passiouns that he myght have it, and also is sori that he hath it not so as he schulde. But to a trewe lovere of Jhesu it is no grete maistrie for to suffren al this, for whi love feighteth for him, and sleeth wondir softeli siche risynges of wraththe and al

2695 malencolie, and maketh his soule so esi, so pesible, so suffrande, and so goodli thorugh the goostli sight of Jhesu, with the feelynge of His blissid love, that though he be dispiced

---

2676 **perfighte**, perfect. 2682 **pesiblité**, peaceability; **lovereden**, love. 2683 **maistrie**, feat of skill. 2685 **anemptis**, in respect to; **disese**, disturb; **unskilfulli**, unreasonably. 2690 **weikeli**, weakly. 2692 **unskilfulle**, irrational. 2693 **maistrie**, feat of skill. 2695 **pesible**, peaceable; **suffrande**, tolerant.

or reprovcd of othere men, or take wronge or harm, or schame or velany, he chargeth it not. He is not mykil stired agens hem, he wil not ben angrid ne sterid agens hem; for yif he were mykil stired he schulde forbeeren the confort that he feeleth withinne in his
2700 soule, but that wole he not. He mai lightliere forgeten al the wronge that is doon to hym, thanne anothir man mai forgeven it, though merci werc askcd. And so he hadde ful lyvere forgeten than forgyven it, for him thenketh it so moste eese to hym.

And love dooth al this, for love openeth the iye of the soule to the sight of Jhesu, and stablith it with the likynge of love that it feelith bi that sight, and conforteth it so myghtili
2705 that it taketh no kepe; whatso men jangelen or don agens him, it hangeth nothynge upon him. The moste harm that he myght havc were a forberynge of the goostli sight of Jhesu. And therfore it is levcrc to him to suffren alle othere harmes than that aloone. Al this mai a soule doo wel and esili, withoute grete trobelynge of the goostli sight, whanne disese falleth al withouteforth and toucheth not thc bodi, as is bakbytynge or scornynge
2710 or spoilynge of siche as he hath. Al this greveth not. But it goth sumwhat neer whanne the flesch is touchid, and he feele smert; thanne it is hardere. Neverthclccs, though hit be hard and impossible to the frele kynde of man for to suffre bodeli peync gladli and pacientli, withouten bittir stirynges of ire, angir, and malencolie, it is not impossible to love (that is, the Hooli Gooste) for to werke this in a soule there He toucheth with His
2715 blissid gifte of love. But He geveth to a soule that is in that plight myghti feelynges of love, and wondirfulli fasteneth it to Jhesu, and departeth the soule wondir feer fro the sensualité thorugh His privei myght, and conforteth it so sweteli bi His blissid presence that the soule feelith litil peyne or ellis noon of the sensualité; and this is the special grace goven to the hooli martires. This grace hadden the apostelis, as Holi Writte seith thus of
2720 hem: *Ibant apostoli gaudentes a conspectu consilii, quoniam digni habiti sunt pro nomine Jesu contumeliam pati* (Acts 5:41). That is, the apostlis yeeden joiande fro the conceil of the Jewes whanne thei weren beten with scourges, and thei weren glaad that thei weren worthi for to suffre ony bodili disese for the name of Jhesu. Thei weren not stired to ire ne to felnesse, for to ben venged of the Jewes that beten hem, as a wordli
2725 man wolde ben whanne he suffreth a litil harm, be hit never so litil, of his even Cristen.

2697–98 he chargeth it not, it does not concern him. **2702 lyvere**, rather; **eese**, comfort. **2706 harm**, injury. **2707 levere**, more desirable. **2709 disese**, trouble; **falleth**, occurs; **withouteforth**, externally. **2710 neer**, nearer. **2719 goven**, given; **hooli martires**, see Pseudo-Augustine, *Sermo de nativitate S. Laurentii* 206 (PL 39:2127); Clark, p. 321n288. **2721 yeeden**, went. **2724 felnesse**, fierceness.

Ne thei were not stired to pride and to heighnesse of hemsilf and to disdeyn and to demynge of the Jewes, as ipocrites and heretikes aren that wolen suffre mykil bodili peyne, and aren redi sumtyme for to suffre deeth with grete gladnesse and with myghti wille as it were in the name of Jhesu, for the love of Hym. Soothli that glaadnesse and

2730 that love that thei han in suffrynge of bodili meschef is not of the Holi Gost. It cometh not fro the fier that brenneth in the highe autier of hevene, but it is feyned by the feend enflawmed of helle. For it is menged with the highest of pride and of presumpcioun of hemsilf, and dispite and demynge and disdeyn of hem that thus ponesche hem. And thei wenen yit that al is charité and that thei suffre al that wronge for the love of God, but

2735 thei aren bigiled bi the myddai feend. A trewe lovere of Jhesu, whanne he suffreth harm of his even Cristene, is so strengthed thorugh grace of the Hooli Goost, and is maad so meke, so pacient, and so peseble, and that sothfastli, that what wronge or harm what it be that he suffre of his even Cristene, he kepeth ai mekenesse. He dispiceth him not, he demeth him not, but preyeth for hym in his herte and hath of hym pité and compassioun,

2740 moche more tendirli thanne of anothir man that nevere dide hym harm; and sothli betere loveth him and more ferventeli desireth the savacion of his soule, bicause that he seeth that he schal have so mykil goosteli profite thorugh his yvel dede, though it be agens his wille. But this love and this mekenesse wirketh oonli the Holi Goost, above the kynde of man, in hem that He maketh trewe loveres of Jhesu.

Chapter Thirty-nine

2745 Hou love sleeth coveitise, leccherie, glotonye, and accidie, and the fleschli savour and delite in alle the fyve bodili wittes in the perfite love of Jhesu softli and esili thorugh a gracious biholdynge of Hym.

Coveitise also is slayn in a soule bi the wirkynge of love, for it maketh the soule so covetous of goostli good and to heveneli richesse so ardant, that it setteth right nought

2750 bi al ertheli richesse. It hath no more deynté in havynge of a precious ston than on a chalke stoon; ne no more love hath he in an hundred pounde of gold thanne in a pounde

---

2726 **heighnesse**, exaltation. 2727 **demynge**, judgment. 2731 **autier**, altar. 2732 **menged**, mingled. 2734 **wenen**, suppose. 2735 **myddai feend**, midday devil; see also *Scale*, II.1518, above. 2750 **deynté**, value.

of leed. It setteth al thynge that schal perisschen and passen at oo price; no more chargeth that oon than that othir as in his love. For it seeth wel that alle thise ertheli thynges that wordli loveris han in so greet price, and loven so deynteli, schullen passen

2755 awey and turne to nought, bothe the thyng in itsilf and the love of it. And therfore he bryngeth it in his thought bityme in that plight that it schal ben aftir, and so he accounteth it at nought. And whan wordli loveres striven and pleten and fighten fore wordli good, who mai first have it, the lovere of Jhesu stryveth with no man, but kepeth himsilf in pees and holdeth hym paied with that that he hath, and he wole stryve for no more; for

2760 hym thenketh hym nedeth no more of alle the richessis in erthe thanne a scant bodili sustenaunce for to save the bodili liyf withal, as longe as God wole, and that mai he lightli have, and therfore wole he no more han. He is wel at ese whanne he hath no more than scanteli him nedeth for the tyme, that he mai be freeli discharged from bisynesse aboute the kepynge and the dispendynge of it, and fulli geven his herte and al his besynesse

2765 aboute the sekynge of Jhesu, for to fynde Hym in clennesse of spirit. For that is al his coveitise, for whi, oonli clene of herte schullen seen Hym.

Also fleschli love of fadir and of modir and of othere wordli frendis hangeth not up hym. It is evene kut from his herte with the swerde of goostli love, that he hath no more affeccioun to fadir ne to modir or to ony wordli frend than he hath to anothir man, but

2770 yif he see and feele in hem more grace and more vertu than in othir men. Outetaken this, that hym were levere that his fadir and his modir hadden the selve grace that summe othere men han; but neverethelees yif thei ben not so, thanne loveth he othere betere than hem, and that is charité. And so sleeth the love of Jhesu coveitise of the world and bringeth into the soule poverté in spirit.

2775 And that dooth love not oonli in hem that han right nought of wordli good, but also in some creatures that aren in greet wordli estate and have dispendynge of ertheli richesse. Love sleeth in summe of hem coveitise, so fer forth that thei han no likynge ne savoure in havynge of hem more than in a stree. Ne though thei ben loste for defaute of hem that schulde kepe hem, thei sette not therbi; for whi, the herte of Goddis lovere is thorugh

2780 gifte of the Holi Goost taken so fulli with the sight and the love of anothire thynge, that

---

2753 chargeth, values. **2754 price**, value; **deynteli**, preciously. **2757 pleten**, debate. **2764 dispendynge**, spending. **2766 coveitise**, desire; **for whi**, for the reason that. **2767 up**, upon. **2770 Outetaken**, Except. **2771 hym were levere**, he would rather. **2776 dispendynge**, spending. **2778 stree**, straw; **defaute**, fault.

is so precious and so worthi, that it wole receyve noon othir love restyngli that is contrarie therto.

And not onli dooth love this, but also it sleeth the likynge of leccherie and al othir bodili unclennesse, and bringeth into the soule veri chastité, and turneth hit into likynge. 2785 For the soule feeleth so grete delite in the sight of Jhesu that it liketh for to be chaste, and it is no grete hardenesse to it for to kepe chastité, for it is the moste eese and the moste reste.

And upon the selve wise the gifte of love sleeth fleschli lustis of glotonie, and maketh the soule sobre and temperat, and berith it up so myghtili that it mai not resten in likynge 2790 of mete and drynke, but it taketh mete and drynke, what it be that leest agreveth the bodili conpleccioun, yif he mai lightli have it, not for love of itsilf, but for love of God. And on this maner wise the lovere of Jhesu seeth wel that hym nedeth for to kepen his bodili liyf with mete and drynk as longe as God wole suffren hem to be togedre. Thanne schal this be the discrecioun of the lovere of Jhesu, as I undirstonde, that hath feelynge 2795 and wirkynge in love; that upon what manere that he mai most kepen his grace hool, and lest be letted fro the wirkynge in hit thorugh takynge of bodili sustenaunce, so schal he doo. That maner of mete that lest letteth and leest troblith the herte and mai kepe the bodi in strengthe — be it fleisch, be it fisch, be it breed and ale — that I trowe the soule chesith for to have yif it mai esily come therbi. For al the besynesse of the soule is for 2800 to thenken on Jhesu with reverent love, ay withoute lettynge of onythynge, yif it myght. And therfore syn that it bihoveth sumwhat be letted and hyndred, the lasse that it is letted and hyndred bi mete and drynk, or bi ony othir thyng, the leverere it is. It hadde leverer taken and usen the beste mete and most of price that is undir sunne, yif it lesse letted the kepynge of his herte, than for to take but breed and watir, yif that letted him 2805 more; for he hath no reward to geten him greet mede for the peyne of fastynge and be put therbi from softenesse in herte. But al his bisynesse is for to kepen his herte as stabli as he may in the sight of Jhesu and in the feelynge of His love. And sotheli, as I trowe, he myght with lasse likynge usen the beste mete that is good in the owen kynde, than anothir man that wirketh al in resoun withoute the special gifte of love schulde mowe 2810 usen the werste, outetaken mete that thorugh craft of curie is oonli maad for lust: that manere of mete mai he not weel acorden withal. And also on that othir side, yif litil mete,

2791 conpleccioun, constitution. **2794 discrecioun**, careful judgment. **2799 besynesse**, activity. **2802 leverere**, more desirable. **2805 reward**, regard. **2806 stabli**, steadily. **2810 outetaken**, except for; **curie**, cooking.

as oonli breed and ale, most helpeth and eseth his herte and kepeth it most in pees, it is thanne most leef to him for to use it so, and nameli yif he feele bodili strengthe oonli of the gifte of love withal.

2815   And yit dooth love more, for it sleeth accidie and fleischli ydelnesse, and maketh the soule lifli and spedi to the service of Jhesu, so fer forth that it coveiteth ai to ben occupied in goodnesse, nameli inward in biholdynge of Him, bi the vertu of whiche sight the soule hath savour and goostli delite in praiynge and thenkynge, and in al othir maner wirkynge that nedeth to be doon, aftir the staat and degree that he stondeth inne

2820   asketh (whethir he be religious or seculer), withouten hevynesse or peynful bittirnesse.

Also it sleeth the veyn likynges of the fyve bodili wittes. First the sight of the iye, that the soule hath no likynge in the sight of ony ertheli thynge, but it feelith rathere pyne and disese in biholdynge of it, be it nevere so faire, ne so precious, ne so wondirful. And therfore as wordli loveres rennen oute sumtyme for to seen newe thynges, for to wondren

2825   in hem, and so for to feden her herte with the veyn sight of hem; right so a lovere of Jhesu is bisi for to rennen awai and withdrawen hym from the sight of sich maner thynges, that the innere sight be not letted, for he seeth goostli anothir manere thynge that is fairere and more wondirfulle, and that wolde he not forbere.

Right on the selve wise it is of spekynge and herynge. It is a peyne to the soule of a

2830   lovere of Jhesu for to speke or heere onythynge that myte letten the fredom of his herte fro thenkynge of Jhesu. What songe or melodie or mynstralsie outeward that it be, yif it lette the thought that it mai not freli and restfulli prayen or thenken on Jhesu, it liketh right nought; and the more delitable that it is to othere men, the more unsaveri it is to him. And also for to heeren ony manere spekynge of othere men but it be sumwhat

2835   touchynge the wirkynge of his soule in the love of Jhesu, it liketh him right nought. He is ellis right soone irke of it. He hadde wel levere ben in pees and speke right nought, ne heere right nought, than for to heere the spekynge or the techynge of the grettest clerke on erthe, with alle the resons that he coude seyn to him thorugh mannys witte onli, but yif he coude speke felandli and stirendli of the love of Jhesu. For that is his craft

2840   principalli, and therefore wolde he not ellis heren ne seen, but that myght helpen him and fortheren him into more knowynge and to betere feelynge of Him. Of wordeli speche it is no doute that he hath no savour in spekynge ne in heerynge of it, ne in wordli talis, ne in tydynges, ne in noon siche veyn jangelynge that longeth not to him.

2815 accidie, sloth. **2816 lifli**, lively; **spedi**, hastening. **2817 nameli**, especially. **2822 pyne**, pain. **2823 disese**, trouble. **2836 irke**, disgusted. **2841 wordeli**, worldly.

And so it is of smellynge and savouryng and touchynge; the more that the thought
2845   schulde be distracte and broken of goostli reste bi the use eithir of smellynge or of
savourynge or of ony of the bodili wittes, the more he fleeth it. And the lasse that he
feeleth of hem, the levere is hym, and yif he myght lyven in the bodi withoute the
feelynge of ony of hem, he wolde nevere feelen hem. For thei troblen the herte ofte
sithes and putten oute fro reste, and thei mowen not ben fulli eschewed. But neverthelees,
2850   the love of Jhesu is sumtyme so myghti in a soule that it overcometh and sleeth al
thynge that is contrarie to it.

Chapter Forty

What vertues and graces a soule receyveth thorugh openynge of the innere iye into the
gracious biholdynge of Jhesu, and hou it mai not be geten oonli thorugh mannes traveile,
but thorugh special grace and traveile also.

2855   Thus werketh love outeward in a soule, openynge the goostli iye into biholdynge of
Jhesu bi inspiracion of special grace, and maketh it clene, sotil, and able to the werke of
contemplacioun. What this openynge of this goostli iye is the grettest clerk in erthe
coude not ymagene bi his kyndeli wit, ne schewe fulli bi his tunge. For it mai not be
geten thorugh studie ne bi mannys traveile oonli, but principali thorugh grace of the
2860   Hooli Goost and with traveile of man. I drede moche for to speke ought of it, for me
thenketh y can nought; it passeth myn assay, and my lippes aren unclene. Neverthelees,
for I hope love asketh and love biddeth, therfor I schal seyn a litil more of it as y hope
love techeth. This openynge of the goostli iye is that lighti merkenesse and that riche
nought that I spak of bifore, and it mai be callide purité of spirit and gosteli reste, inward
2865   stillenesse and pees in conscience, highnesse or deepnesse of thought and oonlynesse
of soule, a liyfli feelynge of grace and priveté of herte, the waker sleep of the spouse
and a taastynge of heveneli savour, brennynge in love, schynynge in light, entré of
contemplacion and reformynge in feelynge. Alle thise resouns aren seid in holi writynge
bi dyvers men, for eche of hem spak of hem aftir his feelynge in grace, and though thei

2848–49 **ofte sithes**, often. 2856 **sotil**, subtle. 2858 **kyndeli**, natural. 2862 **hope₁**, expect.
2863 **lighti**, light-filled; **merkenesse**, darkness. 2864 **nought**, nothing. 2865 **oonlynesse**,
solitude. 2866 **liyfli**, lively; **waker**, wakeful.

2870 aren dyvers in schewynge of wordes, neverethelees thei aren alle oon in sentence of sothfastnesse.

For a soule that thorugh visitynge of grace hath oon, hath alle; for whi, a sighhende soule to see the face of Jhesu, whanne it is touched thorugh special grace of the Hooli Goost, it is sodeynli chaungcd and turned from the plight that it was inne to anothir

2875 maner feelynge. It is wondirfulli departed and drawen first into itsilf from love and likynge of al ertheli thynge, so moche that it hath lost savour of the bodili liyf and of al thynge that is, save oonli Jhesu. And thanne it is clene from al the filthe of synne, so fer forth that the mynde of it, and of alle unordinat affeccions to ony creature, is sodeynli wasschen and wiped awai, that there is no mene lettynge atwixe Jhesu and the soule,

2880 but oonli the bodili liyf. And thanne is it in goostli reste; for whi, alle the peynful doutes and dredis and othere temptaciouns of goostli enemyes aren dryven oute of the herte, that thei troble it not ne synke not thereinne for the tyme. It is in reste fro the noie of wordli besynesse, peyneful tariynge of wikkid stirynges, but it is ful bisi in the free goostli wirkynge of love, and the more it traveileth so, the more reste it feeleth.

2885 This resteful traveile is ful fer fro fleischli ydilnesse, from blynd sikirnesse. It is ful of goostli werk, but it is called reste, for grace looseth the hevy yook of fleschli love fro the soule, and maketh it myghti and free thorugh the gifte of goostli love, for to wirken gladli, softeli, and delitabli in al thynge that grace stireth it for to wirken inne. And therfore it is callid an hooli ydelnesse and a reste most bisi, and so it is, in stilnesse fro

2890 the grete cryynge and beestli noise of fleschli desires and unclene thoughtes.

This stilnesse maketh the inspiracioun of the Hooli Goost, in biholdynge of Jhesu. For whi, His vois is so swete and so myghti that it putteth silence in a soule to jangelynge of alle othere spekeris; for it is a vois of vertu, softeli sowned in a clene soule, of the whiche the prophete seith thus: *Vox domini in virtute* (Psalms 28:4). That is: The vois

2895 of oure Lord Jhesu is in vertu. This vois is a liyfli word and a spedi, as the apostil seith: *Vivus est sermo domini et efficax, penetrabilior omni gladio ancipiti* (Hebrews 4:12). That is: Quyk is the word of Jhesu and spedi, more persynge than ony swerd is. Thorugh spekynge of this word is fleschli love slayn, and the soule keped in silence from alle wikkid stirynges. Of this silence it is seid in the Apocalips thus: *Factum est silencium in*

2900 *celo, quasi dimidia hora* (Revelations 8:1). Silence was maad in hevene as it were half an houre. Hevene is a clene soule, thorugh grace lifted up from ertheli love to heveneli

2876 liyf, life. **2877–78 so fer forth**, to the extent. **2882 noie**, noise. **2883 tariynge**, distress. **2885 sikirnesse**, certainty. **2895 spedi**, advantageous. **2897 persynge**, piercing.

conversacioun, and so it is in silence; but for as moche as that silence mai not lasten hool contynuelli, for corrupcion of bodili kynde, therfore it is likned but to the tyme of half an hour. A ful schort tyme the soule thenketh that it is, be it nevere so longe, and

2905 therfore it is but as half an hour. And thanne hath it pees in conscience; for whi, grace putteth oute gnawynge and prickynge, stryvynge and flitynge of synnes, and bringeth in pees and acord, and maketh Jhesu and a soule bothe at oon in ful accordaunce of wille. There is noon upbraidynge of synnes, ne scharp reprevynge of defautes maad that tyme in a soule, for thei aren kyssed and freendes — al is forgeven that was

2910 mysdoon.

Thus feelith the soule thanne with ful meke sikirnesse and greet goostli gladdenesse, and it conceyveth a ful greet boldenesse of savacioun bi this acord-makynge, for it heerith a privei wittenessynge in conscience of the Hooli Goost, that he is chosen sone to heveneli heritage. Thus Seynt Poule seith: *Ipse spiritus testimonium perhibet spiritui*

2915 *nostro, quod sumus filii dei* (Romans 8:16). That is: The Hooli Goost bereth wittenesse to oure spirit, that we aren Goddis sones. This wittenessynge of conscience, sothfastli feelid thorough grace, is the verri joie of the soule, as the apostil seith: *Gloria mea est testimonium consciencie mee* (2 Corinthians 1:12). That is: My joie is the wittenessynge of my conscience, and that is whanne it wittenesseth pees and acord, trewe love and

2920 frendeschipe bytwixe Jhesu and a soule. And whanne it is in this pees than is it in highnesse of thought.

Whanne the soule is bounden bi love of the world, it is thanne binethe alle creatures; for eche a thynge overgooth it and bereth it doun bi maistrie, that it mai not freeli sen Jhesu ne loven Him. For right as the love of the world is veyn and fleischli, right so the

2925 biholdynge and the thenkynge and the usynge of creatures is fleschli; and that is the thraldom of the soule. But thanne thorough openynge of the goostli yye into Jhesu, the love is turned and the soule is reised up aftir here owen kynde above alle bodili crea- tures; and thanne the bihaldynge and thenkynge and usynge of hem is goostli, for the love is goostli. The soule hath thanne ful grete undeynté for to be buxum to love of

2930 bodili thynges, for it is highe sette aboven hem thorough grace. It setteth right nought bi al the world, for whi, al schal passen and perischen. Unto this highnesse of herte, while the soule is keped thereinne, cometh noon errour ne disceyte of the feend, for Jhesu is sothfastli in the sight of the soule that tyme and al thynge bynethen Hym. Of this

2906 flitynge, contention. **2923 overgooth**, overcomes; **maistrie**, force; **sen**, see. **2926 yye**, eye. **2929 undeynté**, disdain; **buxum**, obedient.

spckcth the prophete thus: *Accedat homo ad cor altum; exaltabitur deus* (Psalms 63:7–
8). Come man to high herte and God schal be highed. That is, a man thorugh grace
cometh to highnes of thought, schal seen that Jhesu is oonli highed aboven alle creatures and he in Hym.

And thanne is the soule aloone, moche straungcd fro felawschipe of wordli loveres,
though here bodi be in myddis amonge hem, ful fer departed from fleschli affeccions of
creatures. It chargeth not though it nevere sighe man, ne speke with him, ne hadde
confort of hym, yif it myght ay be so in that goostli feelynge. It feelith so grete
hoomlynesse bi the blissid presence of oure Lord Jhesu, and so moche savour of Him,
that it mai lightli for His love forgeten the fleschli affeccioun, and the fleschli mynde of
alle creatures. I sei not that it schal not loven ne thenken of othere creatures. But y seie
that it schal thenken on hem in tyme, and seen hem and loven hem goostli and freli, not
fleschli ne peynfulli as it dede biforc. Of this oonlynesse speketh the prophete thus:
Ducam eam in solitudinem, et loquar ad cor eius (Hosea 2:14). I schal leden hire into an
oonli stide, and I schal speken to hire herte. That is, grace of Jhesu ledeth a soule from
noious compaigné of fleschli desires into oonlynessc of thought, and maketh it forgete
the likynge of the world and sounneth bi swettenessc of His inspiracioun wordis of love
in eeres of the herte. Onli is a soule whanne it loveth Jhesu and tendeth fulli to Hym, and
hath lost the savour and the confort of the world; and that it myght the betere kepe this
onlynesse it fleeth companye of alle men yif it mai, and seketh oonlynesse of bodi, for
oonlynesse of bodi moche helpith to onlynesse of soule and to the free wirkynge of
love. The lasse lettynge it hath withouteforth of veyn carpynge, or withinne of veyn
thenkynge, the more free it is in goostli bihooldynge, and so it is in priveté of herte.

Al withoute is a soule while it is overleid and blynded with wordli love; it is as comone
as the highwai. For eche a stirynge that cometh of the flesch or of the feende synketh
in, and gooth thorugh it. But thanne thorugh grace is it withdrawen into privei chambre
into the sight of oure Lord Jhesu, and hereth His pryvy conceiles and is wondirfulli
comforted in the heerynge. Of this speketh the prophete thus: *Secretum meum michi;
secretum meum michi* (Isaiah 24:16). Mi priveté to me, my privyté to me. That is, the
lovere of Jhesu, thorugh inspiracion of His grace taken up from outeward feelynge of
wordli love and ravyssched into priveté of goostli love, yeeldeth thankynges and seiyinge
to Hym thus: Mi pryveté to me. That is, my Lord Jhesu in priveté is schewed to me and

2936 highed, exalted. **2938 straunged**, estranged. **2940 sighe**, saw. **2942 hoomlynesse**,
familiarity. **2946 oonlynesse**, solitude. **2948 oonli stide**, solitary place. **2949 noious**, hurtful.

pryveli hid fro alle the loveres of the world, for it is called hid manna, that mai lightliere be askid than teeld what it is. And that oure Lord Jhesu bihotith to His lovere thus: *Dabo sibi manna absconditum, quod nemo novit, nisi qui accipit* (Revelations 2:17). That is: I schal geven manna hid that no man knowith but he that taketh it. This manna is

2970 heveneli mete and aungelis foode, as Holi Writ seith. For angelis aren fully feed and filled with cleer sight and brennynge love of oure Lord Jhesu, and that is manna. For we moun aske what it is, but not wite what it is. But the lovere of Jhesu is nat filled yit heere, but he is feed bi a litil taastynge of it whiles he is bounden in the liyf of his bodi.

This tastynge of manna is a liyfli feelynge of grace, had thorugh openynge of the

2975 goostli iye. And this grace is not anothir grace than a chosen soule feelith in the bygynynge of his conversioun; but it is the same and selve grace, but it is othirwise schewid and feelid in a soule. For whi, grace wexeth with the soule and the soule wexeth with grace, and the more clene that the soule is, fer departid fro love and likynge of the world, the more myghti is the grace, more inward and more goostli schewand the presence of

2980 oure Lord Jhesu. So that the same grace that turneth hem first from synne and makith him perfite bygynyng and profitynge bi giftes of vertues and exercise of good werkes, maketh hem also perfite, and that grace also is called a liyfli feelynge of grace, for he that hath it feeleth it wele and knoweth it weel bi experience that he is in grace. It is ful lifli to hym, for it quikeneth the soule wondirli and maketh it so hool that he feelith no

2985 peynful disese of the bodi, though it be feble or sekely. For whi, thanne is the bodi mightiest, most hool, and most resteful, and the soule also.

Withoute this grace the soule cannot lyven but in peyne, for it thenketh that it myght ai kepe it and nothynge schulde putte it awai. And neverthelees, yit is it not so, for it passeth awai ful lightli; but neverthelees though the sovereyne feelynge of it passe awai

2990 and withdrawe, the releef leveth stille, and kepeth the soule in sadnesse and maketh it for to desiren the comynge agen. And this is also the waker sleep of the spouse, of the which Holi Writ seith thus: *Ego dormio, et cor meum vigilat* (Canticle 5:2). I slepe and myn herte waketh. That is, I slepe goostli, whanne thorugh grace the love of the world is slayn in me, and wikkid stiringe of fleschli desires aren deeded and so moche that

2995 unnethis I feele hem; I am not taried with hem. Myn herte is maad free, and thane it waketh, for it is scharp and redi for to love Jhesu and seen Hym. The more I slepe from outeward thynges, the more waker am y in knowynge of Jhesu and of inward thynges.

2967 bihotith, promises. **2985 sekely**, sickly. **2990 releef**, remains; **leveth**, lives; **sadnesse**, firmness. **2994 deeded**, made dead. **2995 taried**, troubled.

I mai not waken to Jhesu but yif I slepe to the world. And therfore, the grace of the Hooli Goost sperynge the fleschli iye dooth the soule slepen from worldli vanyté, and openynge the goostli iye waken into the sight of Goddis magesté, helid undir cloude of His precious manhede, as the Gospel seith of apostelis whanne thei were with oure Lord Jhesu in His transfiguracion; first thei slepiden and thanne: *Evigilantes viderunt maiestatem* (Luke 9:32). Thei that wakeneden sighen His majesté. Bi sleep of the apostelis is diynge of wordli love bi inspiracion of the Hooli Goost; bi heer wakyng, contemplacion of Jhesu. Thorugh this sleep the soule is brought into reste fro dene of fleschli lust; and thorugh wakynge it is reysed up into the sight of Jhesu and of goostli thinges. The more that the iyen aren spered in this maner sleep fro the appetite of wordli thinge, the scharpere is the innere sight in loveli biholdyng of heveneli fairheed. This slepynge and this wakynge love werketh thorugh the light of grace in the soule of the lovere of Jhesu.

Chapter Forty-one

Hou special grace in biholdynge of Jhesu withdraweth sumtyme from a soule, and hou a man schal han him in absence and presence of special grace, and hou a soule schal desiren that in it is ai the gracious presence of Jhesu.

Schewe me thanne a soule that thorugh inspiracioun of grace hath openynge of the goostli iye into biholdynge of Jhesu; that is departed and drawen oute fro love of the world, so feer forth that it hath purité and poverté of spirite, goostli reste, inward silence and pees in conscience, highenesse of thought, oonlynesse and privyté of herte, waker sleep of the spouse; that hath loste likynge and joie of this world, taken with delite of heveneli savour, ai thirstande and sothli sighhande the blissid presence of Jhesu; and I dar hardili pronouncen that this soule brenneth al in love and schyneth in goostli light, worthi for to come to the name and to the worschipe of the spouse, for it is reformed in feelinge, maad able and redi to contemplacion. Thise aren the tokenes of

2999 **sperynge**, closing; **dooth the soule slepen**, causes the soul to sleep. **3000 helid**, concealed. **3003 sighen**, saw. **3004 heer**, their. **3005 dene**, din. **3007 spered**, closed. **3016 so feer forth**, to the extent that. **3019 sighhande**, sighing for.

inspiracioun in openynge of the goostli iye. For whi, whan the iye is opened the soule is in ful feelynge of alle thise vertues bifore seid, for that tyme.

3025   Neverthelees, ofte sithes it falleth that grace withdraweth in partie, for corrupcioun of mannes freelté, and suffreth the soule falle into itself in fleschlihede, as it was bifore; and thanne is the soule in sorwe and pyne, for it is blynd and unsaveri and can no good. It is weike and unmyghti, encombred with the bodi and with alle the bodili wittes; it seketh and desireth aftir the face of Jhesu agen, and it mai not fynde it. For Holi Writ

3030 seith of oure Lord thus: *Postquam vultum suum absconderit, non est qui contempletur eum* (Job 34:29). That is: Aftir whanne oure Lord Jhesu had hid His face, there is noon that mai biholde Him. Whanne He schewith Him, the soule mai not unsee Him for He is light; and whanne He hideth Him, it mai not see Him, for the soule is merke. His abidynge is but a sotil assaiynge of a soule; His schewynge is wondir merciful goodnesse in

3035 comforte of the soule.

    Have thou no wondir, though the feelynge of grace withdrawe sumtyme fro a lovere of Jhesu. For Hooli Writ seith the same of the spouse, that sche fareth thus: *Quesivi et non inveni illum: vocavi et non respondit michi* (Canticle 3:1). I sought and I fond not; I callid Him and He answerid not. That is, whan y falle doun to my freelté, than grace

3040 withdrawith; for my fallynge is cause therof, and not His feelinge. But thanne feele I the peyne of my wrecchidnesse in His absence, and therfore y soughte Hym bi sotilté of thought ther I had Hym bifore, and y fond Him nought. I called Him bi greet desirynge of herte, and He gaf to me no felable ansuerynge. And thanne I cried with al myn herte: *Revertere dilecte mi.* (Canticle 2:17). Turne agen, Thou my loved. And yit it semed that

3045 He herde me not. The peyneful feelynge of myself and the assailynge of fleschli loves and dredis in this tyme, and the wantynge of my goostli strengthe, is a continuel criynge of my soule to Jhesu; and neverthelees oure Lord maketh straunge awhile and cometh not, crie I nevere so fast. For He is siker inough of His lovere, that He wil not turne agen fulli to wordli love; He mai no savour have thereinne. And therfore abideth He the lengere.

3050   But at the laste, whanne He wole, He cometh agen, fulle of grace and sothfastnesse, and visiteth the soule that langueschith in desire bi sighhinges of love to His presence, and toucheth it and anoynteth it wel softeli with the oile of gladnesse, and maketh it sodeynli hool from alle pyne. And than crieth the soule to Jhesu in goostli vois with a

3025 ofte sithes, often. **3026 freelté**, frailty. **3028 weike**, weak. **3033 merke**, dark. **3034 sotil**, subtle. **3043 felable**, capable of being felt. **3046 wantynge**, deficiency. **3047 maketh straunge**, remains remote. **3048 siker inough**, certain enough.

glad herte thus: *Oleum effusum nomen tuum* (Canticle 1:2). Oile yoten is Thi name
3055 Jhesu. Thi name is Jhesu, that is heele; thanne as longe as I feele my soule soor and sike
for synne, peyned with the hevy birdyne of my bodi, sori and dredande for periles and
wrecchidnesse of this liyf, so longe Lord Jhesu, Thi name is oile spared, not oile yoten
to me. But whanne I feele my soule sodaynly towchid with the light of grace, heelid and
softid from alle filthe of synne, conforted in love and in light with goostli strengthe and
3060 gladnesse unspecable, thanne mai y seyn with lusti lovynge and gostli merthe to Thee:
Oile yoten is Thyn name Jhesu to me. For bi the effect of Thi gracious visitynge y feele
weel of Thi name the trewe expounyng, Thou arte, Jhesu, heele. For onli Thi gracious
presence heeleth me fro sorwe and from synne.

Blissid is the soule that is feleabli feed in feelynge of love in His presence, or is born up
3065 bi brennynge desire to Him in his absence. A wise lovere is he, and wel taught, that sadli
and reverentcli hath him in His presence, and loveli biholdeth Him withoute dissolute
lightnesse, and pacientli and esili beereth him in His absence withouten venemous dispeir
and over peynful bittirnesse.

This chaungeableté of absence and presence of Jhesu that a soule feeleth is not
3070 perfeccioun of the soule, ne it is not agens the grace of perfeccioun or of contemplacioun;
but in so moche, perfeccion is the lasse. For the more lettynge that a soule hath of itself
fro contynuel feelynge of grace, and though neverthelees yit is the grace in itself grace
of contemplacioun. This chaungeableté of absence and presence fallith as wel in staat
of perfeccioun as in the staat of bigynnynge, but in anothir manere. For right as ther is
3075 diversité of feelynge in the presence of grace atwixe thise two statis, right so is there in
the absence of grace. And therfore he that knoweth not the absence of grace is redi to
be disseyved, and he that kepith not the presence of grace is unkynde to the visitynge,
whethir he be in the staat of bigynneres or of perfite. Neverthelees, the more stabilnesse
that there is in grace, unhurt and unbroken, the loveliere is the soule, more like unto Him
3080 in whom is no maner chaungeableté, as the apostil seith. And it is ful semeli that the
soule-spouse be like to Jhesu-spouse in maneres and in vertues, ful accordande to Him
in stabilnesse of perfite love. But it falleth seldom: nowhare but in the special spouse.

3054 yoten, poured. **3054–55 Thi name Jhesu**, on the association of this verse of the Canticle with devotion to the name of Jesus, see Clark, p. 324n334. **3055 heele**, health; **sike**, sick.
3056 birdyne, burden. **3057 spared**, reserved. **3059 softid**, softened. **3060 unspecable**, unspeakable. **3062 heele**, healing. **3064 feleabli feed**, perceptibly fed. **3065 sadli**, seriously.
3066 hath him, behaves. **3067 beereth him**, conducts himself. **3077 unkynde**, unnatural.

3085

3090

3095

3100

3105

3110

For he that perceyveth no chaungeableté in feelynge of his grace, but ay ilike stable and hool, unbroken and unhurt as him thenketh, he is eithir ful perfight or ellis he is ful blynd. He is ful perfight that is sequestred from alle fleschli affecciouns and comonynge of creatures, and alle menes aren broken awai of corrupcion and of synne atwixe Jhesu and his soule, fulli ooned to Him with softnesse of love. But this is oonli grace above mannes kynde. He is fulle blynd and feyneth him in grace withoute goostli felinge of Goddis inspiracion, and setteth himsilf in manere of a stablenesse, as he were ai in feelynge and in werkynge of special grace, demynge that al is grace that he doth and feelith, withouten and withinnen, thenkynge that whatsoevere he doo or speke is grace, holdynge himself unchaungeable in specialté of grace. Yif there be ony siche, as I hope there is noon, he is ful blynd in feelynge of grace.

But than mvght thou seie thus, that we schulde lyven oonli in truthe and not coveiten goostli feelynges, ne rewarden hem yif thei comen, for the apostil seith: *Justus ex fide vivit* (Hebrews 10:38). That is: The rightwise man lyveth in trouthe. Unto this I seie that bodili feelinges, be thei never so confortable, we schulle not coveiten, ne mykil rewarden hem if thei comen. But gostli feelynges, siche as I speke of now, yif thei comen in the manere as I have seid bifore, we schulen ai desiren that aren sleynge al wordli love, openynge of the goostli iye, purité of spirite, pees in conscience, and alle othere bifore seid. We schullen coveiten to feele ai the liyfli inspiracioun of grace maad bi the goostli presence of Jhesu in oure soule, yif that we myghten; and for to have Him ai in oure sight with reverence, and ai feelen the swettenesse of His love bi a wondirful homlinesse of His presence. This schulde be oure liyf and oure feelynge in grace, aftir the mesure of His gifte in whom al grace is, to somme more and to some lasse; for His presence is feelid in diverse manere wise as He vouchith saaf. And in this we schullen lyven, and wirken al that longeth to us for to wirken, for withouten this we schuld not conne lyve. For right as the soule is liyf of the bodi, right so Jhesu is liyf of the soule bi His gracious presence. And neverthelees this maner of feelynge, be it nevere so moche, it is yight but trouthe as in reward of the fulnesse that schal ben of the selve Jhesu in the blisse of hevene.

Loo, this feelynge schulde we desire, for eche a soule resonable oweth for to coveiten with alle the myghtes of it neighynge to Jhesu and oonynge to Hym, thorugh feelynge of His gracious unseable presence. Hou that presence is feelid, it mai betere be knowen bi

3085–86 comonynge of, communion with. **3094 truthe**, faith. **3095 rewarden**, esteem. **3103 homlinesse**, familiarity. **3106 feelid**, felt. **3107 conne**, know how to. **3109 yight**, yet. **3110 reward**, regard. **3112 neighynge**, approaching; **oonynge**, uniting. **3113 unseable**, invisible.

experience than bi ony writynge; for it is the liyf and the love, the myght and the light,
3115 the joie and the reste of a chosen soule. And therfore he that hath ones soothfastli feelid
it, he mai not forbere it withouten pyne; he mai not undesiren it, it is so good in itsilf and
so confortable. What is more confortable to a soule heere thanne to be drawen oughte
thorough grace fro the vile noie of wordli bisynesse and fro filthe of fleschli desires, and
from veyn affeccioun of alle creatures into reste and softenes of goosteli love, priveli
3120 perceivynge the gracious presence of Jhesu, feleabli feed with favour of His unseable
blissid face? Sotheli nothynge. Me thenketh nothynge mai make the soule of a lovere ful
merie, but the gracious presence of Jhesu as He can schewen Him to a clene soule. He
is nevere more hevy ne sori, but thanne, whanne he is with himsilf in fleschlinesse; he
is nevere ful glad ne merie, but whanne he is out of himsilf fer, as he was with Jhesu in
3125 goostlynesse. And yit is that noo ful myrthe, for ai there hangeth an hevy lompe of
bodili corrupcioun on his soule, and bereth it doun and moche letteth the goostli
gladdenesse, and that mote ai be while it is in this lif.

But nevertheles, for I speke of chaungeableté in grace, hou it cometh and gooth, that
thou mystake it not, therfore y mene not of the comone grace that is had and feelt in
3130 trouthe and in good wille to God, withoute the which havynge, and lastynge therinne,
no man mai be saaf, for it is in the leste chosen soule that lyveth. But I mene of special
grace feelt bi inspiracioun of the Hooli Goost, in manere as it is bifore seid. The comone
grace, that is charité, lasteth hool whatsoevere a man doo, as longe as his wille and his
entente is trewe to God, that he wolde not synne deedli, ne the deede that he dooth
3135 wilfulli is not forbed as for deedli synne, for this grace is not loste but thorugh deedli
synne. And thanne it is deedli synne, whanne his conscience wittenesseth with avisement
that it is deedli synne, and yit neverthelees he dooth it; or elles his conscience is so
blynded that he holdeth it noo deedli synne, though he doo that deede wilfulli, the which
is forboden of God and of Hooli Chirche as deedli synne.

3140 Special grace feelt thorough the unseable presence of Jhesu, that maketh a soule a
perfite lovere, lasteth not ilike hool in the highnesse of feelynge, but chaungeabli cometh
and gooth, as I have seide. Thus oure Lord seith: *Spiritus ubi vult spirat; et vocem eius
audis, sed nescis unde veniat, aut quo vadat* (John 3:8). The Holi Goost spireth wheer
He wole, and thou heerest His vois, but thou wost not fro whennes He cometh or
3145 whider He gooth. He cometh priveli sumtyme whanne thou art leest waar of Him, but

3117 **confortable**₂, comforting; **oughte**, out. **3118 noie**, hurt. **3124 fer**, far. **3141 ilike**, alike.

thou schalt wel knowen Him or He goo, for wondirfulli He stireth and myghtili He turneth thyn herte into biholdynge of His goodnesse, and dooth thyn herte meelten delitable as wex agens the fier into softenesse of His love, and this is His vois that He sowneth. But thanne He gooth or thou wite it, for He withdraweth Him sumwhat, not al, but from

3150 excesse into sobirté. The highnesse passeth, but the substaunce and the effecte of the grace duelleth stille, and that is as longe as the soule of a lovere kepeth him clene and falleth not wilfulli to reccheleshede or dissolucioun in fleschliheed, ne to outewarde vanyté, as sumtyme it dooth, though it have no delite therinne, for freelté of itself. Of this chaungeabilité in grace speke I of now.

Chapter Forty-two

3155 A commendacioun of praiere offrid to Jhesu in a soule contemplatif, and hou stablenesse in praiere is a siker werk to stonden in, and hou every feelynge of grace in a chosen soule mai be seid Jhesu, but the more clene that the soule is, the worthiere is the grace.

The soule of a man, whilis it is not touchid thorugh special grace, is blont and boistous

3160 to goostli werk, and can not thereon. It mai not therof for weikenesse of itself. It is bothe cold and drie, undevout and unsavori in itself. But thanne cometh the light of grace, and thorugh touchynge maketh it scharpe and sotiel, redi and able to gosteli werk, and geveth a greet fredom and an hool redynesse in wille for to be buxum to alle the stirynge of grace, for bi openynge of the goostli iye it is applied al fulli to grace, redi

3165 to werken aftir that grace stireth. And thanne fallith it so somtyme, that grace stireth the soule for to praien; and hou the soule praieth thanne schal I telle thee.

The most special praiere that the soule useth and hath most confort in, I hope, is the Pater Noster, or elles psalmes of the sautier; the Pater Noster for lewid men, and psalmes and ympnes and othere servyce of Holi Chirche for lettred men. The soule praieth

3146 or, before. **3147 dooth,** causes. **3148 sowneth,** sounds. **3149 wite,** know. **3150 sobirté,** soberness. **3151 duelleth,** dwells. **3152 reccheleshede,** recklessness. **3159 blont,** dull, stupid, morally blind; **boistous,** rough. **3160 can not,** knows nothing. **3161 cold and drie,** dominated by bile. **3162 sotiel,** keen. **3163 buxum,** obedient. **3164 iye,** eye. **3168 sautier,** psalter; **lewid,** ignorant.

3170   thanne not in manere as it dide bifore, ne in comone manere of othere men by highnesse of vois or bi renable spekynge oute; but in ful greet stilnesse of vois and softenesse of herte. For whi, his mynde is not trobled ne taried with outeward thynges, but hool gadred togedre in itsilf, and the soule is sette as hit were into goostli presence of Jhesu; and therfore everiche silable and every word is sowned savourli, sweteli and delitabli,

3175   with ful acord of mouth and of herte. For whi, the soule is turned thanne al to fier of love, and therfore eche word that it priveli praieth is like unto a sparcle springynge out of a fierbrond, that clanseth alle the myghtes of the soule and turneth hem into love, and lightneth hem so confortabli that the soule list ai for to praien and to doo noon othere thynge. The more it praieth, the betere it mai, the myghtiere it is. For grace helpeth the

3180   soule weel, and maketh al thynge light and esi, that it list right weel for to psalmen and syngen the lovynges of God with goostli myrthe and heveneli delite.

    This goostli werk is the foode of the soule. And this praier is of moche vertu, for it wasteth and bringeth to nought alle temptacions of the feend, privé and apeert, it sleeth alle the mynde and likynge of the world and of fleschli synnes, it bereth up the bodi and

3185   the soule from peyntul feelynge of wrecchidnesse of liyf, it kepeth the soule in feelynge of grace and wirkynge of love and norischeth ai ilike hoot and fresch as stikkes norischen the fier. It putteth awai al irkynge and hevynesse of herte, and hooldeth it in myrthe and goosteli gladnesse. Of this praier speketh David thus: *Dirigatur oratio mea sicut insensum in conspectu tuo* (Psalms 140:2). That is: Dressed be my praier, Lord, as encense in Thi

3190   sight. For right as encense that is caste in the fier maketh swete smeel bi the reek stiynge up to the iye, right so a psalme savourli and softeli songen or seid in a brennande herte yeldeth up a suete smeel to the face of oure Lord Jhesu and to al the corte of hevene.

    There dare no flesch flie resten upon the pottis brynke boiland over the fier; right so

3195   mai ther no flesch flie delite resten on a clene soule that is lapped and warmed al in fire of love, boilende and plaiand psalmes and lovynges to Jhesu. This is verry praiere. This praiere is evermore herd of Jhesu, and receyveth grace agen. It maketh a soule homli and felawli with oure Lord Jhesu, and with alle angeles of hevene. Use it whoso mai, the werke is good in itsilf and ful gracious.

3171 renable, eloquent. **3172 taried**, disturbed. **3181 lovynges**, praisings. **3183 apeert**, open. **3187 irkynge**, annoyance. **3189 Dressed**, Directed. **3190 reek**, smoke. **3191 stiynge**, rising; **iye**, eye. **3192 suete**, sweet. **3194 flesch flie**, fly (the insect). **3195 lapped**, surrounded. **3196 plaiand**, playing; **lovynges**, praisings. **3197 homli**, familiar. **3198 felawli**, companionable.

3200   And this maner praiere, though al it be not ful contemplacioun in itsilf, ne wirkynge of love bi itsilf, neverthelees it is a partie of contemplacioun. For whi, it mai not be doon on this manere wise but in plenté of grace thorugh openynge of the goosteli iye, and therfore a soule that hath this fredom and this gracious feelynge in praier, with goosteli savoure and heveneli delite, hath the grace of contemplacioun in manere as it is.

3205   This praiere is a riche offrynge filled al in fattenesse of devocion, reseyved bi angelis and presented to the face of Jhesu. The praiere of othere men that are besied in actif werkes is maad of two wordes. For thei ofte sithes formen in here hertis o word thorugh thenkynge of wordli bisynesse, and sownen in here mouth anothir word of the psalme songen or seid; and neverthelees yif her entent be trewe, yit is here praiere good 3210 and medeful, though it lakke savour and swettenesse. But this manere praiere offred of a man contemplatif is maad but of o word. For as it is formed in the herte, right so hoolli it sowneth in the mouth, as it were but o thynge that formeth and sowneth. And soothli no more it is, for the soule thorugh grace is maad hool in itsilf, so fer forth departid from fleschliheede that it is maister over the bodi; and than is the bodi not ellis but as an 3215 instrument and a trompe of the soule, in whiche the soule bloweth swete nootes of goostli lovynges to Jhesu.

    This is the trumpe that David speketh of thus: *Buccinate in neominea tuba, insigni die solempnitatis vestre* (Psalms 80:4). Blowe yee in a trompe in the newe moone. That is, ye soulis that aren reformed in goostli liyf thorugh openynge of the innere iye, blowe 3220 yee devouteli, sownynge psalmes with the trumpe of youre bodili tunge. And therefore, syn this praiere is so plesante to Jhesu and so profitable to the soule, than is hit good to him that is newe turned to God, what that he be, that wolde plesen Hym and coveiteth for to have sum queynte feelynge of grace, for to coveite this feelynge, that he myght thorugh grace come to the liberté of spirit, and offre in his praieres and his psalmes to 3225 Jhesu contynueli, stabli, and devouteli, with hool mynde and brennand affeccioun in Him, and han it neer hand in custom whanne grace stireth him therto.

    This is a siker feelynge and a soothfast. Yif thou may come therto and holden it, thee thar not neden to renne aboute heer and there and aske questions of ech goostli man what thou schalt doon, hou thou schalt love Jhesu, and how thou schalt serve Hym, and 3230 speke of goostli materes that passen thi knowynge, as perchaunce some doon. That manere of doynge is not ful profitable, but yif more neede make it. Kepe thee to thi

3202 **plenté**, fullness. 3206 **besied**, occupied. 3215 **trompe**, trumpet. 3216 **lovynges**, praises. 3223 **queynte**, elegant. 3227–28 **thee thar**, it is necessary for you.

praieris stifli, first with travaile that thou mightest come aftirward to this reestful feelynge of this goostli praiere, and that schal teche thee wisdom inowgh sothfasteli, withoute feynynge or fantasie. And kepe it forth yif thou have it, and leve it not; but yif grace
3235 come othirwise and wil reeve it fro thee for a tyme and make thee for to werken in anothir maner, thanne maight thou leve it for a tyme and aftir turne agen therto. And he that hath this grace in praier asketh not wheereupoun he schal sette the poynt of his thought in his praiere, whether upon the wordes that he seith, or elles on God or on the name of Jhesu, as some men asken. For the feelynge of grace techeth hem wel inowgh.
3240 For whi, the soule is turned al to the iye and scharpeli biholdeth the face of Jhesu, and is maad ful siker that that is Jhesu that he feeleth and seeth. I mene not Jhesu as He is in Himsilf in fulnesse of His blissid Godhede, but I mene Jhesu as He wole schewe Him to a clene soule holden in bodi, aftir the clennesse that it hath. For wite thou weel, that ecche a feelynge of grace is Jhesu and mai be called Jhesu; and aftir that the grace is more or
3245 lasse, so feeleth the soule and seeth Jhesu more or lasse. Yhe, the firste feelynge of special grace of conpuccion and contricion for synnes is verili Jhesu. For whi, He maketh that contricion in a soule bi His presence. But Jhesu is thanne ful boistousli and rudeli feelid and seen, ful fer from His goostli sotilté, for the soule can no betere for unclennesse of itsilf thanne. Neverthelees aftirward yif the soule profite and encrese in
3250 vertues and in clennesse, the same Jhesu and noon othir is seen and feelid of the selve soule whanne it is touchid bi grace. But that is more goostli, nerrere to godli kynde of Jhesu.

And soothli that is the most thynge that Jhesu loveth in a soule, that it mought be maad goostli and godli in sight and in love, like to Hym in grace, to that that He is bi kynde; for
3255 that schal be the ende of alle loveris. Than mait thou be siker that what tyme thou feelest thi soule stired bi grace, speciali in that manere as it is bifore seid, bi openynge of the goostli iye, that thou seest and feelest Jhesu. Hoolde Him faste whiles thou maiste, and kepe thee in grace, and late Him not lightli fro thee. Loke aftir noon nothir Jhesu but the same, bi feelynge of the selve grace more godli, that it mought wexe more and more in
3260 thee; and drede thee nought, though that Jhesu that thou feeliste be not Jhesu as He is in His ful Godheed, that thou schuldest therfore mow ben disseyved yif thou loned to thi feelynge. But truste thou weel, yif thou be a lovere of Jhesu, that thi feelynge is trewe

3235 **reeve**, rob. 3241 **siker**, certain. 3243 **wite**, know. 3246 **conpuccion**, compunction. 3247 **boistousli**, roughly. 3248 **feelid**, felt. 3250 **selve**, same. 3255 **mait**, might; **siker**, certain. 3261 **mow**, be able to be; **loned**, inclined.

and that Jhesu is truli feelid and seen of thee thorugh His grace, as thou maist seen him here. And therefore lene fulli to thi feelynge whanne it is gracious and goostli, and kepe
3265 it tendirli and have grete deynté, not of thi silf, but of it, that thou myghtest seen Jhesu ai betere and betere. For grace schal evene teche thee bi itself yif thou wolte falle therto mekeli, til the ende.

But perchance thou bigynnest to wondren whi y seie o tyme that grace wirketh al this, and anothir tyme I seie that love werketh, or Jhesu werketh, or God wirketh. Unto
3270 this y seie thus, that whanne I seie grace wirketh I meene love, Jhesu, and God: for al is oon, and not but on. Jhesu is love, Jhesu is grace, Jhesu is God; and for he wirketh al in us bi His grace for love as God, therfore may I usen what word I wole of thise foure, aftir my stirynge, in this writynge.

Chapter Forty-three

Hou a soule thorugh openynge of the gosteli iye receyveth a gracious ablenesse for to
3275 undirstonden Holi Writ, and hou Jhesu, that is hid in Hooli Writte, scheweth Hym to Hise loveris.

Whanne the soule of a lovere feelith Jhesu in praiere in manere bifore seid, and thenketh that it wolde nevere feelen othirwise, neverthelees it falleth that some tyme grace putteth silence in a soule to vocal praiynge and stireth the soule for to seen and feelen Jhesu in
3280 othir maner. And that manere is first for to see Jhesu in Hooli Writte; for Jhesu, that is al sothfastnesse, is hid and helid therinne, wounden in a soft sendeel undir faire wordis, that he mai not be knowen ne feelid but of a clene herte. For whi, sothfastnes wole not schewe itself to enemys, but to freendes that loven it and desiren it with a clene meke herte. For sothfastnesse and mekenesse aren ful trewe sustris, festened togidre in love
3285 and charité; and for thi is ther no laynynge of conceiles atwixe hem two. Mekenesse presumeth on soothfastnesse, and nothynge of itsilf; and sothfastenesse trusteth wel on mekenesse, and so thei accorden wondir weel. Thanne for as moche as the soule of a lovere is maad meke thorugh inspiracion of grace bi openynge of the goostli iye, and seeth that it is not in itself, but oonli hangeth on the merci and the goodnesse of God,

3265 **deynté**, value. 3271 **on**, one. 3281 **helid**, concealed; **sendeel**, rich cloth. 3285 **laynynge**, concealment. 3289 **not**, nothing.

3290 and lastyngeli is born up bi favour and helpe of Hym oonli and truli desirynge His
presence: therfore seeth it Jhesu, for it seeth sothfastnesse of Holi Writte wondirfulli schewed
and opened, aboven studie and traveile and resoun of mannes kyndeli wit. And that mai
wel be called the feelynge and the perceyvynge of Jhesu, for Jhesu is welle of wisdom,
and bi a litil heldynge of His wisdom into a clene soule He maketh the soule wise ynowgh
3295 for to undirstonde alle Hooli Writte — not alle at ones in special biholdynge, but thorugh
that grace the soule receyveth a newe ablenesse, and a gracious abite for to undirstonde
it speciali whanne it cometh to mynde.

This openynge and cleernesse of wit is maad bi the goostli presence of Jhesu. For
right as the Gospel seith of two disciplis goynge to the castel of Emaus, brennande in
3300 desire and spekynge of Jhesu, oure Lord Jhesu appered to hem presentli as a pilgrime
and taughte hem the prophecies of Himsilf, and as the Gospel seith: *Apparuit illis
sensum, ut intelligerent scripturas* (Luke 24:45). He opened to hem cleernesse of witte
that thei myten undirstonden holi writynges. Right so the goostli presence of Jhesu
openeth the witte of His lovere that brenneth in desire to Him, and bryngeth to his mynde
3305 bi mysterie of angelis the wordes and the sentence of Holi Writ, unsought and unavised,
oon aftir anothir, and expouneth hem redili, be thei nevere so hard or so privei. The
hardere that thei ben and the ferthere fro mennys resonable undirstondynge, the more
delitable is the trew schewynge of it whan Jhesu is maister. It is expounned, declared
litterali, morali, mistili, and heveneli, yif the mater suffre it. Bi the lettre, that is lightest
3310 and most playn, is the bodili kynde conforted; bi moralté of Hooli Writ, the soule is
enformed of vices and vertues, wiseli to kunne departe the toon from the tother; bi
mystihede it is illumined for to seen the werkes of God in Holi Chirche, redili for to
applien wordes of Holi Writ to Crist oure heved and to Holi Chirche that is His mystik
bodi; and the firthe, that is heveneli, longeth oonli to the werkynge of love, and that
3315 whanne al soothfastenesse in Hooli Writte is applied to love, and for that is most like to
heveneli feelynge, therfore I calle it heveneli.

The lovere of Jhesu is His frende, not for he hath deserved it, but for Jhesu of His
merciful goodnesse maketh him His freend bi trewe acord, and therfore as to a trewe
frend that pleseth Hym with love, not serveth Him bi drede as a thral, He scheweth His

3296 abite, habit. **3307 resonable**, rational. **3309 litterali, morali, mistili, and heveneli**,
literally, morally (or tropologically), mystically (or allegorically), and heavenly (or anagogically);
the traditional four senses of scripture; **suffre**, allow. **3311 kunne departe**, know how to
separate; **toon**, one; **tother**, other. **3312 mystihede**, the mystical.

251

3320   priveté. Thus He seith Himsilf to Hise apostelis: *Iam vos dixi amicos, quia quecumque audivi a patre meo, nota feci vobis* (John 15:15). Now y seie that ye aren frendes, for I make knowen to yow alle thynges that I have herde of My Fader. To a clene soule that hath the palet purified from filthe of fleschli love, Hooli Writ is liyfli foode and sustenaunce delitable. It savoreth wondir sweteli whanne it is weel chewid bi goostli undirstondynge.

3325   For whi, the spirit of liyf is hid thereinne, that quykeneth alle the myghtes of the soule and filleth hem ful of swettenesse of hevenli savour and goosteli delite. But sotheli him nedeth for to han white teeth and scharpe and wel piked that schulde biten on this goostli breed, for fleschli loveres and heretikes mowe not touche the inli flour of it. Here teeth aren blodi and ful of filthe, and therfore aren thei fastynge from feelynge of this

3330   breed. Bi teeth aren undirstonden inli vertues of the soule, the whiche in fleschli loveres and in heretikes aren blodi, ful of synne and of wordli vanyté; thei wolden, and thei kunnen not, come bi the curiousté of her kyndeli wit to the sothfast knowynge of Holi Writ. For here witte is corrupt bi the original synne and actuel also, and is not yit heelid thorugh grace, and therfore thei don but gnawen upon the bark withoute. Carpe thei

3335   nevere so moche thereof, the inli savoure withinne thei feelen not of. Thei aren not meke, thei aren not clene for to seen it; thei aren not frendis to Jhesu, and therfore He scheweth hem not His conceil.

    The priveté of Holi Writ is closid undir keie seelid with a signet of Jhesuis fyngir, that is the Holi Goost; and forthi, withouten His love and His leve mai no man come in. He

3340   hath oonli the keie of connynge in his kepynge, as Hooli Writ seith; and He is keie Himsilf and He leteth in whom He wole thorugh inspiracioun of His grace, and breketh not the seel. And that dooth Jhesu to His loveres; not to alle ilike, but to hem that aren speciali enspired for to seken sothfastnesse in Hooli Writ, with gret devocion in praiynge and with moche bisynesse in studiynge goynge bifore. Thise moun come to the fyndynge

3345   whan oure Lord Jhesu wole schewe it.

    Se now thanne how grace openeth the goostli iye, and clereth the wit of the soule wondirli above the freelté of corrupt kynde. It geveth the soule a newe ablenesse, whethir it wole reden Holi Writ or heeren or thenken it, for to undirstonde truli and

---

3323 **palet**, palate. 3327 **white teeth**, see Augustine, *De doctrina christiana*, 2.6.7; Clark, p. 326n373. 3328 **inli**, inner. 3332 **kunnen**, know how to; **kyndeli**, natural. 3333 **actuel**, actual. 3334 **Carpe**, Speak. 3338 **Jhesuis**, Jesus'. 3340 **connynge**, knowledge. 3347 **freelté**, frailty; **ablenesse**, capability.

savourli the sothfastnesse of it in the manere bifore seid, and for to turnen redili alle
3350 resones and wordes that aren bodili seid into goostely undirstondynge. And that is no
gret mervaile, for the same spirit expouneth it and declareth it in a clene soule in confort
of it, that first made it; and that is the Holi Goost. And this grace mai be, and is, as wel
in lewed as in lettred men, as anemptis the substaunce and the trewe feelynge of
soothfastnesse and of goosteli savour of it in general, though thei se not so manye
3355 resons of it in special, for that nedeth not. And whanne the soule is thus ablid and
lightned thorugh grace, thanne it liste for to ben aloone sumtyme, out of lettynge or
comonynge of alle creaturis, that it myght freli assaien his instrument, that I calle his
resoun, in bihooldynge of soothfastnesse that is conteyned in hooli writynge. And ther
falleth to mynde wordes and resouns and sentence inowgh to occupien it ful ordinatli
3360 and ful sadli.

   And what confort and goostli delite, savour and swettenesse, a soule mai feele thanne
in this goosteli werk thorugh divers illuminacions, inli perceyvynges, privei knowynges,
and sodayn touchynges of the Hooli Goost, bi assai the soule mai witen and elles not.
And I hope that he schal not erren, bi so that his teeth, that aren his inli wittes, be kepid
3365 white and clene from goostli pride and from curiousté of kyndeli witte. I hope that
David feelte ful grete delite in this maner werk whan he seide thus: *Quam dulcia faucibus
meis eloquia tua, super mel ori meo* (Psalms 118:103). Hou swete aren thi spekynges,
Lord Jhesu, to my chekes, or above hony to mouth. That is: Lord Jhesu, Thyn holi
wordes, endited in Hooli Writ, brought to my mynd thorugh grace, aren suettere to my
3370 chekes (that aren affeccions of my soule) than hony is to my mouth. Sothli this is a
faire werke and an honest withoute pyneful travaile, for to seen Jhesu thus.

   This is oo maner sight of Jhesu, as I seide bifore: not as He is, but clothed undir
likenesse of werkes and of wordes, *per speculum in enigmate* (1 Corinthians 13:12), bi
a myrore and likenesse, as the apostil seith. Jhesu is eendelees myght, wisdom and
3375 goodnesse, rightwysenesse, sothfastnesse, hoolinesse, and merci. And what this Jhesu
is in Himsilf mai no soule seen heere, but bi the effecte of His wirkynge he mai seen
thorugh the light of grace, as thus: His myght is seen bi makynge of alle creatures of
nought, His wisdoom in ordinat disposynge of hem, His goodnesse in savynge of hem,
His merci in forgevynge of synnes, His hoolinesse in giftes of grace, His rightwisnes in

3353 **anemptis,** concerning. 3355 **ablid,** empowered. 3356 **lightned,** illuminated; **lettynge,**
hindrance. 3357 **comonynge,** community. 3359 **ordinatli,** regularly. 3360 **sadli,** seriously.
3364 **bi so,** because. 3369 **suettere,** sweeter. 3378 **ordinat,** well ordered.

3380 hard ponyschinge of synne, His soothfastnesse in trewe rewardynge of good werkes. And al this is expressed in Holi Writ, and this seeth a soule in Hooli Writ with alle othere accidentis that fallen therto. And wite thou wel that siche gracious knowynges, in Hooli Writ or in ony othir writynge that is maad thorugh grace, aren not ellis but swete lettres, sendynges maad atwixe a lovend soule and Jhesu loved; or ellis yif y schal seie sothliere,

3385 atwixe Jhesu the trewe lovere and the soulis loved of Him. He hath ful grete tendirnesse of love to alle His chosen children, that aren heere closid in clei of this bodili liyf; and therfore, though He be absent from hem, high hid aboven in bosom of the Fadir, fulfilled in delices of His blissid Godheed, neverthelees yit He thenketh of hem and visiteth hem ful ofte thorugh His gracious goosteli presence, and conforteth hem bi His lettres of

3390 Hooli Writ, and dryveth out of here hertes hevynesse and irkenesse, doutes and dredis, and maketh hem glaad and merie in hem, truli trowande to alle His bihetynges and mekeli abidynge the fulfillynge of His wille.

      Seynt Poul seith thus: *Quecumque scripta sunt, ad nostram doctrinam scripta sunt, ut per consolacionem scripturarum, spem habeamus* (Romans 15:4). Al that is writen, to

3395 oure techynge it is writen, that bi confort of writynge we mai have hope of savacioun. And this is anothir werk of contemplacion, for to seen Jhesu in Scripturis, aftir openynge of the goosteli iye. The clennere that the sight is in biholdynge, the more conforted is the affeccioun in the taastynge. A ful litil savour, feelt in a clene soule of Holi Writ in this manere bifore seid, schulde make the soule sette litil price by knowynge of alle sevene

3400 artes or of alle wordli connynges. For the eende of this knowynge is savacion of a soule in ai lastynge liyf; and the ende of othere as for hemself is but vanité and a passynge delite, but yif thei be turned thorugh grace to this eende.

Chapter Forty-four

Of the privei vois of Jhesu sounned in a soule, wherebi it mai be knowen; and hou alle the gracious illuminaciouns maad in a soule aren called the spekynges of Jhesu.

3405 Loo, thise aren newe feelynges in a clene soule, and yif a soule were fulfilled in siche, it myght be seid, and sothli, that it were sumwhat reformed in feelynge, but yit not fulli.

3386 clei, clay. **3388 delices**, delights. **3390 irkenesse**, weariness. **3391 bihetynges**, promises. **3399 price**, value. **3400 connynges**, knowledge. **3405 clene**, pure.

For whi, yit Jhesu scheweth more and ledeth the soule innere, and bigynneth to speke more homeli and more loveli to a soule, and redi is the soule thanne for to folwe the feelynge of grace. Foɪ the prophete seith: *Quocumque ibit spiritus, illuc gradiebantur et*

3410 *rote sequentes eum* (Ezekiel 1:20). Whidirso yeede the spirit, thider yeeden the wheles folwynge hym. Bi wheles aren undirstonden trewe loveres of Jhesu, for thei aren round in vertues withouten angil of frowardnesse, and lightli whirland thorugh redynesse of wille to stirynge of grace. For aftir that grace stireth and toucheth, so thei folwen and so thei werken, as the prophete seith. But thei han first a ful myghti assai and a trewe

3415 knowynge of the vois of grace, or thei mowen doo so, that thei be not disseyved bi ther owen feynynge, or bi the myddai fend. Oure Lord Jhesu seith thus: *Oves mee vocem meam audiunt, et cognosco eas, et cognoscunt me mee* (John 10:27, 14). Mi scheep heeren My vois, and I knowe hem and thei knowe Me. The privei vois of Jhesu is ful trewe, and it maketh a soule trewe. Ther is no feynynge in it, ne fantasie, ne pride, ne

3420 ypocrisie, but softenesse, mekenesse, pees, love, and charité, and it is ful of lif and of grace. And therfore whanne it sowneth in a soule it is of so greet myght sumtyme, that the soule sodenly leith of hande al that there is   praiynge, spekynge, redynge, or thenkynge in manere bifore seid, and al maner bodili werk — and lesteneth therto fulli, herende, perceyvande in reste and in love the swete stevene of this goostli vois, as it

3425 were ravesched fro the mynde of alle ertheli thynges. And thanne sumtyme in this pees scheweth Jhesu Him, sumtyme as an eighful maister, and sumtyme as a reverent fadir, and sumtyme as a loveli spouse. And it kepeth the soule in a wondirful reverence and in a loveli bihooldyng of Hym, that the soule liketh weel thanne and nevere so weel as thanne. For it feeleth so moche sikernesse and so grete reste in Jhesu, and so moche

3430 favour of His godnesse, that it wolde ai be so and nevere doon othir werk. It thenketh that it toucheth Jhesu, and thorough vertu of that unspekable touchynge it is maad stable and hool in itsilf, reverentli biholdynge oonli Jhesu as yif there were nothynge but Jhesu oo thynge, and it anothir, born up bi the favour and the wondirfull goodnesse of Hym; o thynge that it seeth and feeleth.

3435 And this feelynge is ofte tyme withoute special biholdynge of Holi Writte, ne but with fewe wordes formed in the herte; not but thus among fallen in swete wordes acordynge

---

3410 Whidirso yeede, Wherever went; **wheles,** wheels. **3412 frowardnesse,** perversity. **3413 aftir that,** according to how. **3414 assai,** test. **3415 mowen,** are able to. **3416 myddai fend,** see gloss on II.1518. **3422 leith of hande,** puts aside. **3424 herende,** hearing; **stevene,** sound. **3426 Him,** Himself; **eighful,** terrible.

to the feelynge, eithir lovende or wondrende, or othirwise sounnende as the herte liketh. The soule is ful moche departed fro love or likynge of the world thorugh vertu of this gracious feelynge, and also fro mynde of the world moche in the meene tyme; it taketh

3440 noon heede therof, for it hath no tome therto. But than sumtyme aftir with this fallen into a soule dyvers illuminacions thorugh grace, the whiche illuminacions I calle the spekynges of Jhesu and the sight of goostli thynges. For wite thou weel that al the bisynesse that Jhesu maketh aboute a soule is for to make it a trewe spouse to Him in the highnesse of love. And for that mai not be doon sodeynli, therfore Jhesu, that is love

3445 and of alle loveres the wisest, assaieth bi many wises and bi wondirful menes or it mai comen aboute; and therfore that it myght come to effect of trewe spousage, He hath sich gracious spekynges in likenesse of a wowere to a chosen soule. He scheweth His privei jewelis, moche thinge He geveth and more biheteth, and curtais daliaunce He scheweth. Often He visiteth with moche grace and goosteli confort, as I have bifore

3450 seid. But hou He dooth this in special al fulli can y not telle, for it nedeth not. Neverthelees sumwhat schal I seien, aftir that grace stireth.

The drawynge of a soule fulli to perfite love is first bi the schewynge of goostli thynges to a clene soule, whanne the gosteli iye is opened: not that a soule schuld reste thereinne, and make an ende there, but bi that yit seeke Him and loven Him oonli that is

3455 highest of alle, withouten ony bihooldynge of ony othir thynge than Himsilf is. "But what aren thise goostli thinges?" seist thou; for y speke ofte of goostli thynges. To this I answere and seie that goostli thynge mai be seid al the sothfastnesse of Holi Writte. And therfore a soule that thorugh the light of grace mai seen the sothfastnesse of it, it seeth goostli thynges, as I have bifore seid.

Chapter Forty-five

3460 Hou thorugh openynge of the goostli iye a soule is maad wise, mekeli and sothfastli for to seen Hooli Chirche as travalynge and as blissid, and for to seen angelis kynde repreved for ther malice.

3437 lovende, praising; **wondrende**, wondering. **3440 tome**, leisure. **3445 or**, before. **3447 wowere**, wooer.

Neverthelees, othere goosteli thynges ther ben also, the whiche thorugh light of grace aren schewed to the soule and aren thise: the kynde of alle resonable soules, and the gracious wirkynge of oure Lord Jhesu in hem; the kynde of aungelis, blissid and repreved, and hire wirkynge; and the knowynge of the blissid Trinité, aftir that grace techeth.

Holi Writ seith in the Book of Songes thus: *Surgam, et circuibo civitatem; et queram quem diligit anima mea* (Canticle 3:2). I schal risen and I schal goon aboute the cité, and y schal seken him that my soule loveth. That is, I schal risen into highnesse of thought and goon aboute the cité. Bi this cité is undirstonde the université of alle creatures bodili and goostli, ordeyned and ruled undir God bi lawes of kynde, of resoun, and of grace. I umgo this cité, whanne I biholde the kyndes and the causis of bodili creatures, the giftes of graces and blissis of goosteli creatures; and in alle I seke him that my soule loveth. It is fair lokynge with the innere iye on Jhesu in bodili creatures, for to seen His myght, His wisdoom, and His goodnesse in ordenaunce of here kynde, but it is moche fairere lokynge on Jhesu in goosteli creatures. Firste in the resonable soules, bothe of chosen and reproved, for to seen the merciful callyng of Him to Hise chosene; hou He turneth hem from synne bi light of His grace; hou He helpeth hem, techeth hem, He chastiseth hem, He conforteth hem; He righteth hem, He clenseth hem, He fedeth hem; hou He maketh hem brennende in light bi plenté of His grace. And this dooth He nought to oon soule onli, but to His chosen, aftir mesure of His grace. Also of the reproved, hou rightfulli He forsaketh hem and leveth hem in here synne and doth hem noo wronge; hou He rewardeth hem in this world, suffrynge hem for to have fulfillynge of here wille, and aftir this for to ponysch hem endelesli.

Loo, this is a litil biholdynge of Hooli Chirche whilis it is traveilynge in this liyf; for to seen hou blak and hou foule it semeth in soulis that aren repreved, hou fair and hou loveli it is in chosen soules. And al this goostli sight is not ellis but the sight of Jhesu; not yit in Himsilf, but in merciful pryvey werkes and in His hard rightwise domes, ilke a dai schewed and renued to resonable soules. Also over this for to seen with the goostli iye peynes of the repreved and the joie and the blisse of chosen soules, it is ful comfortable. For sothfastnesse may not be seen in a clene soule withouten greet delite and wondirful softenesse of brennynge love.

Also the sight of angelis kende; first of the dampned, and aftir that of the blissed. It is a ful faire contemplacioun of the feend in a clene soule, whanne grace bringeth the fend

3470 **université**, totality. 3472 **umgo**, go about. 3475 **ordenaunce**, ordered plan. 3488 **domes**, judgments. 3490 **comfortable**, comforting. 3493 **kende**, nature.

3495 to the sight of the soule as a clumsid caitif bounden with the myght of Jhesu, that he mai not deren. Thanne the soule biholdeth hym, not bodili but goostli, seynge his kynde and his malice, and turneth him upsodoun, or spoileth him and rendeth him al to nought. It scorneth him and dispiseth hym and setteth nought bi his malice. Thus biddeth Hooli Writ whan he seith thus: *Verte impium, et non erit* (Proverbs 12:7). Turne the wikked,

3500 that is the feend, upsodoun, and he schal be as nought. Moche wondir hath the soule that the feend hath so moche malice and so litil myght. Ther is no creature so unmighti as he is, and therfore it is grete cowardise that men dreden him so moche. He mai nothynge doon withouten leve of oure Lord Jhesu, not so moche as entre into a swyne, as the Gospel seith. Moche lasse mai he thanne noien ony man.

3505 And thanne yif oure Lord Jhesu geve him leve for to tarie us and troble us, it is ful worthili and mercifulli doon that oure Lord Jhesu dooth. And therfore welcome be oure Lord Jhesu, bi Himself and bi alle His messangeres. The soule dredeth no more thanne the blusterynge of the feend than the stirynge of a mous. Wondir wrooth is the feend yif he durste seie nai; but his mouth is stopped bi his owen malice, his handes aren bounden

3510 as a theef worthi to ben demed and hanged in helle, and thanne the soule accuseth hym and rightfulli deemeth him aftir he hath disserved. Wondre not of this seiynge, for Seynt Poul mened the same whanne he seide thus: *Fratres, nescitis quoniam angelos iudicabimus?* (1 Corinthians 6:3). Bretheren, wite ye not weel that we schullen deeme angelis, that aren wikked spirites thorugh malice, that were maad good aungeles bi

3515 kynde, as who seith. This deemynge is figurid bifore the doom in contemplatif soulis, for thei feelen a litil tastynge, in likenesse of al that schal be doon and aftirward openli bi oure Lord Jhesu in soothfastenesse.

  Schamed and schent is the feend in himsilf greteli whanne he is thus faren with of a clene soule. He wolde fayn fleen awey and he mai not, for the Holi Goost hooldeth hym

3520 stille, and that deereth him more thanne al the fier of helle. Wondir mekeli falleth the soule to Jhesu thanne, with herteli loovynges and thankynges that He so myghtili saveth a sympil soule fro al the malice of so fel an enemy thorugh His grete merci.

3495 clumsid caitif, clumsy wretch. **3496 deren**, harm. **3497 upsodoun**, upside down; **spoileth**, despoils. **3503 entre into a swyne**, see Mark 5.11–13. **3504 noien**, harm. **3510 demed**, judged. **3513 wite**, know. **3518 schent**, injured; **faren**, dealt; **of**, by. **3520 deereth**, harms. **3521 loovynges**, praisings.

Chapter Forty-six

Hou bi the selve light of grace the blissed aungeles kynde mai be seen; and hou Jhesu as man aboven alle creatures, and as God aftir that the soule mai seen Hym heere.

3525 And thanne aftir this bi the selve mai the soule seen goosteli the fairheed of angelis, the worthinesse of hem in kende, the sotilté in substaunce, the confermynge of hem in grace, and the fulnesse of eendeles blisse; the sondriheed of ordres, the distinccion of persoones, hou thei leven al in light of endelees sothfastnesse and hou thei brennen al in love of the Hooli Goost aftir the worthynesse of ordres, hou thei seen and loven and

3530 preisen Jhesu in blissed reste withouten ceesynge. There is noo sight of bodi ne figure in ymaginacion in this maner wirkynge, but al goosteli of goosteli creatures.

Thanne bigynneth the soule for to have grete aqueyntaunce of his blissid spirites, and grete felawschipe. Thei aren ful tendir and ful bisy aboute sich a soule for to helpen it, thei aren maistres for to kenne it, and often thorugh hire goostli presence and touchynge

3535 of her light dryven oute fantoms fro the soule and mynistren to it al that it nedeth. This Seynt Poul seide of hem: *Nonne omnes sunt administratorii spiritus, missi propter eos qui hereditatem capiunt salutis?* (Hebrews 1:14). Wite ye not wel that alle holi spirites aren ministris, sent of Jhesu for hem that taken the heritage of helthe? Thise aren chosen soulis. As who seith, yhis; for wite thou weel, that al this goosteli wirkynge of

3540 wordes and of resounes broughte to the mynde, and sich fair liknesse, aren maad bi the ministerie of aungelis, whan the light of grace abundaunteli schyneth in clene soulis. It mai not be teeld bi tunge the feelynges, the lightnynges, the graces, and the comfortes in special, that clene soulis perceyven thorugh favourable felawschipe of blissed angeles. The soule is wel at ese with hem for to bihoolden hou thei doon, that it wolde tende to

3545 not elles.

But thanne with helpe of aungelis, yit the soule seeth more. For the knowynge riseth aboven al this in a cleene soule, and that is to bihoolden the blissed kynde of Jhesu. First of His glorious manheede, hou it is worthili highed above angelis kynde; and than aftir of His blissed Godheede, for bi knowyng of creatures is knowen the creatour. And

3550 thanne bigynneth the soule for to perceyven a litil of the privetees of the blissid Trinité.

3527 sondriheed, diversity. **3534 kenne**, teach. **3539 yhis**, yes. **3542 teeld**, told; **lightnynges**, illuminations. **3545 not**, nothing. **3547 kynde**, nature. **3548 highed**, exalted.

It mai weel inowgh, for light of grace gooth bifore sche schal not erren as longe as sche hooldeth hire with the light.

Thanne is it opened soothfastli to the iye of the soule the oonheed in substaunce and distinccioun of persones in the blissed Trinité, as it may be seen here, and moche othir
3555 soothfastnesse of the blissid Trinité pertynent to this matier, the whiche is openli declared and schewed bi writyng of holy doctouris of Hooli Chirche. And wite thou weel that the same and the self soothfastnesse of the blisside Trinité that thise hooli doctours, enspired thorugh grace, writen in her bookes in strengthynge of oure trouthe, a clene soule mai seen and knowen thorugh the self light of grace. I wole not expresse to
3560 moche of this matier here, for it nedeth not.

Wonder grete love feeleth the soule with hevenli delite in bihaldynge of this sothfastnesse, whan it is maad thorugh special grace, for love and light goon bothe togidre in a clene soule. There is no love that riseth of knowynge and of special bihooldynge that mai touchen so neer oure Lord Jhesu, as thes love mai; for whi, this knowyng is worthiest
3565 and highest of itsilf oonli of Jhesu God and man, yif it be speciali schewed bi the light of grace. And therfore is the fier of love flaumynge of this more brennende, than it is of knowynge of ony creature bodili or gosteli.

Alle this gracious knowynge feelid in a soule of the université of alle creatures, in manere bifore seid, and of oure Lord Jhesu, makere and kepere of al this faire université
3570 — I calle hem faire wordes in swete spekynges of oure Lord Jhesu to a soule that He wole make His trewe spouse. He scheweth privetees and profreth riche giftes of tresour, and arraieth the soule with hem ful honesteli. Sche daar not be aschamed with the company of hire felawes for to apperen aftirward to the face of Jhesu spouse. Alle thise loveli daliaunces of privei speche atwixe Jhesu and a soule mai be called an hid word, of
3575 the whiche Holi Writ seith thus: *Porro ad me dictum est verbum absconditum, et venas susurrii eius percepit auris mea* (Job 4:12). Sotheli to me is seid an hid word, and the veynes of his rownynges myn eere hath perceyved. The inspiracioun of Jhesu is an hid word, for it is hid from alle the loveres of this world, and schewed to Hise loveres, thorugh the whiche a clene soule perceyveth redili the veynes of His rownynges, that
3580 aren special schewynges of His sothfastnesse. Or eche a gracious knowynge of soothfastnesse, feelt with inli savour and goostli delite, is a privey rownynge of Jhesu in the eere of a clene soule.

3553 oonheed, unity. **3555 matier**, matter. **3558 trouthe**, faith. **3564 for whi**, because. **3569 université**, totality. **3571 privetees**, secrets. **3577 rownynges**, whisperings.

Him nedeth for to han myche clennesse in soule, in mekenesse and in alle othere vertues, and to ben haalf deeff to noyse of wordli janggelynge, that schuld wiseli perceyven
3585   thise swete goostli rounynges. This is the vois of Jhesu, of the whiche David seith thus: *Vox domini preparantis cervos, et revelabit condensa* (Psalms 28:9). The vois of oure Lord Jhesu greithynge hertis, and He schal schewe thikke. That is, the inspiracion of Jhesu maketh soulis light as hertes that stirten fro the herthe of bussches and breres of alle wordli vanité; and He scheweth to hem the thikke, that aren Hise privytees, that
3590   moun not be perceyved but of a scharp iye. Thise bihooldynges maken a soule wise and brennynge in desire to the face of Jhesu. Thise aren the goostli thinges that I spak of bifore, and thei mai be callid gracious feelyngges. And I doo but touche hem a litil, for wissynge of thy soule. For a soule that is clene, stired bi grace to use of this wirkynge, mai seen more in an hour of siche goosteli matier than myght be writen in a grete book.

3587 **greithynge**, preparing; **hertis**, harts; **thikke**, thicket. 3588 **stirten**, start. 3589 **thikke**, thicket; **privytees**, secrets. 3593 **wissynge**, guidance.

Textual Notes

In the following notes, MS indicates the manuscript used in preparing the text of this edition, London, Lambeth Palace, MS 472; C indicates Cambridge, University Library, MS Additional 6686; B indicates Oxford, Bodleian Library, MS Bodley 100.

Book I

4	*thyne.* C: *the.*
79	*desirynge.* C: *yernyng.*
90	*brennynge.* C adds: *love.*
94	*maner.* C: *matier.*
106	*oute.* C omits.
	good. Inserted above the line; C omits.
132	*name.* C adds: *of.*
142	*phalmynge.* For the spelling, see MED under *psalm(e),* n.
155	*bigynnyng.* MS: *bigynnyg.*
170	*deerkenesse.* C: *merkenes.*
179	*contynueli it.* C: *it comunly.*
181	*alle.* Inserted above the line.
209	*bi.* C: *be.*
230	*it.* C omits.
233	*from biholdinge of oure Lord Jhesu Crist and.* C omits.
240	*yif.* C: *thogh.*
245	*dere.* C: *hyndre.*
254	*biginnynge.* C adds: *when it comes.*
257	*the₂.* C adds: *comforth or.*
258	*God.* C adds: *schewed eithir.*
260	*love of.* C: *lovyng.*
	a. C: *bodily.*
261	*ernest.* C: *erls.*
262	*blisse.* C adds: *of heven.*
264	*visited, whanne sche was.* C omits.
266	*legend.* C: *historie.*
274	*for to love and.* C omits.

274	*blisse.* C adds: *gostly.*
275	*goostli that he desireth.* C: *that this desire is.*
275–76	*he desireth.* C: *the desire is.*
277	*fro stable mynde of Jhesu Crist, and.* C omits.
278	*Hym.* C: *Jhesu.*
280	*revelacion.* C adds: *by an aungel.*
284	*thynge.* C: *felinge.*
	felinge. C omits.
286	*sette not to mykil.* C: *thou schalt noght cleve the thoght of.*
287	*hem.* C adds: *but thou schalt foryete hem if thou myght.*
288	*knowe.* C adds: *and fele.*
300	*thise.* C adds: *foure.*
	of. C adds: *alle.*
303	*bravium.* C adds: *thus mykel is this for to sey.*
304	*hyndward.* C adds: *or bakward.*
	unto. C: *out.*
306	*alle₁.* MS: *alld* or *alls*; C: *alle.*
311	*it.* C adds: *is or.*
314	*he.* C: *if it.*
320	*bi strengthe and.* C: *only by.*
325	*swete.* C omits.
326	*into.* C adds: *verrey.*
341	*renne.* C adds: *out.*
343–44	*thorugh stedefaste trouthe. . . othir good werkes.* C omits.
345	*felynge of Hym.* C: *knowyng of God.*
363	*helpe.* Following *helpe* MS has *yng* inserted above the line; C: *helpe.*
375	*knowynge.* MS: *knowyge.*
384	*here.* Inserted above the line; C omits.
399	*of love.* C omits.
418	*no.* C omits.
428	*and.* C adds: *Seint.*
	in tokenynge and. C omits.
472–73	*thorugh devoute biholdynge on His manhede and His mekenesse.* C omits.
478	*as.* C adds: *Seint.*
500	*hath₂.* C adds: *it.*
525	*herte.* MS: *hte*; C: *hert.*
533	*in.* C adds: *alle.*
537	*have drede.* C: *adred of felyng.*
	ne of the feelynge of hem. C omits.

543	*and worschipe.* C omits.
554	*hope.* C: *trouth.*
557	*this.* C adds: *trouth and in this.*
563	*or.* C adds: *elles.*
571	*and hope.* C omits.
581	*oure Lord Jhesu Crist.* C: *hym.*
592	*bodili or.* C omits.
593	*thy Lord Jhesu Crist.* C: *God.*
597	*prikke.* C: *hamere.*
	to₁. C adds: *stirte and.*
598	*into inwarde biholdynge of Jhesu Crist bi praieres or.* C omits.
	bi₂. C: *to.*
599	*dede or.* C omits.
604–05	*fro alle maner of unclennesse.* C omits.
606	*felynge.* C: *knowyng.*
624	*thi Lord Jhesu Crist.* C: *God.*
640	*praier.* MS: *praien*; C: *preyere.*
653	*ony erthly.* C: *a bodily.*
654	*erthli.* C: *bodily.*
656	*Jhesu Crist as yif thu were in His presence.* C: *God.*
657	*as He is in His Godhede.* C omits.
657–58	*thorugh devout biholdynge of His precious manhede.* C omits.
658–59	*of His Godhede.* C omits.
661	*His goostli presence.* C: *God.*
664	*of thi mynde.* C omits.
665	*praier.* C: *it.*
685	*matier.* C: *maner.*
686	*of.* C: *and.*
699	*best.* A preceding *the* has been erased.
700	*bigynnynge.* MS: *bigynnyge.*
731	*to₂.* MS: *to to.*
752	*him.* C adds: *umwhile [in] his bodie.*
760	*it₂.* MS: *hit* with *h* expunged.
792	*smert.* C: *scharp.*
807	*ligna.* MS: *lingua*; C: *ligna.*
812–14	*This reste oure Lord . . . in the blisse of hevene.* Inserted from margin in a different hand; C omits.
882	*fynde.* C: *fele.*
895–96	*with gret conpunccioun and with plenté of teeris.* C omits.

903   *Jhesu Crist.* C omits.

921–22   *to come to.* C: *into.*

922   *Jhesu Crist in His.* C: *the.*

                come. C adds: *comunly.*

923   *comtemplacioun.* An unusual spelling, but see also *comtemplatif* in chapter 92 (line
                2627), below and compare the scribe's common variation *confort/comfort.*

924   *and bi stable trouthe and stidefaste mynde.* C omits.

930   *oure.* C adds: *Lord.*

951   *oonli.* C omits.

952   *for thei trowed not fulli that Jhesu man was God.* C omits.

956   *a litil.* C omits.

985   *maner of.* C omits.

986–87   *putten al hire trust . . . and that thei.* C omits.

992   *litil.* C omits.

992–93   *with a nakid trouthe and stidefaste mynde of Jhesu Crist, so.* C omits.

996   *foulen.* C: *filen.*

1002   *good₁.* C omits.

1008   *uncouth.* C adds: *or worldly.*

                that is to seie, to noon unkunnynge man and worldli. C omits.

1022–23 *stond stifli in hope, and.* C omits.

1057   *Jhesu Crist.* Written following an expunged *God.*

1063   *bigynne.* C adds: *a new gamen and.*

1072   *whanne God wole give it.* Inserted from margin; C omits.

1086   *him.* C: *home.*

1106   *inne.* C adds: *and I hope an heghe plein wey, als mykel as may lye in mannes werk
                to contemplacioun.*

1110   *of synne.* C omits.

1112   *clennesse.* C: *dignité.*

1114   *al.* C adds: *thyng.*

                fro that clennesse. C: *that joye.*

1120–21 *oure Lord Jhesu Crist.* C: *God.*

1121   *ne have hoomlinesse of His gracious presence.* C omits.

1123   *out.* Marginal gloss: *or to drawe up*; C: *up.*

                love₁. C adds: *and felyng of hymself.*

1123–24 *of alle ertheli creatures and from veyn love of himsilf.* C omits.

1124   *schulde.* C adds: *mo.*

1126   *and in the hoomli presence.* C omits.

                Jhesu. C: *God.*

1136   *hate.* C adds: *alle.*

1136–37   *the likynge of.* C: *his bodily felyng for.*

1138–39   *My manhede and of My Godhede.* C: *me.*

1139   *narwe.* C adds: *that no bodily thyng may passe thorogh it.*

1155   *derkenesse.* C: *merknes.*

1158   *of God. God* added above the line; C omits *of God.*
        and. MS: *an.*
        so. C omits.

1196   *saaf.* C adds: *yee and thou schalt be saufe.*

1199   *by.* C: *and.*

1212   *hemself.* Added in margin: *From this to the ende of this chapitille is more than othere bookys have.* (the scribe's notice of the so-called Holy Name passage).

1248   *Jhesu.* C: *savacioun.*

1248–50   *for there may no man be saaf . . . by the merite of His passioun.* C omits.

1253   *in₂.* C adds: *the blis of.*

1263   *are.* C adds: *in this life inperfite and are.*

1309   *of the firste makynge.* C omits.

1319–20   *Crist, that blissid persoone . . . virgyne, that is.* C omits.

1322   *love and to plese.* C omits.

1323   *othir.* C omits.

1328   *thorugh light of Goddis grace.* C omits.

1329   *into₂.* C: *of.*

1330   *ertheli.* C omits.
        thynge. C adds: *that is made.*

1332   *anoynted.* C adds: *in Jhesu.*

1332–33   *and comfortid thorugh gracious presence of oure Lord Jhesu Crist.* C omits.

1339   *the mynde and.* C omits.

1339–40   *thi Lord Jhesu Crist, that blissid maidenys sone.* C: *Jhesu.*

1340   *His Godhede.* C: *him.*

1341   *joie.* C adds: *non othere.*

1342   *to be with Hym wharso He is, and to see Hym and love Hym.* C omits.

1343   *a litil His goostli presence.* C: *him.*

1345   *and wolt no more seken aftir Hym, but.* C: *bot foryete that thou has founden and.*

1348   *in His joie.* C omits.

1350   *blisse.* C adds: *of lovyng.*

1351   *praiers and of.* C omits.

1353   *love.* C omits.

1354   *myghte not seen of His Godhede.* C: *see ryght noght of him.*

1357   *ony.* C omits.

1365   *His grace and of His merciful presence.* C: *him.*

1366	*Hym.* C: *that desire.*
1370	*bi thi desire.* C: *it.*
1370–71	*in thi praieres . . . Lord Jhesu Crist in thi mynde.* C omits.
1372	*from Hym.* C: *therfro.*
	Hym. C: *it.*
1373	*as He sought thee.* C omits.
1379	*and₂.* MS: *and* erased; C: *and.*
1390	*the dragme.* C omits.
1391	*lost.* C adds: *that is for to sey the dragme.*
1404	*into biholdynge of Jhesu Crist.* C omits.
1404–05	*bi Hym (for He is light).* C omits.
1416–18	*that is, yif thou may . . . to the face of thi soule.* C omits.
1418	*glymerynge.* C adds: *of him.*
1444	*betere.* MS: *betetere.*
1458	*lyveré.* C: *lovers;* on C's erroneous reading, see Clark, p. 175n218.
1461	*lyveré.* C: *lovere.*
1463	*of.* MS: *of of.*
1466	*lyveré.* C: *lovers.*
1490–91	*upon thi Lord Jhesu oonly. . . Lord Jhesu Crist.* C: *only Jhesu.*
1492–93	*with stable mynde of Jhesu Crist with besinesse in praieres.* C omits.
1494	*sekest.* Following *sekest* MS has expunged: *but oonli a nakid mynde of his name.*
1504	*steme.* Some MSS (not C) have *stien* ("ascend"), which makes better sense; see Clark, p. 176n232.
1505	*ymage.* MS: *yma*; C: *ymage.*
1512	*lackynge.* Marginal gloss: *merknesse of consciens.*
1513	*God.* C: *gode* ("good"), perhaps a more satisfactory reading; see Clark, p. 176n235.
1515	*clensid and.* C omits.
1516–17	*Jhesu — not oonli . . . thou schuldest fynde.* C omits.
1518	*bi Hym.* C omits.
1519	*of Hym.* C omits.
1524	*smoke.* C: *reke.*
1530	*nought.* Marginal gloss: *merknes of consciens.* The same marginal gloss is found for *nought* in lines 1533, 1537, 1539, and 1541.
1535–36	*not settynge the poynt . . . whiche thou desirest.* C omits.
1543	*hominis.* C omits.
1571	*opyn.* C: *hole.*
1594	*he.* C: *nevertheles it.*
1605	*of.* C adds: *the first.*
1606	*felyng.* An illegible mark after *g* may be a final *e.*

1606	*unwarli.* C omits.
1613	*reste.* C: *end.*
1617	*doth so, ne who.* C omits.
	so. C omits.
1627	*richere and highere than anothir.* C: *then othere.*
1629	*comaundement.* MS: *comaundedement.*
1631	*or₁.* C adds: *lese it eithere of.*
1637	*noithir.* C omits.
1645	*with.* C omits.
1648–49	*he dooth agen that othir and so.* C omits.
1652	*Cristen.* MS: *Criste*; C: *Cristen.*
1653	*and so he synneth deedli.* C omits.
1656	*homni.* sic MS.
1659	*stille.* C omits.
1661	*evere.* C omits.
1663	*while he lyveth heere.* C omits.
1673	*it is sooth, for.* C omits.
	men. C adds: *for that is soth.*
1676	*neer hande.* C omits.
1685	*that he deliteth inne.* C: *and.*
	as₁. C: *that he feles.*
	god. C: *gode.*
	soule. C adds: *whilk is synne.*
1691	*is₁.* C: *schal be.*
1695	*wolde.* C adds: *hold and.*
1711	*and helpe.* C omits.
1717	*as.* C adds: *doun principaly.*
	also. C omits.
	men. C omits.
1722	*myght for.* C omits.
	religious. MS: *religigious.*
1731	*grace and a.* An attempt has been made to erase, but still clearly visible; C omits.
1734	*speke of and.* C omits.
1736	*resoun.* MS: *rosoun.*
	of. C: *and.*
1739	*forsake.* C adds: *al manere of.*
1750	*ony.* C omits.
1751	*of.* C adds: *alle.*
1767	*God.* C adds: *more.*

269

1774	*the love of God.* C: *love.*
1775	*is it.* C: *it may be seid.*
1788	*prefinitum tempus.* C: *ad tempus prefinitum.*
1791	*prophete₂.* C adds: *at the last day.*
	the. C adds: *last.*
1793	*in thy sorte.* C omits.
1795	*worschip.* C adds: *in.*
1797	*this that I have seid.* C: *thise words.*
	thorugh it. C: *trowe hem.*
1802–03	*of the gifte of God as he or sche hath that dwelleth stille in the wordli besynesse.* C: *als fully and als perfitely as a worldly man or woman.*
1804	*dwellith.* C adds: *stille.*
1805	*or sche schal have.* C: *schal.*
1806	*have₁.* C omits.
1807	*wel.* C adds: *meke thiself and*
1808	*is₂.* C adds: *ryght.*
	loke. C omits.
1809	*to.* C adds: *destrue synnes and for to.*
1815	*holde thee.* C omits.
1819	*or disese thee.* C omits.
1820	*anguisch.* C: *angrynes and*
	the persoones. C: *hem.*
1831	*and₁.* C adds: *trewly.*
	in. C adds: *vertue of.*
	mekenesse and. C omits.
1843	*herte.* C adds: *despisyng, bakbityng, unskilfulle blamyng, misseying, unkyndnes, mislikyng, angrynes and hevynes.*
1844	*men.* C adds: *and othere.*
1846	*ponysschid.* C adds: *and chastised.*
1847	*wel.* C adds: *thou schalt fynd it summe tyme*
1860	*prechynge.* MS: *prchynge.*
1862	*kunne.* C omits.
1864	*and women.* C omits.
1868	*vestris.* MS: *vestrs.*
1869	*spiritum.* C adds: *sanctum.*
1875	*badde.* C adds: *to chosen and to reproved.*
1881	*resseyved.* C adds: *if he preche and teche Goddes worde he.*
1883	*Chirche.* C adds: *if thei prechen.*
1894	*and₂.* C adds: *approve and.*

1910   *of₂.* C adds: *alle.*
1912   *hadde.* C adds: *alle manere of.*
1920   *ony.* C adds: *wrecched.*
1927   *he₂.* C adds: *sikerly.*
1936   *philosophie.* C: *philosophers he couthe noght do this; he schuld kun hate the synne of al othere men for he hates it in hymself, but he couthe noght love the man in charité for al his philosophie.*
        of₂. C adds: *alle.*
1939   *techynge.* C: *kennyng.*
1943   *wise.* C adds: *I sey that.*
1945   *y.* C: *thou then.*
1958   *mekenesse.* C adds: *at this tyme.*
1962   *visili.* C: *wisely.*
1967   *for ought that thei dooth agens thee.* Inserted from margin.
1971   *maner of.* Added above the line; C omits.
1974   *cause.* C: *purpose.*
1976   *quenchid.* C: *slekned.*
1977   *wil.* C omits.
1983   *or bi feel.* C omits.
1989–90 *thyn herte in affeccioun and love.* C: *affeccioun of love in thi hert.*
1993   *persequentibus.* C adds: *et calumpniatibus.*
1995   *pursue.* C adds: *and sclaundren.*
1997   *goodli.* C omits.
        was to. C: *loved.*
        Judas. C adds: *whilk was bothe his dedly enmy and a synfulle caytif, how godely Crist was to hym.*
        benynge. C: *benigne.*
1999   *apostelis.* C adds: *He wesch his fete and fede hym with his preciouse bodie, and preched hym als he did to othere apostles.*
2001   *not.* C adds: *openly for it was pryvé, ne mysseid hym noght ne despised hym.*
2002   *nothynge.* C omits.
2008   *goodnes.* C adds: *and forthi it falles to hym to schewe love and godenes.*
        Judas. C adds: *I sey noght that Crist loved hym for his synne, ne he loved hym noght for his chosen as he did Seint Petre, bot he loved hym in als mykel as he was his creature and schewed hym tokens of love if he wold have ben amended thereby.*
2012   *lovere and a.* C omits.
2016   *maliciousli.* C: *malencolious.*
2028   *thisilf.* MS: *silf,* with a preceding caret for an addition, but none is supplied.
2044   *forsaken.* C adds: *clenly.*

2052	*traveiled.* C adds: *and trobled.*
2056	*in thyn herte, and.* C omits.
2058	*gete it.* C omits.
	for. C adds: *to stryve and flite with hym for.*
2065	*pursue.* C adds: *for his godes.*
2067	*hyt.* C adds: *for itself.*
2074	*skilfulli.* C adds: *only for lust and likyng.*
	love. C: *ficche thi love upon.*
2075	*nedith.* C adds: *for itself.*
	that. C adds: *thyng that.*
2076	*it.* C adds: *more then kynde or nede asketh withouten whilk the thyng may not be used it.*
	Soothli. C adds: *in this poynt as I trow.*
	and the likenesse. C omits.
2077	*blyndid in this poynt.* C: *letted.*
2080	*his.* C adds: *love and his.*
2081–82	*the love of ony othir ertheli thynge.* C: *covetise of erthly gode.*
2082	*ellis.* C omits.
2085	*thee.* C adds: *that he loves noght for the.*
2087–88	*it be so moche . . . even Cristen, sothely.* Inserted from margin.
2088	*thee.* C: *hem.*
2092	*or.* C adds: *avere of.*
2095	*me.* C: *my hert.*
2100	*and₃.* C adds: *bodily.*
2109	*sleuthe.* C: *accidie.*
2114	*more.* C adds: *likyng.*
2131–33	*Yif a man wolde oonli take . . . luste from the nede.* C omits.
2140	*herte.* C adds: *that he wold in his hert.*
2145	*likynges.* C adds: *when thei comen.*
2150–51	*so that the dede be not yvel in the silf.* C omits.
2159	*God merci.* C: *aftere merci specialy.*
2160	*fleischli.* C omits.
2161	*forgyveth.* C adds: *swythe.*
2170	*agens.* MS: *aȝns.*
2175	*venial.* C adds: *synne.*
2176	*arise.* C: *travaile.*
	and the₂. C: *of.*
2180	*no.* C omits.
2183	*slee fleischli.* C: *flee.*

2185	*be.* C adds: *mykel.*
2191	*fulli.* C: *felly.*
2197	*delite.* C: *likyng.*
	agrise. C: *ugge.*
2200	*it.* C adds: *more soroe and.*
2209	*or lasse.* C omits.
2210	*synnes, the lasse.* C: *lesse the lesse.*
2215	*hevy.* C adds: *peynfulle.*
2216	*of the gostli presence of Jhesu Crist.* C omits.
2218	*agen.* C adds: *the ground thou schalt noght aryse as I have seid bifore for.*
	that. C omits.
2224	*or₁.* C adds: *bodily.*
2225	*thisilf.* C: *gode rewlyng of hymself.*
2230	*lust.* C: *love.*
2233	*generali.* C: *gladly.*
2235	*mete.* C adds: *as it comes.*
2240	*forgevenesse.* C adds: *and sey thou will amend it and trust of forȝyvenes.*
2248	*more and waxe.* C: *and kepe.*
2249	*and.* MS: *an.*
2256	*hem₂.* C adds: *and if thou may gete hem.*
2259	*hevynesse.* C adds: *ne in lust ne in lyghtnes.*
2266	*grete.* C: *thik.*
2267	*chaos.* C adds: *a grete merknes.*
2272	*Lifte.* C: *Lyght.*
2276	*sight.* C: *eye.*
2277	*tydynges.* C: *thynges.*
2282	*cloude.* C: *mantel.*
2284	*outward.* Written in margin; C omits.
2286	*Lord.* C adds: *manassand.*
2290	*kedis.* C: *gaytes.*
2295	*kides.* C: *gayte.*
2296	*seke.* MS: *begge* inserted over *seke*, apparently as an alternate reading; *begge* is found in other MSS; see Underhill, p. 193.
	withoute. forth added above the line; not in the chapter heading in the Table at the beginning of the book; not in C.
2299	*seke.* C: *beg.*
2300–01	*curtais and free inow.* C omits.
2307	*dronkennesse.* C: *drynkes*
2308	*kynge.* C: *likyng.*

2320	*thus.* C adds: *as I hope thou dos.*
2325	*delite.* C: *an ese.*
2329	*loveth God or wole love soothfastli.* C: *wil sothfastly love God.*
2334	*venyal.* C adds: *and more fle it.*
2345	*that he myght not come.* C omits.
2646	*excusid hym.* C omits.
2347	*oxen.* C adds: *for he is to this purpose.*
2351	*to₂.* C adds: *wilfully.*
2355	*the wise man.* C: *Seint Paule.*
2379	*love.* C omits.
2386	*ne what he wolde.* C: *ne whi he comes.*
2387	*hym₂.* C omits.
2396	*hym.* C adds: *if thou canst.*
2397	*vanytees.* C adds: *of the world.*
2400	*knowe.* C: *kenne.*
2402	*teche₁.* C: *kenne.*
	teche₂. C: *kenne.*
2403–04	*goo his wai.* C: *take his leve.*
2405	*knowen.* C: *kenned.*
	him withal. C: *hem alle.*
2407	*agreef.* C: *of the.*
2409	*alle.* C adds: *othere.*
2420	*into many wrecchidnessis.* C: *in mony fleschly likynges and worldly vanities fro clennes of hert and fro the felyng of gostly vertus.*
2421	*thenketh yvel fore and.* C omits.
2424	*Writt.* MS: *wriit;* C: *writt.*
	dominus. C: *deus.*
2430	*firste.* C adds: *and the principale.*
2432	*extendam.* C: *extendo.*
2441	*ton.* MS: *to.*
2452	*meditacioun.* C adds: *here has thou herd the membres of this ymage.*
2456	*ymage.* C omits.
2457	*luste.* C: *love.*
2469	*of synne.* C omits.
2485	*of.* C adds: *synne and.*
2497	*lyve.* Possibly corrected from *have.*
2500	*comen.* C: *spryngen.*
	filen. C: *defoulen.*
2503–04	*and thyn even Cristene.* C omits.

2509	*Hym.* C adds: *and if thou love hym litel then litel thynkes thou on hym.*
2512	*hou veyn.* C omits.
2513	*malicious.* C: *malencolios.*
2519	*to breke the charge of this veyn.* C: *bere this hevy birthen of this.*
2523	*sorwe.* C adds: *I hope thou feled nevere more.*
2527	*thinge.* C adds: *and fro rest in thin oun bodily felyng.*
2530	*fynde no.* C: *noght lightly fynde.*
2535	*this.* C adds: *false.*
2540	*in.* C: *and.*
2550	*neerhande.* C: *half.*
2554	*of₁.* C: *off.*
2555	*malicious.* C: *malencolie.*
	overmoche. C: *any.*
2570	*to₂.* C adds: *plese hym, for to.*
2574	*teche.* C: *kenne.*
2580	*this felynge and.* C omits.
2585	*alle.* C omits.
	adoune. C: *awey.*
2589	*of.* C adds: *Jhesu.*
2590	*be.* Possibly *bi*; C: *bi.*
2592	*ful.* C omits.
2593	*Christus.* C omits.
2594	*child.* C: *barn.*
2612	*contemplacioun.* C: *contemplatif life.*
2617	*of lif.* C: *of,* partially erased.
2619	*thyn herte.* C: *the.*
2620	*it₁.* C adds: *be so that it.*
2628	*thee.* C adds: *and with hym that writes this boke.*

Book II

9	*and that a worthi image.* B omits.
13–14	*of Him.* B omits.
14	*and schal speken of.* B omits.
15	*liknesse.* B: *ymage.*
18	*myrkenesse.* B: *derknesse*; B consistently uses *derk-* where MS has *myrk-* or *merk-.*
	beestli. B omits.
27	*goodnesse.* B adds: *ferst.*

38	*the trespaas.* B: *hit.*
40	*of.* MS: *of of.*
44	*oweth.* B adds: *of duyté or dette.*
48	*alle.* B omits.
49	*deede.* B: *deth.*
56	*kyndeli.* B omits.
59	*Crist.* B omits.
67	*man.* B omits.
	thingis. B: *God on thyng.*
72	*He was bounde to rightfulnesse, but.* Inserted from margin.
	dyen. B: *deth.*
76	*manere deede.* B: *mannes deth.*
86	*His.* B adds: *preciose.*
99	*troweth.* B: *leeveth* (B regularly uses *leeven* where MS has *trowen*).
111	*untrouthe.* B: *unbyleeve* (here and elsewhere).
115	*other comende or comen.* B: *comande as in the olde lawe or comen as now.*
125	*and paynemes.* B omits.
	kepynge. B: *knowynge.*
126	*and as Cristen men doon.* B omits.
143	*trouthe.* B: *feyth* (here and elsewhere).
149	*whiche.* B adds: *restorynge and.*
150	*in feith.* B omits.
174	*medlere.* B: *medlynge.*
184	*to alle chosen soulis that were lyvande in tyme of His passioun.* Added from margin.
192	*maad.* B omits.
212	*feith.* B adds: *only.*
214	*thorugh lengthe.* B: *by processe.*
216	*yit he mai.* B omits.
217	*not withstondynge al.* Following *withstondynge*, MS has *synne*, which seems to be expunged; B: *aȝeynstondynge.*
222	*reformynge.* MS: *reformyge.*
241	*whiche.* Preceding *whiche* is a decorative filler.
242	*ther.* The scribe's usual usage is the southern forms, *her(e), hire.*
245	*as swithe.* B: *anoon.*
247	*untrouthe.* B adds: *of byleeve.*
272	*mekenesse.* B: *mekenesse and obedience.*
291	*Chirche.* B adds: *and the feyth.*
297	*schrift.* B: *confessioun.*
340	*oonli.* B omits.

343   *unseable.* B: *that is gostly and invisible.*
344   *partener.* Hussey (1992, pp. 103–04) suggests the reading *percener* ("sharer"); see
        the same phrase below in chapter 36 with note.
348   *man.* B: *mannes soule.*
372   *trouthe.* B: *feyth.*
396   *ire.* B: *wreththe.*
        heved. B: *capital.*
399   *as tite.* B omits.
409   *likli.* B omits.
435   *trouthe.* B: *leve or feyth.*
445   *merci.* B adds: *and godnesse.*
459   *desert.* B: *desire.*
468   *hem bihoveth.* B: *moste they.*
470   *neer.* B omits.
473   *fightynge.* B: *chydynge.*
475   *he₁.* MS: *he* preceded by an expunged *thou.*
477   *outetaken.* B: *save.*
478   *werk.* B: *dede.*
486   *feer.* B: *free.*
487   *feer.* B: *free.*
499   *double.* B: *dedly.*
500   *resoun.* Capitalized in MS here and elsewhere, but not consistently. See also, for
        example, line 2080.
524   *light.* B: *sight* (perhaps correctly).
535   *and that he feelith no more of it.* B omits.
538   *and certayn.* B omits.
560   *thee.* B adds: *for* (almost required by the sense).
567   *yif it be gracious.* MS: *yif it be gracicious*; B omits.
569   *God.* B adds: *that is, they ssal see God.*
583   *this.* B adds: *foule.*
603   *defaded.* B: *defaced.*
620   *weike.* B: *fable.*
625   *likynges.* B: *styrenges.*
628   *irketh.* B: *weryeth.*
632   *the.* B adds: *evele.*
        defoulynge. MS: *defoulyge.*
641   *in the whiche he was born in.* B: *the wiche bar hym.*
645   *feelist.* B: *sechest.*
648   *trouthe stilli.* B: *feyth styfly.*

277

651   trouth. B: *byleve, that is trewe feyth.*
665   *God₂.* B: *hym.*
673   *ymage.* B: *lyknesse.*
682   *heveneli.* B: *gostly.*
692   *loveth not. not* written above line; B: *leeveth.*
709   *proud.* B: *mysproude.*
716   *unwillid.* B: *evele willed.*
741   *stangno.* Perhaps an error, but more likely a possible spelling of Vulgate *stagno.*
743   *worschiperis of maumetis.* Inserted from margin.
        dool. B: *here part.*
767   *ugglen.* B: *abhorreth.*
796   *flee.* B: *leeve.*
805   *peyne.* B adds: *he ssal knowen it.*
814   *stoppe.* B: *stoppeth.*
840   *thei han no.* B: *lakkynge of.*
854   *That.* MS: *That* crossed out.
863   *brente.* B: *brought.*
876   *schal langure.* B: *be feble and syklich.*
878   *and reformyd.* B omits.
884   *stele.* B: *gree.*
913   *come to mychil grace.* B omits.
917   *geven.* B adds: *hym besyly.*
920   *foule.* B omits.
943   *yernynge.* B: *covetynge.*
957   *dedli.* MS: *deeli*; B: *dedly.*
960   *first.* Inserted above the line; B omits.
978   *othir wilful custum.* B: *here customes.*
996   *to deedli synne.* B omits.
1019   *and.* MS: *and and.*
1022   *kenne.* B: *teche.*
1025   *lyvynge.* B: *lernynge,* perhaps correctly.
1033   *mykil as.* B omits.
1062   *God.* B omits.
1067   *dedes.* MS: *des*; B: *dedys.*
1074   *biddynge.* B omits.
1099   *the schorteste and the redieste helpe that I knowe in this wirkynge.* B omits.
1134   *bigynnynge.* MS: *bigynnnynge* (otiose abbr. stroke).
1142   *speciali.* B omits.
1145   *strynges.* MS: *stirynges.*

1147	*that₁*. MS: *that that.*
1160	*tome or voide.* B: *empty.*
1172	*lene.* B: *abyde.*
1204	*flawme and the hattere is the.* B omits.
1230	*of the love of Jhesu.* B: *fro the love of God.*
1235	*for to love.* B: *the love of.*
1239	*first and.* B omits.
1260	*a good.* B: *the.*
1277	*oonly.* Inserted above the line; B: *thenk oonly* (perhaps rightly).
1292	*and₁*. B adds: *veyn.*
1315	*thee.* B adds: *charge hit noght, jangle naght therwyth, ne angre the naght.*
1318	*strengthe it.* B adds: *and meynteyne hit.*
1328	*wirkynge.* MS: *wirkyge.*
1343	*therfore see Hym gostly yif thou myght.* Inserted from margin.
1368	*spered.* B: *closed.*
1369	*knowynge.* B: *likynge.*
1378	*thus.* B: *and therfore he that loveth hym he is in lyght everelastynge, as.*
1381	*him bihoveth a while abiden.* B: *he moste abyde a wyle.*
1384	*the affeccioun and.* B omits.
1385	*and loven.* B omits.
1389	*fleschli₂.* B: *bodily.*
1390	*bounden.* B adds: *ne peyned.*
1395	*light.* B: *day.*
1396–97	*werldli desires.* B omits.
1422	*feling of.* B omits.
1427	*chesinge.* B: *clefynde.*
1437	*bryngeth.* B adds: *hit* (perhaps rightly).
1457	*merkenesse.* MS: altered from *mekenesse; ir* inserted above the line between *e* and *k.*
1474	*unseable.* B: *invisible.*
1482	*thee.* B omits.
1486	*To hem that wonen.* B: *that is, wonynge.*
	the. fals inserted here from margin, but expunged.
1500	*thought.* Marginal gloss: *inere* ("inner"); B: *sowth.* Despite the gloss, B's reading is better (see Ezekiel 40:2).
1501	*rodde.* B: *reed.*
1505	*biggynge.* B: *beldenges.*
1508	*liyf.* B: *hylle.*
	iye. B: *syght.*

1509–10 *semeth sumwhat, but it*. B omits.
1523   *of the enemye*. MS: *of enemye*. Emendation may be unnecessary; see the heading for
        I.984 (chapter 38), for *feend* without the article.
1527   *ney. ney* inserted above the line preceding an expunged *newe*; B omits *newe*.
1533   *ben*. B adds: *byfore*.
1534   *hemsilf*. Corrected from *himsilf*.
        thinges. B adds: *outward*.
1537   *wepynge*. B: *wakynge*.
1539   *holi and*. B: *hooly*.
1545   *knowinge*. B: *cunnynge*.
1553   *knowynge*. MS: *knowyge*.
1561   *knowynge*. MS: *knowyge*.
1564   *and*. B: *thorugh*.
1569   *zele*. B: *love*.
1572   *flitynge*. B: *chydynge*.
1573   *that knowynge*. B: *such cunnynge*.
1574   *God*. MS: *good*, with the second *o* expunged; B: *God*.
1577   *the fendes*. B: *comynly*.
1578   *fendes*. B: *feyned*.
1580   *blake*. B omits.
1591   *undirstandynge*. B: *gostly knowynge*.
1598   *risen*. B: *spryngyn*.
1599   *kyndele*. B adds: *or tenden*.
1612   *ne ypocrisies*. B omits.
        into a soule. B: *in*.
1613   *resten*. B: *rysen*.
1639–40 *goo where*. B: *do what*.
1656   *resten*. B: *rysen*.
1684   *mai₁*. B adds: *naght*.
1700   *dyverse*. B: *sondry*.
1701   *seere*. B: *diverse*.
1703   *gate*. B: *way* (and elsewhere in this chapter).
1716   *lif*. B: *love*.
1733   *nought*. B: *nyght*.
1735   *brent*. B: *brought*.
1747   *sadli*. B omits.
        mekeli. B omits.
        fareth bi it. B: *falleth therby*.
1753   *and₁*. MS omits; B: *and*.

1762	*knowynge.* MS: *knowyge.*
1783	*forsakynge.* MS: *forsakyge.*
1799	*bigynnyng.* MS: *bigynnyg.*
1801	*in conpunccion.* B: *of contemplacioun.*
1810	*beykynge.* B: *bethynge.*
1811	*staaf.* B: *stykke.*
1814	*brent.* B: *brought.*
1823	*for it schal not wite where ne how.* Inserted from margin.
1829	*feelynge.* B: *lyvynge.*
1830	*luste.* B: *the love.*
1840	*receyve up hem.* B: *rysen up.*
1842	*knowynge.* MS: *knowyge.*
1847–48	*the soule.* B: *thee.*
1888	*bolneth.* B: *swelleth.*
1920	*falleth.* B: *faryth.*
1948	*thought.* B: *body.*
1953	*and for to love the sovereyn goodnesse.* Inserted from margin.
1962	*undirstondyng.* MS: *undirstondyg.*
1977	*thenkynge.* MS: *thenkyge.*
2001	*worschipen.* B omits.
2005	*is₁.* B adds: *good and.*
2006	*lasse.* B adds: *and* (perhaps rightly).
2017	*in.* MS: *in in.*
2042	*contemplatif.* MS: *conteplatif.*
2068	*heeryng.* MS: *heeryg.*
2096	*reformynge.* MS: *reformyge.*
2103	*schorter.* Last two letters illegible; B: *schortere.*
2149	*hool.* B: *holy.*
2152	*oolde.* B: *holy.*
2166	*blyndli.* B adds: *and nakedly.*
	savourli. B: *unsavourly.*
2180	*eum.* Not in MS; see 1 John 3:2.
2188	*spered.* B: *yclosed.*
2197	*Jhesu.* B adds: *God.*
2205	*thorugh grace.* B omits.
2212	*ferforth.* B: *forward.*
2221	*openynge.* MS: *openyge.*
2240	*worthiere.* B: *worthynesse.*
2264	*privei.* B omits.

2271   *sothfastnesse.* MS: *sostfastnesse.*

2286   *not.* B adds: *speken.*

2296   *aren.* B adds: *temporal and.*

2299–2300 *Thus seith oure Lord.* B omits.

2302   *Jhesu Crist.* B omits.

2306   *love.* A following *of Jhesu* is expunged.

2313   *that.* B adds: *in knowynge.*

2318   *symple.* B: *synful.*

2335   *mekenesse.* B: *mochelnesse.*

2343   *departen.* B: *share.*

2370   *forgyvnesse.* MS: *forȝynesse.*

2377   *biynge.* Corrected from *biggynge* (i.e., "buying").

2406   *wrecchid.* B: *wykkede.*

2429   *streynen.* B: *steren.*

2439   *Jhesu.* B: *God.*

2445   *schewynge of.* B omits.

2460   *fervours.* B: *by fervours.*

2478   *bothe.* B: *god.*

2479   *of God.* B: *goode.*

2483   *for the tyme.* B omits.

2503   *partenere.* B: *takere*; Hussey (1992, pp. 103–04) suggests *percener* ("sharer"); compare the same phrase above in chapter 8; and see Clark, p. 319n263.

2509   *schedynge.* B: *disseveraunce.*

2515–16 *and it schal werken . . . schalt biholden Him.* Interpolated from the margin; B: . . . *biholden Jhesu.*

2518   *Ceese yee.* B: *Taketh heede.*

2521   *God.* B: *God and man.*

2540   *pacience.* B: *of penaunce.*

2549   *alle.* Inserted above the line.

2564   *biholding.* MS: *biholdig.*

2580   *disposeth.* B: *dispyseth.*

2584   *forgyvnesse.* MS: *foryynesse.*

2605   *veyn.* Written over erasure.

2607   *into.* MS: *into into.*

2611   *circumstaunces.* MS: *circustaunces.*

2636   *bihaldynge.* MS: *bihaldyge.*

2645   *ai upon.* B: *evere opene to.*

2646   *snaris.* B adds: *or greves.*

2652   *of God.* B omits.

2660	*passynge.* B adds: *and weyward.*
2694	*risynges.* B: *stirynge.*
2698	*he wil not ben angrid ne sterid agens hem.* Inserted from margin.
2721	*yeeden.* B: *wende or yeeden.*
2734	*wronge.* B omits.
2742	*thorugh his.* B: *of the.*
	dede. B adds: *of that other man.*
2752	*and passen.* B omits.
2773	*the love of Jhesu.* B: *Godes love.*
2792	*Jhesu.* B: *God.*
2815	*accidie.* B: *slouthe.*
2840	*heren.* B: *spekyn, huyren.*
2865	*or deepnesse.* B omits.
2895	*apostil.* B: *gospel.*
2896	*ancipiti.* B omits.
2906	*flitynge.* B: *chydynge.*
2929	*undeynté.* B: *dedeyn.*
2946	*ne peynfulli.* B omits.
	oonlynesse. B: *wyldernesse.*
2947	*an.* B: *wyldernesse or.*
2949	*of thought.* B: *or wyldernesse.*
2954	*oonlynesse of bodi.* B: *that.*
2965	*in.* B: *thy.*
2973	*the liyf of his bodi.* B: *thys bodyly lyf.*
2975	*bygynynge.* MS: *bygynnge.*
2978	*and likynge.* B omits.
2981	*perfite.* B omits.
	bygynyng. MS: *bygynng.*
3003	*that wakeneden.* B: *wakynge.*
3004	*is.* B: *is understonden.*
3005	*dene.* B: *dyynge.*
3007	*wordli.* B: *erthly.*
3019	*sothli.* B: *softly.*
3023	*openynge.* MS: *openyge.*
3033	*abidynge.* B: *hydynge.*
3040	*feelinge.* B: *fleynge*
3043	*herte.* B: *soule.*
3045	*loves.* B: *lustys.*
3049	*to wordli love.* B omits.

3058	*sodaynly.* MS: *sosodaynly; so sodaynly* makes sense, but the second *so* begins the verso and is thus more likely to be a repetition error.
3060	*merthe.* B: *myght.*
3064	*feleabli.* B: *evere.*
3065	*brennynge.* B omits.
3072	*grace.* B adds: *the lasse ys the grace.*
3103	*reverence.* MS: *rereverence.*
3120	*favour.* B: *savour.*
3124	*fer.* B: *fre.*
3139	*and of Hooli Chirche.* B omits.
3169	*lettred men.* B: *lettred.*
3190–91	*reek stiynge.* B: *smoke rysynge.*
3191	*iye.* B: *eyre.*
3194	*flesch flie.* B: *flesschly.*
3196	*plaiand.* B: *reekynge.*
	Jhesu. B adds: *hit yeldeth grace to Jhesu.*
3219	*openynge.* MS: *openyge.*
3229	*Jhesu.* B: *God.*
	Hym. B: *God.*
3246	*special.* B omits.
	of conpuccion. B: *in a bygynnere, that is called grace of contemplacion.*
3248	*and seen.* B omits.
	goostli. B: *godly.*
	betere. B adds: *ne may no betere.*
3261	*loned.* B: *lened.*
3265	*seen.* B adds: *and felen.*
3267	*mekeli, til.* B: *til thou come to.*
3269	*love.* B: *grace.*
3272–73	*I wole of thise foure.* B: *of these foure that me lust.*
3279	*to₁.* MS: *fro* added above the line after *to*, perhaps as an alternative.
3283	*a clene.* B omits.
3286	*trusteth.* B: *troweth or byleveth.*
3289	*God.* B: *Jhesu.*
3290	*favour.* B: *fervour.*
3305	*mysterie.* B: *ministrynge.*
3330	*vertues.* B: *swetnesse.*
3388	*neverthelees yit.* B: *noght for than.*
3405	*aren.* B adds: *fayre.*
3409	*feelynge.* B: *styrynges.*

3413 *stirynge.* B: *the stondynge.*
    toucheth. B: *techeth.*
3414 *myghti.* B: *syker.*
3433 *favour.* B: *savoure.*
3434 *o.* B: *that is, that.*
3437 *wondrende.* B: *worschepande.*
3443 *spouse.* B: *perfyght spouse.*
3444 *highnesse.* B adds: *and the fulnesse.*
3467 *Songes.* B adds: *of the Spouse.*
3472 *umgo.* B: *go aboughte.*
3480 *light.* B: *love.*
3481 *grace.* B: *mercy.*
3496 *deren.* Marginal gloss: *or greve.*
3505 *and troble us.* B omits.
3509 *is.* MS: *his*; B: *is.*
3519 *Holi Goost.* B: *myght of the hygheste.*
3524 *heere.* A following *in this liyf* has been expunged; not in the Table of Contents
    preceding Book II.
3525 *selve.* B adds: *lyght*, perhaps correctly.
3527 *sondriheed.* B: *diversité of sondry.*
3529 *of the Hooli Goost.* B omits.
3531 *maner.* B omits.
3532 *spirites.* Replaces expunged *creatures.*
3535 *soule.* B adds: *and they illumynen the soule gratiously, they conforten the soule with
    swete wordes sodeynly sowned in a clene herte and yyf eny disese falle gostly they
    serven the soule.*
3551 *bifore.* B adds: *and therfore.*
3565 *of₁.* MS: *of in.*
3587 *greithynge.* B: *ordeinynge.*
3588 *stirten fro the herthe of.* B: *lepen over.*
3589 *the thikke, that aren.* B omits.
3590 *bihooldynges.* B adds: *sothfastliche grounded in grace and mekenesse.*
3592 *callid.* B adds: *newe.*

Glossary

adraad *afraid*
agen *again, against*
agenstonde *withstand, resist*
anemptis *regarding*
anoon *at once*
apaid *satisfied*
asketh *requires*
astaat *state, condition*
as tite *immediately*

behight *promised*
ben *are*
besi *diligent*
besynesse, bisynesse *activity, concern*
bihoveth *is necessary (impers.)*
bisili *assiduously, diligently*
bolneth *swells*
boystous *rough*
brennynge *burning*
but yif *unless*
buxum *obedient*
bynemen *take away*

caitif *wretch*
clene *pure*
clennesse *purity*
connynge *ability; knowledge*
couthe *know*
coveityse *covetousness*

daungerous *fastidious, haughty, reluctant*
deceyvable *deceitful*
deed *dead*

defaughtes *faults*
delices *delights*
delitable *delightful*
deme *judge (vb.)*
dere *harm*
disese *discomfort, distress*
doom *judgment*
doute *doubt*
drede *fear*
dweer *doubt*
dylite *delight, pleasure*

even Cristene *fellow Christians*

ficchid *fixed*
fleischli *carnal*
for thi *because*
freel *frail*
freelté *frailty*
fulheed *fulfillment, fullness*

goostli *spiritual*
goven *given*
grucchynge *grudging*

halden *kept*
halewes *saints*
han *have*
heere, here *her*
hem *them*
here *their; her*
hevynesse *sadness*
hire *her*

Glossary

hit *it*
hooli *wholly*
hope *expect, think, suppose*
hym *him*

ilke *same*
inli *inward*
iye *eye*

kenne *teach*
knowelechynge *acknowledging*
kunne *be able, know how to*
kunnynge *teaching, knowledge*
kynde *nature*
kyndeli *natural*

lassed *diminished*
leryd *learned*
letten *prevent, obstruct, hinder*
leve *leave, believe*
lever, lyvere *rather*
lewyd *ignorant*
lightli *easily*
liketh *pleases (impers.)*
liknesse *image, likeness*
likynge *pleasure, attraction*
longeth *belongs*
lo(o)ve *praise*
lo(o)vynge *praising*
lorn *lost*
lowenesse *humility*
lust *desire*

maistrie *difficulty, mastery; feat of skill;*
  force
manhede *humanity*
medle *mix, mingle*
meede *reward*
meedful *deserving, worthy of reward*

meke *humble (vb. and n.)*
merke(nesse) *dark(ness)*
mete *food*
moun, mowe, mowen *can, be able*
mykil *much*
myrke(nesse) *dark(ness)*
myspaide *dissatisfied*

narwgh *narrow*
ne *not, nor*
nedelynges *necessarily*
neer *nearer; near*
not *nought, nothing; know not*

onynge *union*
ooned *united*
or *or; before*
ordaynen *dispose*
ought *ought, was obliged; owed; out*

paid *satisfied, content*
partie *part*
passand *surpassing*
perfight *perfect*
peyne *punishment*
privetees *secrets, mysteries*
profight *profit*
pryvey *secret, hidden*

ransake *examine*
reest *quietness*
reprovede *scorned*
reste *resting-place*
rewardes *concerns, regards*
rightwiseness *righteousness*

saaf *saved*
sadli *soberly*
sautier *psalter*

schryve *confess*
semynge *appearance*
sere *various*
sich *such*
sigh *saw (vb.)*
siker *secure, certain*
sikirnesse *security, certainty*
sithen *since*
sithes *times*
skile *reason*
sleightes *deceptions*
sobirté *soberness*
sone *at once; soon*
sooth, soothfaste *true*
sothfastness *truthfulness*
spedeful *advantageous, profitable*
speryd *locked*
staaf *staff*
staat *estate, standing, status*
stieth *rises*
stiynge *rising*
stoneth *astonishes*
styringe *stirring*
suerd, swerd *sword*
suettenesse *sweetness*
sumdel *somewhat*
sunnere *sooner*
swiche *such*
swithe *much, very*
swynke *work*
syn *since*

taryynge *irritating, hindering*
thenketh *seems (impers.)*
ton *the one*
tothire *the other*
travail *labor; trouble*
trouth *belief*
trowand, trowe *believing, believe*

uggly *horrid, frightful*
uncouthe *unknown*
underneme *rebuke*
unkunynge *unknown, ignorant*
unnethes *scarcely*
unskilful *irrational, unreasonable*
up *according to, up*
upsodoun *upsidedown*
upstiande *ascending*

verili *truly*
verry *true*

waar *aware*
wantynge *lacking*
wenen, wenynge *think, suppose, thinking supposing*
witen, wost *know*
wittes *faculties, senses*
wordli *worldly*
worschipe *honor (n. and vb.)*

ye(e)de *went*
yhe *yea*
yif, yyf *if*
yit *yet*
ympnys *hymns*
ynowgh *enough*
yvel *evil*
yye *eye*

289

Notes

Notes

Notes

Notes

Notes

Volumes in the Middle English Texts Series

The Floure and the Leafe, The Assembly of Ladies, and *The Isle of Ladies*, ed. Derek Pearsall (1990)

Three Middle English Charlemagne Romances, ed. Alan Lupack (1990)

Six Ecclesiastical Satires, ed. James M. Dean (1991)

Heroic Women from the Old Testament in Middle English Verse, ed. Russell A. Peck (1991)

The Canterbury Tales: Fifteenth-Century Continuations and Additions, ed. John M. Bowers (1992)

Gavin Douglas, *The Palis of Honoure*, ed. David Parkinson (1992)

Wynnere and Wastoure and The Parlement of the Thre Ages, ed. Warren Ginsberg (1992)

The Shewings of Julian of Norwich, ed. Georgia Ronan Crampton (1993)

King Arthur's Death: The Middle English Stanzaic Morte Arthur and Alliterative Morte Arthure, ed. Larry D. Benson and Edward E. Foster (1994)

Lancelot of the Laik and Sir Tristrem, ed. Alan Lupack (1994)

Sir Gawain: Eleven Romances and Tales, ed. Thomas Hahn (1995)

The Middle English Breton Lays, ed. Anne Laskaya and Eve Salisbury (1995)

Sir Perceval of Galles and Ywain and Gawain, ed. Mary Flowers Braswell (1995)

Four Middle English Romances: Sir Isumbras, Octavian, Sir Eglamour of Artois, Sir Tryamour, ed. Harriet Hudson (1996)

The Poems of Laurence Minot (1333–1352), ed. Richard H. Osberg (1996)

Medieval English Political Writings, ed. James M. Dean (1996)

The Book of Margery Kempe, ed. Lynn Staley (1996)

Amis and Amiloun, Robert of Cisyle, and Sir Amadace, ed. Edward E. Foster (1997)

The Cloud of Unknowing, ed. Patrick J. Gallacher (1997)

Robin Hood and Other Outlaw Tales, ed. Stephen Knight and Thomas Ohlgren (1997)

The Poems of Robert Henryson, ed. Robert L. Kindrick (1997)

Moral Love Songs and Laments, ed. Susanna Greer Fein (1998)

John Lydgate, *Troy Book: Selections*, ed. Robert R. Edwards (1998)

Thomas Usk, *The Testament of Love*, ed. R. Allen Shoaf (1998)

Prose Merlin, ed. John Conlee (1998)

Middle English Marian Lyrics, ed. Karen Saupe (1998)

John Metham, *Amoryus and Cleopes*, ed. Stephen F. Page (1999)

Four Romances of England: King Horn, Havelok the Dane, Bevis of Hampton, Athelston, ed. Ronald B. Herzman, Graham Drake, Eve Salisbury (1999)

The Assembly of Gods: Le Assemble de Dyeus, or Banquet of Gods and Goddesses, with the Discourse of Reason and Sensuality, ed. Jane Chance (1999)

Thomas Hoccleve, *The Regiment of Princes*, ed. Charles R. Blyth (1999)

John Capgrave, *The Life of St. Katherine*, ed. Karen Winstead (1999)

John Gower, *Confessio Amantis*, Vol. 1, ed. Russell A. Peck (2000)

Richard the Redeless and *Mum & the Sothsegger*, ed. James M. Dean (2000)

Other TEAMS Publications

Documents of Practice Series:

Love and Marriage in Late Medieval London, by Shannon McSheffrey (1995)

A Slice of Life: Selected Documents of Medieval English Peasant Experience, edited, translated, and with an introduction by Edwin Brezette DeWindt (1996)

Sources for the History of Medicine in Late Medieval England, by Carole Rawcliffe (1996)

Regular Life: Monastic, Canonical, and Mendicant Rules, selected with an introduction by Douglas J. McMillan and Kathryn Smith Fladenmuller (1997)

Commentary Series:

Commentary and Notes on the Book of Jonah, Haimo of Auxerre, translated with an introduction by Deborah Everhart (1993)

Medieval Exegesis in Translation: Commentaries on the Book of Ruth, translated with an introduction by Lesley Smith (1996)

Nicholas of Lyra's Apocalypse Commentary, translated with an introduction and notes by Philip D. W. Krey (1997)

Rabbi Ezra Ben Solomon of Gerona: Commentary on the Song of Songs and Other Kabbalistic Commentaries, selected, translated, and annotated by Seth Brody (1998)

To order please contact:

MEDIEVAL INSTITUTE PUBLICATIONS
Western Michigan University
Kalamazoo, MI 49008–5432
Phone (616) 387–8755
FAX (616) 387–8750

http://www.wmich.edu/medieval/mip/index.html